Bali & Lombok

a travel survival kit
Tony Wheeler
Mary Covernton
Alan Samagalski

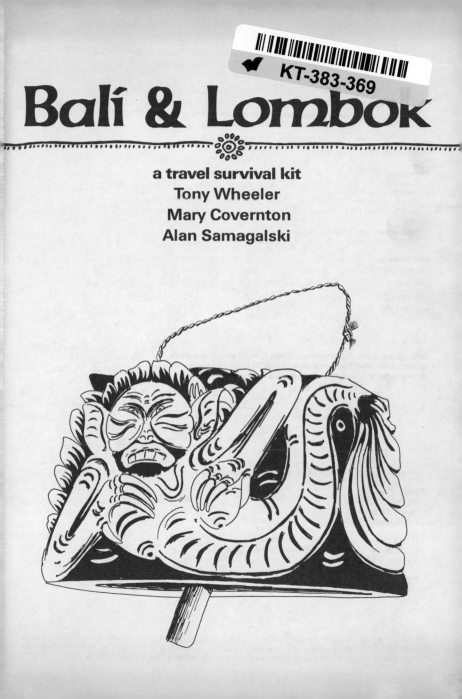

Bali - a travel survival kit
3rd edition

Published by
Lonely Planet Publications
Head Office: P.O. Box 617, Hawthorn 3122, Australia
US Office: PO Box 2001A, Berkeley, CA 94702, USA

Printed by
Colorcraft, Hong Kong

Photographs by
Mary Coventon (MC)
Lachlan Piece (LP)
John Preston (JP)
Tony Wheeler (TW)

Front cover: Rice Terraces, Tirtagangga (TW)
Back Cover: Prahus at the reef off Lovina Beach (TW)

First Published
January 1984

This Edition
June 1989

National Library of Australia Cataloguing in Publication Data

Wheeler, Tony
    3rd ed.
    Includes index.
    ISBN 0 86442 041 2.

    1. Bali (Indonesia) – Description and travel –
    Guide Books –. 2.Lombok (Indonesia) – Description and
    Travel – Guide Books.

    915.98'604
© Copyright Lonely Planet Publications 1983, 1986, 1989

Tony Wheeler

Tony was born in England but spent his youth in places like Pakistan, the West Indies and the US. A degree in engineering and an MBA did nothing to settle him down and he dropped out on the Asian overland trail with his wife Maureen. *Across Asia on the Cheap* was their first book and they've been travelling, writing and publishing guidebooks ever since setting up Lonely Planet in the mid-70s.

Mary Covernton

Mary has lived much of her life in Adelaide where she went to university and worked as an advertising copywriter, journalist and book editor. She has hitch-hiked around Australia and lived in Spain and England for five years. She was also one of the writer-researchers for our Indonesian guidebook.

Alan Samagalski

After escaping the Melbourne Uni Genetics Dept and surviving a long stay in India, Alan joined Lonely Planet and was dispatched north to research Ballarat, Bali and China. After co-writing *China – a travel survival kit*, he did the same to Indonesia and was then sent off on his own to write *Chile & Easter Island* and *Argentina*.

Lonely Planet Credits

Editor	Debbie Rossdale
Cover design & design	Peter Flavelle
Illustrations	Graham Imeson
Typesetting	Ann Jeffree

Thanks also to Susan Mitra for copy editing and Ann Jeffree for additional artwork and illustrations.

Acknowledgements

Three people have had major inputs to this book. In the first edition Tony Wheeler covered Bali while Mary Covernton concentrated on Lombok. Tony continued with Bali for the second edition while Alan Samagalski tackled Lombok while working on *Indonesia – a travel survival kit*. With this third edition Tony covered both Bali and Lombok, accompanied once again by Maureen and their children Tashi and

Kieran, both children on their third visit to Bali.

Additional material for this book was provided by Maureen, who wrote the 'Take the Children' section and Kirk Willcox, who wrote the 'Surfing in Bali' section. The bicycling information is based on Hunt Kooiker's now out of print *Bali by Bicycle*. Mark Balla, Lonely Planet's former linguist-editor, reported on his ascent of the holy mountain Mt Agung. The illustrations of a warung in the introductory section and a losmen scene at the Singaraja beaches were done by Peter Campbell.

As usual our grateful thanks to readers who wrote to us with corrections, suggestions and additions. Thank you to:

Pete Baak (Nl), H C M Beers (Nl), Anne Boadway, P Clarke (Aus), Keith Cranmer (USA), Lyn Dimet (USA), Cecilia Eklund (Sw), Anne Elings (Syr), John Flitcroft (Aus), Robert Gilbride (USA), Melitta Gloor (CH), Stephen Grant (Aus), Russell Gray (NZ), Mal Heyhoe (Aus), Eric & Maureen Hueting (NZ), R Jones (Aus), Valma King (Aus), Sean Robert Lavery (Aus), Kathy Liln (USA), Janet McHenry (USA), Jay Modrall, Brian & Debi Moore (Aus), Michele Mosher (USA), Rob & Claire Napier (UK), Torben Brandi Nielsen (Dk), Irene Osborn, Stephen Pearson (USA), Marion & Peter Phelen (Aus), Tex & Elliot Roperts (USA), Barry Rosenberg (Aus), Sandra Seidita (USA), Karen Shail (UK), Ny Suwela (Indo), A Whybourne (Aus),

Aus – Australia, CH – Switzerland – DK – Denmark – Indo – Indonesia – NI – Netherlands – Sw – Sweden – Syr – Syria – UK – United Kingdom – USA – United States of America

A Warning & a Request

Things change – prices go up, schedules change, good places go bad and bad places go bankrupt – nothing stays the same. So if you find things better or worse, recently opened or long since closed, please write and tell us and help make the next edition better! All information is greatly appreciated and the best letters will receive a free copy of the next edition, or any other Lonely Planet book of your choice.

Extracts from the best letters are also included in the *Lonely Planet Update*. The *Update* helps us make useful information available to you as soon as possible – it's like reading an up-to-date noticeboard or postcards from a friend. Each edition contains hundreds of useful tips, and advice from the best possible source of information – other travellers. The *Lonely Planet Update* is published quarterly in paperback and is available from bookshops and by subscription. Turn to the back pages of this book for more details.

Contents

Introduction

Bali is a tropical island in the Indonesian archipelago so picturesque and immaculate it could almost be a painted backdrop. It has rice paddies tripping down hillsides like giant steps, volcanoes soaring up through the clouds, dense tropical jungle, long sandy beaches, warm blue water, crashing surf and a friendly people who don't just have a culture but actually live it. In Bali spirits come out to play in the moonlight, every night is a festival and even a funeral is an opportunity to have a good time.

A curious mixture of position and events accounts for Bali's relative isolation from Indonesian history and religion, and the amazing vitality of its culture. Six centuries ago Indonesia was still a Hindu nation but when Islam swept across the islands the Majapahits, the last great dynasty on the island of Java, retreated to Bali with their entire entourage of scholars, artists and intelligentsia. Bali's extraordinary fertility had already allowed for the development of a highly active arts and culture and this new injection of energy sparked off a level of activity which has hardly faltered to this day.

The Balinese are a most unusual people. Unlike most islanders they are not great seafarers. In fact they shun the sea as the abode of demons and evil spirits,

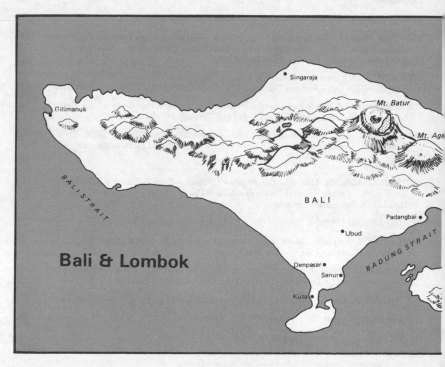

Bali & Lombok

and look toward the holy mountains which rise up in the centre of the island. They're also an unusually friendly and outgoing people – particularly once you get away from the south coast tourist enclaves. Few people manage to spend a week or two in the village of Ubud without falling in love with it.

Although Bali is, for many of its western visitors, simply a place with cheap living and pleasant beaches it's much, much more than that. Festivals, ceremonies, dances, temple processions and other activities take place almost continuously in Bali and they're fun to watch, easy to understand, instantly accessible. It's the great strength of Bali's culture that both makes the island so interesting and also ensures that it will stay that way. 'Has tourism ruined Bali yet?' is the query

every visitor is asked. It may not have done Kuta Beach a lot of good but the answer has to remain 'no, it hasn't'. If it's any consolation Covarrubias, whose pre-war guide to Bali remains the classic book on the island, was worried about tourism ruining the island – at a time when the number of visitors was not 1% of what it is today.

You can go to Lombok to see Bali but you can't go to Bali and see Lombok. The neighbouring island has all the lushness of Bali combined with the primeval starkness of outback Australia. It's an island of contrasts, rimmed with toothpaste-white beaches and tropical coconut palms, dominated by a towering volcano and patchworked with perfect rice terraces. Like its name, which means chilli pepper, it has a harsher side. Parts of Lombok drip

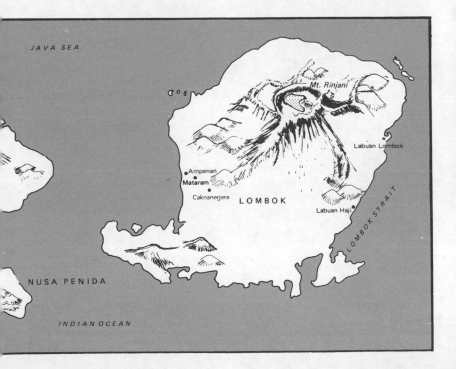

with water while pockets are chronically dry, parched and cracked like a bleached crocodile skin. It's the unpredictability of the rainfall which can cause severe hardship. Droughts on this small island can last for months, rice crops fail and people starve to death in their thousands. In 1966 50,000 people died of starvation and many others only survived by eating mice.

Lombok has an intact Balinese culture with all the splendour and colour of its processions and ceremonies and a number of magnificent, though rather neglected, temples. It also has the secret animist rituals of the Sasaks and the raucous sounds of today's muezzin, the loudspeaker, calling the faithful to prayer. While you shouldn't be taken in by the stories of black magic that the Balinese like to affect about Lombok, it does have a special magic of its own that in some ways is more powerful than the fairy-tale unreality of Bali.

Facts for the Visitor

VISAS

Your passport must have at least six months validity at the time you arrive in Indonesia. For Australians, New Zealanders, British, Americans, Canadians and most western Europeans a visa is no longer necessary for entry and a stay of up to two months provided you have a ticket out of the country. This is a considerable improvement on the previous situation where everybody had to have a visa and it was only valid for one month.

The only minor problem with this new system is that you must enter and leave Indonesia through certain approved 'gateways'. In actual fact 99% of arrivals and departures are through these ports or airports but if Bali is just part of a larger Indonesia trip and you plan to enter or leave through a very strange place (which basically means Jayapura in Irian Jaya) then you'd better check the visa situation before you depart.

In Denpasar the Immigration Office (Kantor Immigrasi) is in the south of Denpasar, just around the corner from the GPO at Jalan Panjaitan 4.

Indonesian Diplomatic Offices

Embassies and consulates include:

Australia
Embassy, 8 Darwin Avenue, Yarralumla, Canberra ACT 2600 (tel 73 3222)
Consulate-General, 238 Maroubra St, Maroubra NSW 2035 (tel 349 7027, 344 9933)
Consulate, 22 Coronation Drive, Stuart Park, Darwin NT 5790 (tel 81 9352)
Consulate, 3rd floor, 52 Albert Rd, South Melbourne Vic 3205 (tel 690 7811)
Consulate, 3rd floor, 34 Gawler Place, Adelaide SA 5000 (tel 223 6300)
Consulate, WA Institute of Technology Building, Kent St, South Bentleigh, WA 6012 (tel 451 8744)
Burma
Embassy, 100 Pyidaungsu Yeiktha Rd, Rangoon (tel 81714, 91358)

Canada
Embassy, 287 Maclaren St, Ottawa, Ontario K2P OL9 (tel 236-7403 to 5)
Consular offices in Toronto and Vancouver
Denmark
Embassy, Orejoj Alle I 2900, Hellerup, Copenhagen (tel 62 44 22, 62 54 39)
Finland
37 Eerikinkatu, 00810 Helsinki 18 (tel 694744)
Hong Kong
Consulate-General, 127-129 Leighton Rd, Causeway Bay, Hong Kong (tel 5 7904421 to 8)
India
Embassy, 50A Chanakyapuri, New Delhi (tel 602352, 602343, 602308)
Consular offices in Bombay and Calcutta
Japan
Embassy, 2-9 Higashi Gotanda, 5-chome, Shinagawa-Ku, Tokyo (tel 441-4201 to 9)
Consular offices in Fukuoka, Kobe and Sapporo
Malaysia
Embassy, Jalan Tun Razak 233, Kuala Lumpur (tel 421011, 421141, 421228, 421354, 421460)
Consulate, Coastal Rd, Karamunsing, Kota Kinabalu (tel 64100, 54245, 55110, 54459, 53571)
Consulate, Jalan Burma 467, Penang (tel 25168, 25162 to 4)
Netherlands
Embassy, 8 Tobias Asserlaan, 2517 KC Den Haag (tel 070-469796)
New Zealand
Embassy, 70 Glen Rd, Kelburn, Wellington (tel 758695 to 9)
Norway
Embassy, Inkonitogata 8, 0258 Oslo 2 (tel 441121)
Papua New Guinea
Embassy, Sir John Guisa Drive, Sel 410, Lot 182, Waigani, Port Moresby (tel 253544, 253116 to 8)
Philippines
Embassy, 185/187 Salcedo St, Legaspi Village, Makati, Manila (tel 85-50-61 to 8)
Consular office in Davao

Singapore
   Embassy, 7 Chatsworth Rd, Singapore 1024
   (tel 7377422)
Sri Lanka
   Embassy, 1 Police Park Terrace, Colombo 5
   (tel 580113, 580194)
Sweden
   Embassy, Strandvagen 47/V, 11456
   Stockholm (tel 63 54 70 to 4)
Switzerland
   Embassy, 51 Elfenauweg, 3006 Bern (tel
   440983 to 5)
Thailand
   Embassy, 600-602 Petchburi Rd, Bangkok
   (tel 252 3135 to 40, 2523177/8)
UK
   Embassy, 38 Grosvenor Square, London
   W1X 9AD (tel 499 7661)
USA
   Embassy, 2020 Massachussetts Ave NW,
   Washington DC 20036 (tel 293-1745)
   Consular offices in Chicago, Honolulu,
   Houston, Los Angeles, New York and San
   Francisco
UN
   UN Building, 325 East 38th St, New York,
   NY 10016 (tel 972-8333 to 49)
West Germany
   Embassy, Bernkasteler Strasse 2, 5300
   Bonn 2 (tel 310091)
   Consular offices in West Berlin, Bremen,
   Dusseldorf, Frankfurt, Hamburg, Hannover,
   Kiel, Munich and Stuttgart

MONEY

Australia	A$1	=	1350 rp
USA	US$1	=	1700 rp
UK	£1	=	2850 rp
New Zealand	NZ$1	=	1050 rp
Singapore	S$1	=	850 rp
Hong Kong	HK$1	=	220 rp
Australia	1000 rp	=	A$0.75
USA	1000 rp	=	US$0.60
UK	1000 rp	=	£0.35
New Zealand	1000 rp	=	NZ$0.95
Singapore	1000 rp	=	S$1.20
Hong Kong	1000 rp	=	HK$4.50

The unit of currency in Indonesia is the
rupiah (rp) – like lire in Italy there is
nothing else. You get coins of 5, 10, 25, 50
and 100 rp but 5s and 10s are really only
found in banks – nothing costs less than 25

rp. Notes come in 100, 500, 1000, 5000 and
10,000 rp denominations. Changing
money is quite easy in Bali. The exchange
rate is usually much the same for cash or
travellers' cheques. In the main tourist
centres of Kuta, Sanur and Ubud there
are lots of moneychangers to back up the
banks and their exchange rates are very
similar to the banks, often better.

Away from the main centres the story is
not quite so simple although it's by no
means difficult. You may not find banks
in all the smaller towns or they may not be
able to exchange foreign currency. Even
Ubud, the major tourist centre after the
Kuta-Sanur area, doesn't have a bank but
the moneychangers there offer rates
almost as good as Kuta.

It's no problem around Kuta, Sanur
and Ubud but out in the sticks beware of
the two standard Asian money problems.
First of all it's difficult to change big notes
– breaking a 10,000 rp note in an out-of-
the-way location can be a major hassle.
Secondly away from the major centres
notes tend to stay in circulation much
longer and tend to get very tatty – when
they get too dog-eared and worn looking
they're difficult to spend. This isn't the
major problem it can be in remote parts of
Indonesia but it's instructive to compare
the age of the notes you get in Kuta with
those you get in less touristed parts of the
island.

In Lombok it's most convenient to take
US dollars cash or travellers' cheques as
they're the most readily exchanged. The
big banks in Mataram are about the only
places you can change money in Lombok
so don't venture far afield without making
sure you have enough currency. Travellers
often seem to find they spend longer on
the Gili Islands than they had planned,
and then have to make a money run back
to Mataram when funds run low. When
you get money changed in Lombok make
sure they give you plenty of smaller
denomination notes. In the villages it's
often very difficult to get change for big
notes.

It is illegal to bring Indonesian currency into or out of Indonesia.

Banking hours are 8 am to 12 noon, Monday to Friday and 8 to 11 am on Saturday although some banks close an hour earlier. Moneychangers are open much longer hours although they tend to open later in the mornings.

COSTS

Bali and Lombok are still great travel bargains. Of course you can spend as much as you want to – there are hotels where a double can be US$100 a night, where lunch can cost US$10 to US$15 per person and they'll even arrange a helicopter for you if you're desperate to see Bali *fast*. But there's absolutely no need to do that. At the other extreme you can find rooms for US$2 and get a filling meal from a warung for a few hundred rupiah – say 25c.

In general travellers who don't need air-con and 24 hour service will discover they can get good rooms almost anywhere on the island for under US$10, sometimes as little as US$3 will get you a fine room. Steering clear of the international air-con places once again, US$10 will get you an excellent meal for two, with a big cold bottle of beer, even at relatively flashy places like Poppies in Kuta. A good meal for two for US$5 is no problem and you don't even have to get into the really rock bottom warungs to eat for under a dollar.

Transport is equally easy – remember that Bali and Lombok are small islands. Bemos cost from around 25 rp a km so a 20 km trip will cost you about 500 rp, say 40c. If you want your own wheels you can hire a motorcycle for around US$6 a day, a jeep for US$35 a day or charter your own bemo for US$20 a day.

Bargaining

Many everyday purchases in Bali require bargaining. This particularly applies to handicrafts, clothes and artwork but can also apply to almost anything you buy in a shop. Meals in restaurants, accommodation and transport are generally fixed price although when supply exceeds demand you may often find hotels willing to bend their prices a little, rather than see you go next door. This particularly applies in Kuta where there are lots of next doors to go to! On the other hand bemos have a well-earned reputation for taking foolish westerners for whatever they're willing to pay. In that case your bargaining has to be a matter of finding the right price and thus beating their excessive demands down to a proper level. The easiest way is simply to ask another passenger what the *harga biasa*, regular price, is. Then you offer the correct fare and don't accept any arguments.

In an everyday bargaining situation the first step is to establish a starting price. It's usually easiest to simply ask them their price rather than make an initial offer, unless you know very clearly what you're willing to pay. You then have to make a counter offer but you can start the psychological game moving your way immediately if you can get the seller to cut his price before you even start. Ask if that is the 'best price' and chances are you'll find it's cheaper straight off. Your counter offer should be a worthwhile notch below what you're willing to pay but not so low as to be ludicrous. If your offer is simply too low then either the seller is going to decide you're just uninterested or you're going to have to start moving in his direction immediately. That is, incidentally, a good way of getting rid of a persistent salesperson – simply make a silly offer. But be careful, lots of people have ended up buying things they didn't want because their silly offer was accepted!

Just what your initial offer should be depends to a large extent on the item for sale and who is selling it. As a rule of thumb your starting price could be anything from a third to two thirds of the asking price – assuming that the asking price is not completely crazy. Then with offer and counter offer you move closer to an acceptable price – they ask 25,000 rp for the painting, you offer 15,000 rp, eventually you compromise at 20,000 rp. Or 22,000 rp if they are better, 18,000 rp if you are. Along the way you can plead your end-of-trip poverty or claim that Ketut down the road is likely to be even cheaper. The seller is likely to point out the exceptional quality and plead poverty too. An aura of only mild interest helps – if you don't get to an acceptable price you're quite happy to walk away. Actually walking away often does help!

A few rules apply to good bargaining. First of all it's not a question of life or death where every rupiah you chisel away makes a difference. Bargaining should be an enjoyable part of shopping in Bali, treat it as such, maintain your sense of humour and keep things in perspective. Remember that 1000 rp is less than US$1. Secondly when you reach a price, you're committed. When your offer is accepted you have to buy it, don't decide then you don't want it after all. Finally the best buy is said to be at the 'morning price'. The seller feels that making a sale to the first potential customer of the day will ensure good sales for the rest of the day. So the trader is more likely to settle for a lower bid from the early morning customer.

Bargaining is nowhere near such an obvious aspect of everyday life on Lombok, nor is it so much fun. Nevertheless you are expected to bargain, particularly for items like antiques, cloth or basketware. If you manage to get the price down to half you can consider yourself a skilful bargainer on Lombok, whereas on Bali this is about the norm. Usually you will end up paying about two-thirds of the starting price on Lombok and sometimes you may only be able to get a nominal amount knocked off the starting figure.

If you have any difficulty knowing when

and where to bargain in Lombok don't be embarrassed to ask. While they are more reserved than the Balinese and may not volunteer this information, they will soon let you know whether it's on or not. In fact they will probably give you a line about special Lombok prices and advise you without so much as a blink of the eye that you will pay twice as much on Bali for a similar item. A very dubious statement! However, there is no doubt that you can get some very good bargains on Lombok if you're prepared to take your time.

As with Bali, restaurant and accommodation prices in Lombok are invariably fixed and, because Lombok is far less popular as a tourist or travel spot, the competition is not so keen and hotels are less likely to drop their prices. Unlike Bali many shops on Lombok have fixed prices but, once again, if you have any doubts ask whether it's permissible to bargain. Nearly every village on Lombok has a market at least once a week where there are numerous stalls selling food, clothes, handicrafts and many other items. Markets are great places for bargaining.

Don't get hassled by bargaining. Remember that no matter how good you are at it there's always going to be someone who is better or will boast about how they got something cheaper than you did. Don't go around feeling that you're being ripped off all the time. There are obviously times when you will be but both Bali and Lombok are very cheap places to travel around and you should remember that in most instances the locals will always pay less than foreigners. Both the Balinese and the Sasaks consider this to be eminently fair as in their eyes all westerners are wealthy.

If you are accompanied by a local on a shopping spree you will find it far harder to get down to bargaining basics. While it is likely that your guide may be getting some commission for taking you there, even if they aren't they don't like to see one of their fellows being put in this position by a westerner, particularly one who is a shrewd bargainer. It reflects on them as well, each loses face. The advantages of finding things more easily and quickly is often outweighed by this local loyalty.

Entry Charges

Nearly every temple or site of touristic interest will levy an entry charge or ask for a donation from foreigners – which means the Javanese just as much as it means you, as any non-Balinese is a foreigner. Usually the charge will be 100 rp, occasionally less, very occasionally more. If there is no fixed charge and a donation is requested 100 rp is also a good figure – ignore the donation book figures indicating that somebody has just paid over 1000 rp. Zeros are easy to add. Entry charges, a few places like Narmada apart, are not so common on Lombok.

At some temples you may be asked to rent a temple scarf, this may sometimes be included in the entry charge or donation. Buy your own at any market or general store, they only cost a few hundred rupiah and if you do much temple visiting they soon pay for themselves as well as allowing you to feel 'well dressed' at temples where scarves are not available.

TIPPING

Tipping is not a normal practice in Bali or Lombok so please don't try to make it one. The expensive hotels slap a 21% service and government tax on top of their bills but there are no additional charges at lower-priced establishments. Beggars are virtually unknown in Bali or Lombok.

TOURIST INFORMATION
Tourist Office

Unlike many other Asian countries Indonesia doesn't have an excellent tourist office pumping out useful brochures and with all the facts at their fingertips. What they do have tends to be piecemeal and variable from place to place. Garuda, the Indonesian airline, has better information brochures than you're likely to find from the government offices. In Bali there is both a Denpasar (Badung) tourist office and a Bali one. The office on the corner of the airport road and Jalan Bakungsari in Kuta is pretty good. The local office in Ubud is also good.

In Lombok the West Nusa Tenggara Regional Tourist Office is at Jalan Langko 70, Ampenan, diagonally opposite the Ampenan post office. It has a couple of coloured brochures with information on places of interest, accommodation, restaurants and so on plus a map of Ampenan, Mataram and Cakranegara.

Foreign Consulates & Embassies

Despite Bali's great number of foreign tourists there is little diplomatic representation there. For most nationalities if your passport is stolen in Bali you have to make the long trek to Jakarta to get another one! Fortunately for the great number of Australian visitors there is an Australian consulate between Sanur and Denpasar. There is a US consular agent at Sanur. Diplomatic offices in Indonesia include:

Australia
Jalan M H Thamrin 15, Jakarta (tel 323109)
Jalan Raya Sanur 146, Denpasar (tel 25997-8) (Denpasar PO Box 243)
Canada
5th floor, Wisma Metropolitan, Jalan Jen Sudirman, Kav 29, Jakarta (tel 510709)

Denmark
4th floor, Bina Mulia Building, Jalan H R Rasuna Said, Kav 10, Jakarta (tel 518350)
India
Jalan Rasuna Said 51, Jakarta (tel 518150)
Japan
Jalan M H Thamrin 24, Jakarta (tel 324308, 324948, 325396, 325140, 325268)
Jalan Raya Sanur Tanjung 124, Denpasar (tel 25611)
Malaysia
Jalan Imam Bonjol 17, Jakarta (tel 3321709, 336438, 332864)
Netherlands
Jalan H R Rasuna Said, Kav S3, Kuningan, Jakarta (tel 511515)
New Zealand
Jalan Diponegoro 41, Jakarta (tel 330552, 330620, 330680, 333696)
Norway
4th floor, Bina Mulia Building, Jalan H R Rasuna Said, Kav 10, Jakarta (tel 517140, 511990)
Papua New Guinea
6th floor, Panin Bank Centre, Jalan Jen Sudirman, Jakarta (tel 711218, 711225/6)
Philippines
Jalan Imam Bonjol 6-9, Jakarta (tel 348917)
Singapore
Jalan Proklamasi 23, Jakarta (tel 348761, 347783)
Sri Lanka
Jalan Diponegoro 70, Jakarta (tel 321018, 321896)
Sweden
Jalan Taman Cut Mutiah 12, Jakarta (tel 333061)
Segara Village Hotel, Jalan Segara, Sanur (tel 8231, 8407)

IT IS SUGGESTED THAT YOU DRESS PROPERLY WHEN VISITING GOVERMENTAL OFFICES AND WE WANT TO HELP YOU, IF YOU DRESS PROPERLY

IT IS SUGGESTED THAT YOU DONOT WEAR THESE DRESSES WHEN VISITING GOVERMENTAL OFFICES AND WE DONOT WANT TO HELP YOU, IF YOU DRESS IMPROPERLY

Thailand
Jalan Imam Bonjol 74, Jakarta (tel 343762, 349180)
UK
Jalan M H Thamrin 75, Jakarta (tel 330904)
USA
Jalan Medan Merdeka Selatan 5, Jakarta (tel 360360)
West Germany
Jalan M H Thamrin 1, Jakarta (tel 323908, 324292, 324357)
17 Jalan Pantai Karang, Sanur (tel 8535)

GENERAL INFORMATION
Post
There are poste restante services at the various post offices around Bali and since the Denpasar post office is so inconveniently situated, you're better off having mail sent to you at Kuta, Ubud, Singaraja or other more convenient locations. Mail should be addressed to you with your surname underlined or in capital letters, then Kantor Pos, the town name, Bali, Indonesia. There's a 50 rp charge for each letter you get through the poste restante.

If you're having mail sent to you on Lombok you may come across a few hassles collecting it. There is only one post office on Lombok with a poste restante service. It's on the edge of Mataram, as inconveniently situated as the one in Denpasar and while there's another post office in Ampenan all poste restante mail is automatically re-directed to the new post office. Other post offices on Lombok are at Cakranegara, Lembar, Narmada, Praya, Tanung and Selong.

Airmail charges for postcards are: Australia 450 rp, Europe 550 rp, and North America 700 rp. Mail charges from Lombok are slightly higher as all mail is sent via Bali.

Electricity
Electricity is usually 220-240 volts AC in Bali and Lombok. In some smaller villages in Bali and many in Lombok voltage is 110 so check first. It's usually fairly reliable too, blackouts are not an everyday occurrence. In many small towns or even in many parts of larger towns electricity is still a fairly futuristic thing – if you travel around very much you're likely to stay in the odd losmen where lighting is provided with oil lamps. Even where there is electricity you're likely to find the lighting can be very dim. Lots of losmen seem to have light bulbs of such low wattage that you can almost see the electricity crawling laboriously around the filaments. If 25 watts isn't enough to light your room it might be worth carrying a more powerful light bulb with you.

Street lighting can also be a problem – there often isn't any. If stumbling back to your losmen down dark gangs in Kuta or through the rice paddies in Ubud doesn't appeal a torch (flashlight) can be very useful.

Time
There are three time zones in Indonesia. Bali and Lombok and the islands of Nusa Tenggara to the east are on Central Standard Time which is eight hours ahead of GMT or two hours behind Australian Eastern Standard Time. The time zone lines have been redrawn since

the previous edition when Bali and Lombok were in different zones.

Thus, not allowing for variations due to daylight saving time, when it is 12 noon in London it is 8 pm in Bali and Lombok, 8 pm in Perth, 10 pm in Sydney or Melbourne, 7 am in New York and 4 am in San Francisco or Los Angeles.

As Bali is close to the equator the days and nights are approximately equal in length. The sun pops up over the horizon at 5 am and drops down the other way at 5 pm. And what sunsets Bali can provide – orange-fire spectaculars!

Business Hours

Most government offices are open from 8 am daily except Sunday. Monday to Thursday they close at 3 pm, Friday at 11.30 am, Saturday at 2 pm. Usual business office hours are 8 am to 4 pm, Monday to Friday. Some also open on Saturday morning. Banks are open 8 am to 12 noon, Monday to Friday and 8 to 11 am on Saturday.

Tourist Seasons

The cool, dry season from April to October is the best time to visit Bali or Lombok but there are also distinct tourist seasons which alter the picture. Remember that Bali is Australia's favourite Asian getaway, a cheap place to laze on the beach. At Christmas time and through January Bali can be packed out with Australians and at that time of year the air fares from Australia are also higher. The early April, late June/early July and late September school holidays also bring Australians flocking in. The European summer holidays also bring crowds –July for the Germans, August for the French.

The Muslim fast of Ramadan applies to Lombok but it is unlikely to pose any major problems. During the month of Ramadan Muslims are not allowed to eat between sunrise and sunset so some restaurants are closed and by the end of the month the people are crabby and unpredictable.

HEALTH

There are no health entry requirements for most visitors to Indonesia but it's wise to be vaccinated against cholera, typhoid and tetanus and have them recorded in a yellow International Health Certificate booklet. You can arrange these vaccinations through your doctor or at a local health centre.

Malaria

Bali and Lombok are officially within the malarial zones but actually the risk of malaria in Bali is very low, particularly in the south Bali tourist enclave. Nevertheless it's wise to take precautions against

malaria by taking either a weekly or daily anti-malarial tablet. Your doctor will probably have a personal recommendation for one form or the other. You have to commence taking anti-malarials before you depart and continue taking them after you return. The period depends on the actual form you're taking.

You can easily take further precautions by avoiding mosquito bites – mosquitoes are the carriers of malaria. In the evening, when mosquitoes are most active, cover bare skin, particularly your ankles. Use an insect repellent and/or burn mosquito coils to repel them and at night sleep under a cover. Actually mosquitoes are not a real nuisance in Bali, at certain times of the year you don't even see them.

Stomach Upsets

The chief health risk to most visitors to Bali or Lombok seems to be the infamous 'Bali Belly'. A lot of visitors get travellers' diarrhoea but it's usually not a serious health risk and with a little care you can generally avoid it completely. I suspect much of it comes from inexperienced travellers whose stomachs are simply rebelling against something new and different. Or people who have just taken foolish risks.

How to avoid Bali Belly? Well be a little careful in what and where you eat – avoid small local warungs if you're not sure your digestive system has built up a little resistance. Water, ice drinks and cooked food that has been left to cool for too long are all big risks. If you're worried about stomach problems then well-cooked food is always safest. Never drink unboiled water – tea or coffee and bottled soft drinks are safe. Major brands of packaged ice cream are usually OK, don't touch the locally made ice cream sold on the street.

Don't go overboard on being careful – you'll miss out on a lot if you view every meal with suspicion. Bali is not an inherently unhygienic place and most of the time you can eat and drink pretty much anything you please with little risk. In Bali I've had an awful lot of salads, had ice in drinks on innumerable occasions and have yet to pay the price!

If worst comes to worst and you do come down with something don't rush straight to the medicine chest. If you can fight it off without the aid of modern medical science you'll have built up some resistance against a repeat performance. The most important precaution is to avoid dehydration by taking frequent drinks –

frequent healthy drinks. If ice juice was what did it to you don't keep drinking it! Fruit juice can aggravate diarrhoea and it's probably better to eat lightly until you've recovered. If you have to resort to outside assistance then Lomotil is generally recommended. It's a prescription drug and usually does the job very efficiently.

Other Precautions

Take great care with small cuts and scratches. They can very easily get infected and can then be extremely difficult to heal. Treat any cut with care; wash it out, preferably with an antiseptic, keep it dry and keep an eye on it. Cuts on your feet and ankles are particularly troublesome – a new pair of sandals can quickly give you a nasty abrasion that can be difficult to heal.

Pharmaceuticals are somewhat up and down in Indonesia. If it's available at all it's likely to be available without prescription but don't count on finding just what you want or, if you do find it, that it will be exactly the same as you're used to. If you have to take some particular medicine it's wise to bring it with you.

Travel Insurance

A travel insurance policy is a very good idea - to protect you against cancellation penalties on advance purchase flights, against medical costs through illness or injury and against theft or other loss of your possessions. Read the small print carefully as it's easy to be caught out by exclusions. As an example some travel insurance policies widely available in Australia specifically exclude motorcycle injuries if you don't hold a current *Australian* motorcycle licence. It's obviously designed to cut out all the people who obtain Balinese licences but could also catch people travelling through Australia who hold, say, a British or American licence.

DRUGS

The old image of floating sky-high over Bali has faded considerably. There's no longer so much about and the authorities are much heavier. The Bali drug scene was basically marijuana and mushrooms but neither are so readily available and it's now not at all safe to buy from a local supplier unless you know him very well. Losmen owners are quick to turn you in as well.

Those who want to go in search of Bali's famed magic mushrooms should remember that their effect is very variable. Some people have stratospheric highs but a lot more suffer deep down lows. And when you come back home remember that drugs may not be so widely available in Bali anymore but nobody has told your friendly local customs department that.

Drugs are absolutely unheard of on Lombok. The closest you would get there would be betel nut. Many of the locals – particularly villagers in the more isolated areas – chew this mild drug constantly.

One drug has, however, been doing very well in Bali of late – alcohol. There are now lots of bars and pubs around and an awful lot more empty beer bottles than there used to be. However, alcohol is scarce on Lombok, largely because the island is predominantly Muslim. Beer, brem and tuak are available at rumah makans in the main centres but in the isolated villages, or more strictly Muslim towns like Labuhan Lombok, forget it.

Western visitors in Bali who fall afoul of the drug laws end up in jail, sometimes for uncomfortably long periods. If you take the Legian Rd from Kuta through Legian and on beyond you'll soon see the Kerobokan jail off to the right of the road. There are quite a number of westerners in there, many of them serving much longer sentences than they would have got for the same offence in the west. Under Indonesian law you can now be convicted for not turning somebody else in for a drug offence. There have been cases of wives going to prison because they did not inform on their husbands. Information on visiting westerners in jail was posted on the notice board in Poppies'

Restaurant in Kuta. They're very happy to have visitors and gifts of books, fruit, yoghurt and other hard to obtain items are much appreciated. Female prisoners get a particularly hard deal as there are fewer of them and their area is much smaller.

FILM & PHOTOGRAPHY

Although film is widely available the cost is generally somewhat higher than in the west. A 36-exposure reel of Kodachrome 64, for example, costs around 17,000 to 20,000 rp in Bali. Developing and printing, on the other hand, is quite good and much cheaper than in the west. You can get Ektachrome slide film developed in two or three days and colour print film can be done the same day through innumerable photographic shops in Kuta and Sanur. An Instamatic film costs about 800 rp to develop plus 150 rp per print, very cheap.

In Lombok colour print film is readily available at numerous outlets in Ampenan, Mataram and Cakranegara including general stores and chemists (drugstores) as well as specialist film and camera shops. There is some colour transparency film around, but it's not so easy to find. The price of film in Lombok is similar to Bali but Lombok does not have the same facilities for developing and printing. You'd do better to wait till you get back there or take it home with you.

Bali is, not surprisingly, very photogenic – you can go through lots of film. There are a number of basic rules for good photographs and good manners in Bali. First of all shoot early or late – from 10 am to 1 or 2 pm the sun is uncomfortably hot and high overhead, you're likely to get a bluish washed-out look to your pictures. If you have to shoot at that time of day a skylight filter will cut the haze. A lens hood will reduce your problems with reflections and direct sunlight on the lens. Beware of the sharp differences between sun and shade – if you can't get reasonably balanced overall light you may have to opt for exposing only one area or the other correctly. Or use a fill-in flash.

Those lush, green, rice fields come up best if backlit by the sun. For those oh-so-popular sunset shots at Kuta or Kalibukbuk set your meter exposures on the sky without the sun making an appearance – then shoot at the sun.

Finally, and most important of all, photograph with discretion and manners. Hardly surprisingly many people don't like having camera lens shoved down their throats – it's always polite to ask first and if they say no then don't. A gesture, a smile and a nod are all that is usually necessary. There's one place not to take photographs at all – public bathing places. Just because the Balinese bathe in streams, rivers, lakes or other open places doesn't mean they don't think of them as private places. Balinese simply do not 'see' one another when they're bathing and intruding with your camera is no different to sneaking up to someone's bathroom window and pointing your camera through.

ACCOMMODATION
Around Bali
Finding a place to stay in Bali is no problem, in fact at the bottom end of the price scale accommodation in Bali is probably the best in the world, for the price. Two or three dollars can still get you a fine room in many places. Ten dollars can get you something terrific.

There are only three areas with hotels of 'international standard'. They are first of all the beach triangle of Kuta-Sanur-Nusa Dua where more than 90% of those air-con, swimming pool, all mod-con places are located. If you want a Hyatt or similar then you'd better head there. You'll also find a couple of upper notch hotels in Denpasar, if for some unearthly reason you wanted to stay there. Finally, Ubud has a few places where you could spend more than US$30 a night. Anywhere else the choice is strictly at the low end of the price scale. In Kuta, Denpasar, Ubud and, to a lesser extent, Sanur you can also find a good selection of middle price hotels. At the beaches they're often done in Balinese bungalow style. Middle price, for this book, will generally be taken as something between US$7 and US$20 per night for a double. Above that is 'top end', below that is 'bottom end'.

If you're going to travel around Bali rather than stay in one place and day-trip (or stay in one place and never move from the beach) then it's the bottom-end places which will be of interest. Cheap hotels in Bali are usually known as losmen and many of them are terrific. A losmen is a small hotel, often family run, and they rarely have more than 10 or 12 rooms.

Losmen are often built in the style of a Balinese home – that is a compound with an outer wall and separate buildings around an inner garden. In Bali you usually live outside – the 'living room' is an open verandah and enclosed rooms are only used for sleeping or specific activities like cooking. Similarly in a losmen your room is generally just that: four walls and a couple of beds. Outside the room there will be a verandah area with chairs and a table.

Apart from the fact that it's pleasant to be sitting out in the garden in any case, this plan has a second very important benefit. You're out there with all the other travellers, not locked away inside a room. So you can talk, meet people and learn more about Bali.

There are losmen all over Bali and they vary widely in standards but not so widely in price. In a few places you'll find a room for as low as 2500 rp but generally they're in the 4000 to 10,000 rp range. Some of the cheap rooms are definitely on the dismal and dull side but others are attractive, well kept and excellent value for money.

Some interesting losmen to try include the places at Penelokan (for the terrific view over the volcano), the water palace losmen at Tirtagganga, a number of the losmen at the Singaraja beaches (for attractive rooms at wonderfully low prices), the Artha Sastra Inn at Bangli and some of the pleasant losmen in Ubud.

Around Lombok

The accommodation picture in Lombok is somewhat different. There is no shortage of accommodation in the main town although there are no big 'international' hotels there. Senggigi Beach is becoming the major beach development on Lombok with a variety of places to stay and the Gili Islands have numerous places, almost all of them at the bottom of the price range. Elsewhere on the island, however, even losmen are scarce.

This is not such a major problem as you can base yourself in the main centres and make day trips to most parts of the island quite easily. If this doesn't appeal and you want to get out and about to see more of the island you are always welcome to stay with the kepala desa or kepala kampung (headman of the village). They are generally very hospitable and friendly, not only offering you a roof over your head but also a minimum of two meals a day – obviously you don't get a room of your own, just a bed. What you pay for this depends on the deal you reach with the kepala desa. Sometimes he may offer it to you for nothing but more often some payment will be expected although it could be as little as 2000 rp.

If you intend to visit remote areas and stay with a kepala desa it is a good idea to have one or two small gifts to offer – cigarettes go down well, as do instant photographs, balloons for the children, soap or foreign coins. That way if he won't allow you to pay for accommodation and food, you will feel happier in being able to reciprocate his kindness in a small way and promote good will for future travellers at the same time.

The cost of a basic losmen on Lombok varies from around 2500 to 7500 rp. As in Bali the quality changes, some are depressing and dirty, others attractive and bright. Many are close to mosques which makes them deafeningly noisy and if you don't like being woken up at 5 am avoid these like the plague. Still others are more or less permanently full with students from out of town or people from villages who have found work in the main centres. They're all interesting and all cheap. Basic hotel accommodation in Lombok is generally slightly more expensive than in Bali.

The Mandi

Successfully coping with the mandi is an important factor in coming to grips with life in a losmen. Running water is not part of everyday life in Indonesia and to get around this many losmen will have a mandi-style bathroom. The word 'mandi' simply means to bath or to wash. Instead of taps and a sink or bath the mandi is a large water tank beside which you'll find what looks like a plastic saucepan. You *do not* climb in the tank. That's the worst error to make! What you do is scoop water out of the mandi tank and pour it over yourself, then soap yourself down and repeat the scooping and showering procedure.

A warning: mandi water is often icy cold, it usually comes from wells way down deep! You will have to get used to cold water because losmen have nothing else, even in most middle price hotels hot water is a rarity. Anyway you're in the tropics and you will soon forget what hot water feels like.

Bathing is a regular and social practice in Bali – every pool, lake, stream or even water channel seems to be in almost constant use as an outside bathhouse. If you're at the *air panas* (hot springs) by Lake Batur try joining the evening bathtime, half the village seems to be there for a social soak and chatter and you're quite welcome to shed your inhibitions and join in. Note, however, that just because the Balinese bathe in public doesn't mean that they don't consider their bathing places to be private. See the important note in the Photography section of this chapter.

The Toilet

In Bali mandis are gradually disappearing

as more places install western-style showers and similarly the old Asian toilets are also fading away, replaced by western-style sit-down toilets. The basic toilets, however, are like those you find everywhere east of Europe – two footrests and a hole in the ground. You squat down and aim. It's basic but you soon get used to it and they have one considerable advantage over western-style toilets – they don't require the same effort to keep clean and when that effort isn't made they are often far more hygienic.

Most losmen on Lombok are still designed with mandis and basic, squat-down toilets. Only at the more expensive hotels will you find western showers and toilet facilities.

As with mandis there is often no running water to flush toilets – Asian-style or western-style. In that case you just reach for that plastic saucepan again, scoop water from the mandi tank and flush it away.

Apart from those places definitely catering to the tourist trade you won't find toilet paper in restaurant toilets – so bring your own. To locate a toilet ask for the *kamah mandi* or the WC (pronounced 'way-say').

FOOD

There's no question that you'll eat well in Bali, the dining possibilities are endless, the prices often pleasantly low and the taste treats terrific. What you're less likely to do is eat Balinese – the places that prepare real Balinese food are few and far between although they certainly are becoming a little more common, particularly in Ubud. Babi guling (spit-roasted suckling pig) and betutu bebek (duck roasted in banana leaves) are probably the only truly Balinese dishes you'll see with any regularity and both of them usually require advance warning to prepare.

A good restaurant with some interesting Balinese dishes is the *Ubud Restaurant* down the Monkey Forest Rd in Ubud. Also see the information in the Ubud section about Ketu Suartana's Balinese feasts.

In many of Bali's touristically inclined eating places not only will you not find Balinese food but you'll be lucky to even find Indonesian food – apart from a token nasi goreng. Some western dishes have been so well assimilated on to the Balinese menu you could almost think they originated here. Jaffles for example! Of

course in places not so squarely aimed at the tourist mainstream you'll find a more normal range of Indonesian dishes.

Food in Indonesia is Chinese influenced although there are a number of purely Indonesian dishes. Some useful food words and some of the dishes you're most likely to find include:

apam – delicious pancake filled with nuts and sprinkled with sugar

asam manis – sweet and sour, for example, ikan asam manis – sweet and sour fish

ayam – chicken, ayam goreng is fried chicken

babi – pork, since most Indonesians are Muslim pork is rarely found elsewhere in the archipelago but in Bali it's a popular delicacy

bakmi goreng – fried noodles

cap cai – usually pronounced 'chop chai' this is a mix of fried vegetables sometimes with meat as well

daging – beef

dingin – cold

dragonflies – a popular Balinese snack, caught with sticky sticks and then roasted!

eels – another Balinese delicacy, kids catch them in the rice paddies at night

enak – delicious

fu yung hai – a sort of sweet and sour omelette

gado gado – another very popular Indonesian dish, steamed bean sprouts, various vegetables and a spicy peanut sauce

garam – salt

gula – sugar

ikan – fish, there's a wide variety of fish available in Bali

kare – curry, as in kare udang – curried prawns

kentang – potatoes

kepiting – crab

kodok – frog, frogs' legs are very popular in Bali, they catch the frogs in the rice paddies at night

krupuk – prawn crackers, they often accompany meals

udang karang – lobster – very popular in Bali and comparatively economical

lontong – rice steamed in a banana leaf

makan – the verb 'to eat' or food in general, *makan pagi* - is breakfast, *makan siang* – is the midday meal

manis – sweet

mee goreng – fried noodles, sometimes with vegetables, sometimes with meat – much the same story as nasi goreng

mee kuah – noodle soup

mentega – butter

nasi campur – steamed rice topped with a little bit of everything – some vegetables, some meat, a bit of fish, a krupuk or two – a good, straightforward, usually tasty and filling meal

nasi goreng – this is the most everyday of Indonesian dishes, almost like hamburgers are to Americans, meat pies to Australians, fish & chips to the British. Nasi goreng simply means fried (goreng) rice (nasi) and a basic nasi goreng may be little more than fried rice with a few scraps of vegetable to spice it up a little. Fancier nasi gorengs may include meat, a 'special' or istemiwa nasi goreng usually means with a fried egg on top. Nasi goreng can range from the blandly dull to the very good.

nasi Padang – Padang food, from the Padang region of Sumatra, is popular all over Indonesia. It's usually served cold and consists of rice (once again) with a whole variety of side dishes. A whole selection of dishes are laid out before you and your final bill is calculated by the number of empty dishes. Nasi Padang is traditionally eaten with your fingers and it's also traditionally very hot (*pedas* not *panas*). It's hot enough to burn your fingers, let alone your tongue.

nasi putih – white (putih) rice – plain boiled or steamed rice

opor ayam – chicken cooked in coconut milk

pahat - no sugar

panas - hot, temperature-wise

pasar malam - night market, often a great source of interesting and economical food stalls

pedas - hot, spicy

pisang goreng - fried banana fritters, a popular streetside snack

rijstaffel - Dutch for 'rice table', Indonesian food with a Dutch interpretation, it consists of lots of individual dishes with rice. Rather like a glorified nasi campur or a less heated nasi Padang. Bring a big appetite.

rumah makan - restaurant, literally 'house to eat' or 'house for food'

sambal - a hot spicy chilli sauce served as an accompaniment with most meals

satay - (sate) one of the best known Indonesian dishes, satay are tiny kebabs of various types of meat served with a spicy peanut sauce. Street satay sellers carry their charcoal grills around with them and cook the satay on the spot.

sayur - vegetables

soto - soup, usually fairly spicy

telur - egg

udang - prawns

warung - food stall combined with a sort of Indonesian small general store.

The only real difference in food between Lombok and Bali is that there are very few tourist restaurants on Lombok - which means you'll be eating local Indonesian dishes wherever you go. In Bahasa Indonesia the word 'lombok' means chilli pepper and they're used liberally in Indonesian cooking so unless you like having your mouth on fire beware of adding even more. Particularly as you can't drink litres of water to cool yourself down!

By and large the Chinese restaurants on Lombok are cleaner and have more variety and tastier food than the Indonesian rumah makan, but as with Bali there is no question that you will eat well and cheaply.

You can get several locally produced brands of ice cream in Kuta and various other well-touristed places. They're safe and while Peters (the locally licensed version of the well-known Australian brand) is quite good, Campina is generally the best. The Indonesians are keen snackers so you'll find lots of street-stall snacks such as peanuts in palm sugar, shredded coconut cookies or pisang goreng.

Fruit

It's almost worth making a trip to Bali or Lombok just to sample the tropical fruit. If you've never gone beyond apples, oranges and bananas you've got some rare treats in store when you discover rambutans, mangosteens, salaks or zurzat. Some of the favourites include:

avocado - avocado enthusiasts can suffer overkill in Bali, they're plentiful and cheap

blimbing - the 'starfruit' is a cool, crispy, watery tasting fruit - if you cut a slice you'll immediately see where the name comes from

durian - the most infamous tropical fruit, the durian is a large green fruit with a hard, spiky exterior. Crack it open to reveal a truly horrific stench. Sewers overflowing? drains blocked up? - no it's just the durian season. Hotels and airlines in Asia often ban durians so it's not surprising that becoming a durian aficionado takes some time! One description of the durian compared it to eating a superb raspberry blancmange inside a revolting public toilet but true believers even learn to savour the smell.

jambu - guava, the crispy, pink, pear-shaped ones are particularly popular

jeruk - jeruk is the all-purpose term for citrus fruit and there is a wide variety available in Bali. They are chiefly grown in the central mountains. The main varieties include the huge *jeruk*

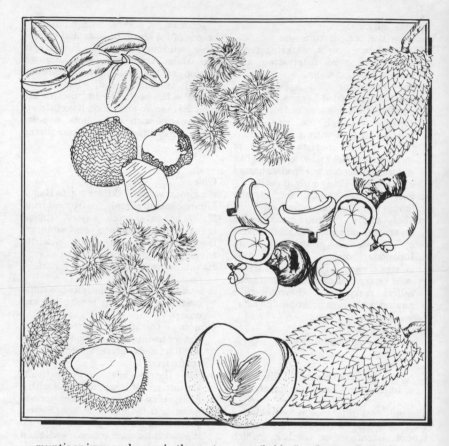

muntis or *jerunga*, known in the west as the pomelo. It's larger than a grapefruit but with a very thick skin, a sweeter, more orange-like taste and segments that break apart very easily. Regular oranges are known as *jeruk manis*, sweet jeruk. The small tangerine-like oranges which are often quite green are *jeruk baras*. Lemons are *jeruk nipis*.

mangosteen – one of the most famous tropical fruits the mangosteen is a small purple-brown fruit. The outer covering cracks open to reveal tasty pure-white segments with an inde-scribably fine flavour. Queen Victoria once offered a reward to anyone able to transport a mangosteen back to England while still edible.

nanas are pineapples

nangcur – also known as jackfruit this is an enormous yellow-green fruit that can weigh over 20 kg. Inside there are hundreds of individual bright-yellow segments with a distinctive taste and a slightly rubbery texture. As they ripen on the tree each nangcur may be separately protected in a bag.

papaya or *paw paw* – these fruits are not that unusual in the west

pisang – are bananas and the variety of *pisang* found in Bali is quite surprising

rambutan – a bright red fruit covered in soft, hairy spines; the name means hairy. Break it open to reveal a delicious white fruit closely related to the lychee.

salak – found chiefly in Indonesia the salak is immediately recognisable by its perfect brown 'snakeskin' covering. Peel it off to reveal segments that in texture are like a cross between an apple and a walnut but in taste are quite unique. Bali salaks are much nicer than any others.

sawo – they look like a potato and taste like a pear

zurzat – also spelt sirsat and sometimes called white mango the zurzat is known in the west as custard apple or soursop. Custard apples I've tried, however, are nowhere near as good as the Indonesian variety. The warty green skin of the zurzat covers a thirst quenching interior with a slightly lemonish, tart taste. You can peel it off or slice it into segments. Zurzats are ripe when the skin has begun to lose its fresh green colouring and become darker and spotty. It should then feel slightly squishy rather than firm.

DRINKS

A variety of the popular western soft drink brands are available in Bali and Lombok – usually in bottles rather than cans. Coca-Cola, 7-Up, Sprite and Fanta are all there. Prices are typically around 300 rp in warungs and much more in the expensive restaurants. Bottled drinking water has become quite the thing in Bali, a 1.5 litre bottle costs 1000 rp.

Beer is comparatively expensive – in some places you can actually get a losmen room for less than the price of a bottle of beer! The three popular brands are San Miguel, Anchor and Bintang. Bintang is often the most expensive. The usual prices are around 1750 to 2000 rp for a large bottle or 1000 rp for a small but you can pay much more in pricier restaurants. In a five-star hotel at Nusa Dua a large beer will set you back 6000 rp.

Some other popular Indonesian and Balinese drinks, both alcoholic and non-alcoholic, include:

air jeruk – lemon juice or orange juice

air minum – drinking water, *air* is water

arak – distilled rice brandy, one stage on from brem and it can have a real kick. It's usually home produced although even the locally bottled brands look home produced. It makes quite a good mixed drink with 7-Up or Sprite.

brem – rice wine, either home produced or the commercially bottled brand Bali Brem. It's a bit of an acquired taste but not bad after a few bottles!

es juice – although you should be a little careful about ice and water the Balinese make delicious fruit drinks which are generally safe to try. In particular the ice-juice drinks are a real taste treat – just take one or two varieties of tropical fruit, add crushed ice and pass through a blender. You can make mind-blowing combinations of orange, banana, pineapple, mango, jackfruit, zurzat or whatever else is available.

es buah – more a dessert than a drink, es buah is a curious combination of crushed ice, condensed milk, shaved coconut, syrup, jelly and fruit. It can be surprisingly delicious.

kopi – coffee, it's grown in Bali and usually served thick and strong, or instant

lassi – a refreshing yoghurt-based drink

stroop – cordial

susu – milk, not a very common drink in Indonesia although you can get long-life milk in cartons

teh – tea, some people are not enthusiastic about Indonesian tea but if you don't need a strong, bend-the-teaspoon-style brew you'll probably find it's quite OK

tuak – palm beer, usually home produced

BOOKS & BOOKSHOPS
Early Books

There are many interesting books on Bali but the best is *Island of Bali* by Miguel Covarrubias. Written by a Mexican artist it was first published in 1937 by Alfred A Knopf and is widely available today as an Oxford University Press paperback. Although it's expensive (around 25,000 to 30,000 rp in Bali) it's a very worthwhile investment for anybody with a real interest in Bali, for few people have come to grips with Bali as well as Covarrubias

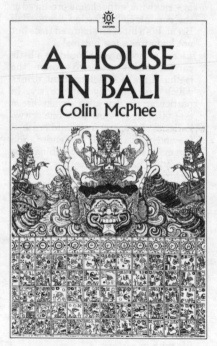

A HOUSE
IN BALI
Colin McPhee

before or since. It's readable yet learned, incredibly detailed yet always full of interest. Every subsequent guide to Bali owes this book a great debt. The closing thoughts (this was written in the 1930s

remember) that tourism may spoil Bali are thought-provoking but it's also a real pleasure to discover how much of Bali is still exactly the way Covarrubias describes it.

There are a number of other early books on Bali still readily available and many have recently been republished. Oxford University Press's Asian based Oxford Paperback series is doing great work in this area. Hickman Powell's *The Last Paradise* (Oxford Paperback) was first published in 1930 and is also very readable but is not on the same level as *Island of Bali*. At times it gets quite cloyingly over-romantic, everything is just too beautiful and too noble.

Colin McPhee's *A House In Bali* (Oxford Paperback again) is a superb, wonderful account of a musician's lengthy stays in Bali to study gamelan music. He's amazingly incisive and delightfully humorous and the book itself is superbly written. Like so many other western 'discoverers' of Bali his stay was in the 1930s but the book was first published in 1947.

Vicki Baum's *A Tale from Bali* is again from that magical time in the 1930s and is also published by Oxford Paperbacks.

K'Tut Tantri's *Revolt in Paradise* (Harper & Row, New York, 1960 and in an Indonesian paperback) tells of life on the island during the Indonesian revolution through the eyes of a western woman. She lived for some time at Kuta Beach in the 1930s, and stayed in Indonesia when the war broke out and suffered at the hands of the Japanese.

Our Hotel in Bali by Louise G Koke (January Books, New Zealand, 1987) is interesting because K'Tut Tantri may have been in partnership with the Kokes in their hotel at some point. Or maybe not, it's very hard to tell from either book! Louise and Robert Koke established the original Kuta Beach Hotel in the mid-30s and ran it until WW II spread to the Pacific. Louise Koke's fascinating account of running their hotel was written during the war but not published until 1987. It's readily available in Bali.

Hugh Mabbett's *The Balinese* (January Books, New Zealand, 1985) is a readable collection of anecdotes, observations and impressions of Bali and its people. See the Kuta section for information on *In Praise of Kuta*, a fascinating book from the same author.

Arts & Culture

For information on Bali's complex and colourful arts and culture look for the huge, and expensive, *The Art & Culture of Bali* by Urs Ramseyer (Oxford University Press). The Oxford Paperback series also includes *Dance & Drama In Bali* by Beryl de Zoete & Walter Spies. Originally published in 1938 this excellent book draws from Walter Spies' deep appreciation and understanding of Bali's arts and culture. He was yet another of the long term western visitors to Bali in the 1930s.

Balinese Paintings by A A M Djelantik (Oxford University Press, 1986) is a concise and handy overview of the field. An economical and useful introduction to Balinese painting can also be found in *Different Styles of Painting in Bali* published by the Neka Gallery in Ubud. It covers the various schools of painting and also has short biographies of well-known artists, including many of the western artists who have worked in Bali.

Modern Guides

Insight Bali (Apa Productions, Singapore) is a cross between a guidebook and a coffee-table paperback with many excellent photographs. Other photographic books on Bali include the coffee-table size *Bali – the Ultimate Island* by Leonard Leuras & R Ian Lloyd (Times Editions, Singapore).

For travel further afield in Indonesia look for Lonely Planet's *Indonesia – a travel survival kit* or *South-East Asia on a Shoestring* which also explore the entire archipelago and the region.

Over the years there have been a number of interesting *National Geographic* features on Bali including an article in the September 1963 issue on the disastrous eruption of Gunung Agung earlier that year.

Phrasebooks

See the language section to be convinced what a wise investment a phrasebook is for Bali. *Indonesia Phrasebook* is a concise and handy introduction to Bahasa Indonesia from the Lonely Planet Language Survival Kit series. There is little opportunity to use Balinese (rather than Bahasa Indonesia) in Bali and it's a far too complicated language to pick up without serious study but a few words can be interesting and fun. You can find a handy little booklet entitled *Balinese Vocabulary – 1000 Basic Words*.

Bookshops

Bali is not well endowed with good bookshops, in fact new books can be quite hard to find. Few places have really comprehensive collections of books on Bali but recently two new bookshops opened in Kuta and Sanur which are far better than the other bookshops. The Krishna Bookshop on the Legian Rd in Kuta and the Family Bookshop on Jalan Tanjung Sari in Sanur have a wide selection of English-language books, particularly on Indonesia.

Good small selections can also be found at the Bali Foto Centre at Kuta, at Murni's Warung in Ubud, and at the Neka Gallery in Ubud. None of them have a lot of books but they all have interesting selections, including some books you won't find elsewhere. You will often find the Oxford in Asia paperbacks already mentioned at these places. Prices of the same book will vary widely so it may be worth shopping around. In some (but not all) of the big hotels the mark-up on books is particularly severe.

If you just want something easy to read on the beach then your best bet will be the numerous second-hand bookshops around

Kuta, Legian and Sanur. You might also find the odd interesting book on Bali in these shops.

In Lombok there are a couple of bookshops on Jalan Pabean in Ampenan and others in Cakranegara but it's virtually impossible to pick up anything in English. Ruma Buku Titian on Jalan Pabean has the English-language *Jakarta Post* and they have a map of the island and English/Indonesian dictionaries. It's not possible, however, to get a Sasak/English dictionary or even a Sasak/Indonesian one.

WHAT TO BRING

As little as possible is the golden rule of good travelling. It's usually better to leave it behind and have to get a replacement when you're there rather than bring too much and have to lug unwanted items around.

You need little more than lightweight clothes – the temperature is uniformly tropical year round so short sleeve shirts or blouses and T-shirts are the order of the day. A light sweater is, however, a good idea for cool evenings and particularly if you're going up into the mountains. Kintamani, Penelokan and the other towns in the central mountain can actually get bloody cold. Up there a light jacket may also be necessary. You'll also need more protective gear if you're going to be travelling by motorcycle. Bare skin is never a good idea and up in the hills travelling by motorcycle can get very chilly indeed.

Even down near the coast a little protection can be a good idea to avoid sunburn. A hat and sunglasses are also useful to ward off that tropical sun. On the beach almost anything – as long as it's something – goes. Bikini tops are a rare sight on Bali's beaches.

Remember that in much of Asia, including Bali and particularly Lombok, shorts are not considered polite attire. At Kuta and the other beach resorts on Bali they've become a part of everyday life and

in any case tourists are considered a little strange and their clothing habits are expected to be somewhat eccentric.

In temples, however, you're expected to be reasonably well dressed and shorts don't fulfil that expectation. To be properly dressed in a temple you should also wear a temple scarf – a simple sash loosely tied around your waist. Many of the larger, more touristically important temples rent them out for 100 or 200 rp but you can buy one yourself for 1000 rp or less. You soon recoup the cost if you visit many temples and in addition you're certain of being politely dressed even at temples where there are no scarves for rent.

The Indonesian authorities have become somewhat fed up with western slobs turning up at public offices dressed in cast-offs. The 'how to dress' posters you see in Bali and Lombok may be amusing but there's a message behind it. If you want to renew a visa or even get a local driving licence ask yourself how you'd dress in a similar situation back home.

TAKE THE CHILDREN

Bali is a great place to travel with children, there can hardly be a place in the world where children are loved as much as they are in Bali. There will always be somebody ready to help you out and always other children ready to play with them. Our children, Tashi and Kieran, have been to Bali three times while we have been researching the three editions of this book. Maureen's notes follow:

Travelling with children anywhere requires energy and organisation, however, in Bali the problems are somewhat lessened by the Balinese affection for children – all children. To the Balinese, children seem to be considered communal property – everyone has a responsibility towards them, and everyone displays great interest in any western child they meet. You will have to learn to give their ages in Bahasa Indonesia (*bulan* means month, *tahun* means year), say what sex they are (*laki* is a boy, *perempuan* is a girl) and if you are feeding your baby (*susu mama*). Actually the women are most surprised if you do feed the child yourself and they will gather around and make comments and approving noises as they are convinced that 'susu mama' is the best.

Health & Food

Health and food are the main concerns of most parents travelling in Asia as there seem to be so many dangers for an adult, yet alone a young child. On our first visit to Bali with the children Kieran, our younger child, was four months old, and on the most recent trip Tashi, the elder one, was seven. With this experience I can say that with a only a little extra care travel in Asia need be no more dangerous than anywhere else.

For travelling babies I think it is essential that they are breast fed until they are 12 months old. Below the age of eight months the problems involved in carrying bottles, sterilising them, keeping them sterile, getting them to the right temperature, preparing formula hygienically, etc, are too mind boggling to consider. With breast feeding it is always there and it is always just right.

For babies from eight months, who are still getting their main nourishment from milk but are also eating, Bali is no problem. Mashed bananas, eggs, peelable fruit, bubur (which is also known as chicken porridge – rice cooked to a mush in chicken stock), and chicken with the skin peeled off, are all generally available. In Kuta, Sanur and probably Ubud you will find jars of baby food if you want something to fall back on. In the travellers' places (Kuta, Sanur, Ubud, Lovina Beach) yoghurt, pancakes, sometimes wholemeal bread, health foods, fruit juices and milk shakes are all available and all suitable as 'tastes' for this age group.

Older children, say one and over, who are really eating will have no problems. If you get away from the tourist areas the local food can be modified. Some children will really enjoy fried rice, others can become 'mee' addicts. Even if these don't appeal, eggs and fruit are a good standby and can be served up in recognisable forms.

All over the island cartons of milk, flavoured and plain, are available from the stores. This is longlife milk that comes in the same sealed boxes as fruit juice, complete with straw. They are a real lifesaver as they don't go off too quickly even when they have been opened, although don't keep them (opened) for more than 24 hours. If your baby uses a bottle, carry bottle sterilising tablets and ask your losmen or restaurant for some boiling water to soak the bottle and teat overnight whenever you think it might be a good idea. I found that the plastic cylindrical container that baby wipes come in was an ideal size for a small bottle and teat. If you clean one of these and take it with you it makes a very compact 'steriliser unit' complete with lid.

The main concern, of course, is that since you have to eat out all the time you have no control over how hygienically the food is prepared. In Bali my experience has been that most of the places that travellers eat in are fairly safe. If you are eating in 'untried' areas then the cardinal rules are don't eat uncooked food and don't drink fruit juices, or any other drinks which use water or ice. Teach your children to always wash their hands after going to the toilet and before meals. Carry baby wipes for occasions when soap and water aren't available.

I always carried a water container which was only used for boiled water, I also dropped a steriliser tab in to make doubly sure. I used this mainly for teeth cleaning but also for drinking when nothing else was available.

In Bali bottled water is available in most places. Ensure that the brand of water is a reputable one, and the seal is intact.

If your child does develop stomach

trouble, it may be no more than 'tourist trots'. This is generally characterised by very loose to liquid stools, frequently passed. If your child does not appear to be suffering pain from stomach cramps, if the stools do not contain blood or mucus, if there is no fever and if your child does not appear to be ill, then don't worry but do take care.

If, however, any of the other mentioned symptoms are present, find a doctor quickly. The major danger is dehydration and it is a good idea to carry an electrolyte mixture with you for such cases. This usually comes in powder form, in individual sachets, and has to be mixed with water so make sure the water is clean. This solution should be given to your child at the recommended intervals. Your child may be tired and not interested in eating, but don't worry, they will soon regain any lost weight once they are well. The main concern is to keep up fluid intake and let the child rest. Ask your doctor to recommend a kaolin mixture for your child before you go, Pepto Bismal is very good for mild runs and can be given to quite young children.

Apart from stomach upsets (although in our trips to Bali our children have had absolutely no stomach troubles) there are not too many other problems health wise.

It is a good idea to treat any cut or scratch with respect, no matter how slight it is. Mercurochrome should be put on immediately. In a tropical climate any scratch can quickly become infected and be very slow to heal. A good antibiotic cream (non greasy) or powder would be a useful addition to the medical kit. Something like Stingose is good for treating mosquito bites and there is an Aerogard lotion which is good and can also be used as a repellent. An antihistamine may also be useful if your child has several bites and is having trouble getting to sleep. Antihistamines are also useful as a preventative for travel sickness.

Still on the subject of mosquitoes Bali is

officially in the malarial zone and although the risk is slight your children should take malarial prophylactics, particularly if you're going to be travelling around. If you're going to Lombok then malarials are definitely required. Some doctors recommend the daily tablets while others advise the weekly one but I strongly recommend that with children you opt for the weekly one. Then you're only going to face a major battle getting the tablet down a protesting toddler's throat once a week instead of every single morning. You can also get anti-malarials for children in syrup form.

You should provide additional protection against malaria by keeping mosquitoes away. Malaria carrying mosquitoes really only appear after dark, so, at night-time use a good insect repellent (lotions and creams last longer than sprays). Loose cotton pyjamas which cover most of the body are a good idea. A mosquito net is good if you can work out a way of stringing it up. Burning mosquito coils may not appeal but they do help to keep the little devils away and a good insecticide which you can spray round your room before you go out for an evening meal helps to keep the mossie population down.

If your child starts running a temperature the main thing is to keep her cool. Bathe her frequently, remove clothes, and administer infant panadol or a similar analgesic every three to four hours. If the temperature does not come down, call a doctor. An infant analgesic, medicine measure or dropper, a thermometer, a bandage and some band-aids are probably all you need to carry. Just about everything is available in Sanur or Kuta and the big hotels will be able to recommend a doctor, whether you are staying there or not.

Never let your child run around in bare feet, remember there are many animals leaving their calling cards all over the walkways, and various worms and other parasites can enter through the feet. While on the subject of animals it is a good idea to instil in your children a healthy respect for the animals that they will encounter. Balinese dogs do not arouse a desire in many adults to pat them, but children are often oblivious to appearances. Rabies is still widespread in Indonesia and monkeys, squirrels and bats can also transmit it.

The sun is another potential hazard. I covered both my children with a total sun block for the first few days, then graduated to a regular protective lotion which for babies should be used just about every time you go out. Both my children seem to tan easily, but I would suggest that protection against the sun be taken at all times. A light caftan is useful, and hats are a must for very small children. Remember a child can burn in a few minutes, even walking to the restaurant just around the corner at lunch time.

If your child gets sunburnt use something like Caladryl which is a calamine lotion, mild antiseptic, antihistamine and skin soother. There is also a gel which is an insect repellent and sun block in one. It would be useful in keeping the flies away at the beach but check to make sure that the sun block is strong enough.

On the whole I found my children have been remarkably healthy during their trips to Bali. At first I worried when Tashi disappeared with the local children to play at their home that she might be offered a drink of well water and become ill, but it never seemed to happen. I think it is important to try and maintain a balance between being overcautious for their safety, which means that your child will miss out on many social experiences, and being too relaxed.

Nappies/Diapers

I carted 80 or so disposable nappies with me on our first 'with the children' Bali trip. They are very light, so it is no problem with your weight allowance, but they are bulky. Disposables are available at Kuta in the European Market, at Sanur and in many other places as well. They're expensive but not astronomically so. I carried a plastic mat, baby wipes, vaseline and a good cream for sore bottoms (all available in Kuta). A number of medium sized plastic bin bags is a good idea to put the dirty nappies in before disposing of them. I have met travelling families who took cloth nappies and washed them each day. I, however, didn't fancy that idea much as having to carry a dirty, soggy nappy with me on a day's trip really did not appeal.

What do the Balinese do about this problem? Basically, like most people in the third world, they don't do anything. Babies often go around bare bottomed and where it happens, it happens. You just hope they aren't sitting on your knee at the time! On the second trip I only carried half a dozen disposables and Kieran was toilet trained by the time we left – a good place to do it!

Social

First of all let us look at your social life. On our first 'with the children' Bali trip, romantic dinners at Poppies seemed to be few and far between. On subsequent trips, however, we organised babysitters regularly. It's easy and cheap. Upmarket hotels and losmen will organise babysitters for you, usually from the workers at the hotel. They will set a rate which is generally not excessive. I have no qualms about leaving children with Balinese child minders, the only problem is they will be very disappointed if the children are asleep when they arrive, and may even want to wake them up to play with them!

If you are staying at more modest losmen you will find little sisters of the losmen owner will haunt your room in order to see and play with your children. Generally speaking any child over nine will be a perfectly responsible child minder and can be trusted. However, if the child cries the Balinese get most upset and insist on finding mother and handing the child over with a reproachful look. I remember pushing Kieran, screaming, in his stroller along one of Kuta's busiest roads. I wasn't allowed to progress very far before several Balinese stopped me and told me the child was crying, and I was expected to do something immediately. No good trying to explain that he would very shortly go to sleep and that I wouldn't let him scream for too long, I had to pick him up there and then.

Your child's social life can be quite hectic. Tashi had a lovely time playing with the Balinese children. It didn't seem to matter that they didn't speak the same language, they communicated beautifully. She learnt to make offerings to the gods, go to the market and help keep losmens clean. She learnt a little Indonesian and on our subsequent trips to Bali she was thrilled to resume a friendship with Ketut whom she remembered well.

You will meet lots of locals who will want to photograph your child. That can be very nice but your toddler may be a bit fed up with all the attention. Tashi learnt to yell 'go away' when they went too far, and I thought that was fair enough. It can become very upsetting for children if they are the centre of too much adult interest.

One thing to be aware of on the beach is that many Balinese children are not good swimmers although they may splash around quite happily in the shallows. If your children can swim well they can easily attract local children in beyond their abilities. You have a responsibility to keep an eye out for them as well!

Equipment
Apart from what I have already mentioned, I think a stroller, or if your child is old enough, a backpack carrier, is essential. It may seem a nuisance to carry on and off planes, buses, bemos, etc, but unless you carry something that your child can sit in, you are condemned to having your child on your knee constantly, at meals and everywhere else. We had a stroller for Kieran on the first trip as he was too young for the back carrier and it was most useful

in restaurants when I wanted to eat a meal in peace. It caused a great deal of amusement amongst the Balinese who obviously thought it was more evidence of our ingenuity, although utterly useless in a Balinese context where a never-ending stream of sisters, brothers, aunts and so on are available to help get Ketut or Nyoman from A to B.

Actually the stroller came in very useful on the plane going to Bali, the Garuda crew were nonplussed to find that the bassinet they produced so proudly did not work. I put the stroller up in front of our seats so that we didn't have to hold Kieran the entire trip to Bali. A few books for older children, their familiar teddy, a bag full of Lego pieces, little people, or various little vehicles, are all the toys they will need. The Balinese children do not have such things and will gather around to watch. You can use these occasions to encourage your children to invite the children to play with them. While your child may not be at an age where sharing appeals, it is worthwhile because the local children are so thrilled with the toys and so pleased to get a chance to play with them. Towards the end of the trip they also make nice presents for any child who has been a particular friend.

Older Children
Problems diminish as your children get older. The more they understand about Bali the more they'll enjoy it so encourage them to learn about Balinese customs, art, dancing and religion. On our second and third 'with the children' trips we seemed to run into many more western children in Bali and each trip seems to have been better and easier than the one before.

SURFING
Bali has long had a reputation as something of a surfing Mecca, an image helped on its way by a number of superb surfing-travelling films. Kirk Willcox, at the time editor of the Australian surfing

Top: Children by the sea, Candidasa, Bali (JP)
Bottom: People arriving at a temple, Ubud, Bali (JP)

Top: Temple offerings, Bedugul, Bali (TW)
Bottom: Getting ready for a procession, Bali (MC)

Bali Bagus

magazine *Tracks*, compiled the following 'Surfer's Guide to Bali'. Since he wrote this for the first edition the island of Nusa Penida has become a new surfing attraction.

Going to Bali and not surfing is akin to going to the snowfields for two weeks and not leaving the bar. Besides all its culture and charm, Bali is surfing. A month here with good swell can provide the surfing holiday of your lifetime. The best way to approach a surfing trip to this lush, tropical isle is to ease yourself into it, familiarise yourself with the numerous breaks, and then cut loose. You will find that you will be able to test, and even stretch, a few of your own limits, especially during bigger swells.

Equipment & Getting it There
To surf the place properly you need the right equipment. For a small board, the one you usually ride in Australia will be adequate. A few inches on your usual length won't go astray. As your knowledge of the island's breaks grows, and the surf increases accordingly, you will find an urge to surf the bigger waves, eight foot and upwards, even if you have never surfed this size before. In Bali, surfing this size on your small board is ridiculous. The main problem is getting into the wave early enough to avoid disaster. It is here that you will need a gun. For a surfer of average height and build a board around the seven foot mark is perfect.

Bali's waves aren't as heavy as Hawaii but they can still pack a punch, especially the reef breaks. But before you start worrying about the live coral reefs you will need to think about your boards and how to get them there in one piece. You will have no opportunity to make a mess of yourself if you don't get your boards there in reasonable condition in the first place.

There are a number of good travel

covers on the market. The best are made in the United States and are quite expensive. Most surfers don't have a lot of money so your best bet is to improvise. Go to your local surf shop and ask them for some bubble plastic which they receive many of their new boards in. Wrap your equipment in this, paying particular care to protecting the nose and tail, and then use a normal cloth board cover on top of this. If you have removable fins, all the better. Take them out and pack them with your luggage, making sure you have the screws in a safe place. And while you're at it, buy an extra fin or two.

When packing your bag, pay attention to some other necessary items which will help you have a good surfing trip. The obvious one is wax. What is not so obvious is the choice of wax and basically it comes down to personal preference. Remember you will be surfing in tepid water and that the sun is extremely hot. (Like what you would surf in your bathtub, or think of a typical hot summer day.) Last trip I found sticky wax to be very good. The best idea is to take a mix and to take a lot, say 10 blocks. What you don't use you can give to the local surfers or board carriers, or to other surfers travelling further on.

In case your board suffers damage, you should pack some resin, hardener, glass and sandpaper. Surfboard materials are quite hard to come by in Bali and it is always advisable to have your own. Even if you don't know what to do with this ding repair equipment, you can always find someone who does. Unfixed dings mean injuries to yourself and others and one of the prime objectives you must keep in mind when surfing in Bali is to avoid injuries. A serious injury can mean the end of a holiday and weeks spent recuperating at home.

To protect your feet take a pair of wetsuit booties. These are extremely useful when you have to walk across the coral reefs at low tide. They also provide some protection in mean wipeouts, especially if you land feet first. If you land

head first, that's a different matter. If you don't like the feel on your board, have a large pocket sewn on your boardshorts and put them on only when you have to traverse the reefs.

A wetsuit singlet vest is also very handy. Not only does it protect you from chills on windy, overcast days (yes, it does occasionally get overcast in Bali) but it also provides some protection to your back and chest during a fall on the sharp, coral reefs. If you are a real tube maniac and will drive into anything no matter what the consequences, you are advised to take a short-sleeved springsuit. If you are an exceedingly poor surfer with a penchant for coral reefs, you are well advised to take a full-length steamer or, better still, think about going somewhere else for your surfing holiday, like Balmoral Beach in Sydney Harbour.

Surviving Surfing

The first thing you will notice about Bali, after the humidity, is the strength of the sun. Unless you have a good tan when you leave home, wear a T-shirt when surfing and take ample supplies of a good sun block. If you don't you will find yourself missing out on a good surf simply because you can't move.

This takes us on to medical matters and your well-equipped medical kit could become your best friend. Not only are the coral reefs a danger but the Balinese have quaint cactus fences along bike trails. Spin out here and you'll end up looking like a pin cushion and feeling much worse. A bottle of surgical spirit is excellent. Splash it liberally on your cuts each night and also take a needle to remove sea urchin spines. You can even get these little gremlins in your fingers while paddling across the shallow reefs, though they usually inflict themselves upon your feet. Decent band-aids that won't come off in the water are also necessary. Elastoplast is excellent. There are fairly well-stocked chemists in Bali but it is easier to take

your own. Don't forget cotton buds for
cleaning wounds.

Take a good pair of joggers for the walk
into Ulu Watu, it's three km and very
rocky. Joggers are also vital equipment on
your bike, if you decide to hire one.
Transporting your board is difficult
unless you have a boardstrap. Just buy a
normal one and add some foam padding
to the shoulder, the more generous the
better. While on the bike with your board
any animal which comes within 20 metres
should be treated as a traffic hazard. Give
the same respect to any car and, more so,
any truck.

If you manage to write yourself off
severely while surfing, or on the way to
surfing, which is just as dangerous, head
to the top hotels where there are good
doctors. There are also private Balinese
doctors' surgeries where you'll be stitched
up with what resembles thick string.
Don't go to the general hospital. It's where
people go when they want to die. If you
don't feel quite like dying, go to the
expensive private annexe. If you nearly
feel that bad, however, get on the next
plane home. You might regret trying to be
a hero. On the same sort of line, brush up
on basic mouth-to-mouth resuscitation.
You will be surprised how often you might
be called upon to use it, especially around
the beachbreaks in the late afternoon
when the swell is a solid six foot. It is a
popular sport among the Europeans and
other foreigners to go to Bali to drown. You
can at least help keep their thrill-seeking
to a minimum.

Where to Surf

Well, after arriving in Bali, finding
accommodation, getting transport and
basically settling in, you are ready for your
first surf in Bali. Taking an educated
guess you are now probably sitting outside
your losmen in the Kuta-Legian region,
taking your board out of its cover. Slowly,
but deliberately, prepare it and yourself
for your first surf. I emphasise slowly,
don't rush into this. Take your time and

take stock of the situation around you. It's
all foreign and different and you should
treat the surf the same way.

Kuta & Legian For your first plunge into the
warm Indian Ocean, try the beachbreaks
around Half-way Kuta, or up at Legian, or
at Kuta Reef. If you are a bit rusty, start at
the beachbreaks. The sand here is finer
than in Australia and consequently is
packed harder so it is harder when you hit
it. Treat even these breaks with respect.
They provide zippering left and right
barrels over shallow banks and can be
quite a lot of fun. Some days you will not
feel like travelling anywhere on the island
looking for surf and you will be content
with little sessions out here.

It is also here that you will encounter
most of the local Balinese surfers. Over
the years their surfing standard has
improved enormously and because of this,
and also because it is their island, treat
them with respect. By and large they're
usually quite amenable in the water,
however, some surfers have found their
holidays cut short by a falling out with the
locals. Avoid getting into fights and give
them the benefit of the doubt on a wave.

To the south of the beachbreaks, about
a km out to sea, lies Kuta Reef, a vast
stretch of coral reef which provides a
variety of waves. The main break is a left-
hander. The easiest way out there is by
outrigger. You will be dropped out there
and brought back in for a fee. Kuta Reef
can be a very fine left, especially around
the five to six foot mark, its optimum size.
Over this it tends to double up and
section. At five to six feet it peels across
the reef and has a beautiful inside tube
section; the first part is a good workable
wave. The reef is well-suited for backhand
surfing. It's not surfable at dead low tide
but you can get out there not long after the
tide turns. The boys on the boats can
advise you if necessary.

When the swell is at its optimum size
here, looking further south along the reef
(remember facing out to the ocean is west)

you will notice another left, usually with fewer surfers out. This wave is more of a peak and provides a short, intense ride. There are even more breaks out there, but that's for you to explore as you get the urge.

Ulu Watu OK, say Kuta Reef is five to six feet today, then Ulu Watu, that most famed surfing break on Bali, will be six to eight feet with bigger sets. Kuta and Legian sit on a huge bay. Ulu is south, way out on the southern extremity of the bay, and it consequently picks up more swell than Kuta. It's about a half-hour journey. If you go by bemo you will have to walk the last part in, about three km. A cap is useful to shade you from the sun. A young Balinese will carry your board and gear (a small backpack is very useful) into Ulu for a fee. He will also wax it, get drinks for you and carry it down into the cave, one of the only ways out to the waves.

Ulu Watu is a phenomenal spot and you will easily see why it has earned its reputation. After the walk through cow paddocks and fields you will get your first glimpse of the ocean. If you go by bike you can ride most of the way in. Walkers use the same track, with a few shortcuts. A concrete stairway leads into the Ulu gorge and in front of you is a sight you will never forget, especially if a decent swell is running. The thatched warungs are set on one side of the gorge, above the cave. One warung is right on the edge of the cliff, which is of The Gap proportions. The Ulu Watu bay stretches out in front of you. In the shade you can eat, drink, rest, even stay overnight. It is one of the best setups for surfers in the world and everything is carried in by the Balinese.

Ulu Watu has about seven different breaks. The most commonly surfed are the Inside Corner and the Peak. If it is your first trip here sit for a while in the shade and survey the situation. See where other surfers are sitting in the lineup and watch where they flick off. The Corner is straight in front of you to the right. It's a fast-breaking, hollow left that holds about six foot. The reef shelf under this break is extremely shallow so try to avoid falling head first. As the tide comes up, the Peak starts to work. This is good from five to eight feet with occasional bigger waves right on the Peak itself. You can take off from this inside part or further down the line. A great wave.

When the swell is bigger, Outside Corner starts operating. This is a tremendous big wave break and on a good day you can surf one wave for hundreds of metres. The wall here on a 10-foot wave jacks up with a big drop and bottom turn then the bowl section. After this it becomes a big workable face. You can usually only get tubed in the first section. When surfing this break you need a board with length, otherwise you won't be getting down the face of any of these amazing waves.

Out behind the Peak, when it's big, is a bombora appropriately called, the Bommie. This is another big left-hander and it doesn't start operating till the swell is about 10 foot. On a normal five to eight foot day there are also breaks south of the Peak. One is a very fast left, and also very hollow, usually only ridden by goofy-footers because of its speed. There is another left running off the cliff which forms the southern flank of the bay. It breaks outside this in bigger swells and once it's seven foot a left-hander pitches right out in front of a temple on the southern extremity. Know your limits.

Observe where other surfers paddle out and follow them. If you are in doubt, ask someone. It is better having some knowledge than none at all. Climb down into the cave and paddle out from there. When it's bigger you will be swept to your right. Don't panic, it is an easy matter to paddle around the whitewater from down along the cliff. Coming back in you have to aim for the cave. When it's bigger, come from the south side of the cave as the current runs to the north. If you miss the cave, paddle out again and repeat the procedure. If you get into trouble ask for help from a fellow surfer and remember not to panic, it's the worst thing you can do.

Padang Padang So, you've survived your first surf at Ulu and now realise, if you've done everything right, that there is no need to be paranoid of the place. Feel like something more of an adrenalin rush? Yes? Well then, you're ready for Padang Padang. This is a super-shallow reef break, again a left, north of Ulu towards Kuta. There are a number of ways to get there. If you are at Ulu you can simply walk along a narrow cliff track and climb down to the beach. Again, check this place carefully before venturing out.

If you can't surf tubes, backhand or forehand, don't go out. Padang is a tube. After a ledgey take-off, you power along the bottom before pulling up into the barrel. So far so good, now for the tricky part. The last section turns inside out like a washing machine on fast forward. You have to drive high through this section, all the time while in the tube. Don't worry if you fail to negotiate this trap, plenty of other surfers have been caught too. After this the wave fills up and you flick off. Not a wave for the faint-hearted and definitely not a wave to surf when there's a crowd.

Canggu After all this you might like a nice, gentle right-hander, with perhaps the choice of a left. The place for you is Canggu. This beach, with a softer reef bottom, is to the north of Kuta, on the northern extremity of the bay. Five to six foot is an optimum size for Canggu. It's a good right-hander that you can really hook into, plus there's the left. There's also a warung or two here. Motorbike is the best way to get to Canggu. You have to walk along the beach if you come by bemo because the track between the rice paddies has eroded away.

Medowi Further up the island is a softer left called Medowi. This wave has a big drop, which fills up then runs into a workable inside section. Worth surfing if you feel like something different, but to catch it you need to get up early in the morning.

These are the waves you usually surf in the dry season. The swells thunder in from the south-south-west and it is often offshore.

Sanur During the wet season, roughly November to March, you surf on the Sanur side of the island. There are some very fine reef breaks over here. Sanur itself is a hollow, right-hand reef which has excellent barrels. From there you can see a number of reefs further offshore and most of them are surfable. The problem with the wet season is getting around safely. Bali's dirt tracks become very muddy and slippery. The main road to Sanur is now very good so the back roads of Kuta are the ones to worry about.

If this is your first trip to Bali I think this is enough grounding. There are many semi-secret spots on the island. Ulu is a definite favourite and is an excellent wave both backhand and forehand. As a surfer you can still do a lot of adventuring in Bali exploring new spots. On days when it seems too flat, or you don't think there is any decent surf around, talk to the locals. They'll be able to point you in the right direction.

If you snap your board in half, there are several surf shops selling second-hand boards. Plans are well underway at the moment for a board factory on the island run by Australians who are teaching some of the locals board-building skills.

Don't approach the surf lacking in confidence, but equally important don't paddle out at new reefs overly confident. Feel the place out. Here your sixth sense is as good as your other five.

DIVING

Bali isn't usually thought of as a great spot for diving but actually it offers some superb diving possibilities. If you just want to do a little snorkelling there's pretty good coral reef at Nusa Dua, Sanur and along the Singaraja beach strip on the north coast. There's also good diving at Padangbai, both off the beach or from boats which can take you out to the fine reefs offshore. Scuba divers can find more demanding possibilities.

The Balina Beach resort between Padangbai and Candidasa caters especially for divers and offers a variety of diving trips for their guests and other visitors. Some of these trips include:

	diving	snorkelling
Pulau Menjangan	US$50	US$20
Nusa Penida	US$45	US$18
Lovina Beach	US$40	US$15
Tulamben	US$35	US$10
Amed	US$32	US$8
Pulau Kambing	US$30	US$7

Two of the most popular diving spots are Pulau Menjangan and Tulamben.

Pulau Menjangan

Off the north-west corner of Bali this totally uninhabited and unspoilt island is a nature reserve and has superb coral. There's accommodation available at Teluk Terima.

Tulamben

On the north-east coast there are two popular diving adventures near here. First there's an amazing reef with a sheer drop of 800 metres. The second attraction is the American ship SS *Liberty*, sunk by the Japanese in 1942 and offering fascinating diving at depths between 10 and 40 metres. Recently a losmen has opened close to the wreck.

Getting There

Flying to Denpasar, the main town and airport of Bali, is slightly complicated by restrictions on flights into Bali. The Indonesians have wanted to ensure that Jakarta, the Indonesian capital, is the gateway to the country and therefore they have restricted the availability of flights into Bali. So from most countries you have to fly to Jakarta and transfer to a domestic flight there. This policy may be relaxed in the future.

The exceptions are when flying Garuda (the Indonesian national airline) or Qantas (the Australian national airline). These two airlines have direct flights into Bali from various places in Australia, and Garuda also has connections from Europe through Jakarta and Denpasar to Australia, and from Los Angeles on the United States west coast to Denpasar via Honolulu and the eastern Indonesian island of Biak.

FROM AUSTRALIA
There are direct flights from Sydney, Melbourne, Brisbane, Perth, Darwin and, believe it or not, Port Hedland. Only Garuda operates the Darwin service and only Qantas flies from Brisbane. Both Garuda and Qantas operate flights on the other sectors.

Both airlines operate direct Melbourne/Denpasar flights some days of the week, and via Sydney on the other days. Some Garuda flights go Melbourne/Sydney/Denpasar while some go Sydney/Melbourne/Denpasar. Flight time Melbourne/Denpasar is about 5½ to 6½ hours; and Sydney/Denpasar is slightly shorter. For West Australians Bali is almost a local resort. Perth/Denpasar flying time is just 3½ hours, less time than it takes to go from Perth to the east coast of Australia.

There's one very interesting alternative to the Garuda or Qantas flights and that is

to take Merpati from Darwin to Kupang on the island of Timor. From Kupang there are regular flights to Bali or you can island-hop through the Nusa Tenggara archipelago to Bali. The Merpati agent in Darwin is Natrabu (tel 81 3695) at 10 Westlane Arcade off Smith St Mall. The Darwin/Kupang fare is A$132 one-way or A$205 return. From there the Kupang/Bali fare is 96,000 rp, about A$70. So you can get from Darwin to Bali for about A$200 one-way or A$350 return. It is a roundabout route but it is certainly much cheaper than the direct Garuda flight.

There are two discount fares available between Australia and Bali. Excursion fares are available to anyone, but the other category, tour inclusive fares, are only available in connection with a holiday package. Both fares have a high and a low season.

The high season means the Christmas holiday period. For an excursion fare that is from 22 November to 15 January, and for the tour inclusive fare it's 10 December to 19 January. At certain times during that peak season, flights to or from Australia are very heavily booked and you must plan well ahead if you want to visit Bali then. In particular getting back to Australia at the end of January, just before Australian schools start after the summer break, can be difficult.

There is no one-way excursion fare to Bali but there is a one-way advance purchase fare. This must be purchased 21 days prior to departure and there are cancellation penalties within that period. This fare is also seasonal and the same season as return excursion fares applies. East coast (Brisbane, Melbourne or Sydney) fares are the same, and fares from Perth or Darwin are also the same. Fares to Denpasar in Australian dollars are:

from	season	one-way	return excursion	package
Melbourne,	high	558	889	791
Sydney or	low	483	782	715
Brisbane				
Perth or	high	351	667	607
Darwin	low	295	591	512
Port Hedland	high	371	698	637
	low	315	621	543

To get the tour inclusive package fare you have to combine the fare with an accommodation package. Some tour operators and travel agents can arrange tour inclusive fare and minimal accommodation packages that cost about the same as the cheapest advance purchase fare. As the package includes accommodation they're particularly good bargains on short trips. Cheap children's tour inclusive fares are also available. Tour inclusive fares for low season departures allow a maximum stay of 45 days; for high season departures the maximum stay is 90 days.

Tour inclusive fares can be offered with 'voucher' tours. You buy a package in Australia which includes air fare and hotel accommodation. You're given vouchers which can be used to pay for accommodation at a number of hotels around the island. Sometimes the vouchers can also be used for motorcycle or bicycle rental, even for meals. Usually the vouchers are good for the cheaper losmen and hotels – don't expect three-star accommodation. The real bargain with this set-up is that the total cost on a short trip can actually be lower than the straight excursion fare. The vouchers are just a useful bonus – you don't even have to use them.

Packages
Complete package tours from Australia can also be a real bargain. There are a variety of tour types available. Straight-forward tours include your air fare, airport transfers, hotel accommodation and perhaps some meals and the odd tour. The price varies depending on when you go, how long you stay and what class of hotel you stay in. The hotels will generally be in Kuta, Sanur or Nusa Dua. Some typical costs from Sydney or Melbourne on a share twin basis are seven days (five nights) from around A$700 to A$1200. Extra nights can cost from as little as A$15 to as much as A$100 per person.

Travel agents and airline offices will have plenty of colourful brochures to whet your appetite. Check a few brochures because costs vary quite a bit from one operator to another – even on packages using the same hotels. Supplementary tours and extensions can be made but a lot of the tours offered can be obtained far more cheaply in Bali. You can rent a whole minibus in Bali for US$25 a day – including driver and fuel. Some packages offer a supplementary visit to Lombok.

FROM NEW ZEALAND
In late '88 Garuda introduced a weekly service from Auckland to Bali, with some talk of increasing this to two flights a week. The fares from New Zealand to Bali operate on a similar system to the Australian fares, but as this is a relatively new service fares and discounts through travel agents should only get better.

The one way fare to Bali is a full economy class fare of NZ$1389. The return excursion fare is NZ$1456 for low season departures and NZ$1586 for high season. Low season is from 1 to 31 March and from 1 to 31 November; high season is from 1 April to 31 August and from 1 December to 28 February. The maximum stay away is 90 days. Check latest fares developments and discounts with Garuda or shop around a few travel agents for any new deals.

FROM EUROPE
Ticket discounting is a long established business in the UK. The various agents

advertise their fares and there's nothing under the counter about it at all. To find out what is available and where to get it, pick up a copy of the giveaway newspapers *Australasian Express* or *LAW* or the weekly 'what's on' guide *Time Out*. These days discounted tickets are available all over England, they're not just a London exclusive. The magazine *Business Traveller* also covers the cheap fare possibilities.

A couple of excellent places to look are Trailfinders (tel 938 3366) at 46 Earls Court Rd, London W8 and STA Travel at 74 Old Brompton Rd, London W7 (tel 581 1022) and at Clifton House, 117 Euston Rd (tel 388 2261).

Garuda is one of the enthusiastic fare discounters in London so it's relatively easy to find cheap fares to Australia with stopovers in Indonesia. It's not, however, such a bargain to go just to Bali or Bali return. A London/Australia ticket with a stopover in Jakarta (and Singapore or Bangkok for that matter) costs around £600, add another £100 to include Bali. London/Denpasar costs around £300 one-way and £580 return.

Another alternative is to fly London/Singapore for around £250 one-way or £475 return and then make your own way down to Bali by air or sea and land.

FROM NORTH AMERICA

You can pick up interesting tickets from North American to South-East Asia, particularly from the US west coast or from Vancouver. In fact the intense competition between Asian airlines has resulted in ticket discounting operations very similar to the London bucket shops. To find cheap tickets simply scan the travel sections of the Sunday papers for agents – the *New York Times, San Francisco Chronicle-Examiner* and the *Los Angeles Times* are particularly good. The network of student travel offices known as Council Travel are particularly good and there are also Student Travel Network offices which are associated with Student Travel Australia.

From the US west coast you can get to Hong Kong, Bangkok or Singapore for about US$500 to US$750 return and get a flight from there to Bali. Discount tickets for a Hong Kong/Denpasar flight can be bought for around HK$2700 to HK$3000, with return fares around HK$4000. You can also find interesting fares from Hong Kong via Bali to Australia. Singapore/Denpasar costs around S$400 one-way and S$550 return.

Alternatively Garuda has a Los Angeles/Honolulu/Biak/Denpasar route which is an extremely interesting back door route into Indonesia and good value at US$472 one-way or about US$800 return. Biak is a no-visa entry point so that's no problem.

FROM ASIA

Although you may find cheap fares from various Asian countries to Bali there are few direct flights. In most cases you will have to enter Indonesia at Jakarta and then fly to Bali. Even flying with Garuda will usually mean a change of aircraft.

FROM/TO JAVA

Air

Garuda fares from Denpasar include Surabaya for 45,000 rp, Yogyakarta for 57,900 rp and Jakarta for 104,000 rp. Merpati and Bouraq also fly from Denpasar to various centres in Java and their fares will always be lower than Garuda's fare. Note that if you want to change your ticket with Garuda there's a 10,000 rp cancellation and reissuance charge.

Bus

The standard travellers' route from Java to Bali is the Surabaya to Denpasar bus. There are numerous bus companies operating on this route, and many of them travel overnight. The fare includes the ferry crossing and often a meal at a rest stop along the way. There are also direct bus services between Yogyakarta and Denpasar.

In Bali you can get tickets from numerous agents around Kuta or Denpasar. You'll also find a collection of bus company offices, and other agents, at the Suci bus station in Denpasar. Fares depend on the bus and cost more with air-con. Buses to Surabaya range in price from 9000 to 11,500 rp and to Yogyakarta they vary from 13,000 to 20,000 rp.

When you book you're assigned a seat number; check the seating chart and I'd advise avoiding the front rows. The night-bus drivers rush along like maniacs and who wants to be first to find out about the accident? In fact the night buses now make the Denpasar to Surabaya trip so rapidly that early evening departures are liable to arrive at an uncomfortably early hour in the morning.

Train

There is no railway in Bali but agents will ticket you by bus and ferry to Banyuwangi, the railhead at the eastern end of Java.

Ferry

The ferry that shuttles back and forth across the narrow strait between Bali and Java is pleasantly cheap and the crossing only takes 15 minutes. For a passenger it's just 395 rp (children 300 rp). You can take a bicycle across for 200 rp, a motorcycle for 875 rp or a car for 4300 to 6200 rp. On the Java side the terminus is not actually in the Java ferry port of Banyuwangi. It's actually right out of the town at Ketapang but there is regular transport into Banyuwangi. Buses to other parts of Java depart straight from the ferry terminal.

FROM/TO LOMBOK

Air

You can fly from Denpasar to Mataram with Merpati. The flight takes less than half an hour and costs 20,000 rp. There are regular flights and extra ones seem to be added as necessary. If you take an early morning flight from Denpasar you can move from the beach at Kuta to a beach on one of the Gili Islands by lunchtime.

Merpati have connections from Mataram to other islands in Nusa Tenggara, the island chain to the east of Bali.

Garuda flies from Surabaya to Mataram for 57,000 rp.

Ferry

There's a twice daily ferry service at around 10 am and 2 pm from the small port of Padangbai, east of Denpasar. The ferry office in Padangbai is at the pier. It's an idea to get there well before departure time as the ferry is sometimes completely full and schedules may be adjusted due to the tides. Anyway Padangbai is a pleasant place to spend a day or two.

First class tickets cost 4775 rp and Ekonomi is 3325 rp. Children are about half price. You can also take bikes, motorcycles and jeeps with you. It costs 500 rp for a bike, 3300 rp for a motorcycle, 38,500 rp for a jeep, and 49,000 rp for a car. The ferry docks at Lembar, south of Mataram-Ampenan, in Lombok.

Food, soft drinks, coffee, tea and cigarettes are available on board from the small bars in 1st and 2nd class or from the numerous hawkers who hang around the wharf until the ferry leaves. The trip takes a minimum of five hours, often up to seven, and the afternoon ferry is always slower than the morning one. On the way across you can buy a ticket for transport into Ampenan, Mataram or Cakranegara. If you're arriving on the afternoon ferry after dark this can be important because there's nothing in Lembar and you may find transport difficult (or expensive) without a ticket.

From Lembar to Padangbai ferries also

depart twice daily and you can buy tickets at the wharf on the day or at the office in Ampenan-Mataram. Bus and bemo drivers drop you off almost directly in front of the office. You can get a cup of coffee and something to eat at the canteen here but don't expect to be able to buy any food from people on the Lembar wharf. They're nowhere to be seen.

FROM/TO OTHER PARTS OF INDONESIA

Air

In some instances it is cheaper to fly to other parts of Indonesia from Bali than from Java. For example, from Denpasar to Ujung Pandang (Sulawesi) the fare is cheaper than from Surabaya to Ujung Pandang. There are flights from Denpasar to other parts of Nusa Tenggara including all the way to Kupang and Dili in Timor.

TICKETS FROM BALI

There are numerous airline ticket discounters around Kuta. Typical fares from Denpasar to Asia include Singapore US$150, Bangkok US$250, Hong Kong US$300, Tokyo US$350. From Denpasar to Australia fares are Darwin or Perth US$210, Sydney or Melbourne US$376. Further afield you can fly from Denpasar to the US west coast for US$550 to US$650 or to London for about US$550.

You can also get tickets ex-Jakarta in Bali. To Asian destinations typical fares include Singapore US$125, Bangkok US$250, Calcutta US$400, Kuala Lumpur US$150, Taipei US$450. You can also hook up on the UTA trans-Pacific services out of Jakarta with good fares to the Pacific and to the US west coast.

DENPASAR AIRPORT ARRIVAL

The airport arrival procedures are fairly typical. There's a hotel booking counter in the luggage arrival hall but they only have the more expensive places on their list, there's nothing much under US$20. Once through customs you're out with the touts and taxi drivers. There's a tourist

information counter inside the arrival area while outside there is a quick and efficient money change desk which may not be open for all international arrivals. The touts will be working hard to convince you to come and stay at their place in Kuta and if you're not sure where you intend to stay they may be worth considering – see the Kuta section for more details.

Transport from the airport is quite simple. To stop tourists being fleeced by taxi drivers there's an official taxi counter where you pay for a taxi in advance. Prices from the airport are:

Kuta Beach	3200 rp
Denpasar	6800 rp
Nusa Dua	9000 rp
Legian	5000 rp
Oberoi Hotel*	7500 rp
Sanur Beach	8700 rp

*beyond Legian

You can, however, start walking towards the gate in which case the taxi drivers will descend upon you independently and they can be negotiated down to slightly lower rates! The truly impecunious should keep walking all the way to the airport gate, a couple of hundred metres from the international terminal. Here you'll find the bemo stop and the standard fare to Kuta should be about 250 rp, and 400 rp to Denpasar. The even more impecunious (and lightly laden) can walk into Kuta although it's a more pleasant stroll along the beach.

If you want to go straight to Ubud from the airport you can easily negotiate a fare with the taxis but count on something in the range of 15,000 to 20,000 rp. Alternatively you can go into Kuta and charter a bemo from bemo corner for around 12,000 to 15,000 rp.

DENPASAR AIRPORT DEPARTURE

Don't forget to reconfirm your flight at least 72 hours before departure. There are Garuda offices in Denpasar and at the

Kuta Beach Hotel in Kuta. Garuda and Qantas both have offices in the Bali Beach in Sanur. Reconfirming is very important in the peak holiday periods when there always seem to be people waiting at the airport hoping for a spare seat. Travel agents will offer to reconfirm for you, for a fee, but some agents have been notoriously lax about actually making reconfirmations.

Come departure time Denpasar airport holds no surprises apart from the fantastic price of drinks at the airport bar. Economically minded drinkers can try the airport snack bar or wait until they've passed through immigration and try the cafeteria bar. There's a duty-free shop and a row of souvenir shops through here where they only accept foreign currency. The departure lounge cafeteria takes rupiah. You can change excess rupiah back into hard currency at a bank counter by the check-in desks.

There's a departure tax on domestic flights (2000 rp) and international (9000 rp) flights. Only children under two years of age are exempt from this.

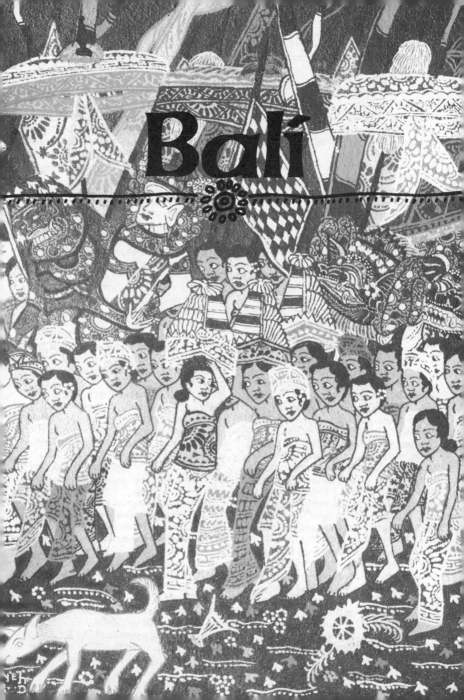

Bali

Facts about Bali

HISTORY

There is no trace of the Stone Age in Bali although it's certain that the island was already populated before the Metal Age commenced here about 300 BC. Nor is much known of Bali during the period when Indian traders brought Hinduism to the Indonesian archipelago. The earliest records found in Bali, stone inscriptions, date from around the 9th century AD and by that time Bali had already developed many similarities to the island you find today. Rice was grown with the help of a complex irrigation system probably very like that employed now. The Balinese had also already started to develop the cultural and artistic activities which have made the island so interesting to visitors right down to the present day.

Hindu Java began to spread its influence into Bali during the reign of King Airlangga from 1019 to 1042. At the age of 16 he fled into the forests of west Java when his uncle lost his throne. He gradually gained support, won back the kingdom ruled by his uncle and went on to become one of Java's greatest kings. Airlangga's mother had moved to Bali and remarried shortly after his birth so when he gained the throne there was an immediate link between Java and Bali. At this time the courtly Javanese language known as *Kawi* came into use amongst the royalty of Bali and the rock-cut memorials seen at Gunung Kawi near Tampaksiring are a clear architectural link between Bali and 11th century Java.

After Airlangga's death Bali retained its semi-independent state until Kertanagara became king of the Singasari dynasty in Java two centuries later. He conquered Bali in 1284 but this period of his greatest power lasted only eight years until he was murdered and his kingdom collapsed. However the great Majapahit dynasty was founded by his son. With Java in turmoil Bali regained its autonomy and the Pejeng dynasty, centred near modern day Ubud, rose to great power. Later Gajah Mada, the legendary chief Majapahit minister, defeated the Pejeng king Dalem Bedaulu in 1343 and brought Bali back under Javanese influence.

Although Gajah Mada brought much of the Indonesian archipelago under Majapahit control this was the furthest extent of their power. In Bali the 'capital' moved to Gelgel, near modern Klungkung, around the late 14th century and for the next two centuries this was the base for the 'king of Bali', the *Dewa Agung*. As Islam spread its appeal into Java the Majapahit kingdom collapsed into disputing sultanates. However the Gelgel dynasty in Bali, under Dalem Batur Enggong, extended its power eastwards to the neighbouring island of Lombok and even crossed the straits to the western end of Java.

As the Majapahit kingdom fell apart many of its intelligentsia moved to Bali including the priest Nirartha (see Ulu Watu and Tanah Lot) who is credited with introducing many of the complexities of Balinese religion to the island. Artists, dancers, musicians and actors also fled to Bali at this time and the island experienced an explosion of cultural activities. The final great exodus to Bali took place in 1478.

Marco Polo, the great explorer, was the first recorded European visitor to Indonesia back in 1292 but the first Europeans to set foot on Bali were Dutch seamen in 1597. Setting a tradition that has prevailed right down to the present day they fell in love with the island and when Cornelius Houtman, the ship's captain, prepared to set sail, half of his crew refused to come with him. At that time Balinese prosperity and artistic activity, at least among the royalty, was at a peak and the king who befriended Houtman had 200 wives and a chariot pulled by two white buffaloes, not to mention a retinue of 50 dwarves whose bodies had been bent to resemble kris handles! Although the Dutch returned to Indonesia, after that first enthusiastic visit, they were interested in profit not culture and barely gave Bali a second glance.

In 1710 the capital of the Gelgel kingdom was shifted to nearby Klungkung but local discontent was growing, lesser rulers were breaking away from Gelgel rule and the Dutch began to move in using the old policy of divide and conquer. In 1846 the Dutch used Balinese salvage claims over shipwrecks as the pretext to land military forces in north Bali. In 1894 the Dutch chose to support the Sasaks of Lombok in a rebellion against their Balinese rajah who capitulated to Dutch demands only for his younger princes to overrule him and defeat the Dutch forces in a surprise attack. Dutch anger was raised, a larger and more heavily armed force was despatched and the Balinese overrun. Balinese power in Lombok finally came to an end when they lost their stronghold at Cakranegara, the crown prince was killed and the old rajah was sent into exile.

With the north of Bali long under Dutch control and Lombok now gone, the south was not going to last long. Once again it was disputes over the ransacking of wrecked ships that gave the Dutch the excuse they needed to move in. A Chinese ship was wrecked off Sanur in 1904, Dutch demands that the rajah of Badung pay 3000 silver dollars damages were rejected and in 1906 Dutch warships appeared at Sanur. The Dutch forces landed against Balinese opposition and four days later had marched the five km to the outskirts of Denpasar.

On 20 September 1906 the Dutch mounted a naval bombardment on Denpasar and then commenced their final assault. The three princes of Badung realised that they were outnumbered and outgunned and that defeat was inevitable.

Surrender and exile, however, was the worst imaginable outcome and they decided to take the honourable path of a suicidal *puputan* or fight to the death. First the palaces were burnt then, dressed in their finest jewellery and waving golden krises, the rajah led the royalty and priests out to face the Dutch with their modern weapons.

The Dutch begged the Balinese to surrender rather than make their hopeless stand but their pleas went unheard and wave after wave of the Balinese nobility marched forward to their death. In all nearly 4000 Balinese died in defence of the two Denpasar palaces. Later the Dutch marched east towards Tabanan, taking the rajah of Tabanan prisoner, but he committed suicide rather than face the disgrace of exile.

The kingdoms of Karangasem and Gianyar had already capitulated to the Dutch and were allowed to retain some of their powers but other kingdoms were defeated and their rulers exiled. Finally the rajah of Klungkung followed the lead of Badung and once more the Dutch faced a *puputan* but with this last obstacle disposed of all of Bali was now under Dutch control and part of the Netherlands East Indies. Fortunately the Dutch government was not totally onerous and the common people noticed little difference between rule by the Dutch and rule by the rajahs. Some far-sighted Dutch officials encouraged Balinese artistic aspirations which together with a new found international interest sparked off an artistic revival. Dutch rule over Bali was short-lived, however, for Indonesia quickly fell to the Japanese after Pearl Harbor in WW II.

When the war ended the Indonesian leader Sukarno proclaimed the nation's independence on 17 August 1945 but it took four years to convince the Dutch they were not going to get their great colony back. In a virtual repeat of the *puputan* of a half a century earlier a Balinese resistance group was wiped out in the

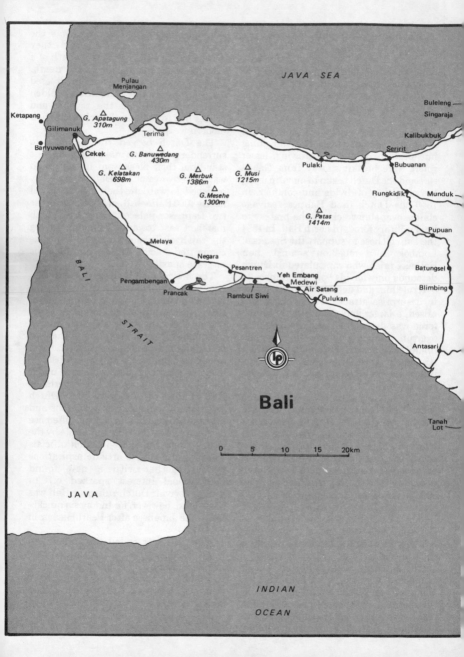

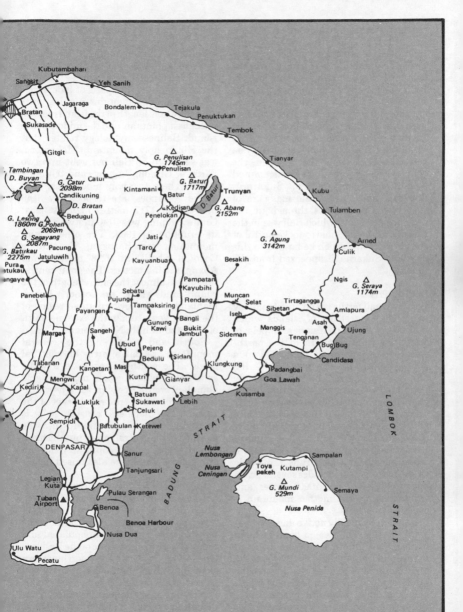

battle of Marga on 20 November 1946 but in 1949 the Dutch finally recognised Indonesia's independence. The Denpasar airport, Ngurah Rai, was named after the leader of the Balinese forces at Marga. Independence was not an easy path for Indonesia to follow at first and Sukarno, an inspirational leader during the conflict with the Dutch, proved less adept at governing the nation in peacetime. The ill-advised 'confrontation' with Malaysia was just one event that sapped the country's energy. In 1965 an attempted Communist coup led to Sukarno's downfall, and a wholesale massacre of suspected Communists throughout the archipelago, events which Bali was in the thick of. General Suharto took control of the government, which he has led to this day, and Sukarno disappeared from the limelight.

GEOGRAPHY

Bali is a small fertile island about midway along the long string of islands which makes up the Indonesian archipelago, stretching from Sumatra in the north-west to Irian Jaya, on the border of Papua New Guinea, in the south-east. It's adjacent to Java, the most heavily populated island, and is the first in the chain of smaller islands comprising Nusa Tenggara. Bali has an area of 5620 square km, measures approximately 140 km by 80 km and is just 8° south of the equator. It's dramatically mountainous, the central mountain chain which runs the whole length of the island includes several peaks approaching or over 2000 metres and Gunung Agung, the 'mother' mountain, is over 3000 metres.

Bali is volcanically active and extravagantly fertile. The two go hand in hand because past eruptions have contributed to the land's exceptional fertility and the high mountains provide the dependable rainfall which irrigates Bali's complex and amazingly beautiful patchwork of rice terraces. Of course that volcanically active nature is a two-edged sword – Bali

has often had disastrous eruptions and no doubt will again in the future. The huge eruption of Gunung Agung in 1963 killed thousands, devastated vast areas of the island and forced many Balinese to accept re-settlement in other parts of Indonesia.

The chain of mountains running east-west the whole length of the island reaches its highest points around the middle of the island. Balinese mythology relates that the Hindu holy mountain, Mahameru, was set down on Bali but split into two parts – Gunung Agung and Gunung Batur. These two holy mountains, both active volcanoes, are respectively 3140 metres and 1717 metres high. At least Gunung Agung was 3140 metres prior to its eruption in 1963. The other major mountains are Batukau, the 'Stone Coconut Shell', at 2278 metres, and Abang, at 2152 metres. The great central range runs almost the entire length of the island and there are other, lesser, highlands in the lower plateau region of the Bukit Peninsula in the extreme south of Bali and in hilly Nusa Penida.

South and north of the central mountains are Bali's fertile agricultural lands. The southern region is a wide, gently sloping area where most of Bali's abundant crop of rice is grown. The south-central area is the true rice-basket of the island. The northern coastal strip is narrower, rising more rapidly into the foothills of the central range, but the main export crops, coffee, copra and rice are grown here. Cattle are also raised in this area.

Despite the fertility of these zones Bali also has arid and lightly populated regions. They include the western mountain region and its northern slopes down to the sea – an area virtually unpopulated and reputed to be the last home of the Balinese tiger. The eastern and north-eastern slopes of Gunung Agung are also dry and barren while in the south the Bukit Peninsula and the adjacent island of Nusa Penida also get receive little rain and have little agriculture.

Districts

Bali is divided into eight *Kabupatens* or districts, which under the Dutch were known as regencies. They are, with their district capitals:

regency	capital
Badung	Denpasar
Bangli	Bangli
Buleleng	Singaraja
Gianyar	Gianyar
Jembrana	Negara
Karangasem	Amlapura
Klungkung	Klungkung
Tabanan	Tabanan

Badung in the south is the most populous district. Each district is headed by a government official known as a *bupati*. The districts are further subdivided into the subdistricts headed by a *camat*, then come the *perbekels*, village headman in charge of a *desa*, and finally there are enormous number of *banjars*, the local divisions of a village.

The Wallace Line

Bali is separated from Java by a narrow strait – just three km wide and with a maximum depth of only 60 metres. The waters between Bali and the next island, Lombok, are not very wide either but they are exceptionally deep. Darwin's contemporary, Sir Alfred Wallace, drew his Wallace line between Bali and Lombok. Here, he postulated, Asia ends and Australasia begins. In Bali you find the last of Asia's flora and fauna while in Lombok you find the first signs of Australasia. Wallace observed that in Lombok and to the east you find thorny plants, more arid country, cockatoos, parrots, lizards and marsupials. By contrast, in Bali and to the west you find tropical vegetation, monkeys and tigers. It's now felt that the line is a fuzzy one though there's certainly a difference – Lombok is drier, dustier and less fertile than Bali.

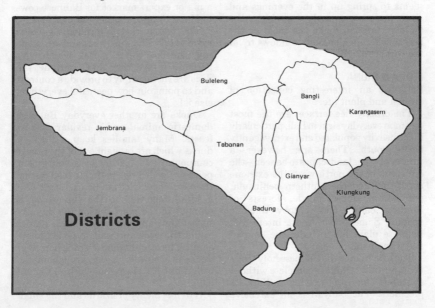

Districts

CLIMATE

Close as they are to the equator Bali and Lombok have climates evenly tropical all year. The average temperature hovers around the high 20°Cs (mid 80°F) year round. There are distinct dry and wet seasons – dry from April to September and wet from October to March – but it can rain at any time of year and even during the wet season rain is likely to be a quickly passing affair. In general May to August are the best months in Bali. At that time of year the climate is likely to be cooler and the rains lightest.

The climate is a gentle one, however, because around the coast sea breezes temper the heat and as you move inland you also move up so the altitude works to keep things cool. In fact at times it can get very chilly up in the mountains and a warm sweater or light jacket can be a good idea in mountain villages like Kintamani or Penelokan or if you climb Rinjani in Lombok. Air-conditioning is really not a necessity in Bali – a cool breeze always seems to spring up in the evenings and since insects are rarely a problem the architecture can make the most of the breeze with open bamboo windows to let the wind through.

FLORA & FAUNA

Bali has an interesting collection of animal and plant life.

The orderly rice terraces are the most common everyday sight in Bali, particularly in the heavily populated and extravagantly fertile south. There are, however, a variety of other landscapes to be seen – the dry scrub of the north-west; the extreme north-east and the southern peninsula; patches of dense jungle, forests of bamboo, barren and scrubby volcanic regions. Some of the most interesting Balinese plant life includes the banyan and frangipani.

The *waringin* is the Balinese holy tree – no important temple is complete without a stately banyan growing within its precincts. The banyan is an extensive shady tree with the exotic feature that it drops creepers down from its branches which take root and can propagate a new tree. Thus the banyan is said to be 'never-dying' since new offshoots can always be taking root.

The shady frangipani trees with their beautiful and sweet-smelling white flowers are almost as common a tree in temples as the banyan.

There are various animals you might come across around the island. Chickens are kept both for food purposes and as pets. A man's fighting cock will be a prized possession, although also one liable to come to a swift end at the next bout.

Balinese cows are nearly as delicate as Balinese pigs are gross. They're fine featured, graceful animals which visitors have often commented seem more akin to deer than cows. Although the Balinese are Hindus they do not generally treat cows as a holy animal but nor are they often eaten or milked. They are, however, used to plough rice paddies and fields and there is a major export market for Balinese cows to Hong Kong and other parts of Asia.

The mangy, horrible mongrels which roam every village on the island are, some say, the one thing in Bali which isn't perfect. In fact, they may continue, the dogs are there simply to provide a contrast and to point out how beautiful everything else is!

Ducks are another everyday Balinese domestic animal and a regular dish at feasts. Many families keep a flock of ducks which are brought out of the family compound and led out to a convenient pond or flooded rice paddy to feed during the day. They're led out using a stick with a small flag tied to the top which is planted in the pond during the day. As sunset time approaches the ducks gather round the stick and wait to be led home again. The morning and evening parade of ducks is a familiar sight throughout the island but it's always one of Bali's small delights.

Bali has plenty of lizards and the small

ones, hanging around light fittings in the evening, waiting for an unwary insect to venture too near, are a familiar sight. Geckoes, on the other hand, are often heard but not so usually seen. A fairly large lizard, the loud and regularly repeated two-part cry 'geck . . . . oh' is an everyday background noise. It's lucky if they repeat it seven times!

The Balinese pig is the animal of the family compound – they clean up all the garbage and eventually end up spit-roasted at a feast. The Balinese pig is a most peculiar creature with some relation to the wild boar. It's black and bristly and has a sway back that droops so low that its stomach almost drags on the ground. But they taste delicious!

Bali certainly used to have tigers but nobody has seen one for a long time although there are periodic rumours of tigers being sighted in the remote north-west of the island. Hickman Powell in *The Last Paradise*, his tale of Bali in the 1920s, tells of an unsuccessful tiger hunt.

Turtles are found in the waters around Bali and are a popular delicacy, particularly for feasts. In several places they are herded and fattened before being slaughtered.

There are also other animals. Bats are quite common, not only in well known haunts like the bat cave at Goa Lawah. They materialise at sunset to start their nocturnal hunt. The little chipmunk-like Balinese squirrels are occasionally seen in the wild, more often in cages. The Balinese have a variety of caged birds they keep as pets. Cats are often kept as domestic animals but they are nowhere near as familiar a sight as those miserable dogs.

ECONOMY

Bali's economy is basically agrarian, the vast majority of the Balinese are still simple peasants working in the fields. Coffee, copra and cattle are major agricultural exports, most of the rice goes to feed Bali's own teeming population. The unusual, for an island people, Balinese tendency to look to the mountains

and away from the sea is carried through to fishing. There are many fishing villages and fish provide a useful part of the Balinese diet but it's not of the scale you might expect, given how much ocean there is around the island. Of course tourism plays a considerable part in the Balinese economy – not only in providing accommodation, meals and services to the many visitors but also selling all those arts and crafts!

Rice

Although the Balinese grow various crops it's rice which is overwhelmingly the most important. It's not just that rice is such an important staple, the whole landscape has been moulded to rice growing. There can be few places where man has played such a large part in how the natural landscape looks yet at the same time made it so beautiful. The terraces trip down hillsides like steps for a giant and in shades of gold, brown and green always different yet always as delicately selected as an artist's palette.

The intricate organisation necessary for growing rice is a large factor in the strength of Balinese community life where the *subak*, the rice growers' association, has to carefully plan the use of the irrigation water. The Balinese do it so successfully that they are reputed to be some of the best rice growers in the world. They manage two harvests a year although there are no distinct times for planting and harvesting the rice.

A legend relates how a group of Balinese

farmers promised to sacrifice a pig if their harvest was good. As the bountiful harvest time approached no pig could be found and they reluctantly decided they would have to sacrifice a child. Then one of them had a brain wave: they had promised the sacrifice after the harvest. If there was always new rice growing then the harvest would always be about to take place and no sacrifice would be necessary. From then on the Balinese have always been planting one field of rice before they have harvested another. It's a delight to the eye because you can always see rice at all different stages of growth.

The process of rice growing starts with the bare, dry and harvested fields. The remaining rice stalks are burnt off and the field is then liberally soaked and repeatedly ploughed. Nowadays this may be done with a Japanese cultivator but more often it will still be done with two bullocks or cows pulling a wooden plough. Once the field is reduced to the required muddy consistency a small corner of the field is walled off and the seedling rice is planted here. The rice is grown up to a reasonable size then dug up and replanted, shoot by shoot, in the larger field. It's easy street for a time after that as the rice steadily matures. The walls of the fields have to be kept in working order and the fields have to be weeded but generally this is a time to practise the gamelan, watch the dancers, do a little wood carving or painting or just pass the time. Finally harvest time rolls around and at this time the whole village turns out for a period of solid hard work. Planting the rice is strictly a male occupation but everybody takes part in harvesting it.

The rice paddies are home for much more than just rice. In the early morning you'll often see the duck shepherds leading their flocks out for a day's paddle around a flooded paddy and at night young boys go out with lights to trap tasty frogs and eels.

POPULATION

Bali has a population of about 2½ million, which makes it a very densely populated island. They're almost all Indonesian – just the usual small Chinese contingent in the big towns, a sprinkling of Indian merchants, plus a number of more-or-less permanent visitors amongst the westerners in Bali.

SOCIAL CUSTOMS

Each stage of Balinese life from soon after conception to after the final cremation is marked by a series of ceremonies and rituals known as *Manusa Yadnya*. They contribute to the rich, varied and active life the average Balinese leads.

Birth

The first ceremony of Balinese life takes place even before birth – when women reach the third month of pregnancy they take part in ceremonies at home and at the village river or spring. A series of offerings are made to ensure the well-being of the baby. Another ceremony takes place soon after the birth, during which the afterbirth is buried with appropriate offerings. Women are considered to be 'unclean' after birth and at 12 days they are 'purified' through another ceremony. The father is also *sebel* or unclean but only for three days. At 42 days another ceremony and a series of offerings are made for the baby's future life.

The first major ceremony takes place half-way through the baby's first Balinese year of 210 days. Then, for the first time, the baby's feet are allowed to touch the ground. Prior to that babies are carried continuously for the ground is impure and babies, so close to heaven, should not be allowed to come into contact with it. The baby is also ceremonially welcomed to the family at this time. Another ceremony follows at the end of the 210-day year when the baby is welcomed to the ancestral temple.

It's said that the Balinese still regard boy-girl twins as a major calamity although according to Covarrubias it has only ever really applied to the ordinary people, not the nobility. The reasoning is that boy-girl twins are said to have committed a sort of spiritual incest while in the womb and that this is dangerous for the whole village. Extensive and expensive rituals and ceremonies must be performed in order to purify the children, the parents and the whole village. Boy-boy and girl-girl twins, however, are quite OK.

Names

The Balinese basically only have four first names. Your first child is Wayan, your second child is Made, your third child is Nyoman and your fourth child is Ketut. And your fifth, sixth, seventh, eighth and ninth; well they're Wayan, Made, Nyoman, Ketut and Wayan again. It's very simple and surprisingly unconfusing although it actually doesn't make their names any easier to remember. Now was he another Made or was he that other Ketut seems to be the order of the day! The only variation from this straightforward policy seems to be that first born boys are sometimes also known as Gede and first born girls as Putu.

The Balinese have a series of titles, depending on your caste. If you're a Brahmana then you can prefix your name with Ida Bagus. If you're a Wesia, the main caste of the nobility, then you're Gusti. The Satria caste are Cokodor but the poor Sudra, the general mass of the Balinese, have no prefix at all.

Childhood

If ever there was a people who love children it must be the Balinese – anybody who visits Bali with their children can attest to that. You'd better learn how to say how many bulan (months) or tahun (years) old your children are because you'll be asked 1000 times! The Balinese certainly love children and they have plenty of them to prove it. Coping with a large family is made much easier by the policy of putting younger children in the care of older ones. One child always seems to be carrying another one around on his or her hip.

Despite the fact that Balinese children are almost immediately part of a separate society of children they always seem remarkably well behaved. Of course you do hear kids crying occasionally but tantrums, fights, screams and shouts all seem to happen far less frequently than we're used to in the west. They say parents achieve this by treating children with respect, showing them good behaviour by example.

After the ceremonies of babyhood the stages of childhood are also marked with ceremonies, including those when the child reaches puberty and the important tooth filing ceremony. The Balinese prize even, straight teeth – crooked fangs are, after all, one of the chief distinguishing marks of evil spirits, just have a look at a Rangda mask! A priest files the upper front teeth to produce an aesthetically pleasing straight line. Today the filing is often only symbolic – one pass of the file.

Marriage

Every Balinese expects to marry and raise a family and they marry comparatively young. Marriages are not, in general, arranged as they are in many other Asian communities although strict rules apply to marriages between the castes. There are two basic forms of marriage in Bali – *mapadik* and *ngrorod*. The respectable form in which the family of the man visit the family of the woman and politely propose that the marriage take place is *mapadik*. The Balinese, however, like their fun and *ngrorod*, marriage by elopement, is a far more exciting way of going about it.

Of course the Balinese are also a practical people so usually nobody is too surprised when the young man spirits his bride-to-be away, even if she loudly protests about being kidnapped. The couple go into hiding and somehow the girl's parents, no matter how assiduously they search, never manage to find her. Eventually the couple re-emerge, announce that it is too late to stop them now, the marriage is officially recognised and everybody has had a lot of fun and games. Marriage by elopement has another advantage apart from being exciting and mildly heroic – it's cheaper.

The Household

Although many modern Balinese houses, particularly in Denpasar or the larger towns are much like houses in the west in their general arrangement, there are still a great number of traditional Balinese homes. Wander the streets of Ubud sometime, nearly every house will follow the same traditional walled design. Like houses in ancient Rome the Balinese house looks inward, outside is simply a high wall. Inside there will be a garden and a separate small building or *bale* for each function. There will be one building for cooking, one building for washing and the toilet, separate buildings for each 'bedroom'. What there will not be is a 'living room' because in Bali's mild tropical climate you live outside – the 'living room' and 'dining room' will be open verandah areas, looking out into the garden.

Covarrubias compares traditional Balinese house design to the human body – there's a head – the ancestral shrine, arms – the sleeping and living areas, legs and feet – the kitchen and rice storage building, even an anus – the garbage pit. There may also be an area outside the house compound where fruit trees are grown or a pig may be kept. Usually the house is entered through a gateway backed by a small wall known as the *aling aling*. It serves a practical and a spiritual purpose – both preventing passers-by from seeing in and stopping evil spirits from entering. Evil spirits cannot easily turn corners so the aling aling stops them from simply scooting straight in through the gate!

Men & Women

Balinese women are not kept cloistered away and social life in Bali is relatively free and easy, but the roles of the sexes are strictly delineated. There are certain tasks clearly to be handled by women, others equally clearly reserved for men. Thus running the household is very much the women's task. In the morning women sweep and clean and put out the offerings for the gods. Every household will have a shrine or god-throne where offerings must be placed, and places on the ground, such as at the compound entrance, where offerings for the demons are derisively cast. While the women are busy attending to these tasks the men of the household are likely to be looking after the fighting cocks and any other pets.

Marketing is also a female job – both buying and selling although at large markets cattle sales are definitely a male job. For the average Balinese peasant the working day is not a long one for most of the year. Despite their expertise at producing large rice crops rice growing doesn't require enormous inputs of labour. Again there's a division of the roles – although everybody turns out in the fields at harvest time planting the rice is purely a male activity.

Once again in their leisure activities the roles are sex differentiated. Both men and women dance but only men play the gamelan. The artistic skills are almost totally left to men although today you do see some women painters, sculptors or wood carvers.

Community Life

The Balinese have an amazingly active and organised village life – you simply cannot be a faceless non-entity in Bali. There's no chance of not knowing who your neighbours are for your life is so entwined and inter-related with theirs. Or at least it still is in the small villages that comprise so much of Bali. Even in the big towns, however, the banjars ensure that the community spirit continues.

The village is known as the desa and in general village plans all follow a similar pattern. In the centre of the village, usually at the crossroads of the two major streets, will be the open meeting space known as the *alun alun*. It's actually more than just a meeting space because you will also find temples, the town market, even the former prince's home. The *kulkul*, warning drum, tower will be here and quite likely a big banyan tree. If you're staying in Ubud notice how the street by the bemo stop in the centre of town has the palace, the banyan tree with its kulkul drums and the temple all close to one another and right across from the market. In Bangli see how the Artha Sastra Inn, in the family compound of the local prince, looks right out on to the main square.

Although village control by the desa authorities is no longer as strict as it once was there is still detailed and careful organisation over land ownership because of the necessary inter-relation of water supply to the rice fields. Each individual rice field is known as a *sawah* and each farmer who owns even one sawah must be a member of his local subak. The rice paddies must have a steady supply of water and it is the subak's job to ensure that the water supply gets to everybody. It's said that the head of the local subak will often be the farmer whose rice paddies are at the bottom of the hill for he will make quite certain that the water gets all the way down to his fields, passing through everybody else's on the way!

Of course Bali being Bali the subak has far more to do than share out the water and ensure that the water channels, dykes and so forth are in good order. Each subak will have its small temple out amongst the rice fields where offerings to the spirits of agriculture will be made and regular meetings held for the subak members. Like every temple in Bali there will be regular festivals and ceremonies to observe. Even individual sawahs may have small altars.

Nor is the subak the only organisation

controlling village life. Each desa is further subdivided into banjars which each adult male joins when he marries. It is the banjar which organises village festivals, marriage ceremonies and even cremations. Throughout the island you'll see the open-sided meeting places known as *bale banjars* - they're nearly as common a sight as temples. They serve a multitude of purposes from a local meeting place to a storage room for the banjar's musical equipment and dance costumes. Gamelan orchestras are organised at the banjar level and a glance in a banjar at any time might reveal a gamelan practice, a meeting going on, food being prepared for a feast, even a group of men simply getting their roosters together to raise their anger a little in preparation for the next round of cockfights.

Death & Cremation

There are ceremonies for every stage of Balinese life but the biggest ceremony is often the last - the cremation. A Balinese cremation can be an amazing, spectacular, colourful, noisy and exciting event. In fact it takes so long to organise a cremation that often years have passed since the death. During that time the body is temporarily buried. Of course an auspicious day must be chosen for the cremation and since a big cremation can be a very expensive business many less wealthy people may take the opportunity of joining in at a larger cremation and sending their own dead on their way at the same time. Brahmanas, however, must be cremated immediately.

Apart from being yet another occasion for Balinese noise and confusion it's a fine opportunity to observe the incredible energy the Balinese put into creating real works of art which are totally ephemeral. A lot more than a body gets burnt at the cremation. The body is carried from the burial ground (or from the deceased's home if it's an 'immediate' cremation) to the cremation ground in a high multi-tiered tower made of bamboo, paper, string, tinsel, silk, cloth, mirrors, flowers and anything else bright and colourful you can think of. The tower is carried on the shoulders of a group of men, the size of the group depending on the importance of the deceased and hence the size of the tower. The funeral of a former rajah or high priest may require hundreds of men to tote the tower.

Along the way to the cremation ground certain precautions must be taken to ensure that the deceased's spirit does not find its way back home. Loose spirits around the house can be a real nuisance. To ensure this doesn't happen requires getting the spirits confused as to their whereabouts, which you do by shaking the tower, running it around in circles, spinning it around, throwing water at it, generally making the trip to the cremation ground anything but a stately and funereal crawl. Meanwhile there's likely to be a priest, half-way up the tower,

hanging on grimly as it sways back and forth and doing his best to soak bystanders with holy water. A gamelan sprints along behind providing a suitably exciting musical accompaniment, camera-toting tourists get all but run down and once again the Balinese prove that ceremonies and religion are there to be enjoyed.

At the cremation ground the body is transferred to a funeral sarcophagus – this should be in the shape of a bull for a Brahmana, a winged lion for a Satria and a sort of elephant-fish for a Sudra. These days, however, almost anybody from the higher castes will use a bull. Finally up it all goes in flames – funeral tower, sarcophagus, body, the lot. The eldest son does his duty by poking through the ashes to ensure there are no bits of body left unburnt.

And where does your soul go after your cremation? Why to a heaven which is just like Bali!

ARTS & CRAFTS

Every Balinese is an artist and craftsman, until the tourist invasion it was just something you did – you painted or carved simply as an everyday part of life. Bali had no art galleries and craft shops in those days, what you produced went into temples or was used for festivals. It's a whole different story now with hundreds, even thousands, of galleries and craft shops in every possible place a tourist might pass. The real problem with Balinese arts and crafts today is that there is simply too much of it, you can't turn around without tripping over more carved Garudas, and in the galleries there are so many paintings that the walls can't accommodate them all and they're stacked up in piles on the floor.

Of course much of this work is rubbish, churned out quickly for people who want a cheap souvenir. It's a shame because there is still much beautiful work produced but you have to sort through a lot of junk to find it. Part of the problem is that

Balinese art has always been something produced today, which deteriorates tomorrow, is worn out the next day and is thrown away the day after. The Balinese were always creators rather than preservers! It's never really been a problem because there is no shortage of time to be spent simply creating more works of art. The fertility of the earth and their own efficiency as farmers gives the Balinese ample time to spend in the pursuit of artistic activities.

Architecture & Sculpture

Of all the Balinese arts it's said that architecture and sculpture have been the least affected by western influence and the tourist boom - nobody's taking temples home and your average stone statue doesn't roll up and stuff in your bag too easily. Architecture and sculpture are inextricably bound together - you don't just put up a temple gateway, you intricately carve every square cm of it and put a diminishing series of demon faces

above it as protection. Even then it's not finished without a couple of stone statues to act as guardians. Thus architecture becomes sculpture and sculpture becomes architecture.

Balinese houses, although often attractive places - due in large part to their beautiful garden, have never had the architectural attention lavished upon *puras* and *puris*, temples and palaces. Nor are palaces everyday constructions these days although some of the flashy new hotels, check the Nusa Dua Beach Hotel at Nusa Dua, are making considerable use of traditional architectural and sculptural features. Basically, however, it's in the temples where you find Balinese architecture and sculpture.

Temples are designed to set rules and formulae, see the section on temples for details. Sculpture serves as an adjunct, a finishing touch, to these design guidelines and in small or less important temples the sculpture may be limited or even nonexistent. In other temples, particularly

some of the exuberantly detailed temples of north Bali, the sculpture may be almost overwhelming in its intricacy and interest.

Sculpture often appears in a number of set places in temples. Door guardians, of legendary figures like Arjuna or other protective personalities, flank the steps to the gateway. Similar figures are also often seen at both ends of bridges. Above the main entrance to a temple Kala's monstrous face often peers out, sometimes a number of times – his hands reach out beside his head to catch any evil spirits foolish enough to try to sneak in. Elsewhere other sculptures make regular appearances – the front of a *pura dalem*, temple of the dead, will often feature prominently placed images of the witch Rangda while sculptured panels may show the horrors that await evil-doers in the afterlife.

Although sculpture in Bali is still very much for internal consumption rather than, as with painting or woodcarving, for visitors to take home, that doesn't mean you can't take a friendly stone demon back with you. Balinese stone is surprisingly light and it's not at all out of the realms of possibility to bring a figure home in your airline baggage. A typical temple door guardian weighs around 10 kg. The stone is also, however, very fragile so packing must be carefully done if you're going to get it home without damage. There are a string of stone sculpture workshops in Batubulan, just outside of Denpasar. Some (but not all of them) will also pack figures very quickly and expertly, usually with shredded paper. With a little negotiation a typical door guardian can be bought for around US$20, including packaging. Scare hell out of your neighbour's garden gnomes.

Painting

Of the various art forms popular in Bali painting is probably the one most influenced both by western ideas and western demand. Prior to the arrival of western artists after WW I painting was,

like other Balinese art, primarily for temple and palace decoration. The influence of western artists not only expanded it beyond these limited horizons it also showed the way to whole new subject areas and, quite possibly most important of all, gave the artists new materials to work with.

Until those fateful arrivals Balinese painting was strictly limited to three basic kinds – *langse*, calendars and *iders-iders*. Langse are large rectangular decorative hangings used in palaces or temples. Iders-iders are scroll paintings hung along the eaves of temples. The calendars pictorially represent the days of the month, showing the auspicious days. Paintings were almost always executed in *wayang* style – that is they were imitative of the *wayang-kulit* shadow puppet players, almost always shown either in profile or three-quarters view. Furthermore the paintings were generally narrative style, rather like a cartoon comic strip with a series of panels telling a story. Even the colours artists could use were strictly limited to a set list of shades. Paintings are still done in these traditional styles – Klungkung is a centre for the wayang style of paintings and you can see a fine original example of the style in the painted ceiling of the Hall of Justice or *Kertha Gosa* in Klungkung. Astrological calendars are also still a popular subject.

Walter Spies and Rudolf Bonnet were the western artists who turned Balinese artists around in the '30s. At that time painting was in a serious decline, the painting styles had become stagnant and since few commissions were forthcoming from the palaces and temples at that time painting was virtually dying out as an art form. The changes Bonnet and Spies inspired were revolutionary – suddenly Balinese artists started painting single scenes instead of narrative tales and using everyday life rather than romantic legends as their themes. Even more important they started painting pictures purely as pictures – not as something to cover a space in a palace or temple. The idea of a painting being something you could do by itself (and for which there might be a market!) was wholly new.

In one way, however, the style remained unchanged – Balinese paintings were packed full, every spare corner of the picture was filled in. A Balinese forest is branches and leaves reaching out to fill every tiny space and then inhabited by a whole zoo of creatures. Idyllic rural scenes from some Balinese arcadia or energetic festival scenes were the order of the day for many of the new artists. Others painted engagingly stylised animals and fish. You can see fine examples of these new styles at the Puri Lukisan museum in Ubud and, of course, find them in all the galleries and art shops.

The new artistic enthusiasm was short lived for WW II interrupted and then in the '50s and '60s Indonesia was wracked by internal turmoil and confusion. The new styles degenerated into stale copies of the few original spirits. A totally new style developed, however, with encouragement from Dutch painter Aries Smit. His 'young artists' painted the typically Balinese rural scenes but in a new naive style and in brilliant technicolour. The name doesn't necessarily mean that the artists are young – it was just what the style was called when it first originated in the '60s. Penestanan, a village just outside Ubud, is where the style developed.

Balinese art today is both strong and weak. It's strong in that there is so much of it going on but weak in that so much of it is all precisely copy-cat alike. It's an unfortunate side of Balinese art that while there are a few truly creative people there are also an enormous number of copyists – some of them excellent, some of them very far from excellent. Doubly unfortunate is that much of the painting today is churned out for the tourist market and much of that market is extremely nondiscriminating about what it buys. Thus the shops are packed full of paintings in the various popular styles –

some of them quite good, a few of them really excellent, most of them uniformly alike and uniformly of poor quality. Even worse many artists have turned to producing paintings purely attuned to tourist tastes and with nothing Balinese about them. It's a sad thing to see instant-Woolworths-art being turned out for the tourist trade although heroic surfing pictures painted to order are at least amusing. It's rare to see anything really new though – painters aim for safety and that means paint what the tourist will buy.

Paintings can be transported in the cardboard tubes which have rolls of wrapped cloth around them, as supplied to drapers. Otherwise you can buy plastic tubes from hardware stores. If you do buy a painting, and can handle the additional weight, consider taking a frame back as well. They're very cheap, especially compared to framing costs in the west.

Woodcarving

Like painting, woodcarving has undergone a major transformation over the past 50 years, moving from being something simply for decoration or other purposes in temples and palaces to something done for its own sake. Wood carving prior to this change of attitudes was chiefly decoration on functional objects – carved doors or columns for examples – or figures such as Garudas or demons with a protective or symbolic nature. There were also minor functional carvings, such as decorative bottle stoppers, but it was the same demand from outside which inspired new carving subjects and styles, just as it had done with painting. It was also some of the same western artists who served as the inspiration.

As with the new painting styles Ubud was a centre for the revolution in woodcarving. Some carvers started producing highly stylised and elongated figures, with the further change that the wood was left in its natural finish rather than being painted. Others carved delightful animal figures, sometimes totally realistic, other times almost caricatures. Other styles and trends developed – whole tree trunks carved into ghostly, intertwined 'totem poles' or curiously exaggerated and distorted figures.

Carving today suffers from the same problems as painting – an overwhelming emphasis on what sells with the successful subjects mimicked by every Wayan, Made and Nyoman on the block. 'Not another technicolour Garuda' could easily be the tourist lament. There's simply too much carving done on the same themes. Still there's always something interesting to see, the technical skill is high and the Balinese sense of humour often shines through. A frog clutches a large leaf as an umbrella or a weird demon on the side of a wooden bell clasps his hands over his ears. You'll even find places which carve perfect replicas of every tropical fruit under the Balinese sun with a complete, life-size banana tree to go with it!

Crafts

Perhaps even more unchanging than stone sculpture are the Balinese crafts basically intended for home consumption. Indeed many of the most intricate crafts are throwaway – they're made today, used tomorrow, chucked out the day after. Notice the beautiful decorations woven of palm leaves for festivals and celebrations – they take a lot of time and energy to produce but a day later they'll be forgotten.

Of course some crafts are not so ephemeral – krises most particularly. The *kris* – often with an ornate, jewel-studded handle and sinister-looking wavy blade – is the traditional and ceremonial dagger of Bali and Indonesia. A kris can be the most important of family heirlooms, a symbol of prestige and honour. Krises are supposed to have great spiritual power and an important kris is thought to send out magical energy waves requiring great care in its handling and use. Even making a kris requires careful preparation, as does

anything in Bali which involves working with the forces of magic.

The wayang kulit shadow puppet figures are also magical items since the plays are again part of the eternal battle between good and evil. The figures are cut from buffalo hide – wayang kulit actually means 'shadow skin'. The intricately lacy figures are carefully cut out with a sharp, chisel-like stylus and the figures are also painted. Although wayang kulit performances usually take place at night there are sometimes daytime temple performances, where the figures are manipulated without a screen. The figures are completely traditional, no variation is made from the standard list of characters and their standardised appearance.

Weaving is a popular craft of everyday use and the standard woven Balinese sarong is not only very useful but also an attractive workaday item. You can use a sarong not only as a comfortable article of clothing but also as a bed top-sheet, a beach towel and for a multitude of other uses. The Balinese also weave a variety of more complex materials for ceremonial and other important uses. *Songket* cloth has gold or silver threads woven into the material for example. In various places in Indonesia you'll find material woven by the complex *ikat* process where the pattern is dyed into the threads *before* the material is woven. Ikat can be of the warp or the weft but in the east Bali village of Tenganan they weave double ikat material where both the warp and weft is pre-dyed. Not surprisingly this extremely complex process takes a long time to complete.

It's the everyday, disposable crafts which are probably most surprising in Bali. Even the simplest activities are carried out with care, precision and the Balinese artistic flair. Just glance at those little offering trays thrown down on the ground for the demons every morning – each one a throwaway work of art. Look at the temple offerings, the artistically stacked pyramids of fruit or other beautifully decorated foods. Look for the *lamaks*, long woven palm leaf strips used as decorations, the stylised female figures known as *cili*. See the intricately carved coconut-shell wall hangings or at funerals simply marvel at the care and energy that goes into constructing huge funeral towers and the exotic sarcophagus, all of which will soon go up in flames.

MUSIC & DANCE

Music, dance and drama are all closely related in Bali – in fact drama and dance are really synonymous. Some dances are more drama and less dance, others more dance and less drama but basically they can all be lumped in together. The most important thing about Balinese dances, however, is that they're fun and they're accessible. Balinese dance is definitely not some sterile art form requiring an arts degree to start to appreciate – it can be exciting and enjoyable for almost anyone with just the slightest effort. As an example when Tashi was 2½ we took her to see a *Kechak* (monkey dance) one night. I spent half an hour beforehand telling her the story behind the dance and she was entranced by the dance – she knew the characters, knew what to expect, understood (as well as a 2½ year old can) what the story was all about and thoroughly enjoyed it. The story of Rama and Sita, which is what the Kechak is based upon, has become one of her favourite bedtime stories.

Nor is it hard to find Balinese dances – they're taking place all the time and everywhere on the island. There are dances virtually every night at all the tourist centres – they generally charge something between 1000 and 3000 rp admission for foreigners. If you're in Bali long enough you're almost bound to be somewhere where a dance is simply taking place, open to anybody, just wander in. Dances are put on regularly at the tourist centres to raise money but they're also a regular part of almost every temple festival and Bali has no shortage of temple festivals. So if you want to see Balinese

dancing you'll have plenty of opportunity. Many of the dances put on for tourists offer a smorgasbord of Balinese dances – a little *Topeng*, a taste of *Legong*, some *Baris* to round it off. A nice introduction perhaps but for some dances you really need the whole thing and it would be a shame if the 'instant Asia' mentality takes too strong a grip on Balinese dance.

The dances take various forms but with a few notable exceptions – in particular the Kechak and the *Sanghyang* trance dance – they are all accompanied by music from the gamelan gong. Some are dances almost purely for the sake of dancing – in this category you could include the technically precise Legong, its male equivalent the Baris or various solo dances like the *Kebyar*. Mask dances like the Topeng or the *Jauk* also place a high premium on dancing ability.

Then there are dances where the story is as important as the dancing, like the Kechak. Or there are dances which move into that important area of Balinese life where the forces of magic, of good and evil, clash. In the *Barong* and *Rangda* dance powerful forces are at work and elaborate preparations must be made to ensure that the balance is maintained. All masked dances require great care as in donning a mask you take on another personality and it is wise to ensure that the mask's personality does not take over. Barong and Rangda masks in particular are treated with great caution. Only an expert can carve them and between performances the masks must be carefully put away, a Rangda mask must even be kept covered until the instant before the performance starts. These masks can have powerful *sakti* and the unwary must be careful of their magical, often dangerous, spiritual vibrations.

The Balinese like, as Covarrubias pointed out, a blend of seriousness and slapstick and this also shows up in their dances. Some dances have a decidedly comic element, with clowns who serve both to counterpoint the staid, noble characters but also to put across the story, for the noble characters may use the high Balinese language or classical Kawi while the clowns, usually servants of the noble characters, converse in everyday Balinese. There are always two clowns, the leader *punta* and his follower *kartala* who never manages to quite carry off his mimicry.

Dancers in Bali are almost always just ordinary folk who dance in the evening or their spare time – just like a painter or sculptor may indulge his artistry in his spare time. You learn dancing by doing it and long hours may be spent in practice, usually by carefully following the movements of an expert. There's little of the soaring leaps of western ballet or the smooth flowing movements often found in western dance. Balinese dance tends to be precise, jerky, shifting and jumpy. In fact it's remarkably like Balinese music with its abrupt shifts of tempo, its dramatic changes between silence and crashing noise. There's also virtually no contact in Balinese dancing, each dancer moves completely independently.

To the expert every movement of wrist, hand and fingers has importance, even facial expressions are carefully choreographed to convey the character of the dance. Don't let these technicalities bother you though – they're just icing on the cake, basically most Balinese dances are simply straightforward 'ripping yarns'. Don't give the dancers your complete attention either – the audience can be just as interesting, especially the children. Even at the most tourist-oriented of dances there will be hordes of local children clustered around the stage. Watch how they cheer on the goodies, cringe back from the stage when the demons appear – how can TV ever win against the real thing?

The Gamelan

Balinese music is based around the instrument known as a gamelan – in fact the gamelan is such a central part of Balinese music that the whole 'orchestra' is also referred to as a gamelan. Gamelan music is almost completely percussion – apart from the simple *suling* flute and the two-stringed *rebab* there are virtually no wind or string instruments in Balinese music. Unlike many forms of Asian music the Balinese gamelan is accessible to ears attuned to western music. It sounds strange – all that noisy, jangly, percussion – with none of the soothing or relaxing passages found in western music, but it's exciting and enjoyable. It also fits Bali perfectly!

The main instruments of the gamelan are the xylophone-like *gangsa* which have bronze bars above bamboo resonators. The player hits the keys with his hammer with one hand while his other hand moves close behind to dampen the sound from each key just after it is struck. Although the *gangsa* make up the majority of the instruments and it is their sound which is most prevalent the actual tempo and nature of the music is controlled by the two *kendang* drums – one male and one female.

Other instruments are the deep *trompong* drums, the small *kempli* gong and the small *cengceng* cymbals used in faster pieces. The whole orchestra is known as a *gong* – an old fashioned *gong gede* or a more modern *gong kebyar*. There are even more ancient forms of the gamelan such as the *gong selunding* still occasionally played in Bali Aga villages like Tenganan.

A village's gamelan is usually organised through a banjar. The members of the banjar will meet to practise, the banjar itself owns the instruments which are stored in the *bale gong*. The musician's club is known as a *seksa*. Gamelan playing is purely a male occupation and all the pieces are learnt by heart and passed down father to son, there is little musical notation or records of individual pieces. The gamelan is also played in Java and Javanese gamelan music is held to be more 'formal' and 'classical' than Balinese. A perhaps more telling point is that

Top: Drummer at a cremation ceremony, Ubud, Bali (JP)
Left: Carrying a gamelan in a procession, Ubud, Bali (TW)
Right: Carved wooden fruit, Ubud, Bali (TW)

Javanese gamelan music is rarely heard apart from at special performances whereas in Bali you seem to hear gamelans playing all the time everywhere you go! In *The Last Paradise* Hickman Powell tells of the cremation of a Rajah of Ubud where as many gamelans in the Ubud area as possible were asked to attend. No less than 126 gamelans turned up!

Kechak

Probably the best known of the many Balinese dances the Kechak is also unusual in that it does not have a gamelan accompaniment. Instead the background is provided by a chanting 'choir' of men who provide the 'chak-a-chak-a-chak' noise. Originally this chanting group was known as the Kechak and they were part of a Sanghyang trance dance. Then in the 1930s the modern Kechak developed in Bona, a village near Gianyar, where the dance is still held regularly to this day.

The Kechak tells a tale from the *Ramayana* about Prince Rama and his Princess Sita. With Rama's brother Laksamana they have been exiled from the kingdom of Ayodya and are wandering in the forest. The evil Rawana, King of Lanka, lures Rama away with a golden deer, in reality his equally evil prime minister who has magically changed himself into the deer. When Rama fails to return Sita persuades Laksamana to search for him and, once she is alone, Rawana pounces and carries her off to his hideaway.

Hanuman, the white monkey god, appears before Sita and tells her that Rama is trying to rescue her. He brings her Rama's ring to show that he is indeed the prince's envoy and Sita gives him a hairpin to take back to Rama. When Rama finally arrives in Lanka he is met by the evil king's evil son Megananda – this story is full of goodies versus baddies – who shoots an arrow at him, which magically turns into a dragon and ties him up. Fortunately Rama is able to call upon the Garuda for assistance and thus

escapes. Finally Sugriwa, the king of the monkeys, comes to Rama's assistance with his monkey army and after a great battle good wins out over bad and Rama and Sita return home.

Throughout the dance the surrounding circle of men, all bare-chested and wearing checked cloth around their waists, provide a non-stop accompaniment, rising to a crescendo as they play the monkey army and fight it out with Rawana and his cronies. The chanting is superbly synchronised, members of the 'monkey army' sway back and forth, raise their hands in unison, flutter their fingers, lean left and right, all with an eerily exciting co-ordination.

Barong & Rangda

The Barong and Rangda dance rivals the Kechak as Bali's most touristically popular dance. Again it's a straightforward battle between good, the Barong, and bad, the Rangda. The Barong is a strange creature, half shaggy dog, half lion, propelled by two men like a circus clown-horse. He's definitely on the side of the good but the Barong is a mischievous and fun-loving creature. The widow-witch Rangda is straightforward, bad through and through and certainly not the sort of thing you'd like to meet on a midnight stroll through the rice paddies.

Barongs can take various forms but in the Barong and Rangda dance it will be as the *Barong Keket*, the most holy of the Barongs. The Barong flounces in, snaps

its jaws at the gamelan, dances around a bit and enjoys the acclaim of his supporters – a group of men with krises. Then Rangda makes her appearance, her long tongue lolling, human entrails draped around her neck and her terrible fangs protruding from her mouth.

The Barong and Rangda duel, using their magical powers, but when things look bad for the Barong his supporters draw their krises and rush in to attack Rangda. Using her magical powers Rangda throws them into a trance and the men suicidally try to stab themselves with their krises. But the Barong also has great magical powers and he casts a spell which stops the krises from harming the men. This is the most dramatic part of the dance. As the gamelan rings crazily the men rush back and forth, waving their krises around, all but foaming at the mouth, sometimes even rolling on the ground in a desperate attempt to stab themselves. There often seems to be a conspiracy to terrify tourists in the front row!

Finally Rangda retires defeated and good has won again. This still leaves, however, a large group of entranced Barong supporters to bring back to the real world. This is usually done by sprinkling them with holy water, sanctified by dipping the Barong's beard in it. Performing the Barong and Rangda dance is a touchy operation – playing around with all that powerful magic, good and bad, is not to be taken lightly. Extensive ceremonies have to be gone through to begin with, a *pemangku* must be on hand to end the dancers' trance and at the end a chicken has to be sacrificed to propitiate the evil spirits.

Legong

The Legong is the most graceful of Balinese dances and to sophisticated Balinese connoisseurs of dancing the one of most interest and discussion. A Legong, as a Legong dancer is known, is a young girl – often as young as eight or nine years, rarely older than her early teens. Such importance is attached to the dance that even in old age a classic dancer will be remembered as a 'great Legong' even though her brief period of fame may have been 50 years ago.

There are various forms of the Legong but the *Legong Kraton* or Legong of the palace is the one usually performed most. Peliatan's famous dance troupe, whom visitors to Ubud often get a chance to see, are particularly noted for their Legong. The story behind the Legong is very stylised and symbolic – if you didn't know the story it would be impossible to tell what was going on.

The Legong involves just three dancers – the two Legongs and their 'attendant', the *condong*. The Legongs are identically dressed in tightly bound gold brocade, they are so tightly encased that it is somewhat of a mystery how they manage to move so rapidly and agitatedly. Their faces are elaborately made up, their eyebrows plucked and repainted, their hair decorated with frangipanis. The dance relates how a king takes a maiden, Rangkesari, captive. When Rangkesari's brother comes to release her, Rangkesari begs the king to let her go rather than go to war. The king refuses and on his way to the battle meets a bird bringing ill omens. He ignores the bird and continues on to meet Rangkesari's brother and gets killed.

That's the whole story but the dance only tells of the king's preparations for battle and it actually ends with the bird's

appearance – when the king leaves the stage it is to the battle that will kill him. The dance starts with the condong dancing an introduction then departing as the Legongs come on. The two Legongs dance solo, in close identical formation and even in mirror image as when they dance a nose-to-nose 'love scene'. The dance tells of the king's sad departure from his queen, Rangkesari's bitter request that he release her and then the king's departure for the battle. The condong reappears with tiny golden wings as the bird of ill fortune and the dance ends.

Baris

The warrior dance known as the Baris is a traditionally male equivalent of the Legong – femininity and grace gives way to energetic and warlike martial spirit. The Baris dancer has to convey the thoughts and emotions of a warrior preparing for action and then meeting an enemy in battle. It's a solo dance requiring great energy and skill. The dancer has to show his changing moods not only through his dancing but also through facial expression – chivalry, pride, anger, prowess and finally a little regret (well war is hell, even in Bali) all have to be there. It's said that the Baris is one of the most complex of the Balinese dances requiring a dancer of great skill and ability.

Ramayana Ballet

The *Ramayana* is, of course, a familiar tale in Bali but the dance has been a relatively recent addition to the Balinese repertoire. It basically tells the same story of Rama and Sita as told in the Kechak but without the monkey ensemble and with a normal *gamelan gong* accompaniment. Furthermore the *Ramayana* provides wide opportunities for improvisations and comic additions. Rawana may be played as a classic bad guy, Hanuman can be a comic clown. Camera-clicking tourists amongst the spectators may come in for a little imitative ribbing.

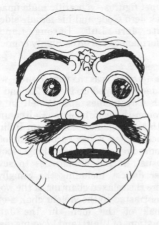

Kebyar

The Kebyar is a male solo dance like the Baris but with greater emphasis on the performer's individual abilities. Development of the modern kebyar is credited in large part to the famous pre-war dancer Mario. There are various forms of Kebyar including the seated *Kebyar Duduk* where the 'dance' is done from the seated position and movements of the hands, arms and torso plus, of course, facial expressions are all important. In the *Kebyar Trompong* the dancer actually joins the gamelan and plays an instrument called the *trompong* while still dancing.

Barong Landung

The giant puppet dances known as *Barong Landung* are not an everyday occurrence – they take place annually on Serangan Island and a few other places in the south of the island. The legend of their creation relates how a demon, Jero Gede Mecaling, popped over from Nusa Penida to cause havoc on Bali. He disguised himself as a standing Barong and to scare him away the people had to make a big Barong just like him. The Barong Landung dances are a reminder of that ancient legend featuring two gigantic puppet figures – a horrific male image of black Jero Gede and his female sidekick white Jero Luh. Barong Landung performances are often highly comic.

Janger

The *Janger* was a new dance which suddenly popped up in the '20s and '30s. Both Covarrubias and Powell in their between-the-wars books on Bali comment on this strange new, almost un-Balinese, dance. Today it has become part of the standard repertoire and no longer looks so unusual. It has similarities to several other dances including the Sanghyang where the relaxed chanting of the women is contrasted to the violent chak-a-chak-a-chak of the men. In the Janger, formations of 12 girls and 12 young men do a sitting dance where the gentle swaying and chanting of the girls is contrasted with the violently choreographed movements and loud shouts of the men.

Topeng

Topeng means 'pressed against the face', as with a mask, and that is what the dance is, a mask dance where the dancers have to imitate the person their mask indicates they are playing. The *Topeng Tua* is a classic solo dance where the mask is that of an old man and the dancer has to dance like a creaky old gentleman. In other dances there may be a small troupe who dance various characters and types. A full collection of Topeng masks may number 30 or 40.

Jauk

The *Jauk* is also a mask dance but strictly a solo performance – the dancer plays an evil demon, his mask an eerie face with bulging eyes and fixed smile, long wavering fingernails complete the demonic look. Mask dances are considered to require great expertise because the dancer is not able to convey the character's thoughts and meanings through his facial expressions – the dance has to tell all. Demons are unpleasant, frenetic and fast-moving creatures so a Jauk dancer has to imitate all these things.

Pendet

The *Pendet* is not normally a major performance, something that requires arduous training and practice. It's an everyday dance of the temples, a small procedure gone through before making temple offerings. You may often see the Pendet being danced by women bringing offerings to a temple for a festival but it is also sometimes danced as an introduction and a closing for other dance performances.

Sanghyang Dances

The Sanghyang trance dances originally developed as religious functions to drive out evil spirits from a village. The Sanghyang is a divine spirit which temporarily inhabits an entranced dancer. The *Sanghyang Dedari* dance is performed by two young girls who dance a dream-like version of the Legong but with their eyes closed. The dancers are said to be untrained in the intricate pattern of the Legong and furthermore they dance in perfect harmony but with their eyes firmly shut. Male and female choirs, the male choir being a Kechak, provide a background chant but when the chant stops the dancers slump to the ground in a faint. Two women bring them round and at the finish a *pemangku* blesses them with holy water and brings them out of the trance. The modern Kechak dance developed from the Sanghyang.

In the *Sanghyang Jaran* a boy in a trance dances round and through a fire of coconut husks riding a coconut palm 'hobby horse'. It's labelled the 'fire dance' for the benefit of tourists. Like other trance dances (such as the Barong and Rangda dance) great care must be taken to control the magical forces at play. Experts must always be on hand to take care of the entranced dancers and to bring them out of the trance at the close.

Other Dances

There are numerous other dances in Bali, some of them only performed occasionally, some quite regularly but not often seen by tourists. Of course old dances still fade out and new dances or new developments of old dances still take place. Dance in Bali is not a static activity. The *Oleg Tambulilingan* was developed in the 1950s, originally as a solo female dance. Later a male part was added and the dance mimics the flirtations of two tambulilingan – bumblebees.

One of the most popular comic dances is the *Cupak* which tells a tale of a greedy coward (Cupak) and his brave but hard-done-by younger brother Grantang and their adventures while rescuing a beautiful princess. The *Arja* is a sort of Balinese soap opera, long and full of high drama. Since it requires much translation of the

noble's actions by the clowns it's hard for westerners to understand and appreciate. *Drama Gong* is in some ways a more modern version of the same romantic themes.

WAYANG KULIT

The shadow puppet plays known as wayang kulit are popular throughout Indonesia, not only in Bali. It's far more than mere entertainment for the puppets are believed to have great spiritual power and the *dalang*, the puppet master and story teller, is an almost mystical figure. He has to be a man of considerable skills and even more considerable endurance. Not only does he have to manipulate the puppets and tell the story he also has to conduct the musical accompaniment, the small gamelan orchestra known as the *Gender Wayang*, and beat time with his

chanting – having long run out of hands to do things with he performs the latter task with a horn held with his toes!

His mystical powers come in to play because the wayang kulit, like so much of Balinese drama, is another phase of the eternal struggle between good and evil. You don't leave that battle to amateurs. The endurance factor comes in because a wayang kulit performance can last six or more hours and the performances always seem to start so late that the drama is finally resolved just as the sun peeps up over the horizon.

Shadow puppets are made of pierced buffalo hide – they're completely traditional in their characters and their poses, there's absolutely no mistaking just who is who. The dalang sits behind a screen on which the shadows of the puppets are cast, usually by an oil lamp which gives a far more romantic flickering light than modern electric lighting would do. Traditionally women and children sit in front of the screen while men sit behind the screen with the dalang and his assistants.

The characters are arrayed right and left of the puppet master – goodies to the right, baddies to the left. The characters include nobles, who speak in the high Javanese language Kawi, and common clowns, who speak in everyday Balinese. The dalang also has to be a linguist! When the four clowns (Delem and Sangut are the bad ones, Twalen and his son Merdah are the good ones) are on screen the performance becomes something of a Punch and Judy show with much rushing back and forth, clouts on the head and comic insults. The noble characters are altogether more refined – they include the terrible Durga and the noble Bima. Wayang kulit stories are chiefly derived from the great Hindu epics, the *Mahabharata* and the *Ramayana*.

RELIGION

The Balinese are nominally Hindus but Balinese Hinduism is a world away from that of India. At one time Hinduism was the predominant religion in Indonesia, witness the many great Hindu monuments in Java, but it died out with the spread of Islam through the archipelago. The final great Hindu kingdom, that of the Majapahits, virtually evacuated to Bali taking not only their religion and its rituals but also their art, literature, music and culture. It's a mistake, however, to think that this was purely an exotic seed being implanted on virgin soil. The Balinese probably already had strong religious beliefs and an active cultural life. The new influences were simply overlaid on the existing practices – hence the peculiar Balinese interpretation of Hinduism. Of course there are small enclaves of other religions in Bali, particularly Muslims whose mosques are often seen at ports and fishing villages all around the coast.

Religion in Bali has two overwhelming features – it's absolutely everywhere and it's good fun! You can't get away from religion in Bali, there are temples in every village, shrines in every field, offerings being made at every corner. The fun element comes in because the Balinese seem to feel that religion should be an enjoyable thing – something the mortals can enjoy as well as the gods. It's well summed up in their attitude to offerings – you make up a lot of fancy food for the gods but once they've eaten the 'essence' you've got enough 'substance' left over for a fine feast.

Basically the Balinese worship the same gods as the Hindus of India – the trinity of Brahma, Shiva and Vishnu – although the Balinese have a supreme god, Sanghyang Widi. But this basic threesome is always alluded to, never seen, in Bali – a vacant shrine or empty throne tells all. Others of the secondary Hindu gods may occasionally appear, such as Ganesh, Shiva's elephant-headed son, but a great many other purely Balinese gods, spirits and entities have far more everyday reality. The widow-witch

Rangda may bear a close relation to Durga, the terrible side of Shiva's wife Parvati, but it's certain that nobody in India has seen a Barong!

To Balinese the spirits are everywhere, it's a reminder that animism is the basis behind much of Balinese religion. The offerings put out every morning are there to pay homage to the good spirits and to placate the bad ones – the Balinese take no chances! And if the offerings thrown on the ground are immediately consumed by dogs? Well so it goes, everybody's suspicious of dogs anyway.

TEMPLES

The number of temples in Bali is simply astonishing, they're everywhere, in fact since every village has several and every home has at least a simple house-temple

there are actually more temples than homes. The word for temple in Bali is *pura* which is a Sanskrit word literally meaning a space surrounded by a wall. Like a traditional Balinese home a temple is walled in so the shrines you see in rice fields or at magical spots such as by old trees are not real temples. You'll find simple shrines or thrones at all sorts of unusual places. They often overlook crossroads, intersections or even just dangerous curves in the road. They protect passers-by, or give the gods a ringside view of the accidents!

Like so much else of Balinese religion the temples although nominally Hindu actually owe much to the pre-Majapahit era. Throughout most of the year the temples are quiet and empty but at festival times they are colourful and active with offerings being made, dances performed, gamelan music ringing out and all manner of activities from cockfights to gambling going on.

All temples are oriented not north-south but mountains-sea. *Kaja*, the direction towards the mountains, is the most important direction so at this end of the temple the holiest shrines are found. The direction towards the sea is *kelod*. The sunrise or *kangin* direction is the second most important direction so on this side you find the secondary shrines. *Kaja* may be towards a particular mountain – as Pura Besakih is pointed directly towards Gunung Agung – or it may just be the mountains in general, which run east-west along the length of Bali.

Temple Types

There are three basic temple types which almost every village will have. The most important is the *pura puseh* or temple of origin which is dedicated to the village founders and is located at the *kaja* end of the village. In the middle of the village is the *pura desa* for the spirits which protect the village community in its day to day life. At the *kelod* end of the village is the

RABIULAKHIR - JUMADILAWWAL
Tahun : Wawu
Jawa : 1921
Arab : 1409

XII DESEMBER 1988

TRI ULAN KE : IV

ÇAKA : 1910
Sasih Kanem, Ngunya : Kaulu, Rah : 2
WINDU : SANGARA
Pangunyan Tahun : ORÉ - WRISABA
TENGGEK : 10

CHAP GWEE - CHAP IT GWEE
BOUW - SIEN : 2539
TAHUN : NAGA

JIE NI GATSU 2648

WUKU	Minggu Ke : 48 2. LANDEP Salah wadi Basah Cenik Bhatara Mahadewa	Minggu Ke : 49 3. UKIR Lanus Bhatara Mahayekti	Minggu Ke : 50 4. KULANTIR Kala Ingsor, Basah Cenik Ehep Bhatara Langsur	Minggu Ke : 51 5. TAULU Was Penganten, Basah Cenik Kala Pati Bhatara Bayu	Minggu Ke : 52 6. GUMBREG Carik walangati, Salahwadi Basah Cenik, Tanpa Guru Bhatara Chandra
AHAD Redite Sunday Niciyobi Sing Chi Rek	Tgl. : PERINGATAN : 10. Hari Hak - Hak Azasi Manusia. 20. Hari Sosial.- 22. Hari Ibu.-	**4** Rabiulakhir 24 Chap Gwee 26 Hari Pare Sato Kajeng Umanis Urukung Jaya 10 Pandita Menga Kala Gigis Watak : Wong - Gajah Lintang : Kala Sungsang 12. Danuh Rasi Sasih Kenem	**11** Jumadilawwal 2 Chap It Gwee 3 Hari Kidang Patra Pasah Pon Paniron Laba 2 Suka Menga Brahma Dangu Watak : Watu - Lintah Lintang : Patrem 19. Danuh Rasi Sasih Kapitu	**18** Jumadilawwal 9 Chap It Gwee 10 Hari Anjing Wong G. Tegeh Kliwon Was Sri 9 Duka Papet Ludra Tulus Watak : Buta - Uler Lintang : Lawean 26. Danuh Rasi Sasih Kapitu	**25** Jumadilawwal 16 Chap It Gwee 17 Hari Lilin Pakai Kajeng Paing Maulu Menala 1 Sri Menga Yama Erangan Watak : Suku - Gajah Lintang : Gajah 5. Makara Rasi Sasih Kapitu
SENEN Coma Monday Getsuyobi Sing Chi Ik	Pengaruh Bintang Panah (Sagitarius) mulai dari tgl : 23 Nopember 1988 s/d tgl : 20 Desember 1988.	**5** Rabiulakhir 25 Chap Gwee 27 Hari Madu Putra Pasah Paing Paniron Menala 11 Duka Pepet Uma Nohan Watak : Buta - Uler Lintang : Kukus 13. Danuh Rasi Sasih Kenem	**12** Jumadilawwal 3 Chap It Gwee 4 Hari Macan Wong Tungleh Wage Was Jaya 3 Dewa Menga Kala Jangur Watak : Buta - Lintah Lintang : Lembu 20. Danuh Rasi Sasih Kapitu	**19** Jumadilawwal 10 Chap It Gwee 11 Hari Naga Pakai Kajeng Umanis Maulu Laba 10 Raksasa Pepet Brahma Dadi Watak : Suku - Uler Lintang : Kalapa 27. Danuh Rasi Sasih Kapitu	**26** Jumadilawwal 17 Chap It Gwee 18 Hari Ulung Mina Pasah Pon Tungleh Sri 2 Pati Pepet Ludra Urungan Watak : Gajah - Lembu Lintang : Kiriman 6. Makara Rasi Sasih Kapitu
SELASA Anggara Tuesday Kayobi Sing Chi El		**6** Rabiulakhir 26 Chap Gwee 28 Hari Kala Wong G. Tegeh Paing Was Sri 12 Pandita Menga Sri Ogan Watak : Wong - Gajah Lintang : Asu 14. Danuh Rasi Sasih Kenem	**13** Jumadilawwal 4 Chap It Gwee 5 Hari Kucing Pakai Kajeng Kliwon Maulu Menala 4 Pati Menga Uma Gigis Watak : Gajah - Lembu Lintang : Dpat 21. Danuh Rasi Sasih Kapitu	**20** Jumadilawwal 11 Chap It Gwee 12 Hari Kambing Mina Pasah Paing Tungleh Jaya 11 Suka Menga Kala Dengu Watak : Watu - Lintah Lintang : Yuyu 28. Danuh Rasi Sasih Kapitu	**27** Jumadilawwal 18 Chap It Gwee 19 Hari Kelapa Taru G. Tegeh Wage Aryang Laba 3 Raja Pepet Brahma Tulus Watak : Watu - Uler Lintang : Jong sarat 7. Makara Rasi Sasih Kapitu
REBO Buda Wednesday Suiyobi Sing Chi San	Disusun Oleh : I Ki : Bangbang Gde Rawi dan Putra - Putranya	**7** Rabiulakhir 27 Chap Gwee 29 Hari Uler Pakai Kajeng Wage Maulu Laba 13 Pati Pepet Indra Erangan Watak : Gajah - Lembu Lintang : Kartika 15. Danuh Rasi Sasih Kenem	**14** Jumadilawwal 5 Chap It Gwee 6 Hari Sampi Mina Pasah Umanis Tungleh Jaya 5 Suka Menga Sri Nohan Watak : Watu - Lintah Lintang : Tangla 22. Danuh Rasi Sasih Kapitu	**21** Jumadilawwal 12 Chap It Gwee 13 Hari Mayang Taru G. Tegeh Pon Aryang Sri 12 Sri Menga Uma Jangur Watak : Suku - Gajah Lintang : Lumbung 1. Makara Rasi Sasih Kapitu	**28** Jumadilawwal 19 Chap It Gwee 20 Hari Bantang Sato Kajeng Kliwon Urukung Jaya 4 Manuh Pepet Kala Dadi Watak : Wong - Lembu Lintang : Tiwa-tiwa 8. Makara Rasi Sasih Kapitu
KEMIS Wraspati Thursday Mokuyobi Sing Chi She	**1** Rabiulakhir 21 Chap Gwee 23 Hari Arang Pakai Kajeng Pon Maulu Menala 7 Manuh Pepet Yama Dadi Watak : Wong - Lembu Lintang : Badé 9. Danuh Rasi Sasih Kenem	**8** Rabiulakhir 28 Chap Gwee 30 Hari Padi Mina Pasah Kliwon Tungleh Jaya 14 Manusa Menga Guru Urungan Watak : Gajah - Lintah Lintang : Naga 16. Danuh Rasi Sasih Kenem	**15** Jumadilawwal 6 Chap It Gwee 7 Hari Kerbao Taru G. Tegeh Paing Aryang Laba 6 Raja Pepet Indra Ogan Watak : Watu - Uler Lintang : Salah Ukur 23. Danuh Rasi Sasih Kapitu	**22** Jumadilawwal 13 Chap It Gwee 14 Hari Gajah Sato Kajeng Wage Urukung Menala 13 Suka Pepet Sri Gigis Watak : Watu - Lintah Lintang : Kumba 2. Makara Rasi Sasih Kapitu	**29** Jumadilawwal 20 Chap It Gwee 21 Hari Hantu Patra Pasah Umanis Paniron Menala 5 Duka Pepet Uma Dengu Watak : Buta - Uler Lintang : Sangka Tikel 9. Makara Rasi Sasih Kapitu
JUMAT Sukra Friday Kinyobi Sing Chi U	**2** Rabiulakhir 22 Chap Gwee 24 Hari Udang Mina Pasah Wagé Tungleh Sri 8 Pandita Menga Ludra Dangu Watak : Wong - Gajah Lintang : Maglut 10. Danuh Rasi Sasih Kenem	**•9** Rabiulakhir 29 Chap It Gwee 1 Hari Ulat Taru G. Tegeh Umanis Aryang Menala 15 Pati Pepet Yama Tulus Watak : Gajah - Lembu Lintang : Banyak angrem 17. Danuh Rasi Sasih Kenem	**16** Jumadilawwal 7 Chap It Gwee 8 Hari Tikus Sato Kajeng Pon Urukung Jaya 7 Duka Pepet Guru Erangan Watak : Buta - Uler Lintang : Prahu Pget 24. Danuh Rasi Sasih Kapitu	**23** Jumadilawwal 14 Chap It Gwee 15 Hari Singa Patra Pasah Kliwon Paniron Laba 14 Sri Menga Indra Nohan Watak : Suku - Gajah Lintang : Udang 3. Makara Rasi Sasih Kapitu	**30** Jumadilawwal 21 Chap It Gwee 22 Hari Arang Wong G. Tegeh Paing Was Sri 6 Manuh Pepet Sri Jangur Watak : Wong - Lembu Lintang : Bubu bolong 10. Makara Rasi Sasih Kapitu
SABTU Saniscara Saturday Doyobi Sing Chi Lioek	**3** Rabiulakhir 23 Chap Gwee 25 Hari Samudra Taru G. Tegeh Kliwon Aryang 9 Raja Pepet Brahma Jangur Watak : Watu - Uler Lintang : Peglangan 11. Danuh Rasi Sasih Kenem	**10** Jumadilawwal 1 Chap It Gwee 2 Hari Kuda Sato Kajeng Paing Urukung Jaya 1 Dewa Menga Ludra Dadi Watak : Buta - Gajah Lintang : Ru 18. Danuh Rasi Sasih Kapitu	**17** Jumadilawwal 8 Chap It Gwee 9 Hari Debu Patra Pasah Wage Paniron Menala 8 Duka Pepet Yama Urungan Watak : Buta - Uler Lintang : Puwuh atarung 25. Danuh Rasi Sasih Kapitu	**•24** Jumadilawwal 15 Chap It Gwee 16 Hari Ikan Wong G. Tegeh Umanis Was Jaya 15 Sri Menga Guru Ogan Watak : Suku - Gajah Lintang : Bgoong 4. Makara Rasi Sasih Kapitu	**31** Jumadilawwal 22 Chap It Gwee 23 Hari Udang Pakai Kajeng Pon Maulu Laba 7 Manusa Menga Indra Gigis Watak : Gajah - Lintah Lintang : Sungenge 11. Makara Rasi Sasih Kapitu
INGKEL :	SATO	MINA	MANUK	TARU	BUKU

ÇAKA : 1910, TAHUN : WRISABA.
Sasih Kanem Kedudukan Nagatahun berada di-Timur, Kepalanya menghadap Lor-Kulon, Ekornya Timur, Perutnya mengadah Selatan, Punggungnya Utara. Kedudukan Kala Wisiya berada di-Utara, Kala Rumpuh berada di-Barat dan Kedudukan Kala Agung berada di - Lor.-

PERINGATAN :
Ek : = Ekajala Resi.
Per : = Pertiti.
Kl : = Kala (Kolo)

Tgl. : Ala - Ayuning Dewasa (Baik - Buruknya Waktu).-
1. Kl : Prawani, Kl : Suwung, Kl : Gumarang, Jiwa menganti, Laku Surya, Satriya wirang, Ek : Suka rahayu, Per : Wedana.-
2. Kl : Siyung, Prawanining ulan, Pati Pata, Kl : Luwang, Tutur mandi, Pepedan, Babi munggah, Laku Pandita Sakti, Sumur sinaba, Ek : Suka pinanggih, Per : Separsa.-
3. Gnirawana, Kl : Kutila, Pepedan, Bojog turun, Laku Bumi, Tunggak semi, Ek : Sida kasobagian, Per : Sedayatana.-
4. Kl : Jengking, Kl : Sor, Kl : Ngunya, Asuasa, Srigati munggah, Laku Pandita Sakti, Sumur Sinaba, Ek : Kinasihaning jana, Per : Namarupa.-
5. Kl : Siyung, Kl : Mangap, Kl : Dangastra, Macekan Wadon, Kl : Buing Rau, Kl : Bangkung, Kl : Ketemu, Laku Bintang, Bumi kapetak, Ek : Buat suka, Per : Wijnyana.-
6. Kl : Temah, Kl : Dangu, Pepedan, Laku Pandita Sakti, Satriya wibawa, Ek : Kinasihaning jana, Per : Saskara.-
7. Gnirawana, Kl : Pati, Gnirawana rangkep, Kl : Empas, Kl : Sor, Aras tuding, Satriya wibawa, Ek : Tininggaling suka, Per : Jati.-
8. Prawani, Karnasula, Kl : Suwung, Kl : Temah, Kl : Buing Rau, Pepedan, Lutung megandong, Tutur mandi, Laku Air, Bumi kapetak, Ek : Rahayu, Per : Bawa.-
9. Amertadewa, Kl : Temah, Kl : Sor, Kl : Ketemu, Titibuwuk, Karnasula, Arastuding, Satriya wirang, Ek : Buat Sebet, Per : Upadana.-
10. Geheng manyinget, Kl : Luang, Kl : Temah, Kl : Pgat, Kl : Rau, Kl : Sor, Kl : Demit, Kajeng rendetan, Pepedan, Kajeng lulunan, Asuajag turun, Laku Api, Satriya wibawa, Ek : Buat astawa, Per : Saskara.-
11. Gnirawana, Karnasula, Dagdig krana, Kl : Mangap, Macekan lanang, Kl : Mues, Kl : Bangkung, Banyu milir, Sampi Gumarang munggah, Aras kambang, Bumi kapetak, Ek : Langgeng, Kayowanaan, Per : Awidiya.-
12. Ayunulus, Sedanayoga, Dewa ngelayang, Subacara, Dauhayu, Amertamasa, Derman bagia, Kl : Was, Karnasula, Laku Api, Wisesa segara, Ek : Werdi Putra, Per : Jeramerana.-
13. Gnirawana rangkep, Kl : Kutilamanik, Kl : Sor, Srigati jenek, Aras tuding, Sumur sinaba, Ek : Manggih suka, Per : Jati.-
14. Amertadewa, Amertamasa, Kl : Temah, Kl : Bangkung, Titibuwuk, Pepedan, Sarik Agung, Aras kambang, Sumur sinaba, Ek : Sida kasobagian, Per : Bawa.-
15. Kl : Mangap, Kl : Dangastra, Banyuurung, Pepedan, Laku Bulan, Lebu Katiup Angin, Ek : Tininggaling suka, Per : Upadana.-
16. Karnasula, Pamacekan Agung, Gnirawana, Kl : Mangap, Kl : Dangastra, Macekan lanang, Dinacarik, Kl : Gumarang, Semut sadulur, Kl : Sor, Pepedan, Laku Bintang, Labu katiup Angin, Ek : Suka pinanggih, Per : Teresna.-
17. Gnirawana, Kl : Luang, Kl : Buing Rau, Kl : Bangkung, Kl : Rau, Semut sedulur, Banyuurung, Babi turun, Laku Bintang, Satriya wirang, Ek : Bagena mapasah.-
18. Kl : Sudukan, Semut sedulur, Kl : Dangu, Pepedan, Bojog munggah, Laku Bintang, Lebu Katiup Angin, Ek : Kemeranaan, Per : Wedana.-
19. Amertadewa, Ayubadra, Kl : Temah, Kl : Ketemu, Srigati turun, Laku Angin, Tunggak semi, Ek : Buat sebet, Per : Separsa.-
20. Gnirawana, Macekan lanang, Gnirawana rangkep, Kl : Mina, Kl : Bancaran, Kl : Beser, Kl : Pacekan, Banyuurung, Pepedan, Aras kembang, Sariya wirang, Ek : Luwih bagia, Per : Sedayatana.-
21. Ayubadra, Kl : Ketemu, Banyuurung, Titibuwuk, Pepedan, Laku Bulan, Bumi Kapetak, Ek : Suka pinanggih, Per : Namarupa.-
22. Geheng manyinget, Kl : Temah, Kl : Mertiyu, Kl : Empas, Kl : Sor, Banyuurung, Aras kambang, Tunggak semi, Ek : Buat suka, Per : Wijnyana.-
23. Prawani, Geheng manyinget, Perabu pindah, Kl : Temah, Kl : Gotongan, Laku Bulan, Wisesa Segara, Ek : Buat manggih suka, Per : Wijnyana.-
24. Sedanayoga, Amerta Pagah, Kl : Wisesa, Kl : Gotongan, Kl : Ketemu, Karnasula, Laku Bulan, Bumi Kapetak, Ek : Suka Pinanggih, Per : Saskara.-
25. Kl : Gotongan, Asuajag munggah, Laku Bulan, Wisesa segara, Ek : Buat manggih suka, Per : Saskara.-
26. Dauhayu, Amertadewa, Kl : Sor, Sampi Gumarang turun, Aras tuding, Sumur sinaba, Ek : Tininggaling suka, Per : Awidiya.-
27. Gnirawana, Amertadewa, Kl : Kutila, Kl : Dangu, Laku Bumi, Lebu katiup Angin, Ek : Buat merang, Per : Jaramerana.-
28. Dauhayu, Kl : Jengking, Kl : Kutila manik, Kl : Sor, Kajeng rendetan, Pepedan, Laku Surya, Lebu Katiup Angin, Ek : Suka pinanggih, Per : Jati.-
29. Geheng manyinget, Banyuurung, Titibuwuk, Laku Bintang, Satriya wibawa, Ek : Buat astawa, Per : Bawa.-
30. Dauhayu, Sedanayoga, Amertayoga, Kl : Buing Rau, Kl : Rau, Banyuurung, Laku Surya, Tunggak semi, Ek : Buat astawa, Per : Upadana.-
31. Dagdig krana, Kl : Dangastra, Kl : Brahma, Kl : Gumarang, Laku Air, Wisesa Segara, Ek : Buat Astawa, Per : Teresna.-

K A L E N D E R   L E N G K A P

Tgl : Hari - Hari Penting Hindu Dharma :
3. Tumpek Landep, melakukan upakara Banten selamatan Sayut Jagrasatru, terhadap alat - alat Senjata Perang, tercapainya jayeng Perang.-
7. Hari Buda Cemeng Ukir.-
9. Hari Tilem Kenem, melakukan Upakara Nangluk merana dari Pantai - Laut, agar terhindar dari Wabah Penyakit dan merana-merana lainnya. Lagi pula hari ini disebut hari Bhatari Sri.-
13. Anggarkasih Kulantir, Kajeng Kliwon Enyitan.-
24. Purnama Sasih Kapitu.-
26. Buda Kliwon Gumbreg, Kajeng Kliwon Uwudan.-

Tgl. : Odalan di - Pura - Pura s.b.b. : Pr = Pura :
3. Pr. Pasek Gelgel Pedungan/Kuta (Badung), Pr : Agung Pasek Tangguntiti Kaler (Tabanan), Pr : Agung Pasek Selemadeg (Tabanan), Pr : Pasek Tangkas Kediri (Tabanan), Pr : Karta di-Banyuning-Barat (Buleleng), Pr : Dalem - Tenggaling Sengguen (Singapadu), Pr : Kawitan Arya Wangbang Pinatih/Peguyangan (Singaraja).-
4. Merajan Geria Sedawa (Gianyar), Sanggah Gde Dukuh - Segening Tegaltugu (Gianyar).-
7. Pr : Desa - Pr : Puseh Bebalang (Bangli), Pr : Dalem Dalem Purancak (Badung), Pr : Pasek Bendesa Hyang Selat Krobokan (Badung), Perhyangan Agung Pr : Ibu Wanasari (Tegal/Badung).-
13. Pr : Penataran Tangkas (Sukawati), Pr : Dalem Lagan Bebalang (Bangli), Pr : Puseh Lambeng (Ketewel), Pr : Pasek Gelgel Penulisan Kerambitan (Tabanan), Pr : Dalem Gandamayu (Klungkung).-
14. Pr : Pasek Tangkas Pasekan Kaler (Tabanan), Pr : Gaduh Benoh/Ubung (Kesiman).-
19. Pr : Puseh/Bale - Agung Ubung Kupang Penebel (Tabanan).-
21. Pr : Catur Buana di - Sanding.-
28. Pr : Pasek Gelgel Kukuh/Marga (Tabanan), Pr : Pasek Gelgel Dukuh/Selemadeg (Tabanan), Pr : Pasek Gelgel Mambang/Selemadeg (Tabanan), Pr : Desa - Pr : Puseh di - Guang (Sukawati).-

Dewasa Ayu Untuk Melakukan s.b.b. :
dan begitu pula, Segenap HASIL PERTANIAN menjadi kebutuhan pokok untuk menunjang Kehidupan MANUSIA setiap waktu, bahkan setiap saat. Andai kata, bilamana - macetnya segenap hasil tersebut, akan menimbulkan Penderitaan dan kesukaran-kesukaran yang amat sulit dikendalikan. Sebagai Pepatah : SEBELUM HUJAN SEDIA PAYUNG.-

Buah nenas ditarik lambat,
Tali benang ikut nyeludup,
Panas terik Hujan lebat,
Kita tenang tinggal hidup.-
Botol gelas makan malas,
Nasi beras bercampur Injin,
Bila malas akan digilas,
Mantap rajin akan dijinjin.-

Mohon ma'af, sekedar Pandangan HIDUP, Eling/ingat : Tegak - Teguh - Teliti - Tenang - Tertib terhadap Swadharmanya.-
BHINNEKA TUNGGAL IKA.

Dewasa Ayu mulai Mewinih tgl : 4 dan 19.-
Dari mulainya menyambut Karya sebaiknya mohon anugrah dari Paduka Tuhan Yang Maha Kuasa berdasarkan hati Suci murni yang mantap, karena itu, kita bisa berusaha, tetapi Tuhanlah yang menentukan.-
Mulai membuka Jalan Air tgl : 25.-

Dewasa mulai MENANDUR menurut Perhitungan Hari : Laki, Perempuan dan Banci yaitu pada tgl : 3, 7, 9, 10, 12, 15, 16, 19, 21, 23, 24, 29, 30 dan 31, tetapi pilih juga Ayuning Dewasa tersebut diatas, begitu pula bijaksana memilih Cocoknya Tanah, Bibit, Musim, Iklim, dan berdasarkan Pemeliharaan yang sebaik-baiknya. Bilamana Pancawiguna diatas ini tidak dipenuhi, kemungkinan tidak dapat diharapkan akan hasilnya, hal ini sangat penting diperhatikan seteliti-telitinya.-
Dewasa Ayu Upakara Biyukukung yaitu pada tgl : 4 dan 19.-
Mulai membuka Jalan Air tgl : 8, 11, 23, 25 dan tgl : 31.-
Mulai nyimpen padi di-Lumbung pada tgl : 4, 13 dan tgl : 19.-
Dewasa Ayu Mantening Padi di-Lumbung pada tgl : 14 dan tgl : 30.-
Mulai mengajar Sapi Godel metekap atau membajak pada tgl : 19.-
Dewasa Ayu Nyula atau Melesin Kucit dan Godel Sapi pada tgl : 12 dan tgl : 30.-
Mulai melangbeng/mengandangkan Babi dan baik pula membuat PALUNGANNYA pada tgl. 17.-
Mulai memelihara Bibit Bangkung pada tgl : 19 dan 25.-
Mulai Nelusuk hidung Godel Sapi pada tgl : 12 dan tgl : 24.-
Dewasa Ayu mulai membakar Genteng, Bata atau membakar Kapur tgl : 3 dan 27.-
Mulai membuat Bubu, Perangkap Ikan pada tgl : 12 dan tgl : 30.-
Dewasa mulai membuat Jaring, Sau, Tepis, Pencar, Anak panah Penangkap Ikan pada tgl : 20, jam : 08.00 pagi.-
Mulai membuat Perau, Janggolan dan Jukung pada tgl : 13, jam : 07.30 pagi.-
Mulai membuat Kolam Ikan pada tgl : 20, jam : 08.00 Pagi dan baik pula membuat Talinpancing.-
Mulai membuat tempat bersarangnya Nyawan atau Laba pada tgl : 4, Jam : 09.00, pagi.-
Mulai membuat Gambelan atau Sani Suara, membuat Bajra, Kendang dan Kentongan pada tgl : 11 dan 12, sama-sama pada jam : 08.30 pagi.
Mulai belajar Menari pada tgl : 28, jam : 07.00 pagi.-
Dewasa Ayu Kawin dan Nikah (Pewarangan dan Wiwaha) pada tgl : 17. Jam : 08.00 siang atau malam waktu setempat dan lagi Ayu juga Pepar Gigi caling atau Metatah, Dewasa diatas ini baik pula melakukan : Mahayu Dewa Pitra dan Manusia.-
Dewasa Upawasa (Berpuasa luar biasa Peribadi) bilamana berminat MULAT SARIRA menuju Kehidupan yang sempurna LAHIR - BATIN dengan jalan berpuasa selama 3 hari mulai dari tgl : 30, 31 dan tgl : 1 Januari 1989 yang akan datang.-

TGL. HARI RAYA TIONGHOA
22 - 23. Tang Ceh.

TGL. HARI RAYA MASEHI UMUM
25. Natal Hari Pertama.

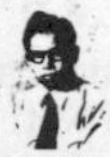

pura dalem or temple of the dead. The graveyard is also located here and the temple will often include representations of Durga, the terrible side of Shiva's wife. Shiva has both a creative and destructive side and it is simply his destructive powers which are honoured here.

Apart from these three basic temple types others include the temples dedicated to the spirits of irrigated agriculture. Rice growing is so important in Bali and the division of water for irrigation purposes is handled with such care that these *pura subak* or *pura ulun suwi* can be of considerable importance. Other temples may also honour dry-field agriculture as well as the flooded rice paddies.

In addition to these 'local' temples Bali also has a lesser number of great temples. Your family worships its ancestors in its family temple, your clan in its clan temple, the village in the pura puseh. Above these come the temples of royalty or state temples and in many case a kingdom would have three of these – a main state temple in the heartland of the state (like Pura Taman Ayun in Mengwi), then a mountain temple (like Pura Besakih or Pura Luhur Batukau) and a sea temple (like Pura Luhur Ulu Watu or Pura Rambut Siwi).

Every house in Bali has its house temple which is at the *kaja-kangin* corner of the courtyard – where the mountain and sunrise sides meet. There will be shrines to the Hindu 'trinity' of Brahma, Shiva and Vishnu, to *taksu*, the divine intermediary, and to the lord of the ground *tugu*.

World Sanctuaries

Certain special temples in Bali are of such importance that they are deemed to be owned by the whole island rather than by individual villages or local community organisations. These *kahyangan jagat* or *sad-kahyangan* include Pura Besakih on the slopes of Gunung Agung. This holiest of Balinese temples encompasses separate shrines and temples for all the clans and

former kingdoms. Pura Besakih is said to be a male temple, its female counterpart is Pura Batur at Kintamani.

Other important temples in this group include Pura Ulu Watu at the extreme southern tip of Bali to the south of Kuta, Pura Goa Lawah also known as the bat cave, Pura Batukau on the side of Gunung Batukau, Pura Pusering Jagat at Pejeng with its enormous bronze drum and the lesser known Pura Lempuyang Luhur at the extreme east of the island.

Temple Design

Balinese temples usually consist of a series of courtyards entered from the sea (*kelod*) side. In a large temple the outer gateway will generally be a *candi bentar*, modelled on the old Hindu temples (*candi*) of Java but split in two and moved apart – hence the name 'split gate'. The first courtyard is used for less important ceremonies, for preparing food, holding meetings and will have a number of open-sided shelters. There will also be a kulkul (alarm drum) tower in this outer courtyard and quite possibly a shady and sweet-smelling frangipani tree.

The innermost and holiest courtyard (small temples may have just two courts) is entered by another candi-like gateway except here there is a passage through the middle of it. It's usually known as the *kori* or *kori agung* and symbolises the holy mountain through which you must pass to enter the inner court. This gateway will be flanked by *dwarapala*, statues of guardian figures, or by small protective shrines known as *pengapit lawang*.

In the inner court there will usually be two rows of shrines – the most important on the mountain (*kaja*) side and the lesser shrines on the sunrise (*kangin*) side. These shrines vary in number and design from temple to temple although there are detailed rules to cover all of them. In the major temples the shrines will include multi-roofed pagodas known as *merus*. The word comes from Mahameru, the Hindu holy mountain. The number of roofs are, apart from some rare exceptions, always odd and the holiest merus in the holiest temples will have 11 roofs. The merus are roofed with long-lasting black sugar-palm.

The inner court may also contain simple little thrones for local and less important gods to use, small wooden shrines which may have little doors to the interior, or *gedong*, made of wood or brick, which a priest may actually be able to enter. Surya, the sun-god, associated with Shiva by the Balinese, usually has his own shrine known as the *padmasana*. This 'lotus throne' has three sections which represent the world's three levels – serpents and the cosmic turtle represent the underworld.

Temple Festivals

For much of the year Balinese temples are deserted, just an empty space. Then every now and then they come alive with days of frenetic activity and nights of drama and dance. Temple festivals come at least once a Balinese year of 210 days. The annual 'temple birthday' is known as an *odalan*. Since most villages have at least three temples that means you're assured of at least five or six annual festivals in every village. But that's only the start – there can be special festival days common throughout the islands, festivals for certain temples, festivals for certain gods, festivals because it just seemed like a good idea to have one.

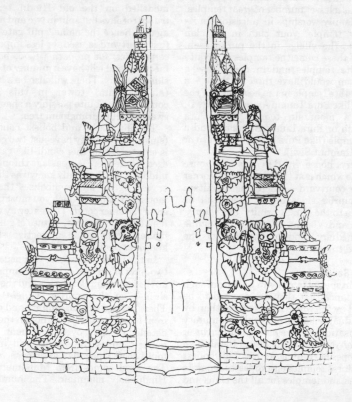

Cockfights are a regular part of temple ceremonies – they're a convenient combination of excitement, sport, gambling and a blood sacrifice all rolled into one. Men keep fighting cocks as prized pets, carefully groomed and cared for, lovingly prepared for their brief moment of glory or defeat. On quiet afternoons the men will often meet in the banjars to compare their roosters, spar them against one another, line up the odds for the next big bout.

You'll often see the roosters by the roadside in their bell-shaped cane baskets – they're placed there to be entertained by passing activity. When the festivals take place the cocks are matched one against another, a lethally sharp metal spur tied to one leg and then, after being pushed against each other a few times to stir up the blood, they're released and the feathers fly. It's usually over in a flash, a slash of the spur and one rooster is down and dying. Occasionally a cowardly rooster turns and flees but in that case they're put in a covered basket together where they can't avoid fighting. After the bout the successful betters collect their pay-offs and the winning owner takes home the dead rooster for his cooking pot.

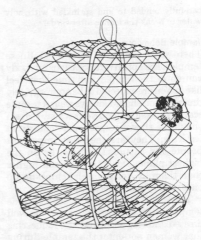

While the men are slaughtering their prized pets the women are bringing beautifully arranged offerings of foods, fruit and flowers to the temple, artfully piled in huge pyramids which they carry on their heads. Outside the temple, warungs offer food for sale and stalls set up to sells toys and trinkets. In the outer courtyard a gamelan provides further amusement.

While all this activity is going on in and around the temple, the pemangkus are suggesting to the gods that they should come down for a visit and enjoy the goings on. That's what those little thrones are for in the temple shrines, they're symbolic seats for the gods to occupy during festivals. Sometimes small images known as *pratimas* are placed on the thrones, to represent the gods.

At some festivals the images and thrones of the deities are taken out of the temple and ceremonially carried down to the sea (or just to a suitable expanse of water if the sea is too distant) for a ceremonial bath. Gamelans follow the merry procession and provide a suitable musical accompaniment.

Back in the temple women dance the stately pendet, an offering dance for the gods, and all night long there's activity, music and dancing. It's just like a country fair with food stands, amusements, games, stalls, gambling, noise, colour and confusion.

Finally, as dawn approaches, the entertainment fades away, the women perform the last pendet, the pemangkus suggest to the gods that maybe it's time they made their weary way back to heaven, and the people wend their weary way back to their homes.

Trances are an everyday feature of Balinese life, particularly at festivals. People seem to be able to go into a trance state in a flash and at that time they're supposed to be a medium of communication for the gods who temporarily possess their bodies. You may see a pemangku go into trance while offering his prayers, a young girl's eye's glaze over as she carries offerings into the temple, or the trance dancers, particularly in the Barong and Rangda dance. It's regarded as a holy state, people in trance are carefully tended to and sprinkled with holy water to break the trance afterwards.

Temple Behaviour

There are a number of rules for Balinese temples. Except on rare occasions anybody can enter the temples anytime they feel like it. You are expected to be appropriately dressed. You should always wear a temple scarf as a sash around your waist. Priests should be shown respect, particularly at festivals. They are the most important people and should, therefore, be on the highest plane. Don't put yourself higher than them by, for example, climbing up on a wall to take photographs.

There will usually be a sign outside temple entrances warning you to be well dressed and respectful and also requesting that women not enter the temple during their periods. The pleasant little lakeside temple up at Bedugul once had the nicest 'no entry' sign in Bali. It announced that 'It is forbidden to enter women during menstruation'. Unfortunately they changed the sign to eliminate that superb double entendre.

HOLIDAYS & FESTIVALS

Balinese calendars, with illustrations for each day indicating what activities that day is auspicious for, are popular souvenirs. Apart from the everyday western calendar the Balinese also use two local calendars, the *saka* and the *wuku* calendar. The *wuku* calendar is used to determine festival dates. The calendar uses 10 different weeks from one to 10 days each, all of which run simultaneously! The intersection of the various weeks determines auspicious days. The seven-day and five-day weeks are of particular importance. A full year is made up of 30 individually named seven day weeks.

The *Galungan* festival is Bali's major feast throughout the island, it comes round once a *wuku* year. During this 10-day period all the gods, including the supreme deity Sanghyang Widi, come

down to earth for the festivities. Barongs prance from temple to temple and village to village.

The last and most important day of the 10-day festival is called *Kuningan*. Forthcoming dates include:

	Galungan	Kuningan
1989	1 February	11 February
	30 August	9 September
1990	28 March	7 April
	24 October	3 November
1991	22 May	1 June
	18 December	28 December

There are numerous festivals around the time of *Galungan* and *Kuningan*. They include:

place	festival	date
Batukau	Pura Luhur	Galungan + 1 day
Serangan	Pura Sakenan	Kuningan & Kuningan + 1 day
Tanah Lot	Pura Tanah Lot	Kuningan + 4 days
Ulu Watu	Pura Luhur	Kuningan + 10 days
Goa Lawah	Pura Goa Lawah	Kuningan + 10 days
Mengwi	Pura Taman Ayun	Kuningan + 10 days

The Hindu *saka* calendar is a lunar cycle that more closely follows our own year in terms of the length of the year. *Nyepi* is the major festival of the *saka* year – it's the last day of the year, the day after the new moon on the ninth month. Nyepi also marks the end of the rainy season and the day before is marked by an island-wide day of purification in which absolutely nothing goes on, a sort of super-Sabbath. That night evil spirits are noisily chased away with cymbals, gongs, drums and flaming torches and on Nyepi everyone stays quietly at home. Nyepi generally falls towards the end of March or the beginning of April.

Certain major temples celebrate their festivals by the *saka* calendar rather than the *wuku* one. This makes the actual date difficult to determine from our calendar since the lunar *saka* calendar does not follow a fixed number of days like the *wuku* one. The full moon around the end of September to beginning of October or early to mid-April are often the time for important temple festivals.

The Balinese also have a major annual festival by the western calendar – Indonesian Independence Day falls on 17 August, celebrating Sukarno's proclamation of independence on that day in 1945. Final freedom from the Dutch did not come until several years later.

LANGUAGE

For a handy introduction to Indonesian see Lonely Planet's *Indonesia Phrasebook*. There are a vast number of local languages and dialects in Indonesia but Bahasa Indonesia, which is all but identical to Malay, is actively promoted as the one national language. Almost anywhere you go in Indonesia, including Bali, people will speak Bahasa Indonesia as well as their own local language. Many of them will also speak English as a third language.

Like any language Indonesian has its simplified colloquial form and its more developed literate language. For the visitor who wants to pick up enough to get by in the common language – 'pasar' or 'market' Indonesian – is very easy to learn. In fact it is rated as one of the simplest languages in the world as there are no tenses, no genders and often one word can convey the meaning of a whole sentence. Furthermore it's an easy language to pronounce with no obscure rules and none of the tonal complications that make some Asian languages very difficult. It can also be a delightfully poetic language – day, for example, is *hari* and eye is *mata*. Therefore *mata hari* is the 'eye of the day', the sun!

Apart from the ease of learning a little Indonesian there's another very good reason for trying to pick up at least a few words and phrases – few people are as delighted with foreigners learning their language as the Indonesians. They don't criticise you if you mangle your pronunciation or tangle your grammar. They make you feel like you're an expert if you know only a handful of words. And bargaining seems to be a whole lot easier when you do it in their language. Few countries in the world repay the effort of learning a little of the language so handsomely and in few countries is it so easy to do.

General Rules

Articles are not used in Indonesian – there's no 'the' or 'a' – nor is the intransitive verb 'to be' used. Thus where we would say 'the room is dirty' in Indonesian it is simply *kamar kotor* – 'room dirty'. To make a word plural in some cases you double it – thus 'child' is *anak*, 'children' *anak anak* – but in many other cases you simply use the same singular form and the context or words such as 'many' (*banyak*) to indicate the plurality.

Probably the greatest simplification in Indonesian is that verbs are not conjugated nor are there different forms for past, present and future tenses. Words like 'already', 'yesterday' (*kemarin*), 'will' (*akan*) or 'tomorrow' (*besok*) indicate the tense. *Sudah*, 'already', is the all purpose past tense indicator. 'I eat' is *saya makan* while 'I have already eaten' is simply *saya sudah makan*.

Except for the adjectives 'all' *semua*, 'many' *banyak* and 'a little' *sedikit*, adjectives follow the noun. Thus a 'big bus' is *bis besar*.

Pronouns & Forms of Address

Pronouns, particularly 'you', are rarely used in Indonesian. Speaking to an older man (or anyone old enough to be a father) it's common to call them *bapak*, 'father' or simply *pak*. Similarly an older woman is *ibu*, 'mother' or simply *bu*. You can call someone of a similar age either *abang* (older brother), *kakak* (younger brother) or *adik* (younger brother or sister). *Tuan* is a respectful term, like 'sir'.

Greetings & Civilities

good morning	*selamat pagi*
good day	*selamat siang*
goodbye (to person staying)	*selamat tinggal*
goodbye (to person going)	*selamat jalan*
good afternoon	*selamat sore*
good night	*selamat malam*
welcome	*selamat datang*
good night (to someone going to bed)	*selamat tidur*

Early morning is *pagi-pagi*. Morning *pagi* extends from about 7 to 11 am. *Siang* is the middle of the day, around 11 am to 3 pm. *Sore* is around 3 pm to 7 pm and *malam* really starts when it gets dark.

thank you	*terima kasih*
please	*silakan*
sorry	*ma'af*
excuse me	*permisi*
how are you?	*apa khabar?*
I'm fine	*khabar baik*
what is your name?	*siapa nama saudara?*
my name is	*nama saya . . . .*
another, one more	*satu lagi*
no, not, negative	*tidak/bukan*
good	*bagus*
good, fine, OK	*baik*

Tidak is used with verbs, adjectives and adverbs, *bukan* with nouns and pronouns to indicate negation.

Hotels & Accommodation

one night	*satu malam*
one person	*satu orang*
sleep	*tidur*
bed	*tempat tidur*
room	*kamar*
bathroom	*kamar mandi*

toilet	*WC (way say)*
soap	*sabun*

Questions & Comments

what is this?	*apa ini?*
how much (money)?	*berapa (harga)?*
expensive	*mahal*
how many kilometres?	*berapa kilometre?*
where is?	*dimana ada?*
which way?	*kemana?*
I don't understand	*saya tidak mengerti*
this/that	*ini/itu*
big/small	*besar/kecil*
finished	*habis*
open/closed	*buka/tutup*

Travelling & Places

ticket	*karcis*
bus	*bis*
train	*kereta-api*
ship	*kapal*
motorcycle	*sepeda motor*
station	*setasiun*
here	*disini*
stop	*berhenti*
north	*utara*
south	*selatan*
east	*timor*
west	*barat*
entry	*masuk*
I want to go to	*saya mau ke . . . .*
street	*jalan*
village	*desa*
town	*kota*
bank	*bank*
post office	*kantor pos*
immigration	*immigrasi*

Numbers

1	*satu*
2	*dua*
3	*tiga*
4	*empat*
5	*lima*
6	*enam*
7	*tujuh*
8	*delapan*
9	*sembilan*
10	*sepuluh*

A half is *setengah* which is pronounced 'stinger', ie half a kg is 'stinger kg. 'Approximately' is *kira-kira*. After the numbers one to 10 the 'teens' are *belas*, the 'tens' are *puluh*, the hundreds are *ratus* and the thousands *ribu*. Thus:

11	*sebelas*
12	*duabelas*
13	*tigabelas*
20	*dua puluh*
21	*dua puluh satu*
25	*dua puluh lima*
30	*tiga puluh*
99	*sembilan puluh sembilan*
100	*seratus*
150	*seratus limapuluh*
200	*dua ratus*
888	*delapan ratus delapan puluh delapan*
1000	*seribu*

Time

when?	*kapan?*
tomorrow/yesterday	*besok/kemarin*
hour	*jam*
week	*minggu*
month	*bulan*
year	*tahun*
what time?	*jam berapa?*
how many hours?	*berapa jam?*
7 o'clock	*jam tujuh*
five hours	*lima jam*

If you ask what time the bus is coming and you're told *jam karet* don't panic, it means 'rubber time', in other words it will come when it comes!

Days of the Week

Monday	*hari senen*
Tuesday	*hari selasa*
Wednesday	*hari rabu*
Thursday	*hari kamis*
Friday	*hari jum'at*
Saturday	*hari sabtu*
Sunday	*hari minggu*

Balinese

Bahasa Indonesian, the national language of Indonesia you hear every day in Bali, is not Balinese. Balinese is another language entirely with a completely different vocabulary and grammar and much more complex rules for its use. Balinese is also much more of a 'spoken' than a 'written' language since it is not taught in schools or, indeed, studied very much at all. It's the language of day to day local contact but exclusively of the Balinese people.

Balinese is greatly complicated by its caste influences. There's high Balinese, low Balinese and even middle Balinese plus a number of variations from those three. Basically when a low caste person speaks to a high caste person he should use high Balinese. Conversely when a high caste person speaks to a low caste person he uses low Balinese. When talking about oneself, however, you talk in low Balinese no matter whom you are talking to! It sounds amazingly complicated, two different languages which you first have to know whom you are talking to before you even know which one to use! Actually it's not quite that complex because the high Balinese words are principally restricted to words about people or their actions.

Middle Balinese has an even more restricted vocabulary. It's mainly used when one wishes to be very polite but doesn't want to emphasise caste differences. How does one Balinese know which level to address another? Well initially a conversation between two strangers would commence in the high language. At some point the question of caste would be asked and then the level adjusted accordingly. But amongst friends a conversation is likely to be carried on in low Balinese no matter what the caste of the conversationalists. In today's world caste differences are increasingly disappearing in the language.

Don't worry about Balinese though, it's interesting to consider, fun to pick up a few words, but you're wiser to put any language learning effort into Indonesian.

Getting Around Bali

BEMOS

Bemos are the favourite local transport. These days most bemos are small minibuses although the old basic bemo, which was a small pickup truck with a row of seats down each side, is still around. Most of them operate a standard route for a set fare picking up and dropping off people and goods anywhere along the way. As a rule of thumb count on about 25 rp a km with a minimum of about 100 rp although, unless you get on at standard starting point A and get off at standard finishing point B the fares are likely to be fuzzy.

The best way of finding out what the fare should be is to ask your fellow passengers what the *harga biasa* (standard price) should be. Bemo drivers are always ready to overcharge the unwary but they're good humoured about it. If they try and ask 200 rp and you know damn well it should only be 100 rp they'll take the correct fare with a grin. Equally if they put up a big protest about the correct fare being 200 rp when you're only offering 100 rp they're probably right. Beware of *harga turis*, or special tourist prices for bemos which are unfortunately becoming increasingly prevalent in Bali.

Around Kuta beware of getting on an empty bemo as there are some unscrupulous bemo drivers who will inform you that they're not just plying the route but that you have chartered the bemo!

As more of the standard bemos are being replaced by minibuses the distinction between bemos and colts is becoming blurred but basically the method of operation and the fares are the same. In a colt-style bemo you probably get a better view and more comfort at the expense of less fresh air and greater difficulty getting on and off.

Warning

Beware of pickpockets – on certain bemo routes they've become notorious. They seem to prey on unwary travellers in particular so you'll find them mainly on the Denpasar to Kuta and Denpasar to Ubud routes. Their mode of operation seems to be for one operator to engage you in friendly conversation, while his accomplice cleans you out, often using a painting, parcel or similar cover to hide the activity. Sometimes half the bemo will be in on the game, and the odds will really be stacked against you.

Chartering Bemos

An excellent way for a group to get around is to charter a bemo. Between half a dozen people it can work out cheaper than hiring a motorcycle by the day and much cheaper than hiring a car. It can also be more convenient for straightforward point A to point B trips. For example to travel by regular bemo from Kuta to Sanur you have to take a bemo into Denpasar, transfer between Tegal and Kereneng stations and then take another bemo out. Alternatively you can, with a little bargaining charter a whole bemo for around 4000 to 5000 rp. Between four people that works out about the same as the roundabout route through Denpasar but it's much faster, more convenient and you can get to-the-door service at your final destination.

Between Kuta and Ubud you should be able to knock the cost down to around 12,000 rp. If you want to make stops on the way – we paused once to buy a stone statue in Batubulan – that will add a little to the cost. Regular bemos carry around 12 people so multiplying the usual fare by 12 should give you a rough idea of what to pay. Denpasar to Ubud is 600 rp therefore 12 times 600 is 7200 rp. Or work on the basis of about 25 rp per km per person, for a full load. Smaller bemos are, of course, cheaper than big ones.

From 20,000 to 25,000 rp per day is probably a good figure to work from although it depends on where you want to go as well. If you're planning to cover an awful lot of territory then you may have to pay more.

COLTS

Colts are small minibuses. The name comes from Mitsubishi Colt minibuses but it's applied to all minibuses, not just Colts. On many transport routes Colts have replaced buses. In comparison with buses Colts are more comfortable and, since they carry fewer passengers, depart more frequently. If there's a choice between a bus and a colt the colt will probably be a bit more expensive, however, a real bemo-bemo and a colt-bemo will be the same price.

HITCHING

Yes, you can even hitch-hike around Bali. Two Dutch travellers reported that while hitching you meet a lot of nice people, can enjoy the scenery and 'it's a good experience to ride around Bali, standing in the back of a truck!'

MOTORCYCLES

Motorcycles are a popular way of getting around Bali but also a controversial one.

They very definitely have their pluses and minuses. The minus points are danger and a distance from certain everyday interactions with the Balinese. There is no denying the dangers of bike riding in Bali and combined with all the normal terrors of motorcycle riding are narrow roads, unexpected potholes, crazy drivers, buses and trucks which through size alone reckon they own the road, children who dart onto the road, bullocks who lumber across, dogs and chickens that run around in circles, unmarked road works, unlit traffic at night and 1001 other opportunities for you to do serious harm to yourself. Every year a number of visitors to Bali come home in a box. Bali is no place to learn to ride a motorcycle.

The distance drawback is that on a motorcycle you forsake many opportunities to get to grips with Bali. You don't meet people the way you do on a bemo, and many things can be missed because you are concentrating on the road. Furthermore motorcycles are an unpleasant intrusion in many places in Bali due to the fact that they can be noisy, distracting, annoying and unwanted.

On the other hand motorcycles also have some important plus points. I have to admit that although I've covered many km around Bali by bus and bemo I've probably covered more by motorcycle. I think I've always ridden carefully and I've never had anything resembling a hairy moment in Bali. I have had some truly beautiful moments biking round Bali, those days when every corner seems to bring another breathtaking chunk of landscape into view; rolling lazily down sweeping, traffic-free roads where the artistry of the terraced rice paddies is pure magic.

The major plus point is the enormous flexibility a motorcycle gives you. Bali may have various not-to-be-missed sights but the best things it has to offer are completely unplanned. You come round a corner and there it is – a procession, a mouth wateringly beautiful piece of scenery, or a temple decked out for a festival. Travelling around on a bike you can stop if you want to and continue on 10 minutes or 10 hours later. If you're travelling in a bemo you may just shoot straight by. That is if you even see it from the bemo. Robert Pirsig in *Zen & the Art of Motorcycle Maintenance* relates driving a car to watching television, whereas riding a bike is being in the picture. Unhappily riding a bemo can be television with a dozen people between you and the screen.

The Bike

Motorcycles for hire in Bali are almost all between 90 and 125 cc with 100 cc as the usual size. You really don't need anything bigger as the distances are short and the roads are rarely suitable for travelling fast. Anyway what's the hurry?

Rental charges vary with the bike and the period of hire. The longer the hire period the lower the rate, the bigger or newer the bike the higher the rate. Typically you can expect to pay around 5000 to 8000 rp a day. A newish 125 cc in good condition might cost 8000 rp a day. If you want a bike for only one day you might have to pay more.

Renting a motorcycle in Bali is not like zipping around to your friendly Avis or Hertz agent with your current rates brochure in hand. The majority of the bikes are rented out by individual owners, probably to raise a little extra money towards paying for it. There are a few places around Kuta which seem to specialise in bike hire but generally it's travel agents, restaurants, losmen or shops with a sign out saying 'motorcycle for hire'. You can ask around or, equally likely, if you've got an 'I need a motorcycle' look about you somebody is likely to approach you. Kuta and Sanur are the main bike hire places but you'll have no trouble finding a motorcycle to rent in Ubud or Singaraja. Check the bike over before riding off – there are some

poorly maintained, rotten old nails around.

Licences

If you have an International Driving Permit endorsed for motorcycles you have no problems. If not, you have to obtain a local licence and this is straightforward and easy but time consuming. The bike owner will take you into Denpasar where you'll probably find 50 or so other bike renters lined up for their licence. You're fingerprinted, photographed, given a written test (to which you are told the answers in advance) and then comes the hard part. After a friendly send off from the police riding tester, who wishes you luck and gives you the cheerful news that if you fail you can always try again, off you go. Ride once round a circle clockwise, once round anti-clockwise, a slalom through a row of tin cans, don't put your feet down and don't fall off. Don't run into the police officer's car either. Eventually everyone passes and is judged fit to be unleashed onto Bali's roads. It costs a healthy 11,000 rp and the whole process takes about four hours.

Apart from your licence you must also carry the bike's registration paper with you. Make sure the bike's owner gives it to you before you ride off.

Insurance

These days insurance seems to be a fixed requirement in Bali. It's quite expensive – it can cost nearly as much as the bike rental itself – and whether it actually does you much good if worse comes to worse I'd hesitate to say. Make sure, however, that your personal travel insurance covers you while you're biking. Some travel insurance policies have some nasty small print that may exclude coverage for motorcycling.

The best advice is don't have an accident, but remember if you do that it was your fault. The logic behind this is Asian and impeccable: I was involved in an accident with you. I belong here, you don't. If you hadn't been here there wouldn't have been an accident. Therefore it was your fault.

On the Road

Once you've got out of the southern Bali traffic tangle the roads are remarkably uncrowded. The traffic is heavy from Denpasar south to Kuta and Sanur; to the east about as far as Klungkung; and to the west about as far as Tabanan. Over the rest of the island the traffic is no problem at all, and in most places it's very light.

Finding your way around is no problem. Roads are well signposted and maps are easily available. Off the main routes roads often become very potholed but they're usually surfaced, there are few dirt roads in Bali. There's a scattering of petrol stations around Bali but they often seem to be out of petrol, out of electricity or simply on holiday. In that case look for the little roadside fuel shops where you fill up with a plastic jug and a funnel. Petrol is still reasonably cheap in Indonesia – it costs around 400 rp a litre.

Although Bali is in the tropics it's still wise to dress properly for motorcycling. Remember that if you fall off your skin and the pavement don't go well together. Thongs, shorts and a T-shirt are not going to protect you. As well as protection against a spill be prepared for the weather. Down on the plains it may be warm all year round but it can get amazingly cold on a cloudy day in the mountains. Coming over the top of Batur you can wish you were wearing gloves. And when it rains in Bali it really rains so be ready for that as well. Don't ignore the sun either, if riding on a hot day you're just holding your uncovered arms out to be sunburnt while your face gets the same treatment so cover up and use a sun block.

Around the Island

Don't plan on any around the island trip in Bali going to schedule – festivals, ceremonies, cremations, processions, almost anything could be there to distract you from your intended itinerary. Given a

minimum of a week a possible round trip route could be:

Day 1	Kuta to Candidasa	110 km
Day 2	Candidasa to Amlapura to Penelokan	140 km
Day 3	on Lake Batur	
Day 4	Penelokan to Kalibukbuk	90 km
Day 5	at the beach	
Day 6	Kalibukbuk to Kuta	140 km

Of course that's a kind of high speed trip and your starting and finishing point doesn't have to be Kuta, it could just as easily be Ubud, Singaraja or anywhere else you choose.

RENTAL CARS

Car rental in Bali has become very easy in recent years. The big international rental operators have a token presence here but they're very expensive and you'll do far better with the local operators. The two most popular vehicles for rent are the small Suzuki jeeps and open VW safari vehicles but you can also find regular cars, minibuses and virtually anything else. Almost anything is fine over Bali's limited distances although the jeeps are small and cramped while the VWs cannot be locked up so you cannot leave things safely inside them. Typical costs are around 25,000 to 30,000 rp a day including insurance and unlimited km. By the week you can expect to get one day free. Kuta and Sanur travel agents will have signs out advertising cars for rent.

Renting a minibus-style bemo is certainly a good way to go. Plenty of bemo drivers are more than happy to take a week off while you drive their bemo around. We met an American family who rented one for a month and we had one for a week while updating this edition. These days tourists driving bemos are a sufficiently 'normal' sight that people don't even bother to flag you down!

BICYCLES

Seeing Bali by pushbike has become much more popular of recent years.

Nowadays more people are giving it a try and more places are renting bikes – some people are even bringing their bikes with them. You can usually bring your pushbike with you in your baggage or some airlines (Qantas for example) may carry it free. Most of the information on renting and using bicycles which follows is based (with necessary updating) on *Bali by Bicycle* by Hunt Kooiker – originally published by the author in 1977 this handy little booklet is now, unfortunately, out of print.

Bicycling in Bali

At first glance Bali does not seem like a place for a bicycle tour: high mountains, narrow bumpy roads, tropical heat and frequent rain showers. However, far from being an obstacle the mountains can be turned into allies. With the judicious help of two short bemo trips to scale the central mountains you can accomplish a beautiful, mostly level or downhill, 200 km circle trip of Bali.

It is true Bali has narrow roads but once out of the congested southern region the traffic is relatively light and the bumpy roads are not a great problem if you invest in a good, padded seat. Since a large part of the trip is level or downhill the tropical heat problem literally turns into a breeze. Frequent roadside foodstalls make it remarkably easy to duck out of a passing rain shower.

The main advantage of seeing Bali by bicycle is the quality of the experience. You can cover many more km by bemo, bus or motorcycle but will you really see more? By bicycle you can be totally accessible to the environment. Without the noise of a motorcycle you can hear the wind rustling in the rice paddies and the sound of a gamelan orchestra practising as you pass by.

The slower speed of bicycling helps to bridge the time warp between the rush of the west and the calm of Bali. You will have time to greet people by the roadside and feel their warm response.

Finding & Equipping Your Bicycle

There is no lack of bicycles for rent in Bali. There are a number of bicycle shops in Denpasar for parts or complete bicycles. Proper 10-speed bicycles are becoming quite common in Bali. There are numerous bike rental shops in Kuta, Legian, Sanur and Ubud. The challenge though is finding one that works! Rental choices run from one-speed clunkers with terrible seats to one-speed clunkers with terrible seats, no reflectors, bell, lights or brakes. Fortunately some of the rental shops are open to special arrangements – Hunt Kooiker gives an example where he arranged to buy a used bike from a shop, spend a little money and rather more time refurbishing it then resold it to them 2½ months later. His 'rental cost' worked out to less than 100 rp per day!

Alternatively if your trip is shorter you can take a bike for the usual rental rates – start bargaining down from around 2000 rp per day. Rates by the week or longer periods are, of course, much cheaper. Instead of agreeing to pay the full amount in cash it's worth bargaining to improve the bike and deduct the cost. Buy a new padded seat in Denpasar, take it to the rental shop and offer to replace their old, distorted, hard-as-tacks seat with the new seat if they'll discount the first part of your rental. Besides making your touring infinitely more enjoyable you will also gain good karma from all the people who rent that bicycle after you!

Another traveller recently suggested that showing the money up front can sometimes have a wonderful effect. Knocking the daily rate down to 1000 rp for a long term rental proved impossible until she produced 90,000 rp (two bikes times 45 days) which the bike renter couldn't resist!

What to Look for in a Bicycle

For touring it is absolutely essential that your bike is in good repair. A checklist of things to look for when picking out your bike includes:

Brakes Both the front and rear brakes must be able to stop your bike individually in case one should malfunction on a steep downhill. Check the brake blocks (the rectangular hard rubber pads which press against the rims) to see that they are symmetrically positioned and show even wear with plenty of rubber left. They should be about 25 mm away from the wheel so that they do not rub any part of the rim when you spin the wheel. The real test is whether or not they can hold the bike still when clamped while you push forward with all your strength. If in doubt buy yourself some new brake blocks, they're very cheap. Do not go into the central mountains without good brakes.

Wheels & Tyres Before agreeing to rent the bike turn it upside down and spin the wheels. Check the rims carefully for deep rust spots which could cause the wheel to buckle under stress. Look at the rim as it moves by the brake shoe. If the wheel wobbles you will have shimmering problems. Also squeeze the spokes to check for loose or broken ones.

Avoid bikes with bald or soft tyres. Sure the shop will offer to pump them up but you're the one who will have to do it every day after that.

Bell, Light & Back Reflector A bell and light are both very useful things to have working. I like the bell positioned out on the handlebar so I can use it with my hand still gripping the brake. Be sure to spin the front wheel with the generator engaged to make sure the light works. A new back reflector is a good investment if there isn't one on the bike.

Seat The condition of your seat depends on the condition of your bicycle seat. Consider buying a new, soft, padded one or at least a tie-on foam seat cover. You can purchase either of these in Denpasar at a bike shop. Invariably the seats will be pushed down to rest on the frame with the correct legroom for a Balinese midget. Ask to have the seat raised so that when you are sitting on it you can straighten your leg fully to touch the lower pedal with your heel. If you are very tall it is worth buying an extra long pipe to raise the seat.

Miscellaneous Accessories A carrier rack over the rear mudguard is ideal for carrying a small bag of belongings. One or two elastic shock cords with hooks at each end help to secure the baggage. Many bikes are equipped with a claw-like key lock which guards against petty theft. A much sturdier steel cable lock may be a worthwhile purchase.

Final Adjustments Most bikes are never oiled by the rental shops and because people ride them on salty beaches they get badly corroded and don't pedal smoothly. Find a can of oil and lightly oil all moving parts including the crankshaft and chain. Check to see if all the nuts are securely tightened especially those to the seat, brake linkage cables and brake rims which tend to vibrate loose.

Bicycles are used extensively by the Balinese themselves and even the smallest village has some semblance of a bike shop. Some shops will allow you to borrow tools to work on your own bike. A small gift of peanuts or an offer of an ice juice is greatly appreciated by the lender. If you're not used to working on bicycles ask the repairman to repair it for you. Labour charges are very low – a flat tyre might cost less than 50c. The best shops for any extensive repairs are in Denpasar.

Packing for Touring
It is quite possible to tour Bali by bicycle with nothing but the clothes on your back – and this book! The distance between losmen is always within a day's ride. Food stalls are numerous and there is no need for actual camping equipment. All losmen provide a sheet which can double as a sarong while you wash your clothes.

However, it's more convenient to carry at least a minimum of gear with you. This would include riding shorts and T-shirt, and a pair of long trousers for temple festivals or cool mountain evenings. Women can consider a skirt and T-shirt, and a nicer shirt or blouse for festivals. Sandals and an optional pair of running shoes are useful if you want to climb Mt Batur. A sash is essential for visiting many temples. You'll also need a swimsuit as skinny dipping is not appreciated.

Other useful things include a torch, mosquito coils, matches, soap, towel, toothbrush, sun hat, and zinc oxide to protect your nose from the sun.

Bring as little as possible. Besides carrying the baggage on your bicycle you may want to park your bike to explore an area on foot. That means either carrying your bag or finding some place to stash it.

The 200 km Circle Trip

This route is designed to take in the greatest number of points of interest with the minimum use of motorised transport and the maximum amount of level or downhill roads. The tour is divided into six days of actual riding in a clockwise direction. Evening stops have been planned where there are convenient losmen. The minimum daily distance is about 20 km, the maximum is 53 km but 20 to 30 km of this latter number will probably be covered by bemo.

Of course there are losmen in other villages along the route and it is also possible to stay in most villages which do not have losmen. Just ask to speak with the headman (kepala desa) of the village. The trip can also be done in reverse. Interposed within the basic six-day tour are suggestions for side trips. These trips, plus extra days spent exploring each area, can easily evolve into a two week trip. An estimated riding time has been given has been given for each day.

Day 1 - Kuta to Bedugul 53 km (the first 37 km by bicycle), riding time seven hours.

The first day is a long one so it is best to get an early start. Leave the tourists and westernised Balinese of Kuta and ride north along the Legian road. Soon the traffic will disappear and you'll be riding along exquisitely terraced rice fields interspersed with small villages. Continue north to Sempidi where numerous roadside foodstalls offer tea, bananas and peanuts to boost your energy reserves.

If you begin your trip at low tide you can do the first seven km north along the beach's firm, moist sand. Turn inland around the Bali Oberoi as further on the sand becomes soft and you'll get bogged down. The hotel's long driveway connects with the main road and you can continue north to Sempidi, the junction with the Denpasar-Gilimanuk road.

Ride west towards Gilimanuk from Sempidi until you reach the turn-off north to Mengwi. The quiet, almost cloistered, Pura Taman Ayun with its surrounding moat is only half a km east of the main road in Mengwi. Continuing north from Mengwi 15 km to Desa Perean you will notice by your breathing that the gentle 1% to 5% gradient is gradually increasing. From Perean to Bedugul is a 700 metre vertical rise over 16 km so this is the place to throw your bicycle into the back of a bemo. Until about 4 pm bemos come along every 10 to 30 minutes. The fare for one bicycle usually equals the fare for one person.

Bedugul has several places to stay. Note the change in vegetation and the sturdier housing construction compared to the lowlands. Small outrigger canoes can be rented by the hour on Lake Bratan. The lake is large enough for skinny dipping out in the middle of the lake. It's a pleasant paddle across from the losmen to the temple of Ulu Danu.

Day 2 - Bedugul to Singaraja 21 km, riding time three hours.

The first km is uphill, followed by a breezy downhill sprint past the Bukit Mungsu market which sells vegetables and wild orchids. For several km the road goes up and downhill. Then there is a three km steep ascent to the unnamed 1400 metre pass – cyclists can usually think of several obscene names for it! From the pass there is a steep 15 km descent to the coastal town of Singaraja. This is where good brakes are most needed. You may want to stop periodically to cool the brake rims and unmould your hands from the brake levers.

Singaraja is a rather hot and dusty town. There are some bicycle repair shops here. There's a wide choice of losmen or you can continue west along the coast to the beach strip around Kalibukbuk (seven to 13 km from Singaraja) or turn east to Yeh Sanih.

Day 3 – Singaraja to Penelokan 56 km (36 km up to Penulisan by bemo then the final 10 km by bike).

Ride 10 km east of Singaraja to Kubutambahan where you find the turn-off heading south to Mt Batur. Visit the Pura Maduwe Karang temple at Kubutambahan before turning inland. It's 36 steep-uphill km from here to Penulisan so once again it's wise to load your bicycle aboard a bemo although there aren't many going this way. Penulisan is the highest point on the ride and it's an easy descent from here to Kintamani (four km) or Penelokan (10 km). The Pura Tegeh Koripan temple at 1745 metres at Penulisan is Bali's highest temple and on a clear day, which is rare, offers a superb panorama of half the island.

Kintamani (1504 metres) has several losmen with fireplaces, and a large and colourful market every three days. Penelokan (1371 metres) has a couple of losmen perched on the rim of the volcano looking down to Lake Batur and Mt Batur. Frequent stops by tour buses encourage swarms of vendors.

Hikes can be made from Kintamani or Penelokan down to the village of Kedisan on Lake Batur and across the lava field to the active volcano. You can also hike round the lake's north shore to the hot springs or round the south shore to the Bali Aga village of Trunyan.

From Penelokan there are at least five routes down the slopes of Mt Batur back to Denpasar. Listed is the route via Klungkung with a side trip to the temple at Besakih. Two alternate routes are listed in the following section – they lead either to the Ubud area or Bangli.

Day 4 – Penelokan to Klungkung 31 km (excluding Besakih), riding time four hours.

Turn left half a km south of the fruit stands which are at the intersection of the road down to Lake Batur. A small sign reads 'Bandjar Abang' and the narrow road leads uphill. If you reach a fork in the main road with a sign for Denpasar and Bangli you've gone too far – retreat. The narrow road goes up and down small hills as it heads east along the south rim of the crater with lovely views of Mt Batur and the lake. Approximately four km along the road is a dip with a sign 'Menanga'. Turn right and continue downhill to Rendang with fine views of Gunung Agung all the way. Rendang is the turn-off for Besakih.

From Rendang to Besakih is six km, mostly uphill. There's a 500 metre rise in eight km. Consider leaving your bike at the crossroads and taking a bemo both ways or putting the bike in a bemo going up and having a nice ride down. Pura Besakih at 1000 metres rests on the misty slopes of Gunung Agung, the 'navel of the world'. Beautiful and eerie, it is considered the mother temple of Bali.

From Rendang to Klungkung is 12 km along a gradual downhill trip through some of the richest rice land in Bali. It's one of the most pleasant bike trips in Bali. Linger at the expensive restaurant at Bukit Jambul – the view is free and magnificent.

Klungkung has several restaurants and places to stay. The the main attraction is the Kerta Gosa at the town's main intersection, with excellent examples of the Klungkung style of painting and architecture. Two km south is the village of Kamasan, known for the wayang style of painting and for its gold and silversmiths.

Day 5 – Klungkung to Denpasar 31 km, riding time six hours.

The entire way is a well surfaced but heavily trafficked road. Although there is a total descent of 70 metres the road crosses several lush river gorges, causing some uphill walking and downhill gliding. Main places of interest along the way are Gianyar (local weaving industry), Batuan (painting and weaving), Celuk (wood carving and silver work), and Batubulan (stone sculpture).

Day 6 – Denpasar to Kuta (via Sanur & Benoa) 24 km, riding time five hours.

Take your life in your hands and head east on the main street of Denpasar, Jalan Gajah Mada. Continue east for six km to Sanur. If you feel enterprising you can even rent your bike to an 'international' hotel guest – they pay about the same per hour as you pay per day. Check out the hotel swimming pools with their swim-up bars and underwater bar stools.

From Sanur the 'superhighway' runs about eight km to the Benoa Harbour turn-off. The sparsely populated marshland around the harbour is worked by the villagers for salt production. Continue south and the road turns into a causeway. To the landlubber Benoa Harbour is not much. There are a couple of small restaurants and several warungs offering the standard fare. If, however, you're looking for a yacht ride out of Bali then this is the place to chat up the owners of visiting yachts which moor just offshore. The village of Benoa is across the bay from the harbour.

After leaving Benoa, backtrack along the causeway and turn west. You can divert off the new highway to the old and now virtually deserted Sanur-Kuta road

which runs parallel to the new road, just north of it. You eventually emerge on the main Kuta-Denpasar road right by the petrol station. You have completed the 200 km round trip and are back at the start. Congratulations!

Alternative Routes from Penelokan to Denpasar
Penelokan to Ubud (via Tampaksiring) 35 km, riding time five hours.

This route used to be pretty rough and ready from Kayuambua down to Tampaksiring but after improvements it's now a fine road. About half a km south of Penelokan the road forks, take the right fork marked 'Denpasar' and nine km later you're in the small junction town of Kayuambua. The left fork leads to Bangli, the right fork takes you to Tampaksiring eight km further on. The road runs down verdant volcano slopes past fields of banana, sweet potato and corn, all partially obscured by roadside groves of bamboo.

At the main intersection in Tampaksiring a road east leads to Tirta Empul with its holy spring. There are lots of warungs and handicraft shops here. Carved chess sets with characters from the Ramayana are a local speciality. Another km down from Tirta Empul is the turn-off to the 11th-century rock-face memorials at Gunung Kawi, about a km off the main road. Back on the road it's an easy 10 km downhill to Bedulu. About a km before Bedulu is the small village of Pejeng with its 'Moon of Pejeng' bronze drum in the Pura Penataran Sasih temple. You turn right at the Bedulu junction and half a km along the road is the Goa Gajah or elephant cave. Then it's on to Peliatan and Ubud.

Ubud to Denpasar 26 km, riding time four hours.

There are several ways down to Kuta from the Ubud area. Heading straight south for four km the road passes through the wood carving village of Mas, another six km is the weaving village of Batuan and then through Celuk, known for its wood carvings as well as fine gold and silversmiths. From Batuan to Denpasar (16 km) there are many trucks, bemos and cars competing for road space which makes that part of the trip mentally exhausting.

An interesting alternative is the less-travelled backroad via Sibang. Except for the first few km, which require some uphill walking, it is an easy descent with little traffic until you are in Denpasar proper. From Denpasar to Kuta is the same as the previous Klungkung route.

Penelokan to Bangli 20 km, riding time three hours.

At the fork in the road half a km south of Penelokan take the left fork marked 'Bangli' and head south. Bangli has an important temple, Pura Kehen, and a couple of places to stay. Continue south from Bangli and you join the Klungkung-Denpasar route about 26 km from Denpasar.

Day Trips out of Kuta

Kuta to Benoa & Sanur This is an 18 km one-way trip. See the round trip details for this route. From Sanur you can either backtrack to Kuta or take the Sanur-Denpasar and Denpasar-Kuta roads although they have very heavy traffic. Or take a bemo back via Denpasar.

Kuta to Ulu Watu This is a 19 km one-way trip. It is a strenuous ride and not recommended for the beginner, anyone not used to tropical heat or for anyone on a bicycle with bad tyres.

Head south to the airport turn-off and continue on the narrow asphalt road to the junction of the Ulu Watu and Nusa Dua roads. The Ulu Watu road is a narrow potholed route that winds up and down, inexorably climbing to the dusty village of Pecatu at 250 metres. This is one-third of the round trip distance and the most arduous part of the route but it is possible to put the bike on a bemo this far.

From Pecatu it is a further five km of going up and downhill to the temple of Ulu Watu, perched on a cliff high above the sea. Return by the same route which will require considerable walking uphill to Pecatu and then mostly downhill and level pedalling back to Kuta.

Distances around Bali in km

Bangli	Besakih	Bedugul	Denpasar	Gianyar	Gilimanuk	Amlapura	Kuta	Kintamani	Klungkung	Negara	Padangbai	Penelokan	Singaraja	Sanur	Tabanan	Ubud	Place
																	Bangli
42																	Besakih
88	109																Bedugul
40	61	48															Denpasar
13	34	75	27														Gianyar
168	89	148	128	155													Gilimanuk
56	40	128	78	51	206												Amlapura
49	55	57	9	36	137	87											Kuta
28	70	116	68	41	196	86	70										Kintamani
18	21	88	40	13	168	38	49	48									Klungkung
135	156	115	95	122	33	173	104	163	135								Negara
36	37	104	56	29	184	24	65	56	16	151							Padangbai
20	62	112	64	33	192	78	73	8	40	159	48						Penelokan
80	122	30	78	93	85	100	87	52	100	112	108	60					Singaraja
43	64	55	7	30	135	81	8	72	43	102	56	71	85				Sanur
61	82	43	21	48	107	99	30	89	61	74	77	85	73	28			Tabanan
23	67	73	25	10	153	61	34	48	23	120	39	40	100	28	46		Ubud
53	74	61	13	40	141	91	4	81	53	108	69	77	91	12	34	38	Airport

Kuta Route along the Beach At low tide short rides along the firm, moist sand can be beautiful. Heading north from Kuta you can ride for up to seven km before the sand changes and will no longer support a bicycle. At that point you can either retrace your tracks or head inland to the road and return via Legian. After tripping along the salty beaches it's wise to throw a few buckets of freshwater on your bike to keep it from rusting.

Several people have written to us with additional thoughts on cycling in Bali:

I had no problems in transporting my bike on Garuda both on international and domestic flights. All I did was remove the pedals from each arm. I did not even have to play around with the handle bars.

I followed the around Bali itinerary which was in the book and did not resort to bemos on the climb to Bedugul and Kintamani. The Bedugul climb is not too steep and I feel that anyone who has an OK bike (10 speed) and is fit can make this climb without a bemo. The Penulisan climb is a completely different story. It's very, very tough going, especially in the tropical heat. Also you cannot get any drinking water until you reach Penelokan so if you intend to ride that stretch carry lots of water –at least four cyclist bottles. I had about 15 warm Sprites that day because I ran out of water!

The ride from Rendang to Amlapura has great scenery and no traffic. Except for a few easy hills between Muncan and Selat it's pretty well downhill all the way. From Amlapura it's not far to Candidasa and dead flat on to Klungkung.

Nigel Daniel, Australia

South Bali

The southern part of Bali, south of the capital Denpasar, is the tourist end of the island. The overwhelming mass of visitors to Bali is concentrated down here. All the higher priced package tour hotels are found in this area and many visitors only get out on day-trips. Some never leave it at all.

The Balinese have always looked towards the mountains and away from the sea – even their temples are aligned in the *kaja* direction (towards the mountains) and away from the inauspicious *kelod* direction (towards the sea). So Sanur and Kuta, the small fishing villages that were to become Bali's major international resorts were not notable places prior to the arrival of mass tourism. Today they're artificial enclaves, not really part of Bali at all. Of course the residents have made the most of their new found opportunities, particularly the people of Kuta where an enormous number of small, locally run losmen and restaurants have sprung up, but many of the Balinese who work at Kuta and Sanur are from other parts of the island. The Indonesian government is determined that the rest of Bali should remain as unspoilt as possible so all future large scale development will be confined to this southern region, particularly the newer tourist enclave at Nusa Dua.

Together with Singaraja in the north the southern region has been most influenced from outside Bali. Even some of Bali's earliest legends relate to this area. The first European to make his mark in the south was Mads Lange, a Danish copra trader who set up at Kuta about 1830. He had some success in persuading local rajahs to unite against the Dutch encroachments from the north but he also made enemies and was poisoned later in the century and buried at Kuta. The Dutch takeover of the south finally took place at Sanur in 1906. The Balinese fell back before them all the way from Sanur to Denpasar and there the three princes of the kingdom of Badung made a suicidal last stand, a *puputan* which wiped out the old kingdoms of the south. When the Japanese left Indonesia after WW II the Dutch again returned to Bali at Sanur.

Sanur was an early home for visiting western artists and is still an artistic centre and famed for its gamelan orchestras. The courtly arja opera and wayang kulit shadow puppets are also popular at Sanur and now a positive mania for flying gigantic kites has swept the region.

An unfortunate side effect of the building explosion in the south has been massive destruction of the coral reefs. Coral makes an excellent building material both ground down to make lime and as actual building blocks. The blocks are very attractive and since the coral grows a little after it has been removed from the water the coral actually locks itself together. But as more and more coral is removed there will be less and less fish and the unprotected beaches can quickly disappear. Some prime offenders where you can literally see stretches of coral reef turned into walls include the Bali Hyatt at Sanur, the Bali Oberoi at Legian and Poppies Cottages at Kuta.

KUTA & LEGIAN

Kuta is the budget beach in Bali. It's only a couple of km from the airport and for many people it's their first taste of Bali. For too many of them it's all they ever see of Bali. Kuta may be good fun and quite a scene but Bali it most certainly is not. If you want to get any taste of the real Bali then you have to abandon the beaches and get up into the hills – where the tourist impact is not so great and where Bali's 'soul' has always been in any case.

Still we all hit Kuta to start with so you might as well enjoy it. Basically Kuta Beach is just that, a strip of pretty pleasant palm-backed beach with some

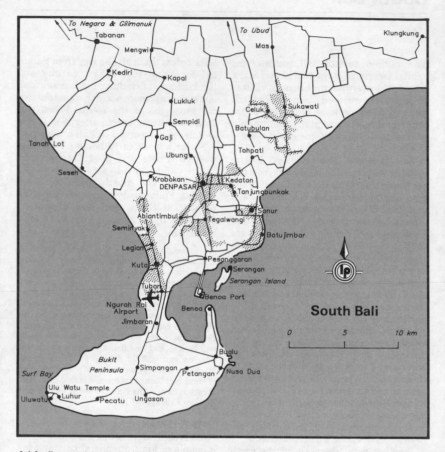

South Bali

fairly fine surf (and tricky undercurrents that take away a few swimmers every year) plus the most spectacular sunsets you could ask for. They were particularly spectacular for the crowds of onlookers who were already eight miles high with a little help from some interesting local mushrooms but naughty substances seem to have all but disappeared from Bali of late – to be replaced by lots of legitimate booze.

Back of the beach a network of little roads and alleys (known as gangs) run back to the biggest collection of small

hotels (known as losmen), restaurants, bars, food stalls (known as warungs) and shops you could possibly imagine. It has been estimated there are over 200 different places to stay at Kuta and Legian and more are still being opened. Kuta is a totally self-contained scene and with so many places to work your way through it's hardly surprising that so many people get stuck there semi-permanently.

Although the original Kuta Beach Hotel was operating in the 1930s and its modern namesake opened in 1959 Kuta only really began to develop as a resort in the late '60s. At first people mainly day-tripped there from Denpasar but gradually losmen opened up and in the early '70s Kuta was an extremely pleasant place to stay with relaxed losmen with pretty little gardens, friendly places to eat and a quite delightfully laid-back atmosphere. Then travellers began to abandon Denpasar as the traffic there became intolerable and Kuta started to grow faster and faster. Legian, the next beach village north, sprang up as an alternative to Kuta in the early '70s. At first it was a totally separate development but gradually Kuta sprawled down towards Legian and Legian spread back towards Kuta until today you can't tell where one ends and the other begins.

Unhappily all this rampant development has taken its toll. Kuta and Legian are nowhere near as relaxed and laid back as they used to be and old hands who first visited Bali in the late '60s or early '70s will find Kuta a rather sad and seedy place. Fortunately new arrivals, and even old hands who avoid making too many comparisons, may still find it just fine – for a short stay.

What's Wrong with Kuta?
What's gone wrong with Kuta? There are many pleasant and beautiful restaurants, the beach and surf can be terrific, the quiet losmen down remote gangs can be relaxed and pleasant but at some time or other you have to venture back on to the Legian road and the traffic down this main street is horrific. The constant stream of sellers importuning you to buy, buy, buy can be a little wearing too but the main problem is planning and people. There's too little of one and too many of the other.

Too little isn't the word for Kuta's planning – there's none at all. Anybody seems to have been able to build almost anything anywhere. The result is that many losmen are only accessible down narrow gangs – which is no problem except that people insist on using these footpaths for motorcycle races and even try to squeeze cars and trucks down them. The Legian road is a typical narrow island road, wide enough for one vehicle or perhaps one and

a half at a squeeze yet it carries a near continuous flow of buses, bemos, taxis, cars, trucks and motorcycles. Recently they've finally realised that it simply cannot operate as a two way road but the solution has been to build a new road virtually on the beach. And the Legian road remains a noisy, confused, evil smelling, frustrating cacophony.

As if that weren't enough there are no parking restrictions along the roads, not even around bemo corner in Kuta where every evening at sunset time there's an unbelievable and quite unnecessary traffic jam. And what are they doing about it? Nothing, just cramming more hotels in anywhere they can.

As for the people, well 15 years ago Kuta was one of the great overland travel stops. One of the three Ks – Kabul in Afghanistan, Kathmandu in Nepal and Kuta. But travellers don't come to Kuta anymore, it's strictly a beach resort for people who want surf and sand, cheap food and plenty of beer. Where you used to get peacefully stoned freaks gazing at the sunset you now have numerous bars where loud-mouthed drunks get ripped every afternoon, clamber clumsily on to their motorcycles and mercifully fall off at the first corner. Fortunately these folk are usually kept right there in Kuta – it's a whole different visitor population up in Ubud.

And on the Beach
Legian beach early in the morning – grey rain clouds even though it's the dry season – the mountains rise up mistily in the background – surfers out after an early break, they're all congregated in the area posted as 'dangerous' – about 20 people are desperately trying to push a minibus out of the sand before the rising tide gets it – already the surf licks at the point where it got stuck and as they heave it up the beach the sand gets softer – motorcycles buzz up and down the beach, some idiots actually riding through the surf, nothing like saltwater for corrosion – joggers pass by – rich Javanese wade, fully dressed, thigh deep into the water – the inevitable anjings run around in packs.

Information & Orientation
You can visit Bali and never have to leave Kuta. There are hotels, restaurants, travel agents, banks, moneychangers, a post office, markets, motorcycle and car rental places, doctors; in fact you name it

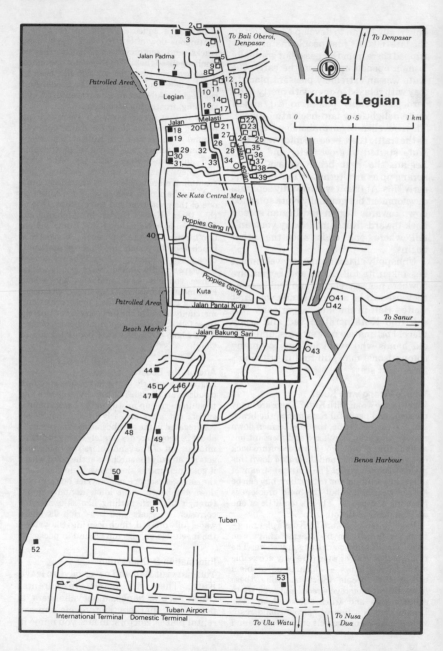

Kuta & Legian

To Bali Oberoi,
Denpasar

To Denpasar

Jalan Padma

Patrolled Area

Legian

Jalan
Melasti

0   0·5   1 km

See Kuta Central Map

Poppies Gang II

Poppies Gang

Kuta

Patrolled Area

Jalan Pantai Kuta

Beach Market

Jalan Bakung Sari

To Sanur

Benoa Harbour

Tuban

Tuban Airport

International Terminal   Domestic Terminal

To Ulu Watu

To Nusa
Dua

and Kuta has it. Kuta and Legian, once separate little villages, are now just the names for different sections of one long and continuous beach. They merge together. An important Kuta landmark is 'bemo corner', the intersection of Kuta Beach Rd (Jalan Pantai Kuta) and the Legian road (Jalan Legian).

On the corner of Jalan Bakung Sari and the airport road the large building has tourist information counters for Bali and also for several other regions of Indonesia. The Bali counter has some brochures and copies of a Bali tourist newspaper.

If you develop a real interest in Kuta read Hugh Mabbett's *In Praise of Kuta* (January Books, Wellington, New Zealand, 1987). It's widely available in Bali and

IN PRAISE OF
KUTA

From slave port to fishing village
to the most popular resort in Bali

Hugh Mabbett

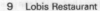

■ HOTELS & LOSMEN		9	Lobis Restaurant
1	Kuta Palace Hotel	11	Norman's Garden Restaurant
3	Orchid Garden Cottages, Sawasdee	12	Sari Restaurant
	Thai Cuisine & Sari Yasa Inn	13	Ned's Place
6	Bali Mandira Cottages	14	Do Drop Inn
7	Legian Village Hotel	15	Goa Indian Restaurant
10	Legian Beach Bungalows	17	Bali Too Restaurant
16	Legian Beach Hotel	20	Legian Garden Restaurant
18	Bali Intan Cottages	21	Orchid Garden Restaurant
19	Bruna Beach Inn	22	Kayu Api
26	Legian Mas Beach Inn	23	Made's Restaurant
29	Bruna Beach Inn	24	Swiss Restaurant
31	Bali Anggrek Inn	25	Rivoli Disco
32	Camplung Mas Bungalows	27	Yudit Bakery
33	Sayang Beach Lodging	28	Il Pirata Pizzeria
44	Kartika Plaza Hotel	30	Southern Cross Restaurant
46	Bali Rani Hotel	35	Monte Carlo Bar
47	Sanika Beach Hotel	36	Depot Viva
48	Raya Beach Cottages	37	Pink Panther Club
49	Bali Bagus Cottages	38	Bali Billabong Restaurant
50	Rama Beach Cottages	39	Mastapa Gardens
51	Mandara Cottages	40	Batu Karang Restaurant
52	Pertamina Cottages	42	Supermarket &
53	Puri Nusantara Hotel		Kentucky Fried Chicken
		45	Godfrey's Bar & Restaurant
□ RESTAURANTS, BARS & DISCOS			
2	Topi Kopi French &	○	OFFICES, SHOPS, ETC
	Yamcha Restaurants, The Club	34	Krishna Bookshop
4	Restaurant Glory	41	Petrol Station
5	Warung Kopi	43	Market
8	Restaurant Happy &		
	Bobbie's Bar & Restaurant		

recounts Kuta's early history and its frenetic modern development. If you want to learn more about Kuta's local entrepreneurs, the development of surfing or what happens if you get caught with drugs then this fascinating book has the goods.

Post There's a post office near the cinema and night market, off the airport road. It's small, efficient and has a poste restante service (50 rp per letter). The post office is open Monday to Thursday 8 am to 2 pm, Friday 8 to 11 am and Saturday 8 am to 12.30 pm. There is also a postal agent on the Legian road, about half a km along from bemo corner. If you want mail sent there have it addressed to 'Kuta Postal Agent, Jalan Legian, Kuta'. These Kuta post offices (or the one in Ubud) are much more convenient than the main Denpasar post office. The information office on the corner of Jalan Airport and Jalan Bakung Sari also has a small post office counter, which is open longer hours than the main post office and is more convenient.

Banks There's a bank on the Legian road but for most people the numerous moneychangers are faster, more efficient, open longer hours and give just as good a rate. If you need a real bank for some complicated money transfer or other bank-like activity you should head for the big bank offices in Denpasar.

A number of the moneychangers have safety deposit boxes where you can leave airline tickets or other valuables and not have to worry about them during your stay in Bali.

Airlines & Travel Agents If you're flying Garuda there's a small Garuda office (tel 24764) where you can make reservations or reconfirmations in the Kuta Beach Hotel at the beach end of Jalan Pantai Kuta. The office sometimes gets hopelessly crowded so it's an idea to arrive before opening time or during the lunch break and be at the head of the queue. It's open

Monday to Friday from 9 am to 12 noon and from 1 to 4 pm. Saturday and Sunday it opens 9 am to 1 pm.

The Bali Qantas office is at the Bali Beach Hotel at Sanur where there is also another Garuda office. The myriad Kuta travel agents will offer to make reconfirmations for you but there's a charge and some agents are said to be less than scrupulous about actually reconfirming.

There are countless tours organised from Kuta which can be booked through the agents. Typical prices for a day trip are around US$7 to US$15. Tours further afield – to places like Lombok, Komodo or Sulawesi – are also offered. They also rent cars, motorcycles and bicycles, sell bus and train tickets to Java and perform other travel agent services.

Theft & Security Kuta developed a bad reputation for theft and rip-offs in the late '70s. Perhaps things have quietened down a bit or perhaps people have just become used to it. Thefts usually take place either on the beach or from losmen rooms. You should always keep your room securely locked as it's quite easy for somebody to just wander into your losmen during the day.

It's equally necessary at night, more than a few people have woken up to find their valuables have disappeared from under their nose. Losmen rooms are not always a safe place to leave money, airline tickets or other valuables. There have also been a number of muggings at Kuta, beware of those dark, lonely gangs (alleys) at night. Take care but don't worry unduly, Kuta is not New York. You'd probably have to spend a lot of dark nights stumbling down a lot of dark gangs before you finally ran into somebody you'd prefer not to! Most people who lose things at Kuta are idiots who leave things on the beach while they're in the water.

Beach Safety Yes, Kuta Beach does have its dangers. Every year there are at least a

Left: Pura Luhur Ulu Watu temple, Bali (TW)
Right: Cliff face at Ulu Watu, Bali (TW)
Bottom: Catching a wave at Ulu Watu, Bali´s prime surfing break (LP)

Left: Multi-roofed *merus* in Pura Taman Ayun temple, Mengwi, Bali (TW)
Right: Launching a giant kite on Sanur Beach, Bali (TW)
Bottom: Ducks in the rice paddies, Ubud, Bali (TW)

half dozen drownings, often of visitors from other Asian countries who are not good swimmers. There is now a Kuta Lifesaving Club at the end of Kuta Beach Rd. Drownings peaked at 18 in 1980, since then it's varied from five to 13 each year so take care in the water especially when the surf is running. There are patrolled areas at Kuta and Legian.

Kuta Beach is much more likely to cost you money than your life, however. First of all it's going to cost 100 rp (50 rp children) just to set foot on the beach. The whole beach is now fenced off and you're charged admission. Secondly there are more sellers on the beach than swimmers – you're constantly importuned to buy anything from a cold drink to a massage or a hair beading job. What can cost you a whole lot more money is to leave things on the sand while you're in the water. Believe it or not this is how a lot of people lose their passports in Bali each year!

Places to Stay

It has been estimated that there are 200 to 300 places to stay at Kuta and Legian. And they're still building more. Surprisingly though it's far from crowded apart from in the heart of Kuta or around Jalan Padma-Jalan Melasti in Legian. Even there you only have to walk a couple of steps back from the main street to find palm trees and open fields. Go back on the other side of the Legian road and there's more open space than anything else.

Once upon a time it was very easy to sum up the accommodation story at Kuta. There were a sprinkling of flashier establishments but everything else was alike as peas in a pod. They all offered much the same standards – spartan little double rooms and a pleasant verandah area outside looking on to a central garden. 'Breakfast' was often thrown in, usually consisting of tea and bananas or black rice pudding. Tea was generally available on call at any time of the day.

These standard losmen were alike in one other way, they all charged the same

standard price. Back in the early '70s (when you got 400 rp to the dollar) they were 400 rp for a double. With time and successive devaluations they crept up to 600 rp, then 750 rp, then 1500 rp and now they're at all sorts of prices from around 4000 to 10,000 rp.

There are still 'standard' losmen around but now there are countless places at all sorts of different standards and also at all sorts of different prices. Even many of the old bottom-bracket losmen have added attached bathrooms, often with showers instead of mandis, or other modern conveniences. Back in the days of the standard losmen you could always be fairly certain they'd be attractive, relaxing places no matter what else. Unfortunately that is no longer always true. There are lots of places at Kuta today which have obviously been thrown together as quickly and cheaply as possible to try and turn over as many rupiah with as little effort as they can manage.

What to look for in a losmen? You can start with that well known advice from real estate agents – location, location, location. Many places are close to busy roads where the traffic noise and exhaust fumes can make you think you're in the centre of some busy western city. On the other hand there are also places so isolated that getting to the restaurants for a meal is a major trek. Where do you want to be – close to the action or away in the peace and quiet? It's often possible to find a good combination of both factors – a place far enough off the main roads to be quiet but close enough so that getting to the shops and restaurants is no problem.

Then you can look at what the rooms are like and how pleasant and generally well kept the losmen is. My ideal losmen would be fairly small and as much like a traditional Balinese home as possible. That is, it should be enclosed by an outer wall and built around a central courtyard-garden. It should be an attractive and peaceful place to sit around and read or

■	HOTELS & LOSMEN	24	Blue Pub
6	Cempaka Losmen	28	Aleang's
9	Puri Rama Cottages	29	Intan Restaurant
11	Poppies Cottages II	30	TJs
12	Barong Cottages	31	Poppies
13	Kuta Seaview Cottages	32	Perama
14	Maharani Bungalows	33	Eldorado Coffee Shop
25	Kempu Taman Ayu	34	Widya Restaurant
26	Sari Yasa Samudra Bungalows	35	Quick Snack Bar
27	Aquarius Beach Inn	39	Kempu Cafe
37	Kubuku Inn	41	Fat Yogi's Restaurant
38	Yasa Samudra Bungalows	43	Made's Juice Shop
40	Rumah Penginapan Walon	44	Melasti Restaurant
42	Poppies Cottages	46	Made's Warung
45	Budi Beach Inn	50	Green House Restaurant
49	Kuta Beach Hotel	53	Suci Restaurant
51	Kuta Cottages	54	Lenny's
52	Yulia Beach Inn	55	Bali Sunrise &
71	Karthi Inn		Daruma Japanese Restaurants
72	Melasti Beach Bungalows	56	Bali Indah, Wayan's & Dayu II
74	Ramayana Seaside Cottages	57	Bagus Pub
75	Kuta Beach Club	59	Pub 41
76	Agung Beach Bungalows	60	Casablanca
78	Losmen Dharma Yudha	61	Serrina Japanese Restaurant
79	Puspa Ayu Beach Bungalows	62	Gantino Baru Padang Restaurant
		67	Dayu I
□	RESTAURANTS, BARS & DISCOS	68	Bamboo Indah
1	Adam Beer Garden	69	Santai (Lucky) Restaurant
2	Angin Laut Restaurant	70	The Pub
3	Fatty Restaurant	73	Yan's Restaurant
4	Norm's Bar	77	Supermarket &
5	Lenny Garden Restaurant		Carolina Fried Chicken
7	Twice Restaurant		
8	Sari Club	O	OFFICES, SHOPS, ETC
15	Aleang's Coffee Shop	10	Kuta Postal Agent
16	Tree House Restaurant	47	Bemo Corner
17	Warung Transformer	48	Kuta Lifesaving Club
18	Wantilan Restaurant	58	Bali Foto Centre
19	The Spotlight Disco	63	Tourist Offices
20	Peanuts Disco, Koala Blu Pub &	64	Police Station
	other bars	65	Post Office
21	Indah Sari Seafood	66	Cinema
22	Mini Restaurant	△	
23	Prawita Garden Restaurant	36	Temple

talk. It should be clean and well kept. And it should be friendly. If they're offering breakfast then find out what it will be. Most important of all remember that there are lots more losmen – if you find you don't like your first choice it's very easy to move somewhere else.

When you first arrive at the airport in Kuta you're liable to be pounced upon by the Kuta hotel touts. They're sometimes local kids out to make a little commission from a losmen owner. Other times they may be the people who actually run the losmen, simply in need of some more business. If you've not got a specific losmen in mind they can often be a good

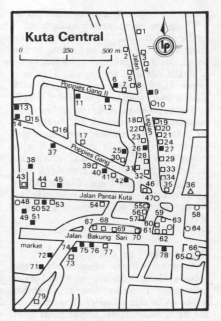

Kuta Central

0   250   500 m

way to find a room – you haven't got to hunt around finding a place with rooms free, if necessary you'll have help carrying your gear and you may even get free transport from the airport. If you don't like the place they take you to you can always say no immediately or just take it for a night while you look elsewhere. I've gone along with a tout at Kuta on many occasions and never found myself at a place which I didn't like. If you just wander around the laneways there'll always be people asking 'want room?' – so you'll have no trouble finding a place.

Places to Stay – bottom end

You can still find basic losmen at around 5000 rp for a double but the prices at Kuta are no longer as cheap as for losmen elsewhere in Bali. In fact compared with some of the very pleasant places up at the Singaraja beaches they're really poor value. Down at this bottom end of the

scale the losmen will be pretty basic, no attached bathrooms, little else apart from the beds in the rooms. There's no reason, however, that they shouldn't be attractive and well kept even at the very bottom of the range. As you move up the scale you get attached bathrooms, western-style toilets, better furnishings and a generally less spartan atmosphere. The prices are likely to be higher closer in to the centre of Kuta compared to further out. Prices for these 'better' bottom-end places could be in the 7500 to 12,500 rp range.

A popular place in the middle of the bottom end range is the long running *Lasi Erawati's*, further down Poppies Gang towards the beach from Poppies itself. It's just far enough out from the centre to be reasonably quiet (although too many motorcycles buzz by). Rooms here cost 5000 and 10,000 rp and Fat Yogi's is a popular place to eat.

A little further down the gang is the *Kubuku Inn* with just four bungalows at 12,000 to 16,000 rp. Just north of Poppies Gang is *Kempu Taman Ayu*, a pleasant and helpful little losmen with rooms with bathrooms for 9000 rp.

Many of Kuta's original losmen can be found along Jalan Pantai Kuta, or Jalan Bakung Sari, such as the *Yulia Beach Inn* down towards the beach end of Jalan Pantai Kuta. Rooms there start from US$3 without bathroom, US$4 to US$8 with bathroom, on up to US$20 for a bungalow with air-con. The *Pendawa Inn* is five minutes from the centre but quiet and good value. Also a little out from the centre the *Cempaka Losmen* is a low priced but pleasant friendly place, down the lane towards the second lot of Poppies Cottages.

In Legian the *Legian Mas Inn* is in a quiet area off the main streets. Right in the middle of things there are a string of places around Jalan Padma including the long running *Three Sisters*, not bad at 4000 to 7000 rp. *Suri Wathi Beach House* on Jalan Padma is a pleasant and quiet losmen. Basically, however, the best way to find losmen around Kuta and Legian is simply to wander around and look in a few. There are countless places to try, something is bound to suit.

Places to Stay - middle

Kuta also has plenty of middle range hotels, from around US$20 to US$40 a night. They include the very beautiful *Poppies Cottages*, just across from Poppies Restaurant on Poppies Gang. The pretty little individual bungalows are dotted around a beautiful garden and even the bathrooms have their own small internal garden. They're very centrally located yet so secluded you can easily forget that noisy Kuta is all around you and there's an equally beautiful swimming pool. This is definitely one of the most attractive hotels in Bali, quite an achievement in a place with so many beautiful hotels. Rooms cost US$36/37. There's also a second Poppies Cottages, along from Kuta towards Legian. Rooms here are US$20/21.

Near the beach market, the *Melasti Beach Bungalows* (tel 51860) on Jalan Kartika has rooms with attached bathroom and fan from US$25, with air-con from US$30. There's a swimming pool, bar and restaurant. In the same vicinity on Jalan Bakung Sari, the *Hotel Kuta Cottages* (tel 51101) has rooms in the same price category, starting from around US$20 and going up to US$40. Again there's a swimming pool.

Along Jalan Legian, the road to Legian, there's the *Puri Rama Cottages* (tel 51591) with a swimming pool and air-con cottages for US$26 to US$32. Also on the Legian road you'll find the similarly priced *Sri Kandi Bungalows*.

The beachfront *Yasa Samudra Bungalows* (tel 51305) has singles/doubles at 15,000/18,000 rp with fan or 22,000/25,000 rp with air-con plus larger family units at 35,000 rp. There's a swimming pool but it's kind of featureless. Right by the beach, between Kuta and Legian, the *Bali Anggrek Inn* (tel 51265) has individual

cottages at US$35/40 and a swimming pool.

There are many other middle bracket hotels at Kuta and Legian like the much cheaper *Bruna Beach Inn*, close to the beach about 100 metres on the Kuta side of Jalan Melasti, in Legian. This is a larger than average small hotel with simple losmen-style rooms from US$10 and some pleasant bungalow-style rooms, complete with verandah and bathroom. Or there's the *Matahari Bungalows* (tel 51616) between Kuta and Legian with rooms from US$8/10 up to US$20/25, all including breakfast. The *Rama Gardens Cottages* at the beach end of Jalan Padma are more expensive. They're related to the *Ramayana Seaside Cottages* in the heart of Kuta.

Places to Stay - top end

Kuta isn't like Sanur where nearly all the hotels are bunched at the upper end of the price range. There are, however, a number of places in this category. They include the *Kuta Beach Hotel*, the original hotel at Kuta and right in the centre of things at the beach end of Jalan Pantai Kuta. Two other upper bracket Kuta hotels are at opposite ends of the strip. The very flashy *Pertamina Cottages* are right down at the airport end of the beach, not the best bit of Kuta Beach. Way beyond Legian is the *Bali Oberoi* – a nicer beach but relatively isolated.

Other more expensive places include the beachfront *Kartika Plaza Hotel*, the *Kuta Beach Club* from US$40 and the *Kuta Seaview Hotel* (also beachfront). Up towards Legian there's the *Bali Intan Cottages* on the beach with a pool and 'motel-style' rooms and individual cottages. In Legian there's the beachfront *Legian Beach Hotel* at the beach end of Jalan Melasti, a popular hotel with rooms at a wide range of prices. The *Bali Mandira Cottages* is at the beach end of Jalan Padma. Further north along the beach is the *Kuta Palace Hotel* and the *Nusa di Nusa*, quiet lower priced bungalows with a swimming pool and bar right on the beach.

There's a 15.5% tax and service charge on top of the room price at these top end places. The vast majority of people staying at them will be on package tours so the regular room rates are really artificial.

Bali Intan Cottages (tel 51770) Jalan Melasti, Legian, PO 1002, Denpasar, 122 rooms, air-con, swimming pool, US$40 to US$60.
Bali Mandira Cottages (tel 51381) Jalan Padma, Legian, 96 rooms, air-con, swimming pool, US$35 to US$50.
Hotel Bali Oberoi (tel 51061) Box 351 Denpasar, directly on the beach beyond Legian, 75 rooms, bungalow-style, air-con, swimming pool, US$80 to US$160, plus villa rooms.
Kartika Plaza (tel 51067) PO Box 84, Denpasar, right on the beach, close to the centre of Kuta, 120 cottages, air-con, swimming pool, from US$41.
Kuta Beach Hotel (tel 51361) PO Box 393, Denpasar on the beach in the centre of Kuta, 32 rooms, air-con, swimming pool US$50 to US$65.
Legian Beach Hotel (tel 51711) Jalan Melasti, Legian, PO Box 308, Denpasar, close to the beach, 118 bungalows, air-con, swimming pool, US$25 to US$51.
Pertamina Cottages (tel 23061) PO Box 121, Denpasar, on the beach at the airport end of Kuta, 178 rooms, air-con, swimming pool, US$84 to US$90.
Santika Beach Hotel (tel 51267) PO Box 1008, Denpasar, air-con, swimming pool, US$49 to US$80.
Sea View Cottage-Kuta (tel 23991) Jalan Pantai, PO Box 36, air-con, swimming pool, US$40 to US$45.

Places to Eat

There are countless places to eat around Kuta, they range from tiny hawker's carts to fancy restaurants, cheap warungs to bars and pubs, steak houses to juice bars. Like so much else about Kuta most of the food here is not Balinese or even Indonesian – you could stay in Kuta for a month, eat in a different place every meal and never ever have to confront so much as a humble nasi goreng. In Kuta the food is pseudo-western top to bottom although

it's always going through some sort of current craze. A couple of years back it was Mexican food, more recently it seems to have been the discovery of pizzas. The cheapest food around Kuta or Legian? Try the night market near the post office and cinema.

Around Kuta With so many places to try the following is just a sparse over-view, a mere handful of places to consider, starting with one of Kuta's most popular upper bracket eating places the still delightful *Poppies*. Situated on Poppies Gang, close to the heart of things but just far enough off the main streets to be calm and quiet, Poppies has a beautiful romantic garden and an extensive menu. It's also squeaky clean, ideal for those who worry about their fragile digestive systems. These days, with so many surprisingly fancy restaurants around Poppies doesn't even seem that expensive. Most meals are 4000 to 6000 rp, desserts 1000 to 2000 rp, a big beer costs 2500 rp, a glass of wine slightly less. Although the food is very straightforward (they do a great hamburger) it's also really very good so Poppies is likely to remain a long term survivor.

A few steps beyond Poppies is *TJ's*, the place in Kuta for Mexican food. Somehow Mexico seems a long way from Bali (well it is!) but they do surprisingly good Mexican food here and its popularity is well deserved. Main courses are generally 4000 to 6000 rp.

Further down Poppies Gang towards the beach there are several popular new places for light meals. *Fat Yogi's* used to be the restaurant for Lasi Erawati's and is still an excellent place for a light meal or breakfast. Their croissants are superb and they also turn out pizzas from their genuine wood-fired pizza oven for 3500 to 5500 rp! Other restaurants down the gang towards the beach include the pleasant *Tree House Restaurant*.

There are plenty of other possibilities around Kuta; particularly along Jalan

Pantai Kuta, Jalan Bakung Sari and right along the Legian road. Starting from bemo corner there's the antiseptic looking *Quick Snack Bar* right on the corner – a good place for a snack or breakfast, good yoghurt.

Going down Jalan Pantai Kuta (Kuta Beach Rd) there's the long running *Made's Warung*. This simple open-front place has been going since the early '70s so it's as much a long term survivor as Poppies. This is probably the place in Kuta for people watching and is a popular hangout for the leading lights of the Kuta rag trade. The food is simple, straightforward but well prepared and there's always somebody strange to watch from first thing in the morning to way late at night.

Further down towards the beach is *Lenny's*, popular for its seafood, and newer restaurants like the *Green House* or the *Suci Restaurant* plus other familiar names like *Made's Juice Shop*.

Along Jalan Buni Sari, which connects Jalan Pantai Kuta at bemo corner with Jalan Bakung Sari, there's a number of long running and popular eating places. In the well liked and crowded *Bali Indah* you can see the food being prepared in their kitchen – 'something not every place would be proud to do'. A couple of doors down there's *Wayan's* and then *Dayu II*, both have been going nearly as long as Kuta has been a travellers' centre.

On this same stretch of road you'll also find some of Kuta's most popular bars, something that certainly didn't exist in the Kuta of 15 years ago. Back then alcohol was definitely not the drug of choice! *The Pub* is the flashiest, cleanest and most expensive of these bars. Across the road is the Japanese *Serrina Restaurant*. Just round the corner on Jalan Bakung Sari there's the *Gantino Baru*, a nasi Padang specialist.

Along the Legian Road There are lots more possibilities down the Legian road. Most of the time the Legian road is an almost continuous traffic jam and a table near the road can mean you have to shout to be heard. Popular places along the Legian road from Bemo Corner include *Aleangs*, where the yoghurt is still pretty good – try the yoghurt, muesli and honey. Next door, however, *Perama's* is just a shadow of the place it once was.

The *Depot Mini Restaurant* is not very 'mini' at all. It's a big, open, basic and busy place serving straightforward food at low prices. A little further along there are several restaurants set back from the road, so they're relatively quiet. The *Wantilan* and *Lenny's Garden Restaurant* are attractive places with lush gardens, good food and, like many Kuta restaurants these days, Australian wine by the glass at quite affordable prices. Like the other Lenny's this one is good for seafood. Between them is the popular *Sari Club*.

Getting down towards Legian you'll find *Il Pirata* which does pretty good pizzas and even has a generator to cope with the odd blackout. Across the road is *Depot Viva*, an open-roofed place which has surprisingly good Indonesian and Chinese food despite its bare, basic and grubby appearance. The prices are pleasantly basic too. *Yudit's* is a bakery with nice looking bread. A little further along is the *Swiss Restaurant*, ideal for homesick German-speakers although the food is not at all bad if you'd like a change from rice and noodles. Next door is *Made's Restaurant* – good steaks and banana fritters.

Around Legian Down Jalan Melasti the *Legian Garden* does a pretty fair 'rijstaffel' although it's really just a glorified nasi campur. The *Orchid Garden* on Jalan Melasti is very pleasant and the food is delicious – try the whole lobster in onion-butter sauce.

The *Do Drop Inn*, between Jalan Melasti and Jalan Padma, is one of Legian's longest running places; ditto for the *Agung Juice Park* a little further up the road. On the corner of Jalan Padma is

Restaurant Happy and nearby is *Bobbies* which is also popular.

Dining out in Kuta

The trouble with Kuta restaurants is that half of them are solid performers like *Poppies* or *Made's Warung* who've been there seemingly for ever and never look any different. The other half are in a constant state of flux, opening, closing, becoming popular and fading away.

So one Kuta night we go in search of new taste treats down Jalan Legian. Yes *Aleang's* and *Perama* look the same as ever, but are pale shadows of their mid-70s peak. *Depot Mini* is doing great business but the *Wantilan*, *Prawita* and *Lenny's* look very nice but very empty. Further down towards Legian the *Goa Indian Restaurant* is new and from the crowds they must be doing something right so we give it a try.

After being told half the items on the menu aren't available we eventually order. And wait. And then wait some more. After an hour I become suspicious and take a wander around. Nobody in this restaurant is eating anything! Eventually a chicken curry, a teaspoonful of raita and two miniature chappatis appear. The vegetable curry has run out we're told and, believe it or not, they've run out of rice! We have found the first restaurant in the entire archipelago of Indonesia to actually run out of rice.

Paying the bill (1500 rp for food, 10,000 rp for all the wine we drank while waiting) we rush hungrily across the road to *Il Pirata* for a pizza but five minutes later the tape deck gives a cautionary hiccup and the power fails. This doesn't deter Il Pirata, however, they have what must be the only generator on the entire Legian Rd so the lights are soon back on and the tape running again. You can't hear it over the generator but never mind.

Twenty-two minutes after we stepped through the door (we're timing it by now) Il Pirata delivers not just the pizza we ordered but two of them! Curiously although they're both ostensibly the same one tastes much better than the other so we eat the better one, leave the other, pay for both and dive out into the darkness of Legian Rd to hold fruitless discussions with the hordes of bemo jockeys and eventually walk home.

Entertainment

Kuta is a good place to get a suntan,

definitely a good place to get pissed, and supposedly a good place to get laid. The beach caters for the first, the numerous bars and discos cater for the second and provide hope for the third.

The nightspots are scattered around Kuta and Legian, many along Jalan Legian. Discos go through strange fads – five nights a week you need a crowbar to clear a space on the dance floor but come back three months later and there's not a lustworthy body in sight. One year you can't even find enough space to park your motorcycle outside – come back next year and there's enough room to dump an elephant. So if the places listed here turn out to be ever so dull and dreary and you don't get laid – don't blame us.

There also seems to have been a long overdue movement to clean up some of the wilder drunken excesses of Kuta. The pub crawls, where bus loads of increasingly noisy and drunken revellers were hauled from one venue to another, have been cut back considerably. Plus many pubs and discos have been closed down and others concentrated into a sort of 'combat zone' on the Legian road. There everybody can get as drunk as they like without bothering other people.

The centre piece of the Jalan Legian entertainment complex is the large *Peanuts* disco – it's rather like an Australian barnyard-pub-venue; which might be why it caught on so quickly. Admission is usually around 3500 rp which includes a couple of drinks. There's a series of open bars flanking the entrance road into Peanuts. These places kick off earlier than the main disco, and continue even after it's in full flight. For some reason *Koala Blu* is (or was) the far and away favourite. Koala Blu T-shirts seem to pop up all over Asia. *Cock n Bull* also attracts some sort of crowds but some of the other bars can be all but empty. After midnight it's quite a scene with music blasting out from every bar, hordes of people, mostly upright but some decidedly horizontal, and out in the parking lot lines of bemos and dokars waiting to haul the semi-conscious back to their hotels.

Other places include *The Spotlight Disco* on Legian Rd or the *Rivoli Disco* which claims to be 'for serious night lifers'. *Kayu Api's*, at the junction of Jalan Legian and Jalan Melasti, has gone through various role changes in its night life.

Bars & Pubs There are numerous regular pubs around Kuta and Legian like the *Bali Aussie,* the *Bali Billabong, Norm's Bar* and *Norman's Garden*. If you can hack it (or even believe it) Wednesday night at the *Casablanca* on Jalan Buni Sari is 'Aussie Party Night' with Aussie beer, Aussie people, drinking contests and other events you'd rather not hear about including ladies' arm wrestling contests, cheese and vegemite sandwich eating contests and other scenes of typical Australian depravity.

Also on Jalan Buni Sari is the *Pub Bagus*, the Buni Sari dancing place, and

The Pub, one of Kuta's original bars. It's still very popular.

At the opposite end of the price (and decor) scale take the little alley beside Made's to Poppies' Gang. Opposite the *Warung Santai* a large and very relaxed Balinese guy ladles rice wine out of a large container, people sit around, guitars are strummed and it's generally a very peaceful and pleasant scene.

Things to Buy

Parts of Kuta are now almost solid shops, in fact they seem to be squeezing out the restaurants and other businesses and over the years they've become steadily flashier and more sophisticated. Lots of the cheaper shops are now crowded together in 'art markets' like the one at the bottom of Jalan Bakung Sari. Popular Kuta buys include painted to order surfing pictures (they'll even paint you into the hero-size waves). You can find all the Balinese arts and crafts from every part of the island. They range from wood carvings to paintings or those delightful wind chimes which you hear all over Bali.

Clothes are another good Kuta buy, there are lots of clothes shops around Kuta and the prices are more than reasonable. You'll probably see the same items later on from Berkeley to Double Bay at 10 times the cost.

Recently there has been a clamp down on the pirate cassette tape business, but it's felt that they'll soon reopen, selling the same pirated tapes at slightly higher prices.

With so many things to buy around Kuta it's very easy to be stampeded into buying things you don't really want during your first days. In fact you need real endurance not to succumb to something, there are so many people trying to sell to you. There are also countless masseurs operating along the beach – they'll quickly prove you have dozens of muscles you never knew existed for a couple of thousand rp.

Getting There & Away

The official taxi fare between the airport and Kuta is 3500 rp. Bemos from Kuta are 250 rp to the airport or 350 rp to Denpasar. There are no direct bemos to Sanur from Kuta, you have to go in to Denpasar, change from the Tegal to Kereneng bemo station and take another bemo out to Sanur. There are some Sanur bound bemos which come round via the Tegal station. Between a few people it would be little more expensive to charter a bemo.

There are almost always lots of bemos around bemo corner if you want to charter one - to Ulu Watu, the airport, Ubud or wherever. See the introductory Getting Around section for details on chartering bemos. To reach most places by regular public bemos you have to go into Denpasar and change.

Getting Around

Bemos shuttle along the Legian road but most of them would rather charter than take you as a regular passenger so beware. There are also lots of places around Kuta and Legian hiring bicycles, motorcycles, jeeps and anything else with wheels you might like to lay your hands on. See the introductory Getting Around section for details. Also there are countless places operating tours around Bali or selling tickets to places further afield in Indonesia or overseas.

Kuta Banjars

Despite all the excesses Kuta is still a village, a place where little offerings are put out in front of house entrances and at tricky gang junctions. It's this part of Kuta which makes it so much more interesting than the antiseptic Nusa Dua.

The banjars are amongst the most visible evidence of Kuta's thriving village life. A banjar is rather like a small town council and the bale banjars are a meeting place, a place for discussions, meetings, ceremonies, dancing or gamelan practice. If you hear a gamelan ringing out over Kuta some quiet evening it's probably a banjar practise session and nobody will mind if you wander in to watch and listen.

Most banjars are little more than an open pavilion or courtyard but they're easy to spot by the warning drum tower and Kuta banjars, with lots of tourist generated rupiah, can afford some pretty fancy warning towers. Check out the one at Banjar Pande Mas next to Made's Warung on Kuta Beach Rd. Or the one at Banjar Buni Kuta next to the Pub. Best of all is the superb new multi-storey tower at Banjar Tegal Kuta, further down the lane from Banjar Buni Kuta.

SANUR

Sanur Beach is the alternative to Kuta for those coming to Bali for sea, sand and sun. The new resort of Nusa Dua is intended to be an alternative to Sanur. Although Sanur is principally the locale for the Hyatts and the like it does have some more reasonably priced accommodation, although not down to the lower Kuta levels. It's got a pleasant beach and the Sanur reef makes for more sheltered water - no big surf here.

What Sanur doesn't have, thank the gods, is the Kuta noise, confusion and pollution. You're not in constant risk of being mown down by motorcycle maniacs, the traffic isn't horrendous and you're not constantly badgered to buy things - badgered yes, but not constantly.

Information

Sanur has travel agents, moneychangers and other facilities just like Kuta. There's a Sanur post office although, of course, you can also have mail addressed to the large hotels. The Denpasar main post office is in a sort of mid-position between Denpasar and Sanur.

Qantas has its Bali office at the Bali Beach Hotel, and it's open Monday to Friday from 8 am to 4 pm, Saturday from 8 am to 2 pm or you can call the airport on 51472. You will also find a Garuda office here although it's not terribly efficient. It's open Monday to Friday from 7.30 am to 4.30 pm and on Saturday, Sunday from 1 to 5 pm. Singapore Airlines, Cathay Pacific, Thai International and Malaysian

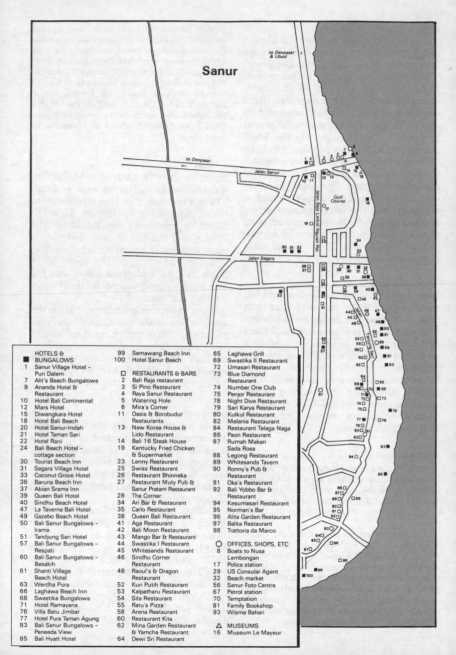

Sanur

to Denpasar
& Ubud

to Denpasar

Jalan Sanur

Jalan Baja Lekod Ngurah Rai

Golf
Course

Jalan Segara

Tanjung Sari

HOTELS & BUNGALOWS		RESTAURANTS & BARS	65	Laghawa Grill
1	Sanur Village Hotel – Puri Dalem	99 Semawang Beach Inn	69	Swastika II Restaurant
7	Alit's Beach Bungalows	100 Hotel Sanur Beach	72	Umasari Restaurant
9	Ananda Hotel & Restaurant	2 Bali Raja restaurant	73	Blue Diamond Restaurant
10	Hotel Bali Continental	3 Si Pino Restaurant	74	Number One Club
12	Mars Hotel	4 Raya Sanur Restaurant	75	Penjor Restaurant
15	Diwangkara Hotel	5 Watering Hole	78	Night Dive Restaurant
18	Hotel Bali Beach	6 Mira's Corner	79	Sari Karya Restaurant
20	Hotel Sanur-Indah	11 Oasis & Borobudur Restaurants	80	Kulkul Restaurant
21	Hotel Taman Sari	13 New Korea House & Lido Restaurant	82	Melanie Restaurant
22	Hotel Rani	14 Bali 16 Steak House	84	Restaurant Telaga Naga
24	Bali Beach Hotel – cottage section	19 Kentucky Fried Chicken & Supermarket	86	Paon Restaurant
30	Tourist Beach Inn	23 Lenny Restaurant	87	Rumah Makan Sada Rosa
31	Segara Village Hotel	25 Swiss Restaurant	88	Legong Restaurant
33	Coconut Grove Hotel	26 Restaurant Bhinneka	89	Whitesands Tavern
36	Baruna Beach Inn	27 Restaurant Muty Pub & Sanur Pratam Restaurant	90	Ronny's Pub & Restaurant
37	Abian Srama Inn	28 The Corner	91	Oka's Restaurant
39	Queen Bali Hotel	34 Ari Bar & Restaurant	92	Bali Yobbo Bar & Restaurant
40	Sindhu Beach Hotel	35 Carlo Restaurant	94	Kesumasari Restaurant
47	La Taverna Bali Hotel	38 Queen Bali Restaurant	95	Norman's Bar
49	Gazebo Beach Hotel	41 Aga Restaurant	96	Alita Garden Restaurant
50	Bali Sanur Bungalows – Irama	42 Bali Moon Restaurant	97	Balita Restaurant
51	Tandjung Sari Hotel	43 Mango Bar & Restaurant	98	Trattoria da Marco
57	Bali Sanur Bungalows – Respati	44 Swastika I Restaurant		
60	Bali Sanur Bungalows – Besakih	45 Whitesands Restaurant	○	OFFICES, SHOPS, ETC
61	Shanti Village Beach Hotel	46 Sindhu Corner Restaurant	8	Boats to Nusa Lembongan
63	Werdha Pura	48 Raoul's & Dragon Restaurant	17	Police station
66	Laghawa Beach Inn	52 Kuri Putih Restaurant	29	US Consular Agent
68	Swastika Bungalows	53 Kalpatharu Restaurant	32	Beach market
71	Hotel Ramayana	54 Sita Restaurant	56	Sanur Foto Centre
76	Villa Batu Jimbar	58 Ratu's Pizza	67	Petrol station
77	Hotel Pura Taman Agung	60 Restaurant Kita	70	Temptation
83	Bali Sanur Bungalows – Peneeda View	62 Mina Garden Restaurant & Yamcha Restaurant	81	Family Bookshop
85	Bali Hyatt Hotel	64 Dewi Sri Restaurant	93	Wisma Bahari
			△	MUSEUMS
			16	Museum Le Mayeur

Airlines agents are also in the Bali Beach Hotel.

There's an Australian consulate (tel 25997) at Jalan Raya Sanur 146; that's actually between Sanur and Denpasar on the back road. The office is open Monday to Friday from 8 am to 2 pm and also will look after British, Canadian and New Zealand citizens although they may still have to go to Jakarta if they need a new passport. The consulates' main problem is people who run out of money – usually through having it stolen. They also warn of the heavy narcotics penalties in Bali and seem to do a lot of marriages – Australian-Indonesian and Australian-Australian.

Around Sanur

There's plenty of opportunity for wandering around Sanur, along the beach or through the rice paddies. The rice farmers of Sanur are said to grow some of the finest rice in Bali. The beach at Sanur is always full of interesting sights such as the colourful prahus known as *jukungs* ready to take you for a quick trip out to the reef. At low tide you can walk across the sand and coral to this sheltering reef. Villagers collect coral here to make building lime.

Beyond the Hotel Sanur at Belanjong there's a stone pillar with an inscription recounting military victories of over 1000 years ago. Tanjung Sari with its coral pyramid was once a lonely temple by the beach.

Museum Le Mayeur

Sanur was one of the places in Bali favoured by western artists during their pre-war discovery of the island. It was still a quiet fishing village at that time but few traces of that Sanur of 50 years ago remain. The exception is the former home of the Belgian artist Le Mayeur who lived here from 1932 to 1958. It must have been a delightful place then, a peaceful and elegant home right by the beach. Today it's squeezed between the Bali Beach Hotel and the Diwangkara Beach Hotel but still maintained by his widow Ni Polok, once a renowned and beautiful Legong dancer. The home displays paintings by Le Mayeur but is also an interesting example of architecture in its own right. Notice the beautifully carved window shutters which recount the story of Rama and Sita from the *Ramayana*.

Admission is 200 rp (children 100 rp) and it's open 8 am to 2 pm Sunday, Tuesday, Wednesday and Thursday, 8 to 11 am Friday and 8 am to 12.30 pm Saturday.

Kites

Asian children don't enjoy the same variety and quantity of toys that children in the west commonly have but they certainly do fly kites. Almost anywhere in Asia the sky is likely to be full of kites of all sizes and types. Bali is no exception – you'll see children flying kites in towns and villages and even in the middle of the rice paddies. At Sanur, however, kite-flying is not just child's play. Here the local banjars compete in kite-flying competitions where size seems to be a major factor.

Their kites are enormous, traffic is halted when they're carried down the road, it takes half a dozen men to launch them, two men to carry the drum of heavy nylon cord and a sturdy tree is needed to tie the kite to once it's up and flying. They're up to 10 metres wide and the cord tensioning the main cross piece (itself a hefty length of bamboo) makes a low 'whoop-whoop-whoop' noise as they fly. Not unexpectedly they're a danger to aircraft – one of these monsters could bring a 747 down – and they've had to restrict kite flying on the airport approaches, particularly across Serangan Island.

Places to Stay

There are no dirt-cheap Kuta-style places around Sanur although there are a handful of medium-price places, a few of them as good or better value than equivalent places at Kuta. Principally, however, Sanur is the high price resort, the place for 'international standard' hotels where the majority of Bali's package tours go. At these upper bracket hotels there will be a 15.5% service charge. The prices quoted here don't include this additional charge.

Places to Stay - middle

At the northern end of Sanur Beach the *Ananda Hotel* (tel 8327) is behind the restaurant of the same name, right by the beach. It's a neat and clean little place with rooms at 15,000/20,000 rp. There are rooms at 15,000 to 25,000 rp at the *Watering Hole*, opposite the Bali Beach Hotel entrance.

In the same price bracket the *Hotel Pura Taman Agung* on Jalan Tanjung Sari is another pleasant place with a pretty garden and well kept rooms with wide verandahs.

On the same side of the road is the *Hotel Ramayana* (tel 8429) with rooms from US$15 to US$25. A little north and on the beach side of the road is the *Werdha Pura*, a government run 'beach cottage prototype'. Further along the road the *Abian Srama Inn* (tel 8415) has rooms from US$12 to US$35.

On Jalan Segara, right next to the Segara Village Hotel and pleasantly close to the beach, the *Tourist Beach Inn* is one of the most economical places at Sanur – straightforward but quite reasonable rooms are 10,000/15,000 rp for singles/doubles including breakfast.

Mrs S Harsojo (PO Box 223, Denpasar) has charming bungalows on the beach at Sanur for US$12 a night including breakfast if you book for a week. The entrance is from Respati Bungalows and it's near the Tandjung Sari's part of the beach. *Swastika Bungalows* near the two Swastika Garden Restaurants has pleasant bungalows around a swimming pool.

On the Jalan Sanur crossroads at the northern end of Sanur the *Mars Hotel* is about a five or 10 minute walk from the beach while across the other side of the crossroads there's the *Hotel Bali Continental* on the Denpasar road.

Other middle bracket places include the *Laghawa Beach Inn*. Finally on Jalan Segara, but across the main road, there are three lower-priced places side by side – the *Hotel Sanur-Indah, Hotel Taman Sari* and the *Hotel Rani*. Rooms are small and simple.

Places to Stay - top end

Sanur's first 'big' hotel and still one of the biggest is the massive *Hotel Bali Beach* from the Sukarno era of the mid-60s. Today it's very out of place in Bali, a Miami Beach-style rectangular block squarely facing the beach. It's got all the usual facilities from bars, restaurants and a nightclub to swimming pools, tennis courts and even an adjacent golf course. The poolside snack bar here is quite reasonably priced. Adjoining the hotel is the newer cottage section.

Almost all the more expensive hotels are on the beachfront. Immediately north of the Bali Beach and adjacent to the Museum Le Mayeur is the slightly secluded *Diwangkara Beach Hotel*. Across the road north again are the cottages of *Alit's Beach Bungalows*. Going south from the Bali Beach you come first to the *Segara Village Hotel* by the beach – it's a more expensive place with motel-style rooms and nicer double-storey cottages in a pleasant garden area. There's a children's playground here. Then there's the *Sindhu Beach Hotel* and *La Taverna Bali Hotel*, both right on the beach. There's also the smaller *Gazebo Beach Cottages* group here with air-conditioned cottages in a lush garden.

There are several groups of *Bali Sanur Bungalows* at Sanur, continuing south you come to the 'Irama', 'Besakih' and 'Peneeda View' bungalows. The 'Puri Dalem' group of bungalows on Jalan Sanur are one of the few top-end places not actually on the beach or close to it.

In between the Irama and the Besakih bungalows is the *Tandjung Sari Hotel*, the name means 'cape of flowers' and they spell Tanjung in the old way. Some of the bungalows in this pleasantly relaxed and fairly expensive place are interesting two-storey buildings.

Then it's the *Bali Hyatt*, one of the biggest hotels along Sanur and an interesting contrast with the Bali Beach of 10 years earlier. The lesson had been learnt in the '60s and a regulation was passed that no hotel could be 'taller than a palm tree'. The Hyatt blends in remarkably well with its sloping balconies overflowing with tropical vegetation. Look for the interesting pottery tiles used as decorations on various walls. There's also Sanur's flashiest and most popular disco here. Right down at the southern end of the beach is the big *Hotel Sanur Beach*.

Alit's Beach Bungalows (tel 8560, 8567) PO Box 102, Denpasar, right on the beach, 98 bungalows, air-con, swimming pool, US$35 to US$40.
Hotel Bali Beach (tel 8511) PO Box 275, Denpasar, right on the beach, 605 rooms, air-con, swimming pools, US$55 to US$75 plus suites, some with kitchenettes.
Bali Hyatt (tel 8271-8277) PO Box 392, Denpasar, right on the beach, 387 rooms, air-con, swimming pool, US$70 to US$120 plus suites.
Bali Sanur Bungalows (tel 8421, 8422) PO Box 198, Denpasar, right on the beach, 160 rooms, air-con, swimming pool, US$40 to US$50.
Beach Hotel Diwangkara (tel 8577, 8591) PO Box 120, Denpasar, right on the beach, 36 rooms, air-con, swimming pool, US$25 to US$38.
La Taverna Bali Hotel (tel 8497) PO Box 40, Denpasar, right on the beach, 34 rooms, air-con, swimming pool, US$50 to US$60.
Hotel Sanur Beach (tel 8011), PO Box 279, Denpasar, right on the beach, 320 rooms plus 26 bungalows, air-con, swimming pool, US$70 to US$75.
Hotel Segara Village (tel 8407, 8408, 8231) PO Box 91, Denpasar, on the beach, 110 bungalows, air-con, swimming pools, from US$85.
Sindhu Beach Hotel (tel 28351) PO Box 181, Denpasar, right on the beach, 50 bungalow rooms, air-con, swimming pool, US$40 to US$50.

Tandjung Sari Hotel (tel 8441), PO Box 25, Denpasar, right on the beach, 25 bungalows, air-con, swimming pool, US$70 to US$80.

Welcome to—
tandjung sari
cape of flowers

Places to Eat
All the top end hotels have their own restaurants, snack bars, coffee bars and bars of course – generally with top end prices too! The food at Sanur is basically western – there's even Bali's centre for homesick pasta lovers, *Trattoria da Marco* down at the southern end of the beach road. You'll also find a number of quite reasonably priced places, very much from the Kuta restaurant mould. Just south of the Bali Beach Hotel there's the slightly more expensive beachfront *Sanur Beach Market*.

For seafood *Lenny's* and the *Kulkul Restaurant* are worth trying. *Kesumasari*, on the beach south of the Bali Hyatt, has good and commendably fresh food. If you continue down towards the south end of the Sanur hotel strip, beyond the Hyatt, there are a number of reasonably priced small restaurants and bars.

On the corner of Jalan Segara and the main road the *Restaurant Bhinneka* has a buffet of over 30 different dishes for 4000 rp.

Things to Buy
There are lots of shops scattered around Sanur, just like at Kuta. Temptation, near the Hotel Ramayana, is particularly interesting with a curious collection of 'artyfacts'.

Getting There & Away
Taxi fare between the airport and Sanur is

9000 rp. A new 'superhighway' runs from the Denpasar-Batubulan road to Sanur and on past Benoa, Kuta, the airport and out to Nusa Dua. It makes transport along this route much faster.

There are two different Denpasar-Sanur bemos operating from the Kereneng bemo station in Denpasar. Coming from Sanur the blue ones go past Kereneng and around the south of town past Tegal (the Kuta station) and then around the north of town through Kereneng. The green bemos *sometimes* go around town but may just go straight to the station. The fare is 300 rp.

To get from Kuta to Sanur you have to go into Denpasar and then out again. It's much faster and, between a few people, not that much more expensive to charter a bemo for a Kuta to Sanur trip.

Getting Around
Small bemos shuttle up and down the beach road in Sanur at a cost of 100 rp. There are numerous places around Sanur renting out cars, motorcycles and bicycles from 1500 rp a day. Tunas Tours & Travel, in the Hotel Bali Beach Arcade, rents mountain bikes for US$7.50 a day and also runs bicycle tours of Bali.

SERANGAN ISLAND
Very close to the shore, south of Sanur and close to the mouth of Benoa Harbour, is Serangan, the turtle island. At low tide you can actually walk across to the island. Turtles are captured and fattened here in pens before being sold for village feasts. The island has an important temple, Pura Sakenan, noted for its unusual shrines known as *candi*. Twice a year major temple festivals are held here, attracting great crowds of devotees. The giant puppet figures known as *Barong Landung* are brought across to the island for these festivals.

Day trips to Serangan have become popular with the travel agents at Kuta and Sanur but Serangan has a very strong tourist trap air and is not terribly popular

with visitors. You're constantly hassled to spend, spend, spend. In fact you get pounced on as soon as the prahu beaches and you're followed, cajoled, pleaded with and abused until you leave.

Getting There & Away
Like Kuta, Serangan has been affected by tourism - badly. It's not a place to waste time or money on but if you do decide to take a look you can either get there on an organised tour or charter a prahu yourself. Beware of rip-offs if you decide to charter, they may start at 25,000 rp but you can eventually knock a boat (big enough for a half-dozen people) down to around 10,000 rp. Charters are available from Suwan, a small mangrove inlet through a rubbish dump. Serangan Island is hard work from start to finish.

JIMBARAN BAY
Just beyond the airport, south of Kuta, Jimbaran Bay is a relatively new development with air-conditioned bungalows at the *Pansea Bali*. There's a bar and restaurant on the beach.

BENOA
The wide but shallow bay off the end of the runway is one of Bali's main ports. It's also the main harbour for visiting yachts and there's nearly always a few overseas vessels moored here. If you're looking for a yacht berth to some place far away you may find notes on various notice boards around Kuta (try Poppies for example) but you might have equally good luck by simply getting a prahu here to paddle you out to the yachts to ask.

Benoa is actually in two parts. The harbour, Benoa Harbour, is on the north side, directly connected with Denpasar. It consists of little more than a wharf and a variety of port offices. Benoa village, where you might see turtles brought in from Serangan, is on the south side of the bay. To get there you have to take the highway to Nusa Dua and then the smaller road along the coast from there.

Boats also shuttle back and forth between Benoa Harbour and the Benoa fishing village.

The village of Benoa has become much cleaner and more affluent looking in recent years and it's something of an activities centre for Nusa Dua. If you want to go windsurfing, para-sailing, scuba diving or indulge in various other water sports, this is the place.

Places to Stay & Eat

Chez Agung Pension/Homestay is a new development with pleasant doubles with bathroom for 16,000 rp. There are several restaurants in Benoa like the *Dalang Sea View Restaurant,* the *Entari Restaurant,* the *Jeladi Suta Restaurant* or the *Rai Seafood Restaurant.*

NUSA DUA

Nusa Dua, 'two islands', is the new Balinese beach resort – the planned resort area where the mistakes of Kuta won't be repeated! The two islands are actually small raised headlands, connected to the mainland by sand-spits. Nusa Dua is south of Kuta and Sanur and the airport, on the sparsely populated Bukit Peninsula.

The beach here is very pleasant and there is often good surf. The development of Nusa Dua was dogged by interminable delays and this is really a place for people who want to get away from Bali. There is no outside development permitted within the compound so you have a km or so walk if you want to get even so much as a coke at non-international-hotel prices. Or a bemo to the rest of Bali.

Places to Stay & Eat

The Nusa Dua hotels all have swimming pools, a variety of restaurants and bars, entertainment and sports facilities and various other international hotel mod cons.

The *Nusa Dua Beach Hotel* (tel 71210) is a huge (450 rooms) and very upper bracket hotel with all the luxuries you could expect and prices from around

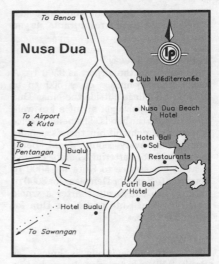

US$70 to US$90 for standard rooms, plus 15.5% service and tax. It's attractively designed using much Balinese architecture and statuary but then how seriously can you take a hotel that promotes itself as being the place where Ronald Reagan stayed when he came to Bali? He probably stayed in the US$1200 a night Nusa Dua Suite.

South of the Nusa Dua Beach Hotel is the 500 room *Hotel Bali Sol* (tel 71510) with regular rooms at US$78 to US$84 and suites at US$138. South again is the *Putri Bali Hotel* (tel 71020, 71420) which has 425 rooms at US$70 to US$88 plus suites, cottages and so on. Just inland from the Putri Bali is the smaller *Hotel Club Bualu* (tel 71310). There are just 50 rooms at this hotel with prices from US$55 to US$70.

Finally at the north end of the Nusa Dua resort area is the *Club Méditerranée Bali* which is strictly an inclusive tour operation.

The hotels offer a wide variety of restaurants but there's not a great deal of choice apart from the hotels since it's a long walk to get out of the resort area. There are some other eating places in the 'amenity core' area but you can't just stroll outside to other restaurants, as you can at Sanur.

Getting There & Away

Taxi fare from the airport is 9500 rp. A bemo from Denpasar costs 500 rp to Bualu, the village outside the Nusa Dua compound. You've got about a km walk from there to the hotels. The bemo service operates on demand but there's usually one about every hour, avoid being pressured into chartering a bemo. There's a hotel bus service to Kuta for 5000 rp return or to Sanur or Denpasar for 8000 rp return. You can easily charter a whole bemo between Kuta and Nusa Dua for around 5000 rp.

ULU WATU

The southern peninsula is known as Bukit, 'hill' in Indonesian. It was known to the Dutch as Tafelhoek. If you follow the road from Kuta around the end of the airport runway it bucks and bounces right down to the end of the peninsula at Ulu Watu. There are plenty of potholes. At times the road climbs quite high, reaching 200 metres, and there are fine views back over the airport, Kuta and southern Bali. Along the roadside you'll notice numerous limestone quarries with large blocks of stone being cut out by hand. Many of the buildings in this area of Bali are constructed of these blocks. This is a dry, relatively sparsely inhabited area – a contrast to the lush rice-growing area which seems to commence immediately north of the airport.

At the southern tip, where the land ends in sheer cliffs which drop precipitously into the clear blue sea, perches the temple of Pura Luhur Ulu Watu. And perches is certainly the word for it – it hangs right over the abyss. The temple has a resident horde of monkeys and is entered through an unusual arched gateway flanked by statues of Ganesh. It's one of several important temples to the spirits of the sea to be found along the south coast of Bali. Others include Tanah Lot and Rambut Siwi.

Ulu Watu, along with the other well known temples of the south – Pura Sakenan on Serangan Island, Pura Petitenget at Krobokan and the temple at Tanah Lot – is associated with Nirartha, the Javanese priest credited with introducing many of the elements of the Balinese religion to the island. He retreated to Ulu Watu for his final days.

Ulu Watu has another claim to fame. It's a Balinese surfing Mecca, made famous through several classic surfing films and a popular locale for the surfers who flock to Bali from all over the world, but particularly from Australia. Just before the Ulu Watu car park a large sign indicates the way to the Suluban Surf Beach, Pantai Suluban. It's two km down a narrow footpath, OK for motorcycles but nothing more. Take care on a motorcycle, the path is narrow, some of the corners are blind and there have been some nasty accidents. From a motorcycle park at the end of the track you continue on foot down to the beach, which is overlooked by a series of warungs catering to the keen surfers who flock here. A letter from a hungry surfer raved on about the *Warung Indra* for three pages!

Top: A hidden away hotel room, Campuhan near Ubud, Bali (TW)
Bottom: Painted panels at Tirta Empul, Tampaksiring, Bali (TW)

Top: The elephant cave, Goa Gajah, Bali (TW)
Bottom: Water spouts held by female figures, Goa Gajah, Bali (TW)

Denpasar

Fifteen years ago, which seems to be a throw-away cliche for too many things about Bali, Denpasar was a pleasant, quiet little town. Today it's a noisy confusion of motorcycles, a polluted disaster area of bemos and buses; not at all a pleasant place to stay. Still, it's the capital of Bali and does have an interesting museum, an art centre and lots of shops. The city has a population of around 200,000. Denpasar means 'next to the market' and the city is sometimes referred to as Badung.

Information & Orientation
The main street of Denpasar is Jalan Gajah Mada, a crowded continuous traffic jam even though it is now one-way. This is the main shopping street of Denpasar but the market, Pasar Badung, is on the outskirts of town. There is also a shopping centre beside the river.

Tourist Office The Badung tourist office is on Jalan Surapati, just past the roundabout and across the road from the Bali Museum. They've got a useful calendar of festivals and events in Bali and a pretty good map. The office is open Monday to Thursday from 7 am to 2 pm, Friday 7 to 11 am, Saturday 7 am to 12.30 pm.

Banks All the major Indonesian banks have their main Bali offices in Denpasar, principally along Jalan Gajah Mada. The Bank Ekspor-Impor Indonesia, which isn't on that main street, is probably the best for transfers from overseas.

Post The Denpasar main post office with poste restante is very inconveniently situated, sort of half-way between Denpasar and Sanur by the back route. Avoid getting mail sent to you here, the offices in Kuta or Ubud are much more convenient.

Immigration The Immigration Office (tel 2439) is at Jalan Panjaitan 4, Sanglah – in the south of Denpasar and just around the corner from the main post office. It's open Monday to Thursday 7 am to 2 pm, Friday 7 to 11 am and Saturday 7 am to 12.30 pm. If you are in the rare circumstances these days of having to make visa changes, get there on a Sanglah bemo and make sure you're prettied up in your best.

PPA The Direktorat Perlindungan dan Pengawetan Alam (Directorate of Nature Conservation & Wildlife Management) is responsible for managing Indonesia's nature reserves and national parks. There is an office outside of Denpasar – you take a Benoa bound bemo from Denpasar and get off at the Kampong Suwang turn-off. Then you walk for 400 metres – the PPA office is on the left-hand side.

Around Town
If you wander down Gajah Mada, past all the shops and restaurants, you come to the towering Guru statue at the intersection with Jalan Veteran. The four-faced, eight-armed statue is of the god Guru, Lord of the Four Directions. He keeps a close eye on the traffic swirling around him.

Beside the intersection is the large Puputan Square, commemorating the heroic but suicidal stand the rajahs of Badung made against the invading Dutch in 1906.

At the junction of Jalan Hasannudin and Jalan Imam Bonjol (the Kuta road) is the Puri Pemecutan, the rebuilt remains of a palace destroyed during the 1906 invasion.

Bali Museum
The museum consists of an attractive series of separate buildings and pavilions. They include examples of the architecture of both the palace (puri) and temple

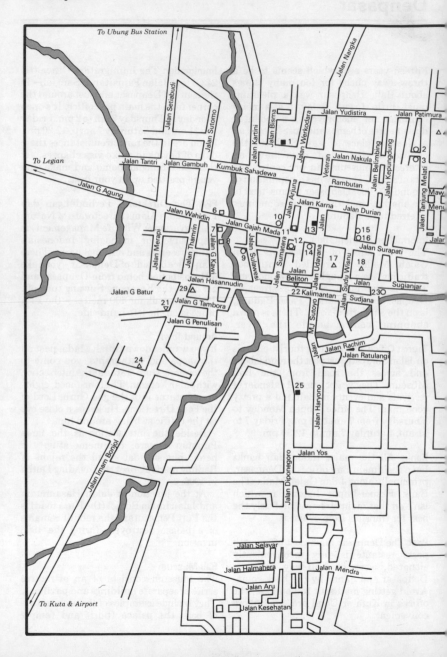

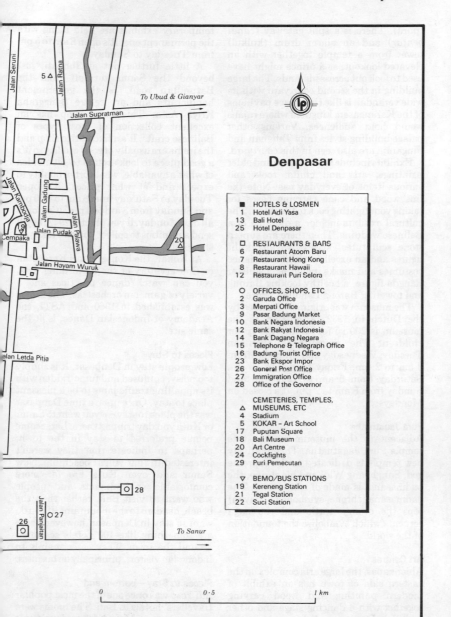

To Ubud & Gianyar

Denpasar

- ■ HOTELS & LOSMEN
  - 1 Hotel Adi Yasa
  - 13 Bali Hotel
  - 25 Hotel Denpasar

- □ RESTAURANTS & BARS
  - 6 Restaurant Atoom Baru
  - 7 Restaurant Hong Kong
  - 8 Restaurant Hawaii
  - 12 Restaurant Puri Selera

- O OFFICES, SHOPS, ETC
  - 2 Garuda Office
  - 3 Merpati Office
  - 9 Pasar Badung Market
  - 10 Bank Negara Indonesia
  - 12 Bank Rakyat Indonesia
  - 14 Bank Dagang Negara
  - 15 Telephone & Telegraph Office
  - 16 Badung Tourist Office
  - 23 Bank Ekspor Impor
  - 26 General Post Office
  - 27 Immigration Office
  - 28 Office of the Governor

- CEMETERIES, TEMPLES,
  △ MUSEUMS, ETC
  - 4 Stadium
  - 5 KOKAR – Art School
  - 17 Puputan Square
  - 18 Bali Museum
  - 20 Art Centre
  - 24 Cockfights
  - 29 Puri Pemecutan

- ▽ BEMO/BUS STATIONS
  - 19 Kereneng Station
  - 21 Tegal Station
  - 22 Suci Station

To Sanur

0   0.5   1 km

(pura). There is a split gateway (*candi bentar*) and an alarm drum (kulkul) tower from a temple together with an elevated lookout, as a prince might have used to look out across his lands. The large building in the second courtyard with its wide verandah is like the palace pavilions of the Karangasem kingdom where rajahs would hold audiences. Various other palace building styles from Tabanan and Singaraja are also seen in this courtyard.

Exhibits include both modern and older paintings, arts and crafts, tools and various items of everyday use. Note the fine wood and cane carrying cases for taking your fighting cock to the event. The cultural exhibits include a diorama of a Balinese wedding. Then there are superb stone sculptures, krises, wayang kulit figures and an excellent exhibit of dance costumes and masks including a sinister Rangda figure, a healthy looking Barong and towering Barong Landung figures.

The museum was originally founded by the Dutch in 1932. Admission to the museum is 200 rp for adults, 100 rp for children. The museum is open on Tuesday, Wednesday and Thursday from 8 am to 2 pm, Friday from 8 to 11 am, Saturday from 8 am to 12.30 pm and Sunday from 8 am to 2 pm. It's closed on Mondays.

Pura Jagatnatha

Adjacent to the museum is the state temple Pura Jagatnatha. This relatively new temple is dedicated to the supreme god, Sanghyang Widi and his shrine, the padmasana, is made of white coral. The padmasana (throne, symbolic of heaven) tops the cosmic turtle and the naga serpents which symbolise the foundation of the world.

Art Centres

Abiankapas, the large arts complex on the eastern side of town has an exhibit of modern painting and wood carving together with a dancing stage and other facilities. Dances are held regularly and temporary exhibits are held along with the permanent one. It's open 8 am to 5 pm from Tuesday to Sunday.

A little further out at Tohpati, just beyond the Sanur turn-off from the Batubulan road, is the government handicrafts and art centre Sanggraha Kriya Asta. This large shop has an excellent collection of most types of Balinese crafts. It's a fixed price shop and the items are usually of good quality so it's a good place to look around to get an idea of what's available, what sort of quality to expect and at what prices. It's open Tuesday to Saturday from 8 am to 4.30 pm and Sunday from 8 am to 4 pm. It's closed all day Monday. If you phone 22942 they'll send a minibus to collect you and take you shopping!

At Kokar, the Konservatori Kerawitan or Conservatory of the Performing Arts, you can watch dance practices and a variety of gamelan orchestras. The centre was established in 1960 and ASTI, the Academy of Indonesian Dance, is at the same site.

Places to Stay

Few people stay in Denpasar. It is simply too noisy, confused and fume-ridden with its appalling traffic jams to be a pleasant place to stay. Once upon a time Denpasar was the place to stay – if you went to Sanur or Kuta you day tripped there. Later some people preferred to stay in the town, perhaps to indicate that they weren't interested in that vulgar beach life. Now Sanur and even Kuta are far more comfortable environments and people who want to visit Bali, rather than the beach, head up to the mountains. If you do want to stay in Denpasar, however, there are something like 100 hotels scattered around the town. They cater mainly to Indonesian visitors, principally on business.

Places to Stay – bottom end

Adi Yasa was once one of the most popular travellers' hotels in Bali. The rooms were arranged around beautiful gardens and it had a delightful easy-going and friendly feel to it. In the evening you could sit around chatting with people from all over the world. It's still well kept but that terrific spirit has just faded away – it's no longer a travellers' centre and without that magic in the air it's just another pleasant enough losmen. Adi Yasa is at Jalan Nakula 11 and rooms are 6000 to 8000 rp including breakfast.

The other hotels which were once travellers' centres have all disappeared. There are plenty of cheap losmen around but Kuta is only a short bemo ride away so why bother.

Places to Stay – top end

There are no real luxury hotels of Sanur standard in Denpasar, but there are a number of places a notch down from that level. The *Bali Hotel* (tel 25681-5) at Jalan Veteran 3 dates from the Dutch days. It's a pleasantly old-fashioned place and centrally situated. Including breakfast singles/doubles cost from 36,000/44,000 rp to 53,000/60,000 rp for rooms with air-con. A suite is 78,000 rp. There's a restaurant, bar and swimming pool and this is a place with a sense of history.

A popular alternative is the *Hotel Denpasar* (tel 26336) at Jalan Diponegoro 103. Singles range from 7500 to 25,000 rp, doubles from 11,500 to 32,500 rp. The more expensive rooms have air-con and there are also some cottage-style rooms.

Places to Eat

There are a number of restaurants along noisy Jalan Gajah Mada although elsewhere in Denpasar the popular travellers' haunts have all disappeared with the city's demise as a travellers' locale.

Up on Gajah Mada the *Atoom Baru* is a big, spartan and comparatively expensive typical Asian Chinese restaurant. Across the road is the *Hong Kong Restaurant* with Chinese and Indonesian food and cafeteria-style self-service or a menu. Prices in either place are quite similar –

around 2000 rp for noodle dishes, from 3000 rp for Chinese dishes. Further down Gajah Mada is the relatively expensive *Puri Selera* which does excellent Chinese food. There are also several Padang food restaurants along Gajah Mada.

At Jalan Kartini 34, just off Gajah Mada, the Depot Mie *Nusa Indah* is a reasonably priced and friendly Indonesian restaurant. At night you'll find excellent and cheap food at the pasar malam stalls by the Suci bus station.

The *Bali Hotel* on Jalan Veteran dates from the Dutch era and in true East Indies colonial style they serve a rijstaffel in their old fashioned dining room. It costs 5500 rp and the service is friendly and efficient.

Entertainment

Dances in and around Denpasar are mainly for tourists only – there are regular performances at the art centre and a Barong dance every morning in nearby Batubulan. Wayang kulit performances can be seen a couple of times a week at the Pemecutan. Near the Kuta bemo station, cockfights used to be held regularly. Officially they're now banned but in practice they probably continue as before.

Things to Buy

Denpasar has no particular crafts of its own although there are numerous 'factories' around town churning out the mass produced handicrafts. Countless craft shops line Jalan Gajah Mada. You can also find an extremely good selection of Balinese crafts just out of town at the Sanggraha Kriya Asta government art centre on the road to Batubulan. It's a fixed price place and an excellent starting point to get an idea of prices and quality, even if you buy elsewhere. They often have articles which you simply may not see anywhere else.

Getting There & Away

Denpasar is the travel centre of Bali – here you'll find buses, colts and minibuses for all corners of the island. Also there are buses for Java, boat tickets, trains tickets and the Garuda, Merpati and Bouraq airline offices here.

See the Getting There chapter for details of transport between Bali and Java and the other islands of Indonesia.

Air Garuda (tel 27825, 22788, 22028) has its office at Jalan Melati 61, near the Kereneng bus station. The office is open Monday to Friday 7.30 am to 4.30 pm, Saturday and Sunday 9 am to 1 pm.

Merpati (tel 22864, 25841) is right next door at Jalan Melati 57. Their hours are Monday to Friday 7 am to 4 pm, Saturday 7 am to 1 pm, Sunday 9 am to 1 pm. Merpati flights are particularly good for the islands of Nusa Tenggara and they have lots of flights to Lombok.

Bouraq (tel 24656) is at Jalan Sudirman 19A. Their fares are the same as Merpati's and they have flights to destinations in Java and Nusa Tenggara.

Bus & Bemo Stations The usual route for land travel to or from Bali is Denpasar-Surabaya by day or night bus. There are a number of bus companies for this run, you find them mainly around the Suci bus station or along Jalan Hasannudin. If you're staying in Kuta, however, there's no need to trek into Denpasar for tickets as there are numerous agents at Kuta.

For travel within Bali, Denpasar has four bus and/or bemo stations so in many cases you'll have to transfer from one station to another if you're making a trip through Denpasar. If, for example, you were travelling from Kuta to Ubud you'd arrive in Denpasar at the Tegal bemo station, transfer to the Kereneng station and take a bemo from there to Ubud. Squadrons of little three-wheeler bemos shuttle back and forth between the various stations and also to various points in the town. The Jalan Thamrin end of Jalan Gajah Mada, for example, is a stop for the transfer bemos. You'll find the

transfer bemos lined up for the various destinations at each of the stations.

Fares vary from around 150 to 300 rp between the stations. You can also charter bemos or even those little three-wheelers (cheaper of course) from the various stations. You could, for example, arrive from Surabaya at Ubung or Suci and charter a mini-bemo straight to Kuta rather than bothering with transferring to Tegal and then taking a bemo to Kuta. Between a few of you it might even be cheaper.

Further afield fares vary with the type of bus you take, the smaller minibuses are more expensive than the larger old buses. The stations and some of their destinations and fares are:

Tegal – south of the centre on the Kuta road. The station for the southern peninsula.

Kuta	300 rp
Legian	400 rp
Airport	400 rp
Nusa Dua	500 rp

Ubung – north of the centre on the Gilimanuk road. This is the station for the north and west of Bali and it is also the main station for buses to Surabaya, Yogyakarta and other destinations in Java. To get to Tanah Lot take a Kediri bemo and another from there for 150 rp.

Kediri	450 rp
Mengwi	400 rp
Negara	1000-1500 rp
Gilimanuk	1500-2000 rp
Bedugul	1000 rp
Singaraja	1500 rp
Lovina Beach	2000 rp

Kereneng – east of the centre, off the Ubud road. This is the station for the east and central area of Bali.

Sanur	300 rp
Ubud	600 rp
Gianyar	500 rp
Tampaksiring	800 rp

Klungkung	800 rp
Bangli	800 rp
Padangbai	1250 rp
Candidasa	1300 rp
Amlapura	1600 rp
Kintamani	1200 rp

Suci – south of the centre is mainly just the bemo stop for Benoa (300 rp) but the offices of many of the Surabaya bus lines and agents for shipping lines are also here. Benoa bemos also leave from the Sanglah Market.

Wangaya – for bemos to Sangeh (450 rp).

Train There are no railways on Bali but there is a railway office where you can get tickets to Surabaya or other centres in Java. This includes a bus ride to Gilimanuk and the ferry across to Banyuwangi in Java from where you take the train.

Boat The usual boat route out of Bali (not counting the short Bali to Java ferry which is included in bus ticket prices) is Padangbai to Lombok. Usually you get tickets for that daily ferry at Padangbai. There's a Pelni agent and other shipping agents at the Suci bus station if you wish to enquire about boat transport further afield.

Getting Around
Small three-wheeler bemos shuttle back and forth between the various Denpasar bus stations and Jalan Gajah Mada. The set fares vary from 150 rp to 300 rp – Tegal to Ubung 300 rp, Ubung to Kereneng 300 rp, Kereneng to Suci 150 rp, Kereneng to Tegal 150 rp. You can also charter these tiny bemos, they'll even buzz you out to Kuta Beach, or you can find taxis. Agree about all prices before getting on board because there are no meters.

Despite the traffic, dokars (horse carts) are still very popular around Denpasar, again agree on prices before departing. Note that dokars are not permitted to go down Jalan Gajah Mada.

Ubud

In the hills north of Denpasar, Ubud is the calm and peaceful cultural centre of Bali. It has undergone tremendous development in the past few years but, unlike at Kuta, this development hasn't ruined Ubud. It has managed to stay relaxed and beautiful, a place where the evenings are quiet and you can really tell you're in Bali. It's worth remembering that electricity only arrived in Ubud in the mid-70s. There's an amazing amount to do in and around Ubud so don't plan to do it in a day trip. You need at least a few days to properly appreciate it and Ubud is one of those places where days can quickly become weeks and weeks become months.

Information

Ubud has a pleasant little post office with poste restante – the letters are just sitting in a box on the counter, you sort through them yourself. There's the usual varied selection of bicycle and motorcycle hire places and a number of shops selling most items you might require. There's no bank but Ubud has a number of money changers and as a result the exchange rates are little worse than those at Sanur or Kuta. The telephone office is on the main road before you reach the post office turn-off from the centre of Ubud.

The Book Shop is a book exchange place on the Monkey Forest Rd or you can find small but excellent selections of new books on Bali at Murni's Warung or the Museum Neka.

Most importantly Ubud has a very friendly and helpful tourist office on the main street. Ubud's survival has been largely due to local efforts. Bina Wisata, the Ubud tourist office is a local venture, not a government one. It was set up in an effort to defend the village from the tourist onslaught – not by opposing tourism but by providing a service aimed at informing and generating a respect amongst visitors for Balinese culture and customs. The British-based magazine *New Internationalist* recounted some of the problems that faced the village:

The locals cursed the tourists, for they disturbed ceremonies and dressed impolitely. Guide books had told their readers about the family events, airlines had promoted Bali with all of its glamorous ceremonies, photographers had made public exhibitions out of private occasions. All of this without asking permission. Foreigners were attracted. They came to Ubud full of expectations. They entered any private house as though the religious ceremonies there were tourist attractions. Conflict after conflict developed, anger mounted.

Boards were put on the gates or walls to warn tourists that the ceremony inside was a private event. 'No Tourist, Please,' 'For Guest Only,' 'This is a Religious Event,' 'Entrance is Forbidden,' 'Only for the Family Members.' It was really ugly to see religious offerings and decorations at a compound entrance disturbed by these emergency boards written in a foreign language. Tempers rose further when a group of tourists were ordered to leave a temple because they were disturbing the praying parishioners. The tourists blamed their guide for not informing them. The guide accused the locals of being unfriendly and uncooperative. The villagers chased the guide away.

In 1981, with the problems of the village so acute, a move was made to revive Ubud's former beauty by extensive tree-planting. Then the tourist office was established – its publications even included an English-language newspaper, probably the first such paper to be produced by a village in Indonesia. In many ways they have been very successful although it takes time for the message to get through – an article in the now defunct Australian newspaper *National Times* summed up the problem:

Some greenhorn visitors frequently think the tourist is a king who can do no wrong, possessing an unlimited right to see anything he or she wants to see and to grab as much as possible with as little expense as possible. 'Do you sell tickets for a wedding tour?' 'I want to see a cremation today.' 'Can you give me a good price?' 'How much do you charge to see a tooth filing ceremony?' . . . . I know the Balinese do not cry. But I do. I cry when visitors think that Bali is a huge open stage on which any local activity is exhibited to collect money . . . .

Museum Puri Lukisan

On the main street of Ubud the Museum Puri Lukisan, Museum of Fine Arts, was established in the mid-50s and displays fine examples of modern Balinese art. It was in Ubud that the modern Balinese art movement started, where artists first began to abandon purely religious and court scenes for scenes of everyday life. You enter the museum by crossing a river gully beside the road and wander from building to building through beautiful gardens with pools, statues and fountains.

It's a relatively small museum and has some excellent art but unfortunately these days the buildings and the gardens are beginning to look rather tired, worn and in need of rejuvenation. Nevertheless this gallery, along with the Museum Neka, is worth looking around before you make any decisions about buying art in Ubud. The museum is open 8 am to 4 pm daily and admission is 200 rp.

Museum Neka

Continue beyond the suspension bridge and Campuhan and a km or so up the road is the Museum Neka. Housed in a number of separate buildings the museum has a diverse and interesting collection, principally of modern art. It also includes an excellent and varied display of works by western artists who have resided in Bali like Arie Smit, Han Snel, Antonio Blanco, Theo Meier and Donald Friend. Admission is 200 rp.

Western Artists

The western artists who 'discovered' Bali and its art between the wars encouraged a massive artistic revival. Prior to their arrival 'art' was purely something for temples and palaces, immovable and rigid in its ideals and format. Walter Spies and Rudolf Bonnet, two of the first western artists to change these attitudes – for better or worse – both lived for some time at Campuhan, near the suspension bridge. Bonnet, a Dutchman, was in Bali from 1928 to 1958 and was imprisoned by the Japanese during WW II. Walter Spies disappeared on a ship during the war.

These original artists have been followed by many others right down to the present day. Just beside the suspension bridge, across the river from Murni's, the driveway leads up to Filipino-born artist Antonio Blanco's superbly theatrical house. Entry to the house and gallery is 200 rp, well worthwhile as it's a beautiful place. His speciality is erotic art and illustrated poetry.

The other well known western artist currently resident in Bali is Dutch-born Han Snel but many others have made their mark. Arie Smit, who is credited with inspiring the 'young artist' school of painting, lived near Penestanan around 1960 and it was his painting instruction to local boys that sparked off the movement. Swiss Theo Meier and the Australian Donald Friend are other well-known western artists who have worked in Bali

Ubud Walks

Ubud is a place for leisurely strolls – wanders through the rice paddies, lazy rambles through the forests, walks to surrounding villages. There are lots of interesting places in the area, including Ubud's famous monkey forest.

Monkey Forest Walks Just wander down the Monkey Forest Rd from the centre of Ubud and you'll arrive in a small but dense forest. It's inhabited by a handsome band of monkeys ever ready for passing tourists who just might have peanuts available for a hand-out. There's an interesting old pura dalem, temple of the dead, in the forest. You can walk to

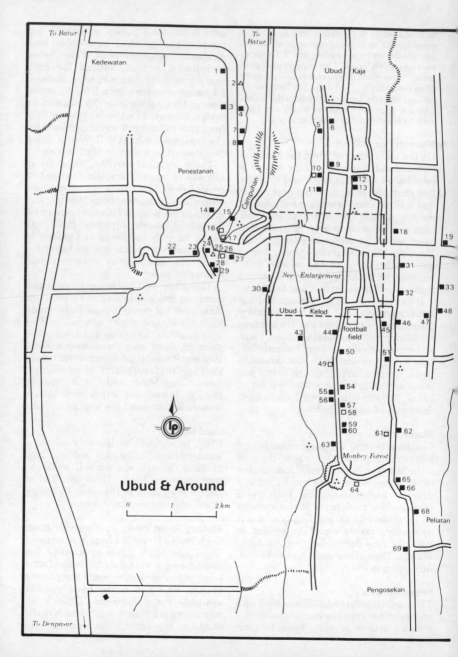

To Batur

To Batur

Kedewatan

Ubud Kaja

1

2

3

4

5   6

7

8

9

10

11

12

13

Penestanan

Campuhan

14   15

16

17

18

19

22   23   24   25   26

27

28

29

31

30

See Enlargement

32

33

Ubud   Kelod

46   47   48

43   44   45

football
field

50   51

49

54

55   56

57

58

59

60

61   62

63

Monkey Forest

64

65   66

68

Peliatan

69

Pengosekan

Ubud & Around

0   1   2 km

To Denpasar

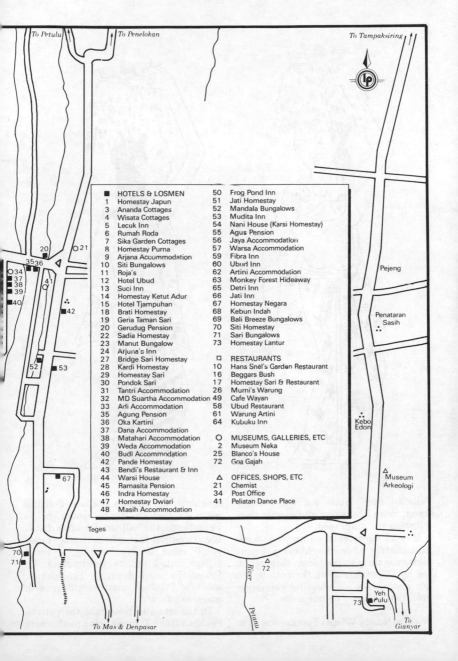

To Petulu
To Penelokan
To Tampaksiring

HOTELS & LOSMEN

1	Homestay Japun
3	Ananda Cottages
4	Wisata Cottages
5	Lecuk Inn
6	Rumah Roda
7	Sika Garden Cottages
8	Homestay Purna
9	Arjana Accommodation
10	Siti Bungalows
11	Roja's
12	Hotel Ubud
13	Suci Inn
14	Homestay Ketut Adur
15	Hotel Tjampuhan
18	Brati Homestay
19	Geria Taman Sari
20	Gerudug Pension
22	Sadia Homestay
23	Manut Bungalow
24	Arjuna's Inn
27	Bridge Sari Homestay
28	Kardi Homestay
29	Homestay Sari
30	Pondok Sari
31	Tantri Accommodation
32	MD Suartha Accommodation
33	Arli Accommodation
35	Agung Pension
36	Oka Kartini
37	Dana Accommodation
38	Matahari Accommodation
39	Weda Accommodation
40	Budi Accommodation
42	Pande Homestay
43	Bendi's Restaurant & Inn
44	Warsi House
45	Ramasita Pension
46	Indra Homestay
47	Homestay Dwiari
48	Masih Accommodation
50	Frog Pond Inn
51	Jati Homestay
52	Mandala Bungalows
53	Mudita Inn
54	Nani House (Karsi Homestay)
55	Agus Pension
56	Jaya Accommodation
57	Warsa Accommodation
59	Fibra Inn
60	Ubud Inn
62	Artini Accommodation
63	Monkey Forest Hideaway
65	Detri Inn
66	Jati Inn
67	Homestay Negara
68	Kebun Indah
69	Bali Breeze Bungalows
70	Siti Homestay
71	Sari Bungalows
73	Homestay Lantur

RESTAURANTS

10	Hans Snel's Garden Restaurant
16	Beggars Bush
17	Homestay Sari & Restaurant
26	Murni's Warung
49	Cafe Wayan
58	Ubud Restaurant
61	Warung Artini
64	Kubuku Inn

MUSEUMS, GALLERIES, ETC

2	Museum Neka
25	Blanco's House
72	Goa Gajah

OFFICES, SHOPS, ETC

21	Chemist
34	Post Office
41	Peliatan Dance Place

Pejeng

Penataran Sasih

Kebo Edon

Museum Arkeologi

Teges

To Mas & Denpasar

River Petanu

To Gianyar

Yeh Pulu

Peliatan from Ubud via the monkey forest, more interesting and quieter than following the main road.

If you turn right down the track immediately after the Monkey Forest Hideaway there's a pool down the gorge on the left. Continue down the path to the left where there's a beautiful swimming hole. Often there's no-one there.

Walks to Nearby Villages Popular strolls to neighbouring villages include Peliatan with its famous dance troupe or to Penestanan, the 'village of young artists'. If you continue through the monkey forest you'll come to Nyuhkuning, a small village noted for its woodcarvers. Or follow the road down to Pengosekan, south of Peliatan, another village with many painters.

In the late afternoon take the path to Petulu, off the Tampaksiring road, where towards sunset every day you can enjoy the spectacular sight of thousands of herons arriving home. Take the trail up beside the river on the Ubud side of Murni's to the beautiful Hill of Campuhan. Or walk to the lovely river Sungai Ayung near the village of Sayan.

Pejeng Walk If you take the road out of Ubud and continue straight on past the *apotik* (pharmacy) at the T-junction there's a wonderful trail that leads through typical Balinese country to the superb gorge of the river that runs by Goa Gajah. Following the trail beyond the river eventually brings you out at Pejeng, a very fine walk. From there you can take a bemo back to Ubud.

Bentuyung Walk Just walk straight north (uphill) from the bemo crossroads through Sambahan and Sakti to Bentuyung. Take the path to the right through the fields and wade across the shallow river. You can continue to Tegal Lantang and Taman or loop back via Junjungan to Kutuh and back to the main road near Peliatan. You can also cross from Junjungan to Petulu to see the herons. This complete loop is about eight km and it's a beautiful walk.

Around Town It's equally interesting just wandering around right in the heart of town. Look around the market in the early morning, it's across the road from the old puri in the centre of town. Or sip a coffee in the *Lotus Cafe* and gaze across the lotus-filled pond a little further up the road.

There are often dances in Ubud – at the Puri Ubud or the Peliatan dance place which is at the turn-off one down from the post office road. Ubud is a great place to study dancing or almost anything to do with Bali. You're likely to meet many travellers here on a long-term visit, studying something about Bali.

If you're wandering the streets of Ubud sometime look for the little black signs by each gateway. They detail the name of the occupant, his occupation and other vital details – like the number of LK (laki means boys), PR (prempuan means girls) and JML (jumlah means total). In one early morning stroll the biggest I saw were 8 + 6 = 14 and 7 + 8 = 15! Few families seem to have less than five or six children.

Places to Stay

Ubud used to have only a handful of accommodation possibilities but there has been quite a boom in new places opening. They are mainly at the cheaper end of the price scale – prices in Ubud generally start lower than in Kuta and stay lower most of the way up. There are only a few 'top end' places and they're really more medium priced in comparison to the real upper bracket hotels of Sanur or Kuta. You'll find places fairly widely scattered around Ubud – there are places along the main road and on the roads leading off it. In particular the Monkey Forest Rd has become a real centre for new places to stay with more places still under construction all the way down to the forest.

There are also lots of places in surrounding villages like Peliatan or Penestanan or simply scattered around the rice paddies. If you are in a remote losmen – and they can be very relaxing, peaceful places to stay – it's probably wise to have a torch (flashlight) with you if you want to avoid actually falling in to the rice paddies on some starry, starry night. Since Ubud is full of artists and dancers you can often find a losmen run by someone involved with the arts – where you can pick up some of the guidelines of Bali's art.

Places to Stay – bottom end

Ubud has a huge choice of places to stay so what follows is really just a sample. There are many other excellent places apart from those mentioned. Cheaper losmen in Ubud generally start around 6000 rp for simple doubles with attached mandi and go up to around 15,000 rp for the flashiest bottom-end places.

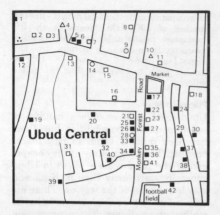

Ubud Central

In Ubud There are lots of places in the bottom end price bracket down the Monkey Forest Rd including, close to the top of the road, one of Ubud's really long runners – *Canderi's*. It's a fairly straightforward losmen-style place with rooms at 5000/7000 rp. Canderi's has been going almost as long as travellers have been staying in Ubud.

There are lots of other places along the Monkey Forest Rd, like *Igna Accommodation*, *Ibu Rai's* or *Sari Nadi*, just round the corner towards the rice paddies with rooms including attached mandi for 6000 rp. A little further down the Monkey Forest Rd is *Warsi's House*, a good friendly place to stay with excellent food. The similarly priced *Karyawan Losmen* is also good and they do great breakfasts, reported one happy visitor.

Continuing down the road towards the monkey forest other places include the *Bendi Inn*, a standard, well kept losmen with rooms at 6000 and 7000 rp. Or there's the very clean and well kept *Frog Pond Inn* with rooms at 5000/8000 rp including an excellent and very filling breakfast. A sign in the entrance area suggests that if there's nobody around you should just find a vacant room and make yourself at home. *Nani's House* is another place which has been recommended. There are rooms from 4000 rp or upstairs rooms at 8000 rp, good for watching the ducks splashing in the rice paddies at sunset.

Right at the bottom, almost in the

forest, is the secluded and pleasant *Monkey Forest Hideaway*. The rooms cost from 12,000 to 15,000 rp and some of them, with balconies looking out over the rice paddies and monkey forest, are quite romantic.

Back up at the main road, down the road opposite the Monkey Forest Rd, the *Suci Inn* is across from the banyan tree. This is a straightforward losmen-style place with simple rooms with bathroom at 6000 rp including black rice pudding for breakfast. The rooms all have small verandah areas looking out on to the central garden and it's a friendly, relaxed place pleasantly quiet yet very central. There are some better rooms at the back at 7500 rp and Ketut, the manager, also has three 12,500 rp rooms at his parent's house further up the road. He's talking of opening a small losmen of his own which, if it eventuates, might be called *Ketut's Place*.

Next door to the Suci Inn is the old *Hotel Ubud*, one of Ubud's oldest places; for many years it was called the 'Hotel Oboed', the Dutch spelling indicating its age.

There are a number of places along the main road through Ubud – like the long running *Geria Taman Sari*, a bit above the road on the left-hand side as you come in from Denpasar. The *Agung Pension* is fairly new, clean and friendly. Or on the post office road there's the reasonably priced *Budi Losmen*, good breakfasts too. *M D Suartha's Losmen* is also excellent value.

Around Ubud There are lots of places around Ubud, either in neighbouring villages or just out in the rice paddies. Cross the suspension bridge by Murni's, for example, and take the steep path uphill by Blanco's house. There you'll find a pretty little group of homestays including the appealing *Kardi* in the rice paddies – secluded and quiet yet really no distance from the road.

In this same area, right behind and above Antonio Blanco's house, is the attractive *Arjuna's Inn*, run by the artist's daughter. The rooms are small but have attached mandi and toilet and cost 6000 to 8000 rp with breakfast. There are more places further up into the rice paddies around Penestanan, or down almost any road into the rice paddies on the south side of the road through Ubud.

You'll find quite a few other places out of Ubud on the Peliatan road. At the junction where the road bends sharp left to Denpasar you'll see a sign for the *Sari Homestay*, just 100 metres or so off the road. It has become somewhat run down over the years but it's still a pretty and popular little place right by the rice paddies and at 2500/3500 rp for singles/doubles the prices are hard to beat. The *Siti Homestay* is a new place with a beautiful garden, charming owners and big breakfasts all for around 4000 rp.

Take the back road from Peliatan to Ubud and you'll pass the *Bali Breeze* with rooms at 12,000 rp or the pleasant *Jati Inn*, two-storey rooms with great views across the rice paddies. Turn down towards the Monkey Forest from this road and you reach *Artini Accommodation* a friendly place with a beautiful garden.

Places along the main road from Peliatan towards Ubud include the pleasant *Mudita Inn* with its shady garden, 'and lovely porridge!' reported one guest. Or there are places still further out from Ubud, like the pleasant little *Homestay Lantur* right where the road ends and you start out through the rice paddies from Bedulu to Yeh Pulu.

Places to Stay – middle

A short distance down the Monkey Forest Rd and off to the right you'll find *Okawati's Homestay*, a very pleasant and clean place right on the rice paddies with doubles at 20,000 to 26,000 rp. The rooms are a definite notch above average with bathrooms, fans, bedside lights and other little luxuries.

A bit further down, almost at the

monkey forest, is the popular *Ubud Inn* with rooms at US$20 and double-storey rooms at US$22 including breakfast. The rooms are brick with carved wood and thatched roofs and they're quite cool, each with a private bathroom. The double-storey rooms have two beds downstairs and two more upstairs and an upstairs verandah ideal for gazing out over the rice paddies. They do excellent Balinese food here if you give them some warning.

On the main road near the Puri Lukisan Museum, the *Mumbul Inn* has rooms at 8000/12,000 rp – self-contained bungalows and close to the centre of Ubud. Some distance out of town, opposite the Museum Neka, *Ananda Cottages* are very calm, relaxed and pretty with rooms at 20,000/25,000 rp including breakfast or big two-storey rooms for 35,000 rp.

Places to Stay - top end

Just up beyond the suspension bridge is the *Hotel Tjampuhan* (or Campuhan if you use the modern spelling). This long-established hotel is beautifully situated overlooking the river and temple. The rooms are individual bungalows in a wonderful garden and cost US$20/30 including breakfast. It's not a hotel for those in search of all the western comforts and modern conveniences although the hotel, owned by a Balinese prince, even has a spring-fed swimming pool on the edge of a cliff. The pool was built by artist Walter Spies back in the '30s. He actually lived for a time in one of the bungalows here. The hotel had become somewhat run down but seems to be going through some renovations.

On the Ubud side of the bridge *Murni's Bungalows* are near the well known Murni's Warung, one of Ubud's most popular restaurants, perched high above the Campuhan River. Follow the river north to *Ulun Ubud* with beautiful bungalows clinging precariously to the steep sides of the ravine. There's a swimming pool here.

Artist Han Snel's luxurious *Siti Bungalows* are well-equipped individual cottages with all mod cons in a beautiful garden for US$35 to US$40. They're pleasantly quiet, back off the main road, but right in the middle of town.

On the main road the pleasant and well kept *Puri Saraswati*, by the palace of that name, has rooms at US$25/30 or bungalows at US$12/15 including breakfast.

The *Hotel Puri Saren Agung*, near the bemo stop in the centre of Ubud, is part of the home of the late head of Ubud's royal family. The bungalows each have a private courtyard and displays of Balinese antiques.

There are some interesting places to try outside Ubud. A visitor wrote to recommend the *Kupu Kupu Barong Bungalows* in Kedewatan, past the Neka Museum, north of Ubud. Six two-storey bungalows perch on the edge of a ravine, each with bedrooms upstairs and downstairs and superb open-air bathrooms, some even with spa baths. There are wonderful views down to the river from the verandah along the front of each bungalow. They're not cheap!

Taman Harum in nearby Mas has also been recommended. Some of the elegant individual bungalows are two-storey with balconies overlooking the rice paddies and there's also a swimming pool. The food, however, did not get such a high rating.

Dogs – if there's one thing wrong with Bali that's what it has to be, those horrible, mangy, flea-bitten, grovelling, dirty, noisy, disgusting *anjings* – that's the Indonesian word for dog, in Balinese a dog is *asu* in high Balinese, *cicing* in low. Or, if you prefer, asu when you're referring to dogs in a good way, cicing in a bad. Dogs are rarely referred to as asu !

Just why does Bali have so many dogs? Well they're scavengers, garbage clearers, and they're simply accepted as part of the picture. It's widely, and probably correctly, thought that demons inhabit them, which is why you often see them gobbling down the offerings put out for the bad spirits. A popular theory is that they were created simply to keep things in balance – with everything so beautiful and picturesque the dogs are put there to provide a contrast. Ubud, incidentally, is particularly well endowed with anjings; terrible, apocalyptic dogs that howl all night long like it's the end of the world.

Places to Eat

In the past Ubud was very restricted in the restaurant department but now you've got a wide choice, some really interesting places and quite probably the best food to be found in Bali.

Happily some of Ubud's 'original' institutions are still going strong. *Okawati's*, a long term favourite, is just off the Monkey Forest Rd and still a pleasant, friendly and economical place to eat. There are no surprises here but for 1000 rp you can have a good mee goreng (fried noodles) or excellent pancakes. Actually on the Monkey Forest Rd, just down from the market, *Canderi's* is another long-running institution which travellers from the early '70s will remember well, although it now has a new restaurant area.

There's plenty of other places to choose along the Monkey Forest Rd. Starting from the main road end you could sample *Harry Chew's* a basic but very popular warung. The food can be rather variable but it always seems to be crowded and the owner is quite a character. A little further down *Lilies* is a new and interesting place with a menu featuring dishes like ayam jeruk (lemon chicken) for 3000 rp or Balinese-style nasi campur for 2000 rp. And a tendency to run out of things!

Further down the Monkey Forest Rd it's an idea to bring a light at night as it can get very dark. *Cafe Wayan* is another relatively new place with some really delicious food including curry ayam (curried chicken) at 3400 rp, saffron chicken at 3500 rp, special dishes like smoked duck or rijstaffel at around 10,000 rp and a famous coconut pie for 1000 rp. Even further down the road you come to the *Ubud Restaurant*, a quiet and peaceful place looking out over the rice paddies. The food here is very well prepared and includes some Balinese dishes – try the coconut satay which is really more than enough for one. They have fine pancakes too.

You'll find a number of good places to eat along the main road of Ubud including one of Ubud's best restaurants, *Murni's*, right down by the suspension bridge. The food here is excellent, the setting is beautiful, there are some interesting arts and crafts on sale and also a small but very good selection of books on Bali. All in all it's well worth the higher prices – satay for 2500 rp served in a personal charcoal holder, a fantastic nasi campur for 1800 rp, even a pretty good burger for 1800 rp. Their cakes are simply superb. Murni's is closed on Wednesdays.

Closer to the centre the *Lotus Cafe* is a relaxed place for a light lunch or a snack any time. It's not cheap but it is very good – their cheesecake at 1500 rp is a real taste treat. They do good Indonesian food from 2000 rp and a variety of western dishes including pastas from 3000 to 5000 rp. It's closed on Mondays. Ubud is something of an international jet setters haven and Murni's and the Lotus are where they're likely to be.

Other places on the main road include the *Puri Pusaka*, opposite the market with a lengthy menu of Indonesian and Balinese specialities. The *Roof Garden Restaurant* has somewhat westernised food and also provides accommodation.

Han Snel's Garden Restaurant, back off the main road, is not cheap by Balinese standards but a great place to eat. A complete meal for two will cost about 20,000 rp – good food, copious quantities, a beautiful setting (frogs croak in the background) and impeccable service. Their 4000 rp 'mini-rijstaffel' is superb. It's closed on Sundays.

There are plenty of other places. Almost in the centre on the main road is *Ary's Warung* with great gado-gado. Round the corner is *Rumah Makan Kartika*. Further down the main road is the *Nomad Restaurant* or back towards the river is the *Griya Barbecue*. Above the bridge, across the river from Murni's, *Beggar's Bush* has a pleasant bar with draught Bintang beer. It's the local Hash House Harriers meeting point. There are also places along the Peliatan road and, of course, countless warungs.

Finding real Balinese food in Bali is often far from easy but Ketut Suartana, the young man who runs the small *Suci Inn*, offers his guests, and others who care to drop by and enquire, an opportunity to sample real Balinese food at its best. He regularly takes groups of visitors back to his parents' home, further up the road from the Suci Inn, and puts on a Balinese feast for 7000 rp per person. You can contact Ketut either through the Suci Inn or the Suci Store, further up the road in front of his parent's house.

A typical meal would include duck or Balinese satay, which is a minced and spiced meat wrapped around a wide stick and quite different from the usual Indonesian satay. A variety of vegetables will include several that we normally think of as fruits – like papaya, nangkur (jackfruit) and blimbing. *Paku* is a form of fern and *ketela potton* is tapioca leaves, both prepared as tasty vegetables. Red onions known as *anyang* and cucumber known as *ketimun* will also feature. Then there will be gado-gado and mee goreng, both prepared in Balinese style, and a special Balinese dish of duck livers cooked in banana leaves and coconut. Of course there will be krupuks (prawn crackers) and rice. To drink there will be *brem* (Bali rice wine) and you'll finish up with Balinese coffee, peanuts and bananas.

The dining area is decorated with palm-leaf decorations, again as for a Balinese feast and a gamelan player tinkles away in the background. It's fun, delicious and a rare chance to sample real Balinese food but it's also a great opportunity to learn more about Bali and its customs as Ketut talks about his house, his family and answers all sorts of questions about life in Bali.

Things to Buy
Ubud has a wide variety of shops and the inevitable art galleries. It's also worth investigating smaller places or places further out from the centre. As elsewhere in Bali so much is completely standard

that it's a real pleasure when you find the odd really different or interesting piece of work. Murni's, down by the river, always seems to have something unusual – pretty cushion covers, carved and painted mirror frames, strange pottery.

Small shops by the market on the Monkey Forest Rd or further down that road often have good wood carvings, particularly masks. M Nama, on the Peliatan corner, also has lots of interesting wood carvings. There are some other good wood carving places along the road from here to Goa Gajah. At Goa Gajah there is a host of stalls selling leatherwork. You'll find good places for paintings along the main road through Ubud or beyond the bridge towards the Museum Neka. The main problem with Ubud is there are simply so many places and it is difficult to find items that rise above the average standard.

Getting There & Away
Bemos from Denpasar to Ubud are 600 rp. The bemos in Ubud start from beside the cinema in the middle of town. Bemos from Kuta can be chartered for 15,000 rp straight off, 12,000 rp with a bit of bargaining.

If you want to go further afield from Ubud you'll have to go down to Gianyar or even back to Denpasar to catch a bus since Ubud is off the main routes to towns in the mountains, to the east and to the north coast. If you're staying in Ubud and have gone to Denpasar or Kuta for the day remember that the last bemo back will probably leave Denpasar's Kereneng station around 4 pm. If you miss it you'll either have to charter one or stay overnight somewhere, which could prove expensive.

Getting Around
To the places around Ubud you can generally count on paying 100 to 250 rp by bemo. Count on about 25 rp a km with a 100 rp minimum. There are a number of places in Ubud where you can hire

bicycles (2000 rp a day) or motorcycles or cars.

One traveller's final memory of Ubud:

.... walking back from a late night festival in Mas along a road surrounded by croaking or squeaking frogs and crickets and lit by glimpses of fireflies. Magic.

DENPASAR TO UBUD

The route from Denpasar to Ubud is heavily trafficked and lined with craft shops and galleries. This is the tourist shopping centre of Bali but there are also alternative, quieter routes between the two towns.

Batubulan

Soon after leaving Denpasar the roadsides are lined with outlets for the Batubulan craft – stone sculpture. This is where those temple gate guardians – seen all over Bali – come from. You'll also find them guarding bridges or making more mundane appearances in restaurants and hotels. The sculpting is often done by quite young boys and you're welcome to watch them chipping away at big blocks of stone. The stone they use is surprisingly soft and even more surprisingly light. If you've travelled to Bali fairly light it's quite feasible to fly home with a demonic stone character in your baggage!

Not surprisingly the temples around Batubulan are noted for their fine stone sculptures. Pura Puseh, just a couple of hundred metres from the road, is worth a visit. There is also a Barong dance, popular with tourists, held in Batubulan every day.

Celuk

Travelling on from Batubulan to Celuk takes you from stone to filigree for Celuk is the silverwork centre of Bali. The craft shops that line the road here are dedicated to jewellery. Other centres for silverwork in Bali include Kamasan near Klungkung and Kuta.

Batuan & Sukawati

Further on, before the turn-off to Mas and Ubud, are the villages of Batuan and Sukawati. Sukawati is a centre for the manufacture of those noisy wind chimes you see all over the island. Batuan is a noted painting centre.

Mas

Mas means 'gold' but it's wood carving which is the craft here. The great priest Nirartha once lived here and Pura Taman Pule is said to be built on the site of his home. Again the road through Mas is almost solidly lined with craft shops and you are welcome to drop in and see the carvers at work, as well as inspecting the myriad items for sale.

Blahbatuh

Although the most direct route to Ubud is to turn off the main road at Sakah and head north through Mas, you can continue on a few km to the turn-off to Blahbatuh and go via Kutri and Bedulu before turning off again for Ubud. In Blahbatuh the Pura Gaduh has a metre-high stone head said to be a portrait of Kebo Iwa, the legendary strongman and last king of the Bedulu kingdom (see Bedulu). Gajah Mada, the Majapahit strongman, realised that he could not conquer Bedulu, Bali's strongest kingdom, while Kebo Iwa was there so he lured him away to Java (with promises of women and song) and had him killed.

The stone head is thought to be very old, possibly predating Javanese influence in Bali, but the temple is a reconstruction of an earlier temple destroyed in the great earthquake of 1917.

Kutri

Just beyond Blahbatuh you can climb the hill from Pura Bukit Dharma and find a hill-top shrine with a stone statue of Durga thought to date from the 11th century and showing strong Indian influences. Between here and Klungkung the road crosses a series of deep gorges, the bridges rising high above the valleys below.

AROUND UBUD

The Pejeng region encompasses many of the most ancient monuments and relics in Bali, some of them well known and very much on the beaten track, others relatively unknown and little visited.

Getting There & Away

You can reach the places around Ubud by bemo and on foot. If you're planning to see a lot of them it's a good idea to go straight up to Tampaksiring to start with, then any walking you have to do is back downhill. It's only a km or two downhill from Tirta Empul at Tampaksiring to Gunung Kawi, and you can follow the path beside the river and come out right in Gunung Kawi.

From there you can take bemos back down to Pejeng, Bedulu, Goa Gajah and on to Ubud. Pejeng to the Bedulu turn-off is only about a km and from there it's a half km or so to Yeh Pulu and a similar distance to Goa Gajah. Alternatively from Pejeng you can cut across country directly to Ubud, a pleasant walk with fine views. See the Ubud Walks section for more information.

Goa Gajah

Only a short distance beyond Peliatan, on the road to Pejeng and Gianyar, a car park on the north side of the road marks the site of Goa Gajah. The elephant cave is carved into the rock face, reached by a flight of steps down from the other side of the road. There were never any elephants in Bali, the cave-hermitage probably takes its name from the nearby Petanu River. You enter the cave through the cavernous mouth of a demon, while gigantic fingertips pressed beside the face push back a riotous jungle of surrounding stone carvings.

Goa Gajah was certainly in existence at the time of the Majapahit take over of Bali. It probably dates back to the 11th century and shows elements of both Hindu and Buddhist use. In front of the cave are two square bathing pools with water gushing into them from water spouts held by six female figures. These were only uncovered in 1954. You can clamber down through the rice paddies to crumbling rock carvings of stupas on a cliff face and a small cave. Admission to Goa Gajah is 200 rp (children 100 rp).

Yeh Pulu

Although it's only a km or so from Goa Gajah to Yeh Pulu few visitors get there – it's amazing the difference between a place with a car park beside it and a place you have to walk to through the rice paddies! It's quite easy to find your way there. At the end of the road there's a sign which points to the path that follows the small cliff face most of the way. It's as picturesque as any tramp through the paddies in Bali – there are ups and downs, small streams gurgling by and Heath Robinson bamboo contraptions channelling water across gullies from one series of paddies to another.

Eventually a small gateway leads to the ancient rock carvings at Yeh Pulu. Only excavated in 1925 these are some of the oldest relics in Bali. The carved cliff face is about 25 metres long and is believed to be a hermitage dating from the 14th century. Apart from the figure of elephant-headed Ganesh, the son of Shiva, there are no religious scenes here. The energetic frieze includes various scenes of everyday life – two men carrying an animal slung from a pole, a man slaying a beast with a dagger (and a frog imitating him by disposing of a snake in like manner – clearly the Balinese sense of humour is not new!), and a man on horseback pulling a captive woman along behind him.

On the way through the rice paddies to Yeh Pulu you pass a bathing place with female fountains remarkably similar to those at Goa Gajah. The Ganesh figures of Yeh Pulu and Goa Gajah are also quite

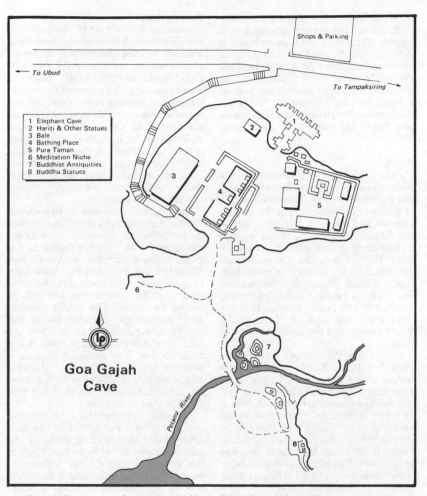

To Ubud

To Tampaksiring

Shops & Parking

1 Elephant Cave
2 Hariti & Other Statues
3 Bale
4 Bathing Place
5 Pura Taman
6 Meditation Niche
7 Buddhist Antiquities
8 Buddha Statues

Goa Gajah
Cave

Petanu River

similar, indicating a close relationship between the two sites.

Bedulu
Just beyond Goa Gajah is the road junction where you turn south for Gianyar or north for Pejeng and Tampaksiring. It's hard to imagine Bedulu, the small village at the junction, as the former capital of a great kingdom. The legendary Dalem

Bedaulu ruled the Pejeng dynasty from here and was the last Balinese king to withstand the onslaught of the powerful Majapahits from Java. Finally in 1343 he was defeated by Gajah Mada and the capital shifted several times, eventually ending up at Gelgel and then Klungkung.

A legend relates how Bedaulu possessed magical powers which even allowed him to have his head chopped off and then replaced. Performing this unique party trick one day the servant entrusted with lopping off his head and then replacing it unfortunately dropped it in a river and to his horror watched it float away. Looking around in panic for a replacement he grabbed a pig, cut its head off and popped it upon the king's shoulders. Thereafter the king was forced to sit on a high throne and forbid his subjects to look up at him.

Pejeng

Up the road to Tampaksiring from the Bedulu junction you soon come to Pejeng and its famous temple. There are a couple of places of interest between the Bedulu junction and there. First on your right is the Museum Arkeologi. Then a little further along on your left is the temple of Pura Kebo Edan, the Crazy Buffalo Temple, with it's nearly four-metre-high statue of Bima, liberally endowed with no less than six penises! Other interesting temples in the Pejeng area include the Pura Puser ing Jagat or Navel of the World temple and the monastery of Goa Garba.

As you enter Pejeng itself the temple of Pura Penataran Sasih, once the state temple of the Kingdom of Pejeng, is on your right. In the inner courtyard, high up in a pavilion where you really cannot see it very well, is the huge bronze drum known as the 'Moon of Pejeng'. It is believed to be over 1000 years older than the Kingdom of Pejeng itself, a relic from the Bronze Age in Indonesia. The hourglass-shaped drum is over three metres long, the largest single piece cast drum in the world.

A Balinese legend relates how the drum came to earth as a fallen moon, landing in a tree and shining so brightly that it prevented a band of thieves from going about their unlawful purpose. One of the thieves decided to put the light out by urinating on it but the moon exploded, killed the foolhardy thief and fell to earth as a drum – with a crack across its base as a result of the fall.

Gunung Kawi

Continuing up the road to Tampaksiring you pass through pleasant rice land along a steady upward climb which continues all the way to the rim of the crater at Penelokan. In the small town of Tampaksiring a sign points off the road to the right to Gunung Kawi. From the end of the access road a steep stone stairway leads down to the river, at one point making a cutting through an embankment of solid rock. There, in the bottom of this lush green valley with beautiful rice terraces climbing up the hillsides, is one of Bali's oldest, and certainly largest, ancient monuments.

Gunung Kawi consists of 10 rock-cut *candis*, memorials cut out of the rock face in imitation of normally constructed monuments – in a similar fashion to the great rock-cut temples of Ajanta and Ellora in India. The *candis* are believed to be memorials to members of the Balinese royalty of the 11th century but little is known for certain. The *candis* stand in seven-metre-high sheltered niches cut into the sheer rock cliff faces. There are four on the west side of the river which you come to first. You cross the river on a bridge to a further group of five on the east side. A solitary *candi* stands further down the valley to the south, reached by a trek through the rice paddies.

Legends relate that the whole group of memorials were carved out of the rock faces in one hard working night by the mighty fingernails of Kebo Iwa. Each of the sets of memorials has a group of monks' cells associated with it, including one on the east side with the only 'no shoes, sandals, boots may be worn' sign I've ever seen in Bali. There are other similar groups of *candis* and monks' cells within the area of the ancient Kingdom of Pejeng – but none of them so grand or on so large a scale.

Tampaksiring – Tirta Empul

Continuing through the actual town of Tampaksiring the road branches, the left fork running up to the grand palace once used by Sukarno while the right fork goes to the temple at Tirta Empul and continues up to Penelokan. You can look back along the valley and see Gunung Kawi from this road, just before you turn into Tirta Empul. The holy springs at Tirta Empul are believed to have magical powers so the temple here is an important one.

Each year an inscribed stone is brought from a nearby village to be ceremonially washed in the spring. The inscription on the stone has been deciphered and indicates that the springs were founded in 962 AD. The actual springs bubble up into a large, crystal-clear tank within the temple and gush out through water-spouts into a bathing pool. According to legend the springs were created by the god Indra who pierced the earth to tap the 'elixir of immortality', *amerta*. Despite its antiquity the temple is glossy and gleamingly new – it was totally restored in the late '60s.

The springs of Tirta Empul are a source of the Pakrisan River, which rushes by Gunung Kawi only a km or so away. Between Tirta Empul and Gunung Kawi is the temple of Pura Mengening where you can see a *candi* similar in design, but free-standing, to the *candis* of Gunung Kawi. There is a spring at this temple which also feeds into the Pakrisan. Overlooking Tirta Empul is the Sukarno palace, a grandiose structure built in 1954 on the site of a Dutch rest-house.

The car park outside Tirta Empul is surrounded by the usual unholy confusion of souvenir and craft shops. Chess sets and bone carving are popular crafts here. There is an admission charge to Tirta Empul and you have to wear a temple scarf.

Places to Stay & Eat Tampaksiring is an easy day trip from Ubud or even Bangli but it is possible to stay here. In the village itself there's the small *Homestay Gusty* and the *Homestay Tampaksiring*.

Apart from the usual selection of warungs there's also the expensive *Tampaksiring Restaurant* for tourist parties, some distance below the village.

UBUD TO BATUR

The usual road from Ubud to Batur is through Tampaksiring but there are other lesser roads up the gentle mountain slope. If you go out of Ubud to the road junction but turn away from Peliatan, towards Petulu, this road will bring you out on the crater rim just beyond Penelokan towards Batur. It's a surfaced road all the way except for a few km near the top where it's cobbled and fairly rough. Along this road you'll see a number of woodcarvers producing all those beautiful painted ducks, birds, frogs, Garudas and tropical fruit. Tegalalang and the nearby village of Jati, just off the road, are noted woodcarving centres. Further up, other specialists carve stools and there are a couple of places which carve whole tree trunks into whimsical figures.

Another route from Ubud to Batur can be followed by taking the road through Campuhan and Saggingan and then turning up the hill, instead of down towards Denpasar, at Kedewatan. On this route you pass through Payangan, the only place in Bali where lychees are grown. It's possible to get bemos some distance up the road on both these routes but at the very top finding public transport can be difficult. The roads, once quite rough, are not bad now.

Of course you could walk up to Batur from Ubud too. If you take the path from near the temple down by the suspension bridge and followed it steadily uphill you'd pass through unspoilt villages like Bangkiang Sidem, Keliki and Sebali. They'd make a nice walk in themselves and from Sebali you can cut across to Tegalalang and get a bemo back to Ubud. And if you keep walking? Well it's 30 km to Batur, uphill all the way.

East Bali

The eastern end of Bali is dominated by mighty Gunung Agung, the 'navel of the world' and Bali's mother mountain. Towering 3140 metres high Agung has not always been a kind mother – witness the disastrous 1963 eruption. Today Agung is again a quiet though dominating mountain and the mother temple Pura Besakih, perched high on the slopes of the volcano, attracts a steady stream of devotees . . . . and tourists.

The east has a number of places of great interest. Here you'll find Klungkung, former capital of one of Bali's great kingdoms. From here the road runs close to the coast past interesting fishing villages like Kusamba, the bat infested cave temple of Goa Lawah, the beautiful small port of Padangbai, the pretty little Bali Aga village of Tenganan, the popular beach centre of Candidasa, and finally reaches Amlapura, another former capital.

At Amlapura you can about turn and retrace your route or take an alternative route higher up the slopes of Agung to Rendang. From Rendang you can turn north to Besakih, south to Klungkung or continue west on a pretty but lesser-used route to Bangli. As a third alternative you can continue right round the coast from Amlapura to Singaraja in the north. See the north Bali section for more details on this lightly populated coastal route.

The 1963 Eruption

The most disastrous volcanic eruption in Bali this century took place in 1963 when Agung blew its top in no uncertain manner and at a time of considerable prophetic importance; 8 March 1963 was the culmination of *Eka Desa Rudra*, the greatest of all Balinese sacrifices and an event which only takes place every 100 Balinese years. The sacrifices had not been made 100 years previously so it was now 115 of our years since the last *Eka Desa*

Rudra. Naturally the temple at Besakih was a focal point for the festival but Agung was already acting strangely as preparations were made in late February. Agung had been dormant since 1843 but by the time the sacrifices commenced the mountain was belching smoke and ash, glowing and rumbling ominously.

On 17 March 1963 it exploded in a catastrophic eruption that killed more than 1000 people and destroyed entire villages. Streams of lava and hot volcanic mud poured right down to the sea at several places in the south-east of the island, completely covering roads and isolating the whole eastern end of the island for some time thereafter. The entire island was covered in ash and crops were wiped out everywhere. Torrential rainfall that followed the eruptions compounded the damage as boiling hot ash and boulders known as *lahar* were swept down the mountain side, wreaking havoc on many villages like Subagen, just outside Amlapura and Selat, further along the road towards Rendang. All Bali suffered a drastic food shortage and many Balinese, whose rice land was completely ruined, had to be resettled in Sulawesi.

Although Besakih itself is high on the slopes of Agung, only about six km from

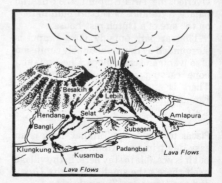

the very crater, it suffered little damage from the eruption. Volcanic dust and gravel flattened timber and bamboo buildings around the temple complex but the stone structures came through unscathed. The inhabitants of the villages of Sorga and Lebih, also high up on Agung's slopes, were all but wiped out. Most of the people killed at the time of the eruption were burnt and suffocated by searing clouds of hot gas that rushed down the volcano slopes. Agung erupted again on 16 May, with serious loss of life but not on the same scale as the March eruption.

The Balinese take signs and portents seriously – that such a terrible event should happen as they were making a most important sacrifice to the gods was not taken lightly. The interrupted series of sacrifices were finally recommenced 16 years later in 1979.

Getting There & Away

Buses for the east of Bali generally depart from the Kereneng bus station in Denpasar. Fares include Klungkung 800 rp, Padangbai 1250 rp, Amlapura 1600 rp and Bangli 800 rp. To get to Besakih take a bus or colt to Klungkung and another colt from there for 500 rp. Klungkung to Amlapura costs about 700 or 800 rp, then from Amlapura to Singaraja buses cost 1800 rp. From Culik, a little beyond Tirtagangga, to Kubutambahan, it's 1500 rp and takes about 3½ hours. Bemos run locally from Amlapura including some going to Tirtagangga.

GIANYAR

On the main road from Denpasar, and still in the region of south Bali plagued by heavy traffic, Gianyar has a number of small textile factories on the Denpasar side of town. You're welcome to drop in, see the materials being woven and even make a purchase. It takes about six hours to weave a complete sarong.

Right in the centre of town the old palace is little changed from the time the Dutch arrived in the south and the old kingdoms lost their power. It's a fine example of traditional palace architecture, surrounded by high brick walls. You can look in through the gates.

SIDAN

Continuing beyond Gianyar you come to the turn-off to Bangli at Sidan, just a few km out of town. Go up the road less than a km from the junction and at a sharp bend you'll find the Sidan Pura Dalem, a good example of a temple of the dead. Note the sculptures of Durga with children by the gate, and the separate walled in enclosure in the front-left corner of the temple – this is dedicated to Merajapati, the guardian spirit of the dead. If you continue up this road to Bangli there's another interesting Pura Dalem at Penunggekan, just before you reach Bangli. See the Bangli section for more details.

BONA

The village of Bona, on the back road between Gianyar and Blahbatuh, is credited with being the modern home of the Kechak dance. Kechak and other dances are held here every week and they're easy to visit from Ubud – tickets inclusive of transport from Ubud are around 4000 rp. Bona is also a basket-weaving centre.

KLUNGKUNG

Klungkung was once the centre of Bali's most important kingdom and a great artistic and cultural focal point. The Gelgel Dynasty, which was the most powerful kingdom in Bali, held power for about 300 years, until the arrival of the Dutch. It was here that the Klungkung school of painting, with its characters all presented in side-profile wayang kulit style, was developed. Today Klungkung-style paintings are still produced but a few km outside Klungkung in Kamasan.

Klungkung is a major bus and colt crossroads – from here you can find transport up to Besakih or further east to

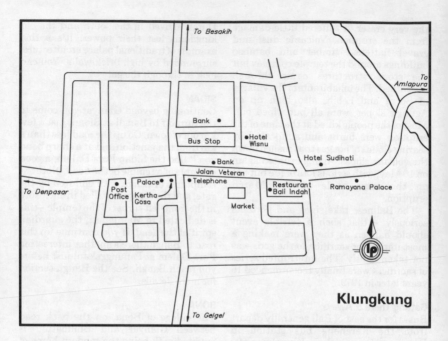

Klungkung

Padangbai, Candidasa and Amlapura. A new bridge crosses the river beyond Klungkung and until its construction in 1985 there were often lengthy traffic jams.

Kertha Gosa

Right beside the road as you reach the centre of town from Denpasar stands the Kertha Gosa or Hall of Justice. Surrounded by a moat this open pavilion is a superb example of Klungkung architecture and the roof is completely painted inside with fine paintings in the Klungkung style. The paintings, done on asbestos sheeting, were installed in the 1940s, replacing cloth paintings which had deteriorated.

This was effectively the 'supreme court' of the Klungkung kingdom, where disputes and cases which could not be settled at the village level would eventually be brought. The defendant would be brought before the three priests who acted

as judges and his gaze could wander to the ceiling where wrongdoers were tortured by demons while the innocent enjoyed the pleasures of Balinese heaven. The capital of the kingdom was shifted to Klungkung from nearby Gelgel in the early 1700s and the Kertha Gosa was probably constructed around the end of that century.

Palace

Adjoining the Kertha Gosa is the palace with its beautiful Bale Kambang or Floating Pavilion. Its ceiling is also painted in Klungkung style, having been repainted in 1945. Around the Kertha Gosa and the Bale Kambang note the statues of top-hatted European figures, an amusing departure from the normal statues of entrance guardians. Admission to the palace and Kertha Gosa is 200 rp (children 100 rp).

Kamasan Paintings

The village of Kamasan, a few km outside of Klungkung, has long been a bastion of traditional painting – the origins of which can be traced back at least 500 years. Highly conventionalised, the symbolism of equating right and left with good and evil, as in the wayang puppet shows, is evident in the compositions and placement of figures in Kamasan paintings. Subject matter derives largely from Balinese variations of the ancient Hindu epics, the Ramayana and the Mahabharata. *Kakawins*, poems written in the archaic Javanese language of Kawi, provide another important source, as does indigenous Balinese folklore with it's pre-Hindu/Buddhist beliefs in demonic spirit forces. The style has also been adapted to large versions of the zodiacal and lunar calendar, especially the 210-day *wuku* calendar which still regulates the timing of Balinese festivals.

The earliest paintings were done on bark cloth, said to have been imported from Sulawesi – though a coarse handspun cloth and later machine-made cloth was used as support. Kamasan art is essentially linear – the skill of the artist was judged by his draughtsmanship and by the sensitivity of his line. The colouring was of secondary importance and left to apprentices, usually the artist's children. Members of the family would assist in preparing the colours, stiffening the cloth with rice paste and polishing the surface smooth to receive the fine ink drawing.

Paintings were hung as ceremonial backdrops in temples and houses and they were also sufficiently prized by the local rulers that they were acceptable gifts to rival royal households. Whilst they were traditionally patronised by the ruling class, paintings also helped fulfil the important function of imparting ethical values and customs – *adat* – to the ordinary people, in much the same way as traditional dance and wayang puppetry. In fact, it is from the wayang tradition that Kamasan painting takes its essential characteristics – the stylisation of human figures, their symbolic gestures, the treatment of divine and heroic characters as refined and evil ones as vulgar and crude, and the primary function of narrating a moral tale.

It's worth noting that there are striking similarities between Kamasan paintings and a now almost totally abandoned form of wayang theatre, the *wayang beber*. The slender horizontal format of Balinese paintings almost certainly derives from the *wayang bebe*, which is a large handscroll, held vertically and unrolled and expounded upon by the puppet-master, accompanied by the gamelan orchestra The wayang beber was still being performed during the Dutch occupation, but a performance now is very rare, although craftsmen in East Java are still producing scenes from such scrolls in the traditional style for the tourist trade.

The wayang style can be traced back to 9th century Javanese sculpture, and its most mature form can be seen at the 14th-century temple complex at Panataran in East Java. The relief sculptures at Panataran display the characteristic wayang figures, the rich floral designs, the flame-and-mountain motifs – all vital elements of Balinese painting. There's a gallery at Banjar Siku selling good quality Kamasan paintings.

Places to Stay & Eat

There are a couple of accommodation possibilities in Klungkung. Close to the centre, just back from the bus station, *Hotel Wishnu* has fairly average rooms at 3000/6000 rp for singles/doubles. It's brighter upstairs than downstairs.

Towards the bridge on the road out of town to Amlapura the *Ramayana Palace* has rooms at 4000/6000 rp. It's a much more pleasant place and set back far enough from the busy main road to be quiet. It also has its own restaurant.

There are several other places around town to eat including the Chinese *Restaurant Bali Indah*.

Things to Buy

There are a number of good shops along Jalan Veteran in Klungkung selling Klungkung-style paintings and some interesting antiques. Klungkung is also a good place for buying temple umbrellas – several shops sell them.

KUSAMBA

Beyond Klungkung the road crosses lava flows from the '63 eruption of Agung and is now much overgrown. The road comes back to the coast at the fishing village of Kusamba. Turn off the main road and go down to the beach to see the lines of colourful fishing prahus lined up on the beach. Fishing is normally done at night and the 'eyes' on the front of the boats help them to see through the darkness. You can charter a boat out to Nusa Penida, clearly visible opposite Kusamba. Regular trips are made out to the island carrying supplies so you can try to get on one of these cargo prahus. The crossing takes several hours.

Just beyond Kusamba you can see the thatched roofs of salt-panning huts along the beach. Saltwater-saturated sand from the beach is dried out around these huts and then further processed inside the huts. You can see the same process being carried out beside the Kuta-Sanur road.

GOA LAWAH

The road continues to run close to the coast beyond Kusamba and after a few km you come to the Bat Cave, Goa Lawah. A cave in the cliff face here is packed, crammed, jammed full of bats. There must be untold thousands of the squeaking, flapping creatures, tumbling and crawling over one another and occasionally launching out of the cave only to zip straight back in as they realise it's still daytime. The cave is, of course, part of a temple and is said to lead all the way to Besakih but it's unlikely anybody would be too enthusiastic about investigating! Entry to the bat cave temple is 200 rp (100 rp children) and it costs another 150 rp to park in the car park.

PADANGBAI

Padangbai is the port for the ferry service between Bali and Lombok. Along with Benoa it's the principal shipping port in the south of the island. Padangbai is a couple of km off the main road, a scruffy little town situated on a perfect little bay, one of the very few sheltered harbours in Bali. It's very picturesque with a long sweep of sand where colourful outrigger fishing boats are drawn up on the beach.

Padangbai can be an interesting place

to spend a day or so if you don't want to simply arrive in the morning and depart straight for Lombok. If you walk round to the right from the wharf and follow the trail up the hill it leads to an idyllic little beach on the exposed coast outside the bay.

The coral reefs around Pulau Kambing, off Padangbai, offer excellent diving possibilities. Gili Toapekong, with a series of coral heads at the top of the drop off, is apparently the best site. The currents here are strong and unpredictable and there are also sharks – it's recommended for experienced divers only.

Cruise ships visiting Bali usually use Padangbai but have to anchor offshore outside the harbour as only small ships can actually enter the bay.

Information

There are no banks or moneychangers in Padangbai so whether you're planning to stay here or continuing on to Lombok make sure you've changed enough money before you get here. Otherwise you may have to backtrack to Klungkung to the nearest bank or continue to Candidasa to find a moneychanger. Johnny, at Johnny's Warung, will sometimes change cash US$ or A$ (not travellers' cheques) into rupiah at a discount.

Places to Stay

On the main street of the small port, just a few steps back from the wharf entrance, *Hotel Madya* has rooms around the courtyard at 6000 rp, each with an attached bathroom and verandah. There may still be some older rooms in the main building, but they're pretty basic.

Most visitors to Padangbai stay at the pleasant beachfront places – go down to the wharf and you'll find them a couple of hundred metres to the left along the beach. First there's the *Rai Beach Inn* with two-storey rooms at 10,000 rp. Next to it is *Sedani Kerthi Beach Bungalows* with rooms at 5000 rp. Finally there's the *Padangbai Beach Inn*, a quiet little

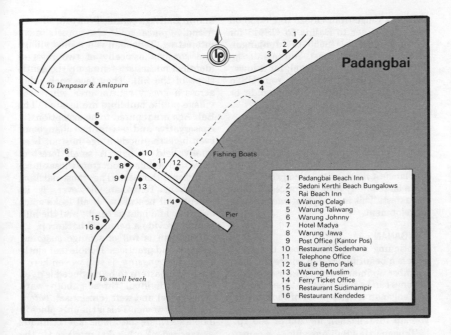

To Denpasar & Amlapura

Padangbai

Fishing Boats

Pier

To small beach

1	Padangbai Beach Inn
2	Sedani Kerthi Beach Bungalows
3	Rai Beach Inn
4	Warung Celagi
5	Warung Taliwang
6	Warung Johnny
7	Hotel Madya
8	Warung Jawa
9	Post Office (Kantor Pos)
10	Restaurant Sederhana
11	Telephone Office
12	Bus & Bemo Park
13	Warung Muslim
14	Ferry Ticket Office
15	Restaurant Sudimampir
16	Restaurant Kendedes

homestay with thatched roof bungalows and attached bathroom at 5000 rp. Padangbai's beach is lovely and with all the colourful fishing boats drawn up it's very picturesque as well.

Places to Eat
Padangbai has a number of restaurants including the *Rumah Makan Candra* at the Hotel Madya. A major road widening project demolished all the places on the northern side of the road so it remains to be seen if restaurants there will re-open. *Johnny's Warung, Warung Jawa* and the *Warung Muslim* are other small places. On the beach near the cluster of losmen is the *Warung Celagi*.

Getting There & Away
See the introductory information on the ferry service between Bali and Lombok for details on the daily ferry from Padangbai.

The ticket office is down by the pier. Buses meet the ferry and go straight to Denpasar. There are also connections from Padangbai right through to Surabaya (13,000 rp) and Yogyakarta (17,500 rp) in Java. Padangbai is a couple of km off the main Klungkung-Amlapura road, 54 km from Denpasar.

BALINA BEACH
It's 11 km from the Padangbai main road turn-off to Candidasa and between the two, about seven km from the turn-off and four km from Candidasa is Balina Beach. This is strictly a one resort development and it is probably the major scuba diving centre for Bali. They have diving equipment for rent and organise snorkelling and diving trips all around Bali including to Nusa Penida or the north coast.

Diving trips including transport and a

full tank range from US$25 to US$35 on the trips closer to Balina to US$45 for Nusa Penida or US$50 to Menjangan Island on the north coast. You can also go on the same trips to snorkel, for a lower cost. Snorkelling trips start from US$5 and go up to U$18 for Nusa Penida or US$20 for Menjangan.

Places to Stay

Balina Beach Bungalows have rooms at a host of prices from as low as US$6/8 for singles/doubles right up to US$22/25 for the fanciest rooms with balcony or US$35 for a large family unit. All prices include breakfast. This is a large, attractive new development.

TENGANAN

Continuing from Padangbai the road enters a beautiful stretch where the hills clamber up inland while glimpses of fine beaches can be seen below. At the turn-off to Tenganan a little posse of motorcycle riders wait by the junction, ready to ferry you up to Tenganan for 200 or 300 rp.

Tenganan is a Bali Aga village, a centre of the original Balinese prior to the Majapahit arrival. Unlike that other well

known Bali Aga centre, Trunyan, this is a friendly place and also much more interesting. Tenganan is a walled village and consists basically of two rows of identical houses stretching up the gentle slope of the hill. They face each other across a grassy central area where the village public buildings are located. The Bali Aga are reputed to be exceptionally conservative and resistant to change but even here the modern age has not been totally held at bay. A small forest of television aerials sprout from those oh-so-traditional houses! The most striking feature of Tenganan, however, is its exceptional neatness – it all looks spick and span and neat as can be and the hills behind provide a beautiful backdrop.

Tenganan is full of strange customs, festivals and practices. Double ikat cloth, known as *gringsing*, is still woven here – where the pattern to be produced is dyed on the individual threads, both warp (lengthwise) and weft (crosswise), *before* the cloth is woven. This is the only place in Indonesia where the double ikat technique is practised, all other ikat produced in the archipelago is single ikat where only the warp or weft, never both, is dyed.

Candidasa

To Tenganan

Denpasar 65 km sign

To Denpasar

	HOTELS & LOSMEN		
1	Pelangi & Homestay Taruna	31	Homestay Sasra Bahu
2	Gotya Homestay	33	Pondok Bamboo Seaside Cottages
3	Catra Homestay	35	Homestay Nakula
4	Saputra Beach Inn	36	Puri Amarta Beach Inn
5	Bambu Garden Bungalows & Restaurant	38	Homestay Natia
6	Homestay Sri Artha	39	Cantiloka Beach Inn
7	Candidasa Beach Bungalows	41	Homestay Ida
10	Homestay Geringsing	42	Homestay Kelapa Mas
13	Homestay Segarawangi	45	Dewi Bungalows
14	Homestay Ayodya	46	Rama Homestay
16	Puri Bali	47	Sindhu Brata Homestay
18	Wiratha's Bungalows	51	Purwa Beach Inn
21	Pandan Losmen & Restaurant	52	Pandawa Homestay
23	Big New Hotel	53	Srikandi Bungalows
25	Homestay Lilaberata	54	Ramayana Guest House
30	Homestay Agung	55	Nani Beach Inn
		56	Puri Pondok Bungalows
		57	Orchid Bungalows

A magical cloth known as *kamben gringsing* is also woven here – a person wearing it is said to be protected against black magic! A peculiar old-fashioned version of the gamelan known as the *gamelan selunding* is still played here and girls dance an equally forgotten dance known as the *Rejang*. At the *Usaba sambah* festival once a year around June or July men fight with their fists wrapped in sharp-edged pandanus leaves – similar events occur on the island of Sumba, far to the east in Nusa Tenggara. At this same festival small man-powered ferris wheels are brought out and the village girls are ceremonially twirled round. There are other Bali Aga villages in the vicinity including Asak where the even more ancient *gamelan gambang* is played.

If you walk right up through the village to the road off to the right you'll see a sign pointing to the home of I Made Muditadnana who produces lontar palm books – the traditional Balinese palm-leaf books. He's a friendly man and well worth visiting but if you're thinking of buying one of his books check the prices at the village handicraft shops first!

There's a delightful legend about how the villagers of Tenganan came to acquire their land. It's a story that in slightly different forms pops up in various places in Indonesia. The Tenganan version relates how Dalem Bedaulu (the king with a pig's head – see the Bedulu section for details) lost a valuable horse and offered to reward the villagers of Tenganan who had found its carcass. They asked that they be given the land where the horse was found – that is all the area where the dead horse could be smelt. The king sent a man with a keen nose who set off with the village chief and walked an enormous distance without ever managing to get away from the foul odour. Eventually accepting that enough was enough the official headed off back to Bedaulu, scratching his head. Once out of sight the village chief pulled a large hunk of dead horse out from under his clothes.

CANDIDASA

Less than a km beyond the turn-off to Tenganan and about 13 km before Amlapura the road runs right down to the coast at Candidasa. In 1983 it was just a quiet little fishing village but two years later a dozen losmen and half a dozen restaurants had sprung up and this was suddenly *the* new beach place in Bali. Fortunately it's still a quiet, relaxed little resort, this isn't Kuta.

Beyond Candidasa the road spirals up to the Pura Gamang pass from where there are fine views down to the coast.

Information

Homestay Kelapa Mas has a book exchange. At night dance performances are often put on at the Pandan Harum dance place. Candidasa has shops, moneychangers and other facilities.

The Beach & the Sea

The beach is great, when the tide's out. When the tide's in it almost completely disappears and you have to take refuge up on the bank behind the beach. Unfortunately the villagers have been attempting to preserve their suddenly valuable strip of beach by building ugly concrete walls

	RESTAURANTS		
8	Yasa Garden Restaurant	43	Warung Rasmini
9	Made's Restaurant	44	Lila Arnawa Stage Restaurant
11	Candidasa Restaurant	48	Budi's Restaurant
12	Cafe Sayang	49	Pizzeria Candi Agung
15	TJ's Restaurant	50	Ngandi Restaurant
17	Ayu Seaside Restaurant		
20	Gusti Restaurant & Pub	●	OTHER
22	Camplung Restaurant	19	Pandun Harum dance place
24	Tunjung Restaurant		
26	Warung Chandra		
27	Depot Sumber Rasa		
28	Hawaii Restaurant		
29	Pandawa Restaurant		
32	Tropical Bar		
34	Pondok Bamboo Restaurant		
37	Murni Restaurant		
40	Sri Jati Restaurant		

against the sea. The most probable result will just be an acceleration of the usual erosion. Still, the water's fine, sheltered, relatively calm and great for children. If you swim out a couple of hundred metres to where the waves break there's good coral and lots of colourful fish.

Just beside the road, at the lagoon, there's a temple built up the hillside. The fishing village, just beyond the lagoon, has colourful fishing prahus drawn up on the beach. In the early morning you can watch them coasting in after a night's fishing. Outriggers regularly appear at Candidasa beach to take snorkellers out to the reef and the nearby islets.

If you follow the beach round from Candidasa towards Amlapura a trail climbs up over the headland with fine views over the rocky islets off the coast. From the headland you can see that although they look as if they're in a straight line, from Candidasa beach it's actually one cluster of the smaller ones plus the solitary larger island isolated off to the east. There's good diving around these islands.

Looking back inland there's no sign at all of the village below or the road – just an unbroken sweep of palm trees. If it's clear Agung rises majestically behind the range of coastal hills. Round the headland there's a long sweep of beach – as wide, black and shadeless as Candidasa is narrow, white and shady.

Places to Stay

Candidasa's losmen are mainly out of the same mould – simple rooms with attached bathroom and a small verandah area out front. They start from the Tenganan turn-off and extend right through the tourist part of the village to the original fishing village, hidden in the palm trees where the road turns away from the coast. Typical prices are from 6000 rp for basic doubles but as at Kuta or Ubud there are so many places to choose from the best advice is simply to wander around and have a look at a few rooms.

Starting at the Denpasar side the *Candidasa Beach Bungalows* are pleasant if a little tightly packed together and cost a rather expensive 30,000 rp. Next to it *Homestay Geringsing* has rooms at 10,000 or at *Wiratha's Bungalows* pleasant rooms with attached mandi are 6000 rp. In between them *Puri Bali's* 12,000 rp rooms are good value, they're simple but clean and well kept.

The *Pandan Losmen* has simple solid rooms at 22,000 rp. *Homestay Lilaberata* is a rock bottom place but quite popular with rooms at 5000, 6000 and 10,000 rp and a discount for longer stays. A big new hotel was built in 1988 between these two.

Pondok Bamboo Seaside Cottages has doubles at 26,000 rp and a beachfront restaurant. *Puri Amarta Beach Inn* has 6000 rp rooms out of the usual construct-a-losmen box plus larger ones with a small attic-type room above – ideal for families. The larger rooms are 15,000 and 20,000 rp.

Homestay Ida, close to the lagoon, definitely doesn't fit the usual pattern, with pleasantly airy bamboo cottages dotted around a grassy coconut plantation. Smaller rooms are 15,000 or 18,000 rp, the larger rooms with mezzanine level are 35,000 rp, all including breakfast. Next door is the *Homestay Kelapa Mas* and then the small lagoon.

There are plenty of small losmen beyond the lagoon. These include *Dewi Bungalows, Rama Homestay* and the *Sindhu Brata Homestay*, three fairly standard losmen right beside the lagoon. Several more can be found further along the beach.

Places to Eat

Restaurants are dotted along the road although curiously there are not a great number right on the beach. The fish is usually good at Candidasa. The *Hawaii Restaurant* has good food at reasonable prices and the *Camplung Restaurant* is popular, particularly for breakfast. *Warung*

Top: Evil-doers pay for their misdeeds in the afterlife on the ceiling of the Kerta Gosa, Hall of Justice, Klungkung, Bali (TW)

Bottom: Bat cave, Goa Lawah, Bali (TW)

Top: Looking down on the lagoon at Candidasa (JP)
Bottom: Ujung water palace, Bali (TW)

Chandra and *Depot Sumber Rasa* are both straightforward places with simple menus and low prices attracting a steady stream of customers.

There are some places on the beach like the *Pondok Bamboo's* with fairly standard food including quite good sandwiches. *Ayu Seaside Restaurant* seems to have its ups and downs, definitely down when I tried it.

Puri Amarta has quite good food, they have a restaurant by the road and a second, open area down by the beach. There are plenty of other possibilities like the *Gusti Restaurant & Pub, Murni's Restaurant* and *TJs*. The *Arung Restaurant* has excellent food. Down towards the lagoon the *Sri Jati Restaurant* has good straightforward Indonesian food.

Beyond the lagoon and the temple, towards Amlapura, there's *Budi's*, the *Pizzeria Candi Agung* and the *Ngandi Restaurant* on the inland side of the road, the *Lila Arnawa Stage Restaurant* on the coast side.

Getting There & Away

Candidasa is on the main route between Amlapura and Denpasar so any bus or bemo coming by will get you somewhere!

AMLAPURA

The main town at this end of Bali and capital of the Karangasem regency this is also the 'end of the road' travelling east. A road continues from Amlapura down to the coast at Ujung and beyond but basically at Amlapura you change directions, turn north and then bend round west to follow the coast to Singaraja on the north coast. This road is now in much better condition than it was in the '70s and the route to Singaraja is no problem at all.

The kingdom of Karangasem broke away from the Gelgel kingdom in the late 17th century and a century later had become the most powerful kingdom in Bali. Amlapura used to be known as Karangasem, the same as the regency but it was changed after the '63 eruption of Agung in an attempt to get rid of any influences which might provoke a similar eruption!

Palace

The palace, Puri Agung Karangasem, is an imposing reminder of Karangasem's period as a kingdom although it actually dates from the 20th century. Take a look at the three-tiered gate and the beautiful sculptured panels on the outside of the main building, which is known as the Bale London because of the British Royal Crest on the furniture. Because Karangasem co-operated with the Dutch during their take-over of the island the rajah of Karangasem was able to retain his old power, at least for a while.

Ujung

A few km beyond Amlapura, on the road down to the sea, is the Ujung Water Palace, an extensive, picturesque and crumbling complex. It has been crumbling away for some time but a great deal more damage has been done to it since the mid '70s. The last king of the Kingdom of Karangasem, Anak Agung Anglurah, was obsessed with moats, pools, canals and fountains and he completed this grand palace in 1921. You can wander around the pleasant park, admire the view from the pavilion higher up the hill above the rice paddies or continue a little further down the road to the fishing village at the coast.

Places to Stay

Amlapura has a few places to stay but most travellers prefer to stay out of town, either in Tirtagangga or at Homestay Lila, a short distance down the road towards Rendang. If you do want to stay in Amlapura there are two options only a few steps apart and another just out of town.

On your left, just as you enter town, the *Lahar Mas Inn* has rooms with bath at

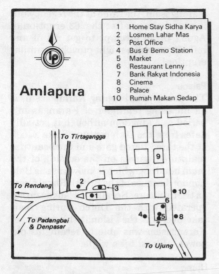

Amlapura

1 Home Stay Sidha Karya
2 Losmen Lahar Mas
3 Post Office
4 Bus & Bemo Station
5 Market
6 Restaurant Lenny
7 Bank Rakyat Indonesia
8 Cinema
9 Palace
10 Rumah Makan Sedap

To Tirtagangga

To Rendang

To Padangbai
& Denpasar

To Ujung

5000/6000 rp including breakfast – bread, an egg and coffee. They're around a large common room area and quite comfortable. The Lahar Mas backs on to the rice paddies and visitors report that it's a pleasant place with friendly people.

On the other side of the road a short distance in towards the centre, *Homestay Sidha Karya* was the original losmen in Amlapura but most visitors deserted it as soon as the Tirtagangga water-palace inn opened. Rooms here are 3000/4000 rp, again including breakfast. A third possibility is the *Losmen Kembang Ramaja*, just out of Amlapura on the Rendang road.

Places to Eat

There's the usual collection of rumah makans and warungs around the bus station plus the *Restaurant Lenny* and the *Rumah Makan Sedap* on the main street. Amlapura tends to shut down early so don't leave your evening meal until too late.

Getting There & Away

Although Amlapura is the 'end of the road' for bus services from Denpasar, you can continue round the coast all the way to Singaraja in the north.

TIRTAGANGGA

Amlapura's water-loving rajah, having constructed his masterpiece at Ujung, later had another go at Tirtagangga. This water palace, built around 1947, was damaged in the 1963 eruption of Agung and during the political events that wracked Indonesia around the same time. Nevertheless it's still a place of beauty and solitude and a reminder of the power the old Balinese rajahs once had. There's a swimming pool here as well as the ornamental ponds. Entrance to the water palace is 200 rp (children 100 rp) and another 500 rp (children 200 rp) to use the fine swimming pool (300 rp for the lower one, children 100 rp).

The rice terraces around Tirtagangga are reputed to be some of the most beautiful in Bali. They sweep out from Tirtagangga almost like a sea surrounding an island. A few km beyond here, on the road round the east coast to Singaraja, there are more dramatically beautiful terraces.

Places to Stay & Eat

Right by the water palace is the peaceful *Losmen Dhangin Taman Inn* with rooms at 3000, 4000, 5000 and 10,000 rp. Breakfast is included. The most expensive rooms are large and have an enclosed sitting area. You can sit in the courtyard, gazing across the rice paddies and the water palace while doves coo in the background. The losmen owner here is very amusing and the food is not bad although the warung nearest the losmen also does excellent food.

Actually within the palace compound the *Tirta Ayu Homestay* has pleasant individual bungalows at 7000, 8000 and 10,000 rp. Alternatively you can continue 300 metres beyond the water palace and climb the steep steps to the *Kusuma Jaya Inn*. The 'Homestay on the Hill' has a fine view over the rice paddies and rooms at 3000/6000 rp including breakfast and tea. Other meals are also available and they have information about local walks.

Across the road from the palace the *Rijasa Homestay* is a small and simple place with rooms at 2500/3000 rp or 3000/4000 rp, all including breakfast and tea. There's another losmen here, the *Taman Sari Inn*, but it is closed down at present.

Getting There & Away

Tirtagangga is about five or six km from the Amlapura turn-off on the road that runs around the eastern end of Bali. Bemos from Amlapura cost 200 rp. Buses continue around this way to Singaraja. See the section on the east coast under North Bali.

AMLAPURA TO RENDANG

The Amlapura-Rendang road branches off from the Amlapura-Denpasar road just a km or two out of Amlapura. The road gradually climbs up into the foothills of Gunung Agung, running through some pretty countryside. It's a quiet, less travelled route than the relatively busy Amlapura-Denpasar road – very busy between Klungkung and Denpasar. At Rendang you meet the Klungkung-Besakih road close to the junction for the very pretty minor road across to Bangli.

The road runs through Bebandem, with a busy market every three days, Sibetan and Selat to Rendang. Sibetan and Rendang are both well known for the salaks grown there. If you've not tried this delicious fruit with its curious 'snakeskin' covering then this may be the time to do so. It's worth diverting a km or so at Putung to enjoy the fantastic view down to the coast, only here do you realise just how high up you have climbed.

Shortly before Selat you can take a road south-west through Iseh and Sideman to the Amlapura-Klungkung road. The German artist Walter Spies lived here for some time from 1932. Later the Swiss painter Theo Meier, nearly as famous as Spies for his influence on Balinese art, lived in the same house.

Although the route from Amlapura to Rendang is fine with your own transport it can be time consuming by bemo, requiring frequent changes and lots of waiting. Taking the busier coastal route to Gianyar is much faster.

Places to Stay

Three km along the Rendang (or Bebandem) road from the junction as you leave Amlapura, *Homestay Lila* is a very pretty little place just off the road but right in the rice paddies. It's quiet and well away from everything, an ideal place to relax. The individual bungalows have bathrooms and a verandah out front, but no electricity. Singles/doubles cost 3000/5000 rp including breakfast – there's no where else to eat around here but the homestay also does other meals. It's a half-hour walk from here to Bukit Kusambi.

Further along towards Rendang, 11 km beyond Bebandem, you can turn off the road a km or so to the superbly situated *Putung Bungalows*. On the edge of a ridge they look out over the coast far, far below. You can see large ships anchored off Padangbai and across to Nusa Penida. They have two-storey bungalows, with a bathroom and small sitting area downstairs and also 'losmen class' rooms. Prices are from 8000 rp and there's also a restaurant in the complex.

BANGLI

Half-way up the slope to Penelokan the town of Bangli, once the capital of a kingdom, is said to have the best climate in Bali. It also has a very fine temple and quite a pleasant place to stay. Bangli is a convenient place to visit Besakih from, so it's quite a good base for exploring this area.

Pura Kehen

At the top end of the town Pura Kehen,

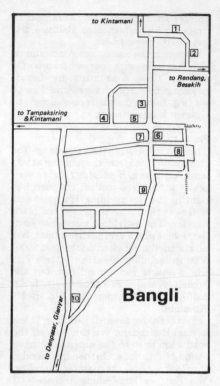

Bangli

1 Pura Kehen
2 Art Centre
3 Losmen Dharmaputra
4 Post Office
5 Cinema
6 Artha Sastra Inn
7 Bus Stop
8 Market
9 Telephone Office
10 Pura Dalem Penunggekan

the state temple of the Bangli kingdom, is terraced up the hillside. A great flight of steps leads up to the temple entrance and the first courtyard, with its huge banyan tree, has colourful Chinese porcelain plates set into the walls as decoration. Unfortunately most of them are now damaged. The inner courtyard has an 11-roof meru and a shrine with thrones for the three figures of the Hindu trinity – Brahma, Shiva and Vishnu. This is one of the finest temples in Bali. There's a large arts centre just round the corner from the Pura Kehen.

Bukit Demulih

If you take the Tampaksiring road out of Bangli about three km, the hill of Bukit Demulih is just off the road to the left (south side). There's a sign pointing to it or local children will direct you. You can make the short climb to the top where there's a small temple and from there you can look back over Bangli. Or walk along the ridge line to the end of the hill where all of south Bali spreads out below. You can see the long sweep of Sanur Beach with the Bali Beach Hotel, a minuscule rectangular box, far away.

Pura Dalem Penunggekan

Just below Bangli, right beside the road down to Gianyar, there's an interesting temple of the dead, the Pura Dalem Penunggekan. Along the front the reliefs illustrate particularly vivid scenes of wrong-doers getting their just deserts in the afterlife. In one panel a demon rapes a woman while other demons simultaneously stab and castrate a man. Elsewhere in the same panel demons gouge out eyes and a particularly toothy demon takes a bite out of some ne'er-do-well. On an adjoining panel unfortunate sinners are hung by their heels from a tree branch and roasted over a fire.

Places to Stay & Eat

The *Artha Sastra Inn* is a former palace residence and still run by the grandson of the last king of Bangli. Rooms, some with private bathrooms, cost 5000 to 8000 rp. It's a pleasant, friendly place, quite popular and very centrally located – right across from the bus station and main square.

The Bangli alternative is the youth

hostel connected *Losmen Dharmaputra*, a short distance up the road towards Kintamani. It's cheaper but also fairly basic. Rather drab singles/doubles cost 3000/4000 rp and you can also get food here.

Bangli has a good night market in the square opposite the Artha Sastra and there are some great warungs but they all close early. One catch in Bangli – 'the dogs are even worse than Ubud'.

BESAKIH

Perched nearly 1000 metres up the side of Gunung Agung is Bali's most important temple, Pura Besakih. In all it comprises about 30 separate temples in seven terraces up the hill, all within the one enormous complex. The temple was probably first constructed 1000 or more years ago. It was the state temple of the powerful Gelgel and Klungkung kingdoms 500 years ago and today is the 'mother temple' of all Bali. Every regency in Bali has its own shrine or temple at Besakih and just about every Balinese god you care to name is also honoured. Apart from its size and majestic location Besakih is also probably the best kept temple you'll see on the island. This is not a temple simply built and then left to slowly decay.

Besakih is the Balinese mother temple and also the mother of Balinese financial efforts. You pay to park, pay to enter, pay to rent a scarf and then have to brave the usual large collection of souvenir sellers. After which it's quite possible you'll find the inner courtyards are all closed to visitors!

The temple is definitely impressive, but you do not need a guide to see it. So if someone latches on to you and begins to tell you about the temple, let them know quickly if you don't want their services. If you don't they will expect to paid at the end, and whatever you do give them is certainly not going to be enough – they have no qualms about asking for more.

Places to Stay

About five km below Besakih the *Arca Valley Inn* has rooms and a restaurant. It's prettily situated in a valley by a bend in the road. This could be a good place to stay if you wanted to climb Gunung Agung from Besakih and would like to make an early morning start. There is also a losmen very close to the temple entrance.

Getting There & Away

The usual route to Besakih is by bus or bemo to Klungkung from where there are regular bemos up the hill to the temple for 500 rp.

If you go up to Besakih with your own wheels take the left fork about a km before the temple. There may be a 'No Entry' sign on the left fork, ignore it. This brings you to a car park close to the entrance. The right fork ends about a half km from the temple – leaving you with a long walk up the entrance road or a little hassling with the motorcycle gang who'll offer to ferry you up there. Extortionate first price – 1000 rp. You can't take your own bike up the entrance road.

The 'guardhouse' on the right fork is a bit of a scam as well, here they'll try and get you to sign a visitor's book where you'll find that lots of previous foreign guests have dispensed little donations, like 50,000 rp! Taking the left road not only brings you out closer to the temple it also bypasses the souvenir sellers and the 'donation' collectors.

GUNUNG AGUNG

If you want to climb Gunung Agung from Besakih you must leave no later than 6.30 am, it's a pretty tough climb. It's easy to get lost on the lower trails so hire a guide, which can cost anything from 10,000 to 20,000 rp depending on the size of your party, plus a few thousand as a tip. Take plenty of food and water, an umbrella, raingear, a warm woollen sweater and a torch (flashlight) with extra batteries – just in case you don't get back down by nightfall. An Agung climber's account of the ascent:

We were approached by a young man named Gede who told us that he could take us up Gunung Agung the next day. He took us to a losmen near the temple entrance for the night. It would be unwise to attempt Agung without a guide, as there are numerous trails leading in all directions in the early stages of the climb. In the later stages there are a few choices, some of them less dangerous, some more time consuming. In general the guides have all been to the top on a number of occasions. They are all particularly strong and will carry your daypack for you.

The cost of a guide depends on how many are going to climb and on how hard you bargain. We met a New Zealander who had bargained for about one hour to get the price down to 10,000 rp plus water and lunch. In effect that meant 12,000. Two of us paid 12,000 plus lunch between us although we also gave Gede a well earned tip at the end of the day. We also met another party of three on their way down. They had started climbing at 1 am and given up at 7 am, only an hour or two from the top. Their guide had cost them 22,000 rp.

Our daypack contained three litres of water, three packs of Marie biscuits, half a dozen bananas and a few fistfuls of boiled sweets as we set out from our losmen at 5.15 am. It was cold so we were glad of our woollen sweaters. After walking through the temple we hit upon a very narrow path. It was very dark and humid here and we would have been lost without our torches (flashlights). Our guide was setting a roaring pace, so it wasn't long before our sweaters became a burden. Gradually the path steepened and it became lighter. The vegetation was very thick and we would often lose sight of our guide as he surged ahead. Eventually it became so steep in this jungle that we had to grab onto roots or branches to pull ourselves up the track.

After about three hours of oppressive humidity there was a rather sudden change in terrain. The vegetation all but disappeared and we found ourselves at the base of a slope made entirely of small fragments of volcanic rock. Perseverance saw us struggle successfully through this slippery avalanche scenario to a point where we had to haul ourselves up onto a ledge above the slope. Briefly the ground levelled out for the first time in around three hours – a great relief! This was where we met the vanquished trio who had started out at 1 am. To come so far and then to turn back must have been very painful I'm sure. I found it hard to imagine that the climb could become more difficult, yet our guide assured us that 'most' people turned back somewhere between our present position and the top.

A 10 minute rest was followed by a new phase in the ascent. The next hour was spent scrambling up a slope which appeared to have no end. There was no path to follow, it was just a matter of clawing your way from one rock to the next. There was only one way to go – up. Looking back down the 'hill' only bought fear to my heart as I became convinced I would fall off the mountain into oblivion. The ground was made of an apparently sturdy lichen covered rock which unfortunately was not as sturdy as it looked. On many occasions during that hour I would grab a rock only to find it crumble in my hand. It's important to be alert on this section which is probably the steepest part of the climb.

Finally the summit was in view – or so we thought. It was with an incredible sense of frustration that we reached the top of the lichen field. It was no longer as steep, but the way had become very narrow. This was the beginning of the summit ridge which was no wider than two metres and in some places less than a metre across. It took about half an hour to the top, from both sides of the ridge the mountain dropped away alarmingly steeply. The wind was particularly strong up here and we began to notice the altitude, needing to catch our breath every five minutes or so. With the thought of plunging off the mountain into infinity ever present, we pressed on.

There was only room for one person to stand on the actual summit. From Besakih we had climbed some 2200 vertical metres to an altitude of around 3150 metres (10,300 feet). One step in any direction would take you to a lower point, either along the ridge or over the edge. The wind was positively biting but the view was breathtaking. It was also brief. We reached the summit at around 10 am, looked at the view for no more than a few seconds when the clouds rolled in. An icy dew formed on our arms and legs. Our guide showed us his thermometer. It read 3°C! There was nowhere to hide from the cold and the wind, so we headed off along the ridge toward the crater some 10 to 15 minutes away.

I peered nervously over the edge into the

gaping abyss. There appeared to be no bottom. My nose, ears and hands were stinging and I wanted desperately to get off the summit ridge and out of the cold. This was a frighteningly hostile place.

We arrived back in Bekasih at 3 pm after some four hours of slipping and sliding our way down Agung. Our knees were quite visibly swollen and distinctly painful. Our arms and legs were covered in small cuts and abrasions

and we were covered from head to toe in grime. We felt decidedly like heroes returned from battle and indeed we were given a heroes welcome by everyone we passed on our way through the temple. To an inexperienced mountaineer like myself this had been an epic climb. I number it among the great experiences of my life and I wouldn't do it again if you paid me.

Mark Balla

South-West Bali

Most of the places regularly visited in the south-west of Bali, like Sangeh or Tanah Lot, are easy day trips from Denpasar. The rest of the west tends to be a region travellers zip through on their way to or from Java. In the latter half of the last century this was an area of warring kingdoms but with the Dutch takeover the princes' lands were re-distributed amongst the general population. With this bounty of rich agricultural land the region around Tabanan quickly became one of the wealthiest parts of Bali.

Further west there are two spectacular roads up into the hills and across to the north coast but still further west the rugged hills are sparsely populated and the agricultural potential limited due to the low rainfall. This is the area where periodic rumours tell of the continued existence of the Balinese tiger. Along the south coast there are long stretches of wide black-sand beach and rolling surf. Countless little roads run down to the coast from the main road, which runs close to the coast but never actually on it.

Getting There & Away
Buses to the west of Bali generally go from the Ubung station in the north of Denpasar. It's around 2500 rp to Gilimanuk, 400 rp to Mengwi.

SEMPIDI, LUKLUK & KAPAL
Kapal is the garden gnome and temple curlicue centre of Bali. If you're building a new temple and need a balustrade for a stairway, a capping for a wall, a curlicue for the top of a roof, or simply any of the countless standard architectural motifs then the numerous shops which line the road through Kapal will probably have what you need. Or if you want some garden ornamentation, from a comic book

deer to a brightly painted Buddha then again you've come to the right place.

Lukluk's Pura Dalem and Sempidi's three desa temples are all worth inspecting but Kapal's Pura Sadat is the most important temple in the area. Although it was restored after WW II, following its destruction in an earthquake earlier this century, this is a very ancient temple, possibly dating all the way back to the 12th century.

TANAH LOT
The spectacularly placed temple of Tanah Lot is possibly the best known and most photographed in Bali. It's almost certainly the most touristed – the crowds here are phenomenal, the gauntlet of souvenir hawkers to be run is appalling and the commercial hype is terrible. Signs direct you to the best place for photographs and even where to catch the sunset. In fact sunset time has definite overtones of Australia's Ayers Rock with the faithful lined up, cameras at the ready, for the hallowed moment.

It's easy to see why it's such an attraction because Tanah Lot's setting is fantastic. It's perched on a little rocky islet, connected to the shore at low tide but cut off as the tide rolls in. It looks superb whether it's delicately lit by the dawn light or starkly outlined at sunset.

It's also an important temple – one of the venerated sea temples respected in similar fashion to the great mountain temples. Like the equally spectacularly situated Ulu Watu, at the southern end of the island, Tanah Lot is closely associated with the legendary priest Nirartha. It's said that Nirartha passed by here and, impressed with the tiny island's superb setting, suggested to local villagers that this would be a good place to construct a temple. Entry to the temple is 200 rp.

Getting There & Away

Tanah Lot is reached by turning off the Denpasar-Gilimanuk road at Kediri and taking the road straight down to the coast. You can reach it by bemo but if you're going with your own wheels this would be a good place for which to make a very early start – and miss the tourist jam. If you go out by bemo note that there is no regular service, and come sunset time when all the visitors flock back you may find the car park quickly empties and you only have a choice of chartering or walking.

MENGWI

The huge state temple of Pura Taman Ayun, surrounded by a wide moat, was the main temple of the kingdom which ruled from here until 1891. The kingdom split off from the Gelgel dynasty, centred near Klungkung in east Bali. The temple was originally built in 1634 and extensively renovated in 1937. It's a very large, spacious temple and its elegant moat gives it a very fine appearance. The first courtyard is a large, open grassy expanse while the inner courtyard has a multitude of shrines and merus.

In a beautiful setting across the moat from the temple is a rather lost looking art centre. Built in the early '70s it became an almost instant white elephant and today seems forgotten and neglected and is already beginning to take on the ageless look of all Balinese architecture. There's also a small museum here and the Mandala Wisata, *Water Palace Restaurant*, overlooking the moat, is not a bad place for lunch.

BLAYU

In Blayu, a small village between Mengwi and Marga, traditional songket sarongs are woven with intricate gold threads. These are for ceremonial use at festivals, not for everyday wear.

MARGA

Near Mengwi stands a peculiar memorial to Lt Colonel I Gusti Ngurah Rai who in 1946 led his men in a futile defence against numerically superior and better armed Dutch forces. The Dutch were trying to recover Bali after the departure of the Japanese. They even called in air support but the Balinese refused to surrender and in an outcome similar to the *puputans* of 40 years before all 94 of his men were

killed. Denpasar's airport is named Ngurah Rai in his memory.

SANGEH

North of Denpasar stands the monkey forest of Bukit Sari. It is featured, so the Balinese say, in the *Ramayana*. To kill the evil Rawana, king of Lanka, Hanuman had to crush him between two halves of Mahameru, the holy mountain. Rawana, who could not be destroyed on the earth or in the air, would thus be squeezed between the two. On his way to performing this task Hanuman dropped a piece of the mountain here, complete with a band of monkeys. Of course this sort of legend isn't unique, Hanuman dropped chunks of landscape all over the place!

There's a unique grove of nutmeg trees in the monkey forest and a temple, Pura Bukit Sari, with an interesting old Garuda statue. Plus, of course, there are lots of monkeys. They're very worldly monkeys, very aware of what visiting tourists have probably bought from the local vendors – peanuts. Take care, they'll jump all over you if you've got a pocketful of peanuts and don't dispense them fast enough. The Sangeh monkeys have also been known to steal tourists hats, sunglasses and even, as they run away, their thongs!

There are also plenty of Balinese jumping on you, clamouring to sell you anything from a sarong to a carved wooden flute. This place is geared to tourists.

Getting There & Away

You can reach Sangeh from Denpasar, bemos run directly there, but there is also a road across from Mengwi and from Ubud.

TABANAN

Tabanan is in the heart of the south Bali rice-belt, the most fertile and prosperous rice-growing area in the island. It's also a great centre for dancing and gamelan playing. The renowned dancer of the pre-war period, Mario, who perfected the Kebyar dance and is featured in Covarrubias' classic guide to Bali, was from Tabanan.

AROUND TABANAN

Near Tabanan is Kediri, where Pasar Hewan is one of Bali's busiest markets for cattle and other animals. A little beyond Tabanan a road turns down to the coast through Krambitan, a village noted for its beautiful old buildings and also its interest in ancient Javanese and Balinese literature.

About 10 km south of Tabanan is the village of Pejaten, which is a centre for the production of traditional pottery including elaborate, ornamental rooftiles. Recently they have started to make porcelain clay objects for purely decorative use. They can be seen in the Pejaten Ceramics Workshop.

TABANAN TO NEGARA

There's some beautiful scenery but little tourist development along this stretch of coast, the road running for 74 km from Tabanan to Negara.

Lalang-Linggah

The *Balian Beach Club* overlooks the Balian River and is surrounded by coconut plantations. There are bunk beds for 4000 rp plus bungalows at 6000/10,000 rp or a pavilion for 15,000 rp. To get there from Denpasar take any Negara or Gilimanuk bus and ask to stop at Lalang-Linggah, by the 49.6 km post.

Rambut Siwi

Between Air Satang and Yeh Embang a short diversion off the main road leads to the beautiful coastal temple of Pura Luhur at Rambut Siwi. Picturesquely situated on a clifftop overlooking a long, wide stretch of beach this superb temple with its numerous shady frangipani trees is one of the important coastal temples of south Bali.

Before you reach Rambut Siwi, at 22.5

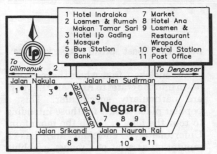

1 Hotel Indraloka	7 Market
2 Losmen & Rumah Makan Tamar Sari	8 Hotel Ana
	9 Losmen & Restaurant Wirapada
3 Hotel Ijo Gading	
4 Mosque	10 Petrol Station
5 Bus Station	11 Post Office
6 Bank	

km before Negara, a large sign announces the Medewi Surfing Point. Beyond Rambut Siwi, just seven km before Negara, there's the Delod Brawah Beach, two km off the main road, which is reputed to be good for windsurfing.

NEGARA

The capital of the Jembrana regency, Negara comes alive each year when the bullock races take place between July and October. The normally docile creatures, pulling tiny chariots, charge down a two-km stretch of road. Their riders often stand on top of these chariots forcing them on. This is still Bali, however, so it's not necessarily first past the post which wins. Style also plays a part and points are awarded for the most elegant runner!

Places to Stay & Eat

On Jalan Ngurah Rai, the main street, just on the Denpasar side of the centre, *Hotel Ana* is a standard losmen with rooms from around 3000 rp. Just down

from it is the *Losmen & Restaurant Wirapada* (tel 161) at Jalan Ngurah Rai 107 which is more expensive.

The Denpasar-Gilimanuk road actually bypasses the town centre. There are several accommodation possibilities along this road including, on the Gilimanuk side of town, the *Hotel Indraloka* at Jalan Nakula 13-15. The friendly *Losmen & Rumah Makan Taman Sari* at Jalan Nakula 18 has rooms at 4000 rp. Or there's the *Hotel Ijo Gading* at Jalan Nakula 5.

GILIMANUK

Right at the western end of the island Gilimanuk is the terminus where ferries shuttle back and forth across the narrow strait to Java. It's of little interest apart from this, just an arrival and departure point.

Gilimanuk is actually off the main road around the island. About a km on the Denpasar side from the junction there's a curious new temple like a pagoda with a spiral stairway around the outside. For more information on the north coast route to Gilimanuk see the North Bali section.

Places to Stay

Most people simply zip straight through Gilimanuk but if you do have a reason to stay there are several places along Jalan Raya, the main road into the port. They're all about a km from the ferry dock. First there's the *Homestay Putra Sesasan* at No 1, then a *Rumah Makan Padang* and *Homestay Kartika Candra*. At No 24 there's the *Homestay Gili Sari* and at No 12 the *Homestay Surya*.

The Central Mountains

Bali, as you'll quickly realise from a glance at one of the three-dimensional maps so popular with Balinese hotels, has lots of mountains. They effectively divide the gentle sweep of fertile rice land to the south from the narrower strip to the north. From the east there's a small clump of mountains right at the end of the island, beyond Amlapura. Then there's the mighty volcano Gunung Agung, the island's mother mountain. North of Agung rises the great crater of Batur with its lake and smaller volcano inside. Finally another series of mountains marches off to the west, a region sparsely inhabited and little visited.

The popular round trip to the north coast takes you up across the mountains on one route and back on the other thus covering most of the mountain region. It's often said the Balinese look away from the sea and towards the mountains; how the mountains are the abode of the gods and the sea is the home of demons and monsters. It's true enough but in reality the Balinese look towards them rather than actually live on them. The true Balinese heartland is the gentle, fertile rising land sweeping up to the mountains. The villages up in the mountains are strange, often chilly and cloudy places.

PENELOKAN

The roads up to Batur from Bangli and from Tampaksiring meet just before they finally reach the crater rim at Penelokan. This is an incredibly spectacular place, the age old crater rim is quite narrow and the road runs right along it with superb views down into the crater to Lake Batur and Mt Batur. Penelokan appropriately means 'the place to look'. In many places you can see down the other side as well and at the far end of the crater road, at Penulisan, you can look back into the crater or turn the other way and see the

north Bali coast spread out at your feet, far below.

At Penelokan, from where the road runs down into the crater to Kedisan, the views are particularly spectacular. This a popular place to stay for those intending to tour the lake or climb the mountain. Unfortunately Penelokan also has a reputation as a bit of a money grubbing place where you're constantly importuned to buy things and where you need to keep an eye on your motorcycle or other gear. It can get surprisingly chilly up here so come prepared. Clouds often roll in over the crater, sometimes getting hung up along the rim and making all the crater rim towns cold and miserable places to be. The Balinese here look very different to those from the warm lowlands.

Places to Stay

There are several places to stay in Penelokan, a couple of them teetering right on the edge of the crater with tremendous views. If hotels could sell their views these places would be five-star. As it is they're just standard little losmen charging standard little prices. Take care though, the Penelokan business attitude carries over to the losmen and they'll charge whatever they reckon the market will bear.

First of the Penelokan places if you arrive from the south is the newer *Caldera Batur* with rooms at 15,000 rp. A little further along the *Lakeview Homestay* clings to the crater rim and has standard rooms at 5000 rp and also more comfortable bungalow-style rooms complete with bathroom for rather more money. The standard rooms are impossibly small – if the beds weren't so tiny and narrow they wouldn't be able to get two in a room. Ah, but the view, the view . . . .

Continuing a little further, past the road down to Kedisan inside the crater, you come to *Losmen Gunawan* – almost an exact duplicate of the Lakeview. Again the view is terrific, the rooms are tiny (they cost 6000 rp) and the bungalow-style rooms are rather better at 10,000 rp and up. A little further along the expensive *Danau Batur Restaurant* may have rooms available at the back of the building. No crater view though.

Places to Eat

Almost everywhere in Bali where there's a major tourist attraction there will also be a major restaurant, somewhere you can pour the tour group into for lunch before it's back to the bus for the afternoon activities. Along the road between Penelokan and Kintamani there is quite a crowd of them, all with fine views over the crater and Mt Batur. They generally do buffet-style lunches at prices suitable for international tourist standards. The restaurants, from Penelokan to Kintamani, include the *Batur Garden*, the *Danau Batur*, the *Puri Selera*, the *Puri Aninditha* and the *Kintamani Restaurant*. Lunch costs from around 7500 to 10,000 rp. The Kintamani Restaurant is the most expensive and possibly the best.

Of course there are also cheap warungs along the main road like the *Warung Makan Ani Asih* or the *Warung Makan Sederhana* The Penelokan losmen also have reasonably priced places to eat.

Getting There & Around

To get to Penelokan you'll probably have to take a bemo first from Denpasar to Gianyar or Bangli and another from there up the mountain. From Ubud go first to Gianyar. Bemos shuttle back and forth regularly between Penelokan and Kintamani (200 rp) and down to the lakeside at Kedisan (300 rp).

From Penelokan you can hike around the crater rim to Gunung Abang (2152 metres), the high point of the outer rim. Or you can follow the road which starts out around the crater rim then drops down to Rendang, joining the Rendang-Besakih road at Menanga. If it's clear there are fine views of Gunung Agung along this route.

The two main routes up the mountain to Penelokan are through Gianyar and Tampaksiring, meeting just before you get to Penelokan. There are, however, several lesser routes, OK for motorcycles but with very little public transport. See the Ubud section for details. The country off to the west of Batur is remote and not visited much.

BATUR & KINTAMANI

Batur and Kintamani virtually run together, it's impossible to tell where one ends and the other begins but the village of Batur used to be down in the crater. Batur had a violent eruption in 1917 which killed thousands and destroyed over 60,000 homes and 2000 temples. Although the village of Batur was wiped out the lava flow stopped at the entrance to the villagers' temple. Taking this as a good omen they rebuilt their village only for Batur to erupt again in 1926 and this time the lava flow covered all but the loftiest temple shrine. The shrine was moved up to the crater rim and placed in the new temple Pura Ulun Danu, where its construction commenced in 1927 and still continues. Mt Batur is the second most important mountain in mountain-conscious Bali, only Agung outranks it, so the temple here is of considerable importance.

Kintamani is a long spread out town, just one main street right along the rim. It's often cold and grey and Kintamani is far from the most attractive place in Bali. This is, however, a major centre for growing oranges and you'll often see them on sale. Kintamani is famed for its large and colourful market, held every three days. Like most markets throughout Bali it starts and ends early – by 11 am it's all over. The high rainfall and cool climate up here makes this a very productive fruit and vegetable growing area. Kintamani is also another place challenging for the hard fought title of 'miserable howling dog capital of Bali'.

Places to Stay & Eat

There are a number of losmen along the main street of this volcano-rim town but they don't have the spectacular setting of the Penelokan places and most of them are pretty drab and dismal. There's not much incentive for staying here longer than you need to.

Starting from the Penelokan end of town there's *Losmen Superman's* with rooms with bathroom at 4000 rp. It's OK, nothing special but survivable.

If you continue in to town, past the Batur temple, you come to *Losmen Batur Sari* – very drab and plain, with rooms at 5000 rp. A little further along is the *Losmen Lingga Giri* which is also very drab and plain but also very cheap at around 2500 rp for a tiny room. The beds and blankets 'are designed for midgets and there's a warming open fire in the evenings – which no longer adequately compensates for the rather run down and grubby surrounding'. The food is, however, quite good so this is the popular gathering place in the evenings.

Almost next door is the *Hotel (ex-Losmen) Miranda*. Rooms here cost from 2000 to 5000 rp, the most expensive have attached bathrooms. It's a bit better than the general run of Kintamani accommodation and has good food and an open fire at night. Made Senter who runs it also acts as a mountain guide.

Continuing along the road, beyond the main 'centre' of Kintamani, if this strung out little town can be spoken of as having such a thing, you come to *Losmen Kencana*. It's rather brighter and airier than the other places, quite pleasant in fact. Next to it is the *Losmen Sasaka*.

Finally a bit further along again a sign points off the road to the *Hotel Puri Astini* – it says 200 metres but it's probably more like four times that distance. Rooms with attached bathrooms are 10,000 to 20,000 rp including breakfast. That's a big price

jump since the last edition although the somewhat remote location, OK if you've got your own wheels, is compensated for by the crater-rim position and the fine sunset views. *Wisma Ardi* is next door to the Puri Astini.

Getting There & Away

From the south coast you get up to Penelokan by bus or bemo then take a bemo to Kintamani for 200 rp. Buses run between Kintamani and Singaraja on the north coast.

PENULISAN

The road continues along the crater rim beyond Kintamani, gradually climbing higher and higher. Sometimes if you come up from the south you'll find yourself ascending through the clouds around Penelokan and Kintamani then coming out above them as you approach Penulisan. There are more fine views down over the crater, this time looking across the land to the north of Mt Batur. Sometimes you can even see Rinjani in Lombok.

At a bend in the road at Penulisan a steep flight of steps leads to Bali's highest temple, Pura Tegeh Koripan at 1745 metres. Inside the highest courtyard there are rows of old statues and fragments of sculptures in the open bales. Some of them date back as far as the 11th century. The views from this hilltop temple are superb, looking to the north you can see down over the rice terraces clear to the Singaraja coast.

Towering over the temple, however, is a shrine to a new and powerful god – Bali's television repeater mast!

LAKE BATUR & MT BATUR

The crater rim from Penelokan through Batur and Kintamani to Penulisan offers superb views. However the real thrill is the descent into the massive outer crater, a trip across Lake Batur and an ascent of Mt Batur.

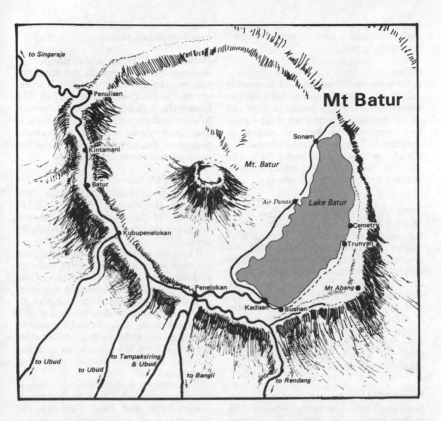

Kedisan

A winding road hairpins down from Penelokan to Kedisan on the shore of the lake. From there you can take a boat across the surprisingly large and very deep lake to Trunyan, and to the hot springs at Tirtha. From Kedisan or Tirtha you can climb to the summit of Mt Batur in just a couple of hours.

Places to Stay There are several losmen in Kedisan including the new *Segara Homestay* just on the Toyah Bungkah side of the junction. Rooms cost 12,000 rp.

Trunyan

On the shore of Lake Batur the village of Trunyan is squeezed tightly between the lake and the outer crater rim. This is a Bali Aga village, inhabited by remnants of the original Balinese, the people who pre-date the Majapahit arrival. Unlike the other well known Bali Aga village, Tenganan, this is not an interesting and friendly place. Trunyan is just a scruffy little village inhabited by a rather unfriendly and pushy bunch of people. It's famous for its four-metre high statue of the village's guardian spirit, Ratu Gede Pancering Jagat – but you're unlikely to be allowed to see it. About all you do get to do at Trunyan is sign the visitors' book, make a donation and be told you can't visit the temple.

Kuban

A little beyond Trunyan, and accessible only by the lake – there is no path – is the village cemetery. The people of Trunyan do not cremate or bury their dead – they lie them out in bamboo cages to decompose. Despite their secretiveness in the village they're quite happy for you to visit the cemetery although it's got a definite tourist trap feel about it.

Tirtha – Toyah Bungkah

Directly across the lake from Trunyan is the small settlement of Tirtha, also known as Toyah Bungkah, with its famous hot springs (air panas). The springs bubble out in a couple of spots and are captured in bathing pools before flowing out into the lake. If you stay here, perhaps to climb Mt Batur in the early morning, you can join half the village for a sunset bath – women at one end, men at the other. The water is soothingly hot, ideal for aching muscles after you've climbed the volcano.

Places to Stay There are a number of places to stay in Tirtha Just as you come into the village there's the Under the Volcano Homestay with rooms at 4000, 5000, 10,000 and 15,000 rp. The rooms are standard value for money and it's quite a pleasant place with a popular restaurant.

Across the road is the small and basic Siki Inn with rooms at 3000/5000 rp. Other cheaper losmen are the Losmen Tirta Yatra right by the lake or also on the lakeside, above the hot springs, Losmen Amertha with rooms at 5000/6000 rp. Kardi's Mountain View Losmen is back from the lake, at the far side of the small village.

The Balai Seni Toyabungkah Art Centre is a pleasant place with rooms at 15,000 and 20,000 rp, definitely a cut above the other small losmen. There's an excellent library there.

Places to Eat There are a number of warungs including, just as you enter the village, the Nyoman Pangus Warung which does good barbecued fresh fish. The Under the Volcano Homestay's Rumah Makan Sederhana restaurant section is also pretty good and the art centre restaurant has surprisingly good food but at commensurately higher prices.

Ascending Mt Batur

Soaring up in the centre of the huge outer crater is the cone of Mt Batur (1717 metres). It has erupted on several occasions this century, most recently in 1963.

There are several routes to the top but it's most interesting to take one route up and another one down. At several of the losmen there will be people who volunteer as guides although finding your way up Mt Batur by yourself is no problem at all – there are plenty of paths and the way to the top is clear as day. Two popular guides are Made from the hot springs or flute-playing Gede (he's quite a character) from Kintamani.

The shortest and most direct route is probably from the hot springs. Just take a straight line and head right up the mountain, it gets pretty steep towards the top. The most popular route is probably from Kedisan – it's quite a beaten track and there are even a number of refreshment stops along the way. If there are no local children running them they will be operated on the honour system – leave your money in the jar and help yourself to the pause that refreshes! This is quite an interesting route, winding across the lava flows to the west of Mt Batur and climbing across the smaller cone, created by the most recent eruption. A third possibility is to ascend from Kintamani, first descending the outer crater rim and then climbing up the inner cone.

It's possible to walk right around the

Top: Pura Luhur temple, Rambut Siwi, Bali (TW)
Left: Sculptured panels in the beautiful coast temple of Pura Luhur,
    Rambut Siwi, Bali (TW)
Right: Rice fields beside the Pulukan-Pupuan road in central Bali (TW)

Top: Mt Batur, Bali (TW)
Bottom: Cows going for a paddle in Lake Batur, Bali (TW)

rim of Mt Batur, or even descend into the crater and up the other side. Wisps of steam issuing from fissures in the rock and the surprising warmth of many stretches of the thinly crusted ground indicate that things are still happening down below. A possible round trip could be to climb Mt Batur from the hot springs, follow the rim round to the other side or cut across through the crater, then descend on the regular route back to Kedisan. Climbing up, spending a reasonable time on the top and then strolling back down can all be done in an easy four or five hours.

Down to the East Coast

The rough old jeep track across the lava field has been surfaced not only to the hot springs but beyond to Sonam and right to the very edge of the outer crater. From the temple at the crater edge you can climb to the top of the crater rim in just 15 minutes and from there you can see the east coast, only about five km away. It's an easy downhill stroll to the coast road.

Getting Around

Getting across the lake was at one time Bali's great rip-off. After negotiating a sky-high price your boatmen would then want to renegotiate half-way across. Meanwhile your motorcycle was being stripped back at Kedisan. It got so bad that the government took over and everything is now at set prices. At Kedisan, where the boats depart from, there is a boat office, car park and the usual assortment of rumah makans and warungs. Your motorcycle will be safe here!

Standard prices vary with the route you want to take – there are charges for the charter of a whole boat or per person. A boat will carry about 12 people. If you can't get a group together then try tagging on to one of the many Indonesian tourist groups. Charter prices are in the 7000 to 9000 rp range, for 9000 rp you can make the whole lake circuit Kedisan-Trunyan-

Kuban-Tirtha-Kedisan. Per person costs range from 875 to 2000 rp.

If you want to do it on the cheap don't consider the alternative of hiring a dugout canoe and paddling yourself. For a start the lake is much bigger than it looks from the shore. More important it can quickly get very choppy if a wind blows up – in those conditions the middle of the lake can be a very dangerous place. A better alternative is to walk, the road continues from Kedisan to Buahan and from there you just follow the good footpath around the lakeside to Trunyan, an easy hour or two's walk. From Trunyan you should be able to negotiate a cheaper fare to the cemetery and hot springs. You can walk from there back across the lava field to Kedisan, it's about four km along a surfaced road. Or why not spend the night at the *air panas*, climb Mt Batur in the morning and descend from there back to Kedisan?

BEDUGUL

The serenely calm Lake Bratan is on the road from Denpasar to Singaraja. You can also reach Singaraja from Denpasar via Penelokan and Kintamani but the Bedugul route is faster. The climb to Bedugul is like the one to Penelokan, you gradually leave the rice terraces behind and ascend into the cool, damp mountain country. Gunung Bratan, overlooking the lake, is 2020 metres high.

At Candikuning, on the shores of the lake, with one courtyard actually isolated on a tiny island right in the lake, is the temple of Ulu Danu. This temple is dedicated to Dewi Danu the goddess of the waters. It has classical thatched-roof merus and an adjoining Buddhist stupa. Admission is 200 rp (children 100 rp). There are several places to stay near the lake and this can be an excellent base for walking trips into the surrounding hills. If you descend from Bedugul to Lake Buyan you can make a fine walk around the southern lakeside of Buyan and over the saddle to the adjoining, smaller Lake

Tamblingan and from there to Munduk. It takes about two to three hours from Lake Buyan to Munduk and from there you can take the road back to the starting point or continue to Seririt on the north coast. The road around the north side of the lake is now sealed and makes an interesting descent from Munduk through picturesque villages to the coast.

Near Bedugul the market of Bukit Mungsu is noted for its wild orchids. The orchid plantation near here is being developed as a botanical garden. The road beyond Bedugul descends past an expensive golf course, opened in the mid-70s, and Lake Buyan. There's a beautiful waterfall near the road at Gitgit.

It's possible to hire a prahu for 2500 rp an hour (but we got the same rate for a half day) and paddle across Lake Bratan from the lakeside just below the Lila Graha to some caves which the Japanese used during WW II. You can also walk there in about an hour. From there a very well marked path ascends to the top of Gunung Catur. It takes about two hours for the climb up and an hour back down, the final bit is steep and you should take some water but it is well worth the effort. There is an old temple on the summit with lots of monkeys.

Anne Whybourne & Peter Clarke,
Australia

Places to Stay & Eat

There are now several places to stay dotted along the road up to Bedugul from the Denpasar side as well as a number of places around the lake. There's a 200 rp entry charge to the lakeside at the Denpasar end of the lake. Here you'll find the *Bedugul Hotel* with rooms at 15,000, 20,000 and 25,000 rp. On the main road just by the turn-off is the *Hadi Raharjo*, a fairly basic and straightforward losmen with rooms at 6000 rp.

Continuing north the road climbs higher up the hillside to the turn off for the new and expensive *Bukit Mungsu Indah Hotel*. Rooms here cost from US$25 to US$40. The road then turns the corner and drops down towards the lake, passing

the turn-off to the *Lila Graha*, which is also expensive at 30,000 rp. They do have hot showers though!

In Candikuning you can eat at the *Restaurant Pelangi*, the *Rumah Makan Mini Bali* or others in the same area.

Just north of Bedugul is the *Bali Handara Country Club*, situated at Bedugul's lush green golf course.

MT BATUKAU

West of the Mengwi-Bedugul-Singaraja road rises 2093 metre Mt Batukau, the 'coconut-shell mountain'. This is the third of Bali's three major mountains and the holy peak of the west end of the island.

Pura Luhur

On the slopes of the mountain Pura Luhur was the state temple when Tabanan was an independent kingdom. The temple has a seven-roof meru to Maha Dewa, Mt Batukau's guardian spirit, as well as shrines for the three mountain lakes Bratan, Tamblingan and Buyan.

There are several routes to Pura Luhur but none of them are particularly high class roads – it's a remote temple. You can reach the temple by following the road up to Penebel from Tabanan. Or turn off the Mengwi-Bedugul road at Baturiti near the 'Denpasar 40 km' sign and follow the convoluted route to Penebel. Wongaya Gede is the nearest village to the forest-surrounded and often damp and misty temple.

Jatuluih

Also perched on the slopes of Gunung Batukau, but closer to Bedugul and the Mengwi-Bedugul road, is the small village of Jatuluih, whose name means 'truly marvellous'. The view truly is, it takes in a huge chunk of south Bali.

ROUTES THROUGH PULUKAN

Although the routes through Kintamani and Bedugul are the two most popular roads over the mountains, between the south and north coast there are two other routes. One starts from Pulukan, the other from Antosari, both on the Denpasar-Gilimanuk road, and they meet at Pupuan before dropping down to Seririt, to the west of Singaraja. They're interesting and little used alternatives to the regular routes.

The Pulukan-Pupuan road climbs steeply up from the coast with fine views back down to the sea. The route runs through spice-growing country and you'll often see spices laid out on mats by the road to dry – the smell of cloves rises up to meet you. At one point the narrow and winding road actually runs right through an enormous banyan tree which bridges the road. Further on the road spirals down to Pupuan through some of the most beautiful rice terraces on the island.

North Bali

The north of Bali, the regency known as Buleleng, makes an interesting contrast with the south of the island. For a start it's physically separated from the south by the central mountains and that short distance, only a few hours by bus, keeps the tourist hordes at bay. Along the coast near Singaraja there's a string of popular beaches with a varied collection of places to stay and eat but it's nothing like the hassle and confusion of Kuta, and nowhere near the expense of Sanur. Most visitors to the north are attracted by the peaceful beaches but there are also a number of other features worth visiting.

The north has been open to influence from the west far longer than the south of Bali. While the Dutch had established full control of north Bali by 1848-49, it was not until the beginning of this century that they extended their power to the south.

Having first encountered Balinese troops in Java in the 18th century, the Dutch were the main purchasers of Balinese slaves – many of whom served in the East Indies Company armies. The Dutch did not become directly involved with internal affairs of the island, as they had in Java, although in 1816 they made several unsuccessful attempts to persuade the Balinese to accept their authority. Various Balinese kings continued to provide the Dutch with soldiers but in the 1840s disputes over the looting (salvaging?) of shipwrecks, together with fears that other European powers might establish themselves in Bali, prompted the Dutch to make treaties with several of the Balinese rajahs. The treaties proved ineffective, the plundering continued and in 1844 disputes arose with the rajah of Buleleng over the ratification of agreements.

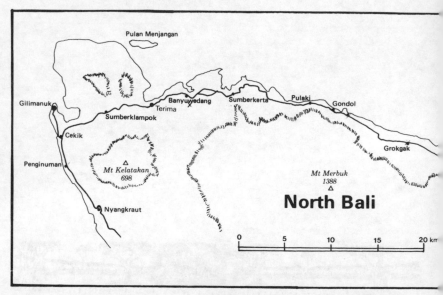

In 1845 the rajahs of Buleleng and Karangasem formed an alliance, possibly to conquer other Balinese states but equally possibly to resist the Dutch. In any case the Dutch attacked Buleleng and Karangasem in 1846, 1848 and 1849, and in the third attempt they finally took control of the north. The western regency of Jembrana came under Dutch control in 1853, the rajah of Gianyar surrendered his territory in 1900 but it was not until 1906 that they finally subdued the south. The last confrontation was in 1908 when Klungkung rebelled – unsuccessfully.

From the time of their first northern conquests the Dutch interfered more and more in Balinese affairs. It was here that Balinese women first covered their breasts – on orders from the Dutch to 'protect the morals of Dutch soldiers'.

SINGARAJA

For years Singaraja was the usual arrival point for visitors to Bali. All those pre-war travel books start at Singaraja because at that time land transport through Java was slow and circuitous and there was certainly no busy airport near Denpasar. Singaraja is hardly used as a harbour anymore due to lack of protection from bad weather. Shipping for the north coast now generally uses the new port at Celukanbawang where you might be lucky enough to find a Bugis schooner willing to take you to Surabaya, or further afield. The cruise ships that include Bali on their itinerary use Padangbai, in the south, as their entry point.

The centre of Dutch power, throughout their rule in Bali, was Singaraja and it remained the administrative centre for the Nusa Tenggara islands (Bali through to Timor) until 1953. With a population of around 15,000 it's still a busy little town although a long way behind Denpasar in the cosmopolitan metropolis stakes. It has some pleasant tree-lined streets and dokars are still an everyday means of transport. The 'suburb' of Beratan to the

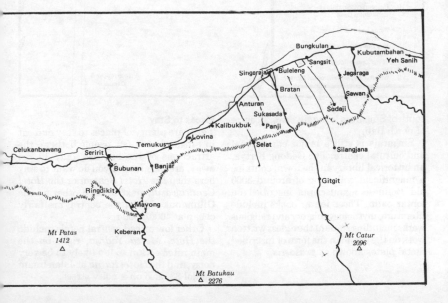

Singaraja

to Kalibukbuk

to Kintamani & Amlapura

to Bedugul & Denpasar

1 Bus Station – Kalibukbuk,
   Gilimanuk, Denpasar
2 Petrol Station
3 Hotel Saka Bindu
4 Hotel Gelarsari
5 Hotel Garuda
6 Hotel Duta Karya
7 Bank Dagang Negara
8 Hotel Sentral & Hotel Cendrawasih
9 Mosque
10 Restaurant Gandhi
11 Bank Bumi Daya
12 Mosque
13 Ratna Losmen
14 Cinema
15 Bus Station – Kintamani, Amlapura
16 Post Office
17 Telephone & Telegraph Office
18 Hotel Sedana Yoga
19 Gedung Kirtya – Historical Library

south of Singaraja is the silverwork centre of north Bali.

Singaraja is still a major educational and cultural centre. The Gedong Kirtya, an historical library in the town, contains a magnificent collection of around 3000 old Balinese manuscripts inscribed on lontar palm. These lontar books include literature, mythology, history and religious works including some of the oldest written work on the island in the form of inscribed metal plates known as *prasastis*.

Places to Stay

There are plenty of places to stay and eat in Singaraja but few people bother – the attractions of the beaches, only 10 km away, are too great. If you do want to stay here then the *Hotel Sentral* or the *Hotel Cendrawasih*, next to each other on the Gilimanuk side of the centre, are fairly cheap at 4000/5500 rp.

Other low priced central hotels include the *Hotel Merta Yadnja*, right on the main intersection so it's likely to be very noisy, and the *Hotel Ratna* at Jalan Imam Bonjol 33, also on a noisy street.

As in Denpasar there are many other hotels, most of them rather more expensive and principally used by local business travellers. You'll find a string of them further along Jalan Jen Achmad Yani from the Sentral and Cendrawasih – like the *Hotel Duta Karya* with rooms at a variety of prices from 8500/10,000 rp up to 15,000/18,000 rp. Plus many others in other parts of town – like the neat and clean *Hotel Sedana Yoga* on Jalan Imam Bonjol near the telephone office with rooms from 5000/8000 rp up to 15,000/20,000 rp with air-conditioning.

Places to Eat

There are plenty of places to eat around Singaraja including a batch of places in the small Mumbul Market, on Jalan Jen Achmad Yani. You'll find the popular *Restaurant Gandhi* here, a good Chinese menu and glossy clean surroundings. Across the road is the *Restaurant Segar II*. There are also a few restaurants along Jalan Imam Bonjol.

Getting There & Away

Singaraja is the main transportation centre for the north coast. There are bus stations on the east and west side of the town for travel in the various directions. To Denpasar minibuses leave about every half hour from 6 am to 4 pm, the fare is around 1500 rp and they go via Bedugul. Some other typical fares around Bali from or to Singaraja are Amlapura 1200 rp, Gilimanuk from 1000 rp (takes two hours), Kintamani and Bedugul also cost from around 1000 rp depending on the vehicle. Buses to Amlapura run around the coast now that the road is so much improved.

There are also direct buses to or from Surabaya which saves going down to Denpasar. You'll find a number of ticket offices near the junction of Jalan Jen Achmad Yani and Jalan Diponegoro but you can also arrange tickets from the Lovina Beach places. There aren't direct buses to Yogyakarta but it is possible to arrange to connect with a direct Denpasar-Yogyakarta bus in Gilimanuk.

SINGARAJA BEACHES

To the west of Singaraja is a whole string of popular beaches – Happy Beach, Lovina Beach, Kalibukbuk. They developed as a resort much later than Sanur and Kuta and their development has been a lot slower – which is just fine as this area is relaxed and unhassled. The continuous string of shops which seem to line Sanur and, to an even greater extent, Kuta simply does not exist here. Nor are you endlessly hassled on the beaches to buy things, have a massage or do anything more than simply laze there.

The beaches here are black sand, not the white stuff you find at Sanur or Kuta. Nor is there any surf, a reef keeps it almost flat calm most of the time. Generally the water is very clear and the reef is terrific for snorkelling. It's not the best coral you'll ever find but it's certainly not bad and getting out to it is very easy. In many places you can simply swim out from the beach, elsewhere a prahu will take you out there and they should know the best places for diving. All the hotels seem to have their own boats or access to one or you can simply ask in the various fishing villages. There always seems to be someone ready to cater to snorkelling enthusiasts and the standard price is about 3000 rp per person.

This is a wonderful place to introduce children to snorkelling. Out on the reef the water is calm, clear and relatively shallow and even beginner swimmers can easily have a good look around and have the prahu outrigger to hang on to for security. My son Kieran can boast that he first went diving on a coral reef at the age of four.

The beach also provides plenty of local entertainment with goats and ducks making a morning and evening promenade along the sand. The sunsets along here are every bit as spectacular as Kuta and there's quite a programme of entertainment around sunset time. As the sky reddens

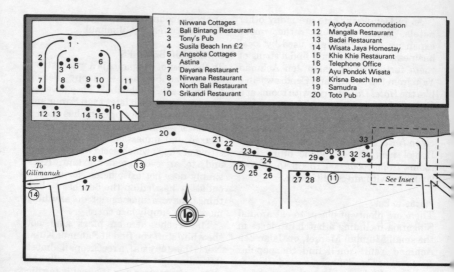

1	Nirwana Cottages	11	Ayodya Accommodation
2	Bali Bintang Restaurant	12	Mangalla Restaurant
3	Tony's Pub	13	Badai Restaurant
4	Susila Beach Inn £2	14	Wisata Jaya Homestay
5	Angsoka Cottages	15	Khie Khie Restaurant
6	Astina	16	Telephone Office
7	Dayana Restaurant	17	Ayu Pondok Wisata
8	Nirwana Restaurant	18	Krisna Beach Inn
9	North Bali Restaurant	19	Samudra
10	Srikandi Restaurant	20	Toto Pub

the bats come out to play and then the lights of the fishing boats appear as bright dots right across the horizon. Earlier in the afternoon, at fishing villages like Anturan, you can see the outriggers being prepared for the night's fishing. It's quite a process bringing out all the kerosene lamps and rigging them up around the boat.

Information

There are a couple of good bookshops beside the Badai Restaurant at Kalibukbuk.

Places to Stay

The Singaraja beach strip hasn't had the explosion of accommodation construction which you find at Kuta-Legian or even Ubud but there certainly are far more places than a few years ago and more are gradually being added. Unlike Kuta it's not a compact cluster of losmen, here they are strung out along the beach for several km. The first place is soon after the six km marker, the last at nearly 14 km. You might find one place, then nothing for a half km or so, then a small cluster of places.

Singaraja to Anturan As with almost anywhere in Bali these days prices are very variable with season and demand. Starting from the Singaraja end the first place is the somewhat higher priced *Baruna Beach Cottages*. There are individual cottages and rooms in a larger two-storey block. All have bathrooms and including breakfast costs range from around 12,000 to 15,000 rp. It's quite nice and has a bar/restaurant on the beach but is not the best value to be found.

Next up is the *Suci Jati Reef*, also higher priced, a series of cottage complexes right in the rice paddies close to the beach. They're quite comfortable with double rooms with those bathroom-gardens at around 5000 to 10,000 rp. The reef off the beach here is reputed to be the best along the Singaraja beach strip.

Anturan Continuing along the road you come to the turn-off at the scruffy little fishing village of Anturan, where there is a small cluster of lower-priced places and lots of local colour. Closest to the village is *Mandhara Cottages*, a neat little complex at 6000/10,000 rp for singles/doubles with

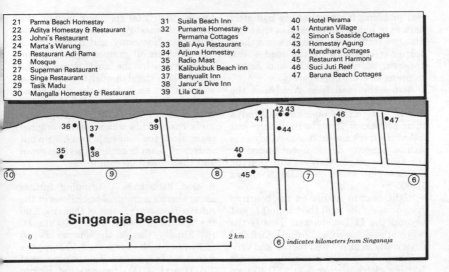

21	Parma Beach Homestay	31	Susila Beach Inn	40	Hotel Perama
22	Aditya Homestay & Restaurant	32	Purnama Homestay &	41	Anturan Village
23	Johni's Restaurant		Permama Cottages	42	Simon's Seaside Cottages
24	Marta's Warung	33	Bali Ayu Restaurant	43	Homestay Agung
25	Restaurant Adi Rama	34	Arjuna Homestay	44	Mandhara Cottages
26	Mosque	35	Radio Mast	45	Restaurant Harmoni
27	Superman Restaurant	36	Kalibukbuk Beach inn	46	Suci Juti Reef
28	Singa Restaurant	37	Banyualit Inn	47	Baruna Beach Cottages
29	Tasik Madu	38	Janur's Dive Inn		
30	Mangalla Homestay & Restaurant	39	Lila Cita		

Singaraja Beaches

0   1   2 km

⑥ indicates kilometers from Singanaja

bathrooms. Further round the beach is *Simon's Seaside Cottages* which was rebuilt and renovated after becoming somewhat run down.

Next door again is the very neat and clean little *Homestay Agung* complex. There are rooms from 5000 up to 7500 rp, the more expensive rooms are interesting 'two-storey' places with double bunk beds. The food at Agung can be quite good. *Homestay Sri* is a newer place on this same bit of beach. It's very plain but rooms with attached mandi are just 3000/4000 rp.

Anturan to Kalibukbuk Pressing on from Anturan you pass the *Hotel Perama* up on the main road and then come to the *Lila Cita* down from the turn-off, a simple but very friendly and popular place. Everyone who stays here seems to like it. Rooms are 6000/7500 rp or 7500/10,000 rp with mandi and you could hardly get any closer to the beach. Made, who runs it, is a pleasant guy with family up at Tirtha (the hot springs) at Lake Batur.

Continue along the road to the next turn-off where you'll find the *Kalibukbuk*

Beach Inn right down by the beach. Rooms with bath are 10,000 rp, very plain but they have nice verandahs and it's quite a pleasant place to stay. Back a bit from the beach is the *Banyualit Inn* with rooms at 12,500 rp and the new *Janur's Dive Inn* with rooms at 6000 and 7000 rp.

Kalibukbuk A little beyond the 10 km marker you come in to the village of Kalibukbuk itself. Here you'll find *Ayodya Accommodation*, a traditional but truly delightful place. It's a beautiful, spacious, wonderfully furnished old Balinese house – clean, friendly and extremely well run. The rooms cost 3000 and 4000 rp and are generally bare and functional, but you sit outside and take your meals there. In the evening, with the bamboo gamelan tinkling in the background, you can really appreciate one traveller's description of Ayodya as 'Gothama's stately home – taking in guests'. Unfortunately Ayodya has one drawback – it's right by the road and in recent years the traffic on this road has increased so much as to make the noise a real problem. It's particularly bad after dark as in Indonesia so much of the long-distance traffic runs at night when there are fewer obstacles on the road – less children, animals, bicycles and bemos stopping at every opportunity.

Across the road from Ayodya is the small *Wisata Jaya Homestay* and a little further along on the same side as Ayodya there's *Srikandi*. Down by the beach – just follow the track almost beside Ayodya – is *Astina*, a newer development owned by the Ayodya people. Gardens surround the cottages here which cost 6000, 8000 and 12,000 rp.

Right next to Astina on the beach is *Nirwana*; on the road the turn-off is just beyond the 11 km marker. This is the biggest development at Lovina Beach and deservedly so as it's well placed and very well run. They have a variety of rooms starting with basic rooms at 3000/4000 rp and 8000/12,000 rp plus some even nicer ones at 10,000/12,000 rp in a new development beside Astina. Then there are three double-storey cottages which are quite delightful and cost US$16/18. They have a bedroom upstairs with a double bed and are surrounded on all sides by screened windows, without glass. Downstairs there are two single beds and a bathroom and outside there's a spacious verandah. These cottages are ideal for families. In the newer development at Nirwana there are four new double-storey cottages of different design, only completed in 1988.

Right behind Nirwana are the *Angsoka Cottages*, a small place with simple but pleasant rooms with bathroom for just 6000 rp, excellent value for money. There are also some new rooms here at 9000, 10,000 and 12,000 rp. The 12,000 rp upstairs rooms are very good. The small *Susila Beach Inn 2*, beside the Angsoka, is a straightforward losmen with rooms at 4000 rp.

Back on the main road there is a string of lower priced places beyond the Nirwana/Angsoka turn-off with prices as low as 2500/3500 rp. They include the *Arjuna Homestay, Permana Cottages, Purnama Homestay* and *Susila Beach Inn* which are all grouped together in one little clump by the road. Some of the places here extend through to the beach so you can get away from the road noise. There is also the *Mangalla Homestay* with rooms at 3000/4000 rp and up. Next up is *Tasik Madu* which was the original place along the Singaraja beach strip but in recent years became rather run down and then closed up completely.

Beyond Kalibukbuk Continuing further along there's a group of bungalows at the *Aditya Homestay*, some of them right on the beach and costing from 10,000/12,000 rp. Finally there's the *Parma Beach Homestay* with rooms from 5000 rp, the *Samudra Inn,* surprisingly expensive at 25,000 and 30,000 rp, and the *Krisna Beach Inn* 3000 rp or 4500 rp with bathroom, midway between the 13 and 14 km marker from Singaraja. In all the Singaraja beach strip extends seven km from just after the six km marker.

Places to Eat
Most of the places to stay along the beach strip also have restaurants and snack bars and you're generally welcome to visit other losmens for a meal, you don't have to be staying there. There are also a handful of restaurants and warungs. Starting once again from the Singaraja end the small *Homestay Agung* has a good reputation for its food and people from other losmen often drop in here. On the main road nearby there's the *Restaurant Harmoni* which does great fresh fish and other seafood.

Right on the edge of Kalibukbuk village there's the *Khie Khie Restaurant* with a reputation for good seafood. At the turn off to the Nirwana and Angsoka cottages is the extremely popular *Badai Restaurant*. In the evening its long tables are a convivial meeting place for travellers. It's a relaxed, friendly place and the food is pretty good too with some excellent 'order a day in advance' dishes like fish curry, duck (6000 rp for two) or Hidangan Jawa (like a rijstaffel) for 4000 rp for two. The Badai also has a useful bulletin board.

The open double-storey Nirwana Restaurant across the road is closed down but at *Nirwana Cottages* the restaurant area overlooking the beach is very popular. On the road down to the beach there's also the *Bali Bintang Restaurant* on one side and *Tony's Pub* on the other. The Bintang is good, relatively cheap and happy to tackle food not featured on the menu.

Back at the main road you'll find the *Mangalla Restaurant* next to the Badai and *Jacky's Pub* across the road. Next to it the *Dayana Restaurant* has good

seafood at reasonable prices. Then there's the *Bali Ayu Restaurant* with good food and regular Balinese dance performances. Further along you come to the *Singa Restaurant* and the *Superman Restaurant* followed by a couple of small warungs – the popular *Marta's Warung* and then *Johni's Restaurant* with an extensive menu and pretty reasonable food. The *Aditya Restaurant* also has dance performances.

Getting There & Away
To get to the Singaraja beaches from the south of Bali you first have to get to Singaraja, then take a bemo out from there. The regular bemo fare from Singaraja to Kalibukbuk in the middle of

the beach strip is 250 rp. See the Singaraja section for details of buses.

There are buses direct between Surabaya and Singaraja and if you're coming in from Surabaya you can get off along the beaches rather than have to backtrack from Singaraja. You can also be picked up there and save going in to Singaraja to start with. The Mangalla Restaurant is one place where you can get tickets and arrange to be collected. Night buses to Surabaya cost 9500 rp, through to Yogyakarta 13,000 rp.

AROUND SINGARAJA – WEST

There are numerous places of interest around Singaraja both to the east and the west. Heading west you'll find several places worth a visit between the Kalibukbuk beach strip and the junction town of Seririt.

Waterfalls

At the village of Labuanhaji, only just beyond the end of the Singaraja beach strip, there's a sign to the Singsing Air Terjun – Daybreak Waterfalls – about a half km off the road. It's about 200 metres through the fields, along a concrete path, to the first falls which cascade down the hill into a deep pool. Balinese kids will leap from a tree high up the hill side into the deep water – for a fee.

You can clamber further up the hill side to the higher Singsing Dua falls. Again they cascade into a deep pool – which is much deeper in the wet season of course. You can swim in either pool.

Buddhist Monastery & Hot Springs

About a half km beyond Banjar Tega (which is about two steeply uphill km off the main coast road) is Bali's only Buddhist monastery. It's indeed vaguely Buddhist-looking with its bright orange roof and Buddha statues but overall it's very Balinese with the same decorative carvings and door guardians. From the walls you can see the sea, beyond the rice paddies far below. The road continues

past the monastery, winding further up into the hills.

The hot springs, *air panas*, are only a short distance from the monastery. If you head back down to Banjar Tega, turn left in the centre and cut across to Banjar. It's then only a very short distance uphill again before you see the 'air panas one km' sign. Follow the dirt trail to the inevitable motorcycle park and on down to the lukewarm baths by the riverside. The water pours into the bath and overflows into the river. Bring your swimming gear if you want to try them, there's a small changing enclosure.

Getting There & Away The monastery (*wihara*) and the *air panas* are both signposted from the road. If you've not got your own transport it's probably easiest to first continue beyond the Banjar Tega turn-off to the Banjar turn-off (around the 18 km marker) where there are horse carts that can take you up to the *air panas* path. Then you can walk across to the monastery and back down to the main road afterwards.

SERIRIT TO GILIMANUK

Seririt is little more than a junction town for the roads that run south over the mountains to Pulukan or Bajera, on the way to Denpasar. On to Gilimanuk, the ferry port for Java, the road runs either close to or right by the coast and there are a few places of interest.

Seririt

Seririt has a reasonable selection of shops, though not as good as Singaraja, but if you're staying at the beaches and need something unobtainable at the local shops this might be a place to try. You can stay here in the *Losmen Singarasari* but with the pleasant Singaraja beach hotels so close there's little reason to do so.

Celukanbawang

Celukanbawang is now the main port for the north coast of Bali, and it has a large wharf. You may see the odd Bugis schooner here.

Pulaki

Pulaki is famous for its coastal monkey temple which has been rebuilt. The village of Pulaki seems to be entirely devoted to grape growing, the whole village is almost roofed over with grapevines. For some reason grape growing has become popular at several locations on the north coast in recent years. They'll be making wine next! There are several hot springs close to the road on this route, one is a km or so beyond Pulaki and a half km off the road, and another one further on.

Terima

This national park in the north-west corner of Bali includes Pulau Menjangan, an unspoilt and uninhabited island with excellent diving around it. There's a 500 rp entry charge to the park, payable to the PPA Kantor. At Labuhan Lalang, 16 km from Gilimanuk, there's a dock for boats to the island. A motor prahu costs 25,000 rp for four hours, 5000 rp for each additional hour. There are also coral formations close to the mainland and since this area of Bali is lightly populated, and now protected in the national park, the variety of both fish and coral is amazing. Day trips can be arranged to the island by the various diving centres.

The outcrop of land between Terima and Gilimanuk is also protected and a 25 km walking track skirts the coast. It's a hot walk so take plenty of liquids.

Places to Stay At the 13 km marker before Gilimanuk there's a place to stay at Teluk Terima where *P T Margarana Accommodation* is just off the road. It's clean and has good showers and rooms for 6000 rp plus a small restaurant area. Otherwise there are just some basic warungs with chicken and rice, drinks and some snacks.

AROUND SINGARAJA FAST

There are a number of places of interest close to the coast road between Singaraja and the turn-off to Kintamani, including some of north Bali's best known temples. The north coast sandstone used in temple construction is very soft and easily carved and this has allowed local sculptors to give a free rein to their imagination, to an even greater extent than in the south. You'll find some delightfully whimsical scenes carved into a number of the temples here. Overall the exuberant, even baroque, style of the north makes temples in the south appear almost restrained in contrast.

Although the basic architecture of the temples is similar north or south there are some important differences. Whereas the inner courtyard of southern temples usually houses a number of the multi-roofed meru towers together with other structures, in the north everything will be grouped on a single pedestal. On the pedestal you'll usually find houses for the deities to use on their earthly visits and also for storing important religious relics. Also there will probably be a padmasana or 'throne' for the sun god.

Sangsit

Only a few km beyond Singaraja you'll find an excellent example of the north's colourful architectural style at Pura Beji at Sangsit. This is a subak temple, dedicated to the spirits which look after irrigated rice fields, about a half km off the main road on the coast side. The sculptured panels along the front wall set the tone with their Disneyland demons and amazing nagas (snakes).

It's just the same on the inside, with a variety of sculptures covering every available space. Like many other northern temples the inner courtyard is spacious and grassy, shaded by a frangipani tree.

Continue beyond Sangsit to Bungkulan where there is another fine temple with an interesting kulkul drum.

Jagaraga

Only a couple of km off the main road as you enter the small village of Jagaraga there's a temple to the left of the road. This small and otherwise unprepossessing temple has a number of delightful sculptured panels along its front wall both inside and out. On the outer wall look for a vintage car driving sedately past, a steamer at sea and even an aerial dogfight between early aircraft. Jagaraga is also famous for its legong troupe, said to be the best in the north of Bali. It was the capture of the local rajah's stronghold at Jagaraga that marked the arrival of Dutch power in Bali in 1849. A few km further along on the right hand side look for another small temple with ornate carvings of a whole variety of fish and fishermen.

Sawan

Sawan, several km further inland, is the centre in the north of Bali for the manufacture of gamelan gongs and complete gamelan instruments. You can see the gongs being cast and the intricately carved gamelan frames being made. It's very much a local cottage industry and they don't get many visitors so they're usually pleased to see you and show you around.

Kubutambahan

Only a km or so beyond the Kintamani turn-off at Kubutambahan, is the Pura Maduwe Karang temple, beside the coast side of the road. Like Pura Beji at Sangsit it's dedicated to agricultural spirits, but this one looks after unirrigated land. The temple is usually kept locked but ask in the shop opposite, they'll have the key.

This is one of the best temples in the north and particularly noted for its sculptured panels, including the famous bicycle panel with a gentleman riding a bicycle with flower petals for wheels. It's on the base of the main plinth in the inner enclosure but there are other panels worth inspecting in this peaceful and pleasant temple.

YEH SANIH

Only about 15 km east of Singaraja this is a popular local spot where freshwater springs are channelled into a very pleasant swimming pool before flowing into the sea. It's right by the sea and the small centre is very attractively laid out with pleasant gardens, a restaurant and a couple of places to stay. It's well worth a visit and admission to the springs and pool is 150 rp (children 100 rp). On the hill overlooking the springs is the Pura Taman Manik Mas temple.

Places to Stay & Eat

There are a couple of places to stay right by the springs. In fact the *Bungalow Puri Sanih* is actually in the springs complex. It's got a very pretty garden and doubles at 8000, 10,000 and 15,000 rp – the most expensive rooms are little two-storey bungalows. Just beyond the springs is the *Yeh Sanih Seaside Cottages* with very pleasant rooms at 20,000/25,000 rp.

The Puri Sanih also has a restaurant looking out over the springs and the gardens. There are a number of warungs across the road from the springs.

YEH SANIH TO AMLAPURA

Beyond Yeh Sanih the road runs close to the north-east coast, although rarely right beside it, to Culik where it turns inland towards the south-east coast. It climbs over a small range of hills then drops down to Tirtagangga and Amlapura. This used to be a rough route but with improvements it's now no problem at all. There are a number of villages along the way but this part of Bali is relatively dry and you see none of the usual rice paddies until just before Tirtagangga – and there you'll see some of the most spectacular rice terraces in Bali. Not far beyond Yeh Sanih you can turn inland to the interesting village of Sembiran; a little further on at Tejakula there's a famous horse bath; and there's a good beach near Culik.

The main feature of this route is the superb view of Gunung Agung. Along this coast Bali's mightiest mountain descends right down to the sea and its slopes beckon enticingly to climbers. The road crosses a great number of dry riverbeds, most of them too wide to be easily bridged and, in the dry season at least, showing no sign of water. They're probably similar to many rivers in Australia, running briefly during the heavy rains of the wet season but remaining dry for the rest of the year.

Tulamben

The American ship SS *Liberty*, sunk by the Japanese in 1942, lies just off the beach at Tulamben. You can snorkel over it, only 50 metres off-shore. The beach here is pebbles rather than sand but the water is clear and the snorkelling good. In June and July there's good windsurfing. The recently constructed losmen makes this an interesting place to pause on your way around the east coast. It's a long way from anywhere on this barren coast.

Places to Stay & Eat

Until recently there was no place to stay anywhere along the east coast from Yeh Sanih until you reached Tirtagangga. Now there's the *Paradise Palm Beach Cottages* at Tulamben and Bali being Bali more places will no doubt spring up along the coast. Rooms in this cheerful little losmen right on the beach cost 10,000/15,000 rp with breakfast. There's electricity at night.

Nusa Penida

Clearly visible from Sanur, Padangbai, Candidasa or anywhere else along the south-east coast the rocky island of Nusa Penida is beginning to attract increasing numbers of visitors for its seclusion, surf and snorkelling. The island has a population of around 40,000 and was once used as a place of banishment for criminals and other undesirables from the Kingdom of Klungkung. It's still part of the regency of Klungkung. Nusa Penida is also the legendary home of the demon Jero Gede Macaling who inspired the Barong Landung dance.

The island has some interesting temples including Pura Ped near Toyapakeh and Pura Batukuning near Sewana. There is also a huge limestone cave, Goa Karangsari, about a km from Sewana. The mountain village of Tanglad in the

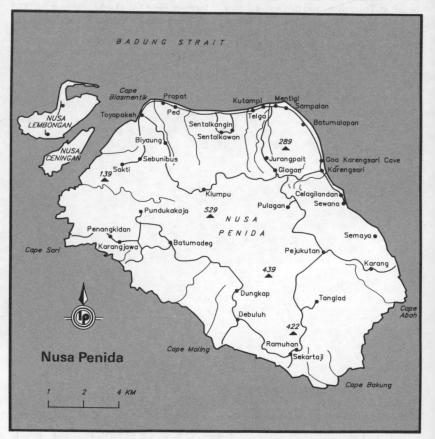

Nusa Penida

Top: Walking oxen along the beach at Kalibukbuk, Bali (TW)
Bottom: Kerosene lamps are set up on fishing boats in preparation for a night's fishing
        off the north coast, Anturan, Bali (TW)

Left: Temple carving, Kubutambahan (AS)
Right: Rice terraces spilling down a hillside near Tirtagangga, Bali (TW)
Bottom: The famous bicycle rider sculpture, Pura Maduwe Karang, Kubutambahan, Bali (TW)

south-east with its throne for the sun-god Surya is also interesting. Salak, a village on the south coast, is spectacularly situated on a cliff top high above the sea.

Rice terraces on the island are all faced with stone and at some villages a unique ikat cloth is woven. When making an animal offering to propitiate evil spirits a certain type of chicken raised on the island is supposed to be particularly efficacious. Nusa Penida is also the sole home for Rothchild's Mynah, one of the world's rarest birds.

On some approaches to Denpasar airport or from Bali-Lombok flights you may get a good view of the island. It's surprisingly hilly, especially along the south coast where high cliffs falls precipitously into the sea. From the air it looks completely uninhabited. The ferry to and from Lombok also passes quite close to it but you'd need binoculars to get a good look.

The tourist development at Nusa Penida has, so far, all been on the adjoining smaller island of Nusa Lembongan where there are a variety of losmen to choose from. The surfing here is world class and there's also some fine snorkelling. Prahus will take you out to the reef.

Places to Stay & Eat

Nusa Lembongan Bungalows are at Jungutbatu on the island of Nusa Lembongan, just offshore from Nusa Penida itself. They have singles/doubles at 15,000/19,500 rp including breakfast. You can book the bungalows from Kuta and they will arrange transport out to the island. *Wayan's Restaurant* at the Bungalows is definitely *the* place to eat with excellent food at reasonable prices, however the popularity means that service can be slow.

Nusa Lembongan has various other cheaper losmen from around 3000 rp including the *Mainski Inn*, but *Johnny's Losmen* on the left end of the beach, one of the pioneers here, seems to have fallen from favour.

Getting There & Away

There are twin-engined prahus out to Nusa Penida from Sanur every morning around 7 to 9 am. The fare is about 7000 to 8000 rp per person and the trip takes a couple of hours. They come back at various times during the day.

It's also possible to reach Nusa Penida from Kusamba, on the south-east coast of Bali. Boats make regular trips across bringing supplies because the island is dry and relatively uncultivated. The crossing takes about two hours. Sampalan is the main port and the usual arrival point.

Lombok

Facts about Lombok

HISTORY

The earliest recorded society on Lombok was the relatively small kingdom of the Sasaks. They were agriculturalists and animists who believed in the innate liveliness of inanimate objects as well as trees, plants and living creatures, and they practised ancestor and spirit worship. These original Sasaks are believed to have come overland from north-west India or Burma in waves of migration that predated most Indonesian ethnic groups. Few relics remain from the old animist kingdoms and the majority of Sasaks today are Muslim although animism has left its mark on the culture. Not much is known about Lombok before the 17th century, at which time it was split into numerous, frequently squabbling, petty states each presided over by a Sasak 'prince' – disunity which the neighbouring Balinese exploited.

In the early 1600s the Balinese from the eastern state of Karangasem established colonies and took control of west Lombok. At the same time the roving Makassarese crossed the straits from their colonies in western Sumbawa and established settlements in east Lombok. This conflict of interests ended with the war of 1677-78 which saw the Makassarese booted off the island, and east Lombok temporarily reverting to the rule of the Sasak princes. Balinese control soon extended east and by 1740 or 1750 the whole island was in their hands. Squabbles over royal succession soon had the Balinese fighting amongst themselves, and Lombok split into four separate kingdoms. It was not until 1838 that the Mataram kingdom subdued the other three, reconquered east Lombok (where Balinese rule had weakened during the years of disunity) and then crossed the Lombok Straits to Bali and overran Karangasem, thus reuniting the 18th-century state of Karangasem-Lombok.

While the Balinese were now the masters of Lombok the basis of their control in west and east Lombok was quite different and this would eventually lead to a Dutch takeover. In west Lombok, where Balinese rule dated from the early 17th century, relations between the Balinese and the Sasaks were relatively harmonious. The Sasak peasants, who adhered to the mystical Wektu Telu version of Islam, easily assimilated Balinese-Hinduism, participated in Balinese religious festivities and worshipped at the same shrines; intermarriage between Balinese and Sasaks was common. The western Sasaks were organised in the same irrigation associations (the subak) that the Balinese used for wet-rice agriculture. The traditional Sasak village government, presided over by a chief who was also a member of the Sasak aristocracy, had been done away with and the peasants were ruled directly by the rajah or a land-owning Balinese aristocrat.

Things were very different in the east, where the recently defeated Sasak aristocracy hung in limbo. Here the Balinese had to maintain control from garrisoned forts and although the traditional village government remained intact the village chief was reduced to little more than a tax collector for the local Balinese district head *(punggawa)*. The Balinese ruled like feudal kings, taking control of the land from the Sasak peasants and reducing them to the level of serfs. With their power and land-holdings slashed the Sasak aristocracy of east Lombok were hostile to the Balinese; the peasants remained loyal to their former rulers and this enabled the aristocracy to lead rebellions in 1855, 1871 and 1891.

The Balinese succeeded in suppressing the first two revolts but the uprising of 1891 proved fatal. Towards the end of 1892 it too had almost been defeated, but the

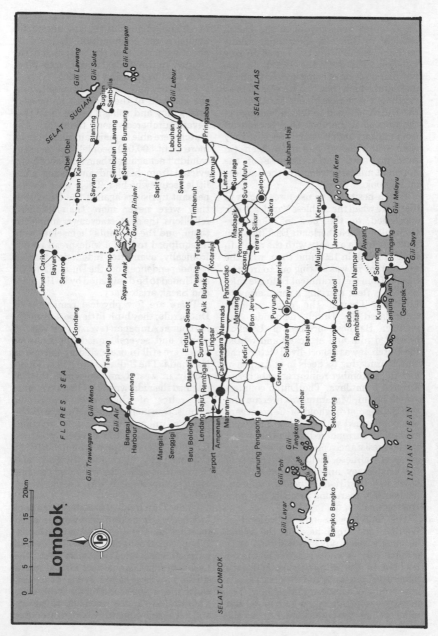

Lombok

Sasak chiefs sent envoys to the Dutch resident in Buleleng (Singaraja) asking for help and inviting the Dutch to rule Lombok. This put the Dutch in the peculiar position of being invited to storm an island which they had barely taken so much as a sideways glance at. Although the Dutch planned to take advantage of the turmoil in Lombok they backed off from military action – partly because they were still fighting a war in Aceh (in Sumatra) and partly because of the apparent military strength of the Balinese on Lombok.

Dutch hesitancy to use force began to dissipate when the ruthless Van der Wijck succeeded to the post of Governor-General of the Netherlands East Indies in 1892. He made a treaty with the rebels in East Lombok in 1894 and then, with the excuse that he was setting out to free the Sasaks from the tyrannical Balinese rule, he sent a fleet carrying a large army to Lombok. Though the rajah quickly capitulated to Dutch demands, the younger Balinese princes of Lombok overruled him and attacked and routed the Dutch. It was a short-lived victory; the Dutch army dug its heels in at Ampenan and in September reinforcements began arriving from Java. The Dutch counter-attack began, Mataram was overrun and the Balinese stronghold of Cakranegara was bombarded with artillery. The rajah eventually surrendered to the Dutch and the last resistance collapsed when a large group of Balinese, including members of the aristocracy and royal family, were killed in a traditional suicidal *puputan*, deliberately marching into the fire from Dutch guns.

The Dutch were now in control of Lombok and from here on the island becomes a case study in callous and inept colonial rule. A whole range of new taxes resulted in the impoverishment of the majority of peasants and the creation of a new strata of Chinese middlemen. The peasants were forced to sell more and more of their rice crop in order to pay the taxes and as a result the amount of rice available for consumption declined by about a quarter from the beginning of the century to the 1930s. Famines took place from 1938 to 1940 and in 1949.

For nearly half a century, by maintaining the goodwill of the Balinese and Sasak aristocracy and using a police force that never numbered more than 250, the Dutch were able to maintain their hold on more than 500,000 people! The peasant wouldn't act against them for fear of being evicted from his land and losing what little security he had. There were several peasant uprisings against the Dutch but they were never more than localised rebellions, the aristocracy never supported them, and the peasants themselves were ill-equipped to lead a widespread revolt. Ironically, even after Indonesia attained its independence from the Dutch, Lombok continued to be dominated by its Balinese and Sasak aristocracy.

There are few physical reminders of Dutch rule; they built little apart from the harbour at Ampenan (even then it was too small) and several aqueducts, some of which are still in use including the one at Narmada. The Balinese can still be found mostly in west Lombok, where they've retained their idiosyncratic Hindu customs; the relics of their occupation and colonisation include their influence on the Sasak's unique Wektu Telu religion. Other leftovers of the Balinese presence include the temples they built at Cakranegara, Narmada, Lingsar and Suranadi, as well as the temple processions and ceremonies still seen on the island today.

Under Dutch rule the eastern islands of Indonesia – from Bali on – were grouped together as the Lesser Sunda Islands. When Sukarno proclaimed Indonesian independence on 17 August 1945, the Lesser Sunda Islands were formed into a single province called Nusa Tenggara, which means the islands of the south-east. This proved far too unwieldy to govern and it was subsequently divided into three separate regions – Bali, West Nusa Tenggara and East Nusa Tenggara. Thus Lombok became part of West Nusa Tenggara in 1958.

GEOGRAPHY

Lombok is one of the 13,677 islands of Indonesia, all of which lie between continental Asia and Australia forming a barrier between the Pacific and Indian Oceans. It is one of the two main islands of the province of West Nusa Tenggara, which is situated about half-way along the archipelago. Immediately to the west of Lombok is Bali, while to the east is Sumbawa, the other main island of West Nusa Tenggara. Lombok is 8° south of the equator and stretches some 80 km east to west and about the same north to south.

Like Bali, Lombok is dominated by one of the highest mountains in Indonesia. Soaring to 3726 metres Gunung Rinjani can be seen, when not covered in cloud, from any point on the island. Situated in the north and well inland, Mt Rinjani is an active volcano, but it last erupted over 80 years ago in 1901. It has a large caldera, the bottom of which drops 200 metres below the rim to a crater lake, Segara Anak, with a new cone in the centre.

The south of Lombok is similar to Bali with rich alluvial plains, but in the far south it changes to dry, scrubby, barren hills, which look strikingly similar to parts of Australia's outback. The majority of the population is concentrated in the fertile but narrow east-west corridor sandwiched between the dry southern region and the slopes of Rinjani to the north. The continuous alluvial fan – an extension of the mountain slope – often gets little rain causing droughts that can last for months.

Districts

Lombok is divided into three *Kabupaten* which are West Lombok (capital Mataram), Central Lombok (capital Praya) and East Lombok (capital Selong). Mataram is also the administrative capital of the West Nusa Tenggara Province.

CLIMATE

In Lombok in the dry season – from April to September – the heat can be so scorching that even in the mountains a sunshade or at least a broad-brimmed hat may be handy, while at night the temperature drops so drastically that a jumper (sweater) and light jacket is necessary. The wet season extends from October to March and January is often very stormy. Crossing from Bali by ferry during this period can be very unsettling with particularly rough seas, so if you've got a weak stomach, don't attempt it.

FLORA & FAUNA

Apart from banana and coconut palms which grow in profusion over most of Lombok, the forests here are confined largely to the mountain regions where they are extensive and dense. Among the timber that grows here is teak and mahogany. Other native trees include bintangur, kesambi, bungur and fig, all of which are used widely for building houses and furniture. Much of the rest of the island is devoted to cultivating rice and the rice fields here are every bit as picturesque as Bali's (though you don't see so many geese and ducks being taken out for their daily paddle in Lombok).

Several species of deer, including barking deer, as well as wild pigs, porcupines, snakes, numerous kinds of lizards – both large and small, frogs, turtles, long-tailed monkeys, civets and feral cattle are found here. Lombok is the furthest point west of Australia that the sulphur-crested cockatoo can be found.

ECONOMY

Lombok's economy is based on agriculture and the rice grown here is noted for its excellent quality. However, the climate in Lombok is drier than Bali's and they can only produce one crop a year. Poor rains and basic shortage of water in some years can lead to not enough rice being produced or complete crop failure, and consequently spiralling price rises and unstable markets. In 1973 rice on Lombok was twice as expensive as it was on Bali. Though rice is the staple crop there are small and large plantations of coconut palms, coffee, kapok, tobacco and cotton. New crops such as cloves, vanilla and pepper are gradually being introduced.

The people of Lombok do not have the same qualms about the sea as the Balinese, and fishing is carried out around the coastlines which, edged by coral, are good spawning areas. Stock-breeding on Lombok is only done on a small scale.

Attempts are being made to promote Lombok as a tourist resort and money is being invested in upgrading facilities, particularly hotels and roads. The development of Senggigi Beach has been the first sign of national intent in this direction and at the same time the Gili Islands have become a real travellers' centre. Still, it will be a long time, if ever, before Lombok becomes as touristed as Bali.

POPULATION

Lombok has a population of just over two million people, the majority being congregated in and around the main centres of Ampenan, Cakranegara, Mataram, Praya and Selong. Almost 80% of them are Sasak, about 20% are Balinese, who are concentrated in the west, and there are minority populations of Chinese, Javanese and Arabs.

Basically hill people, the Sasaks are now spread over central and east Lombok, heavily Islamic and generally much poorer than the Balinese. Most of the Chinese in the east were killed in 1965-66 as suspected sympathisers in the wave of hysterical reprisals following the abortive Communist coup in 1965.

In 1966 a grand-scale natural disaster occurred when the rice crop failed through drought and 50,000 people starved to death in villages all across the island, many more only survived by eating mice.

PEOPLE
Sasaks

The Sasaks are predominantly hill tribes with dark brown skin, long curly black hair, high cheek bones and Caucasian appearance. They are assumed to have originally come from north-west India or Burma and the clothing they wear even today – particularly the women – is very similar to the peoples from these areas. Sasak women traditionally dress in black in long sarongs called *lambung* and short-sleeved overblouses with a V-neck. The sarong is held in place by a four-metre long scarf known as a *sabuk*, trimmed with brightly coloured stripes. They wear very little jewellery and never any gold ornaments.

The Sasaks retain their own customs and culture and survive by cultivating rice, tobacco and various vegetables. They also keep small herds of cows, water buffaloes and a few horses. Officially most Sasaks are Muslims, but unofficially they retain many of their ancient animist beliefs and practices, though for an outsider to witness any other than the extraordinary trial of strength, known as *peresehan*, or weaving techniques would be sheer luck. Unlike the Balinese they have not developed their dances or religious rituals as tourist attractions. However, while their customs are more secret – indeed in many ways completely different from the Balinese – many have become intermixed with Muslim ideology.

There are a number of traditional Sasak villages scattered over the island; the easiest to get to that are still intact and unspoilt are Sukarara, Rembitan and Sade in the south and Bayan and Senaro in the north. Typical Sasak huts are square or rectangular and constructed of wooden frames daubed with lime and covered with grass. Some sit squat on the ground but generally they are on stilts and have a high, thatched roof. Usually the village is surrounded and protected by a high paling fence and the houses are built in long, straight lines. The Sasaka Beach Cottages on the coast near Ampenan, were designed in this traditional style.

Balinese

The Balinese settled in the west of Lombok and the majority still live there today. They have kept their idiosyncratic Hindu customs, life style and traditions unadulterated. Historically, in their role as conquerors of Lombok they ruled as feudal overlords and this, combined with their attitude of treating it as a kind of penal colony for undesirable Balinese, caused friction and ill-will with the Sasaks. Even today, the Sasaks regard the Dutch as liberating them from an

oppressive power. Occasionally you may still witness some animosity directed towards the Balinese, but it is rare to hear any criticism against the Dutch. The word *Belanda* (Hollander) is often called out as a welcome to westerners passing through small villages.

By and large, however, the Balinese and Sasaks have assimilated amicably and the Balinese have made strong cultural contributions to the island. One of these contributions was the effect Balinese Hinduism had on the emergence of the Wektu Telu religion, a unique mix of Islamic and Hindu philosophies, peculiar to Lombok. Other areas of influence include the spectacular temples they built at Cakranegara, Narmada, Lingsar and Suranadi which add greatly to the interest and beauty of the architecture and relics in Lombok. The Balinese temple ceremonies and processions also contribute to the liveliness and attraction of the island.

Chinese

The Chinese first came to Lombok with the Dutch as a cheap labour force, to work as coolies in the rice paddies. Later they were given some privileges and allowed to set up and develop their own businesses, primarily restaurants and shops.

When the Dutch were ousted from Indonesia in 1948, the Chinese stayed and continued to expand their business interests. Many were killed in vicious reprisals following the abortive Communist

...ever,
...ch an
...ok as
...u can
...stivals

...l by the
...which
...nvolves
...l of, the
...led *adi*
...t during
...siblings

Cakranegara. Almost every ...
every second restaurant in Cakra is run or
owned by the Chinese.

escape from ... ...d by the
blood, the fertilised egg, the fluid that
protects the foetus during pregnancy and
the placenta. If the afterbirth is treated
with deference and respect the four
siblings will not cause harm to the
newborn child or its mother. The placenta
is buried close to the main entrance of the
house, on the left-hand side if it's a girl
child, on the right if it is a boy. Then
follows a kind of 'christening' characterised
by a ritualistic scattering of ashes known
as *buang au* during which the priest
names the newborn child. When the child
is 105 days old it has its first haircut in
another ceremony called the *ngurisang*.

Arabs

In Ampenan there is a small Arab quarter
known as *Kampung Arab*. The Arabs
living here are devout Muslims who follow
the Koran to the letter. They have no
particular customs of their own but are
inclined to hold themselves aloof from the
other peoples of Lombok and marry
amongst themselves. They are well
educated and relatively affluent; many
follow professions such as teaching and
medicine, others are insurance agents or
office workers. They tend to adopt small
western affectations like wearing sunglasses
and are extremely friendly towards
foreigners, welcoming the chance to
practise their English. Often they will go
out of their way to take you for sightseeing
trips around the island.

SOCIAL CUSTOMS

Traditional law or *adat* is still fundamental
to the way of life on Lombok today,
particularly customs relating to courting
and marriage rituals, and circumcision
ceremonies. Life is complex, rich and
varied because both Balinese and Sasak
adat systems are followed. In western
Lombok you can see the dances, colourful
processions with their decorative offerings
of flowers, fruit and food, and the temple
ceremonies of Bali as well as the

Circumcision

The laws of Islam require that all boys be
circumcised (*nyunatang*) and in Indonesia
this is usually done somewhere between
the ages of six and 11. Much pomp and
circumstance mark this occasion on
Lombok. The boys are carried through the
village streets on painted wooden horses
and lions with tails of palm fronds. The
circumcision is performed without
anaesthetic as each boy must be prepared
to suffer pain for Allah, and as soon as it is
over they all have to enact a ritual known
as the *makka* – a kind of obeisance with a
drawn kris dagger held unsheathed.

The makka ritual is upheld as a
singular honour for the boys because it is
regarded as a mystical rite, and apart

from this occasion, is performed solely by adult men and even then only rarely. Traditionally such an occasion would be a vow of loyalty to their king in which they state their willingness to die in his defence. After the ritual a party is held to celebrate the ceremony. If possible this is put on straight after a wedding, so that the same decorations – the marquee of bamboo supports and thatched palm, glasses, plates and chairs – can be used again.

Courting

Once again there's much pageantry in Sasak courting mores. Traditionally teenage girls and boys are kept strictly apart except on certain festival occasions – weddings, circumcision feasts and the annual celebration of the first catch of the strange nyale fish at Kuta. On these occasions they are allowed to mingle with each other freely. However, if at one of these occasions a girl publicly accepts a gift from a boy – food for example – she is committed to marrying him.

Harvest time is another opportunity for courting. Traditionally the harvesting of rice was done with a razor-sharp bamboo cutter, and each head of grain was cut from the plant separately. This was the women's work; the men carried the sheaves away on shoulder-poles. Under the watchful but busy eyes of the older men and women, a group of girls would approach the rice paddy from one side, a group of boys from the other. Each group would sing a song, each would applaud the other and each had a chance to circumspectly flirt with one another. This courtship ritual is still carried on in the more isolated, traditional villages.

Marriage Rituals

When the time comes to get married young couples have a choice of three rituals: the first is an arranged marriage, the second a union between cousins, the third involves eloping. The first two are simple and uncomplicated: the parents of

the prospective bridal couple meet to discuss the bride's dowry and sort out any religious differences. Having handled the business arrangements, the ceremony, sorong serah, is performed.

The third method is far more complicated and dramatic. Theoretically a young girl is forbidden to marry a man of lower caste, but this rule can be broken through kidnapping and eloping. As a result, eloping is still a widespread practice in Lombok, despite the fact that in most instances the parties involved – parents of both bride and groom and the couple intending to marry – are in the know. Originally it was used as a means of eluding other competitors for the girl's hand or in order to avoid family friction but it also minimised the heavy expenses of a wedding ceremony!

The rules of this ritual are laid down and must be followed step by step. After the girl is spirited away by the boy, he is required to report to the kepala desa – head of the village – where he has taken refuge. He receives 44 lashes for such a 'disrespectful' action and has a piece of black cotton string wound around his right wrist to indicate to all that he has kidnapped his future bride. The kepala desa then notifies the girl's family through the head of the village that they live in. After this a delegation from the boy's family visits the girl's parents, and between them they settle on a price for the bride, which is distributed among members of the bride's family in recompense for losing her.

Traditionally dowries are worked out according to caste differences; the lower his caste and the higher hers, the more he has to pay. There are four forms of payment: bolongs which are old Chinese coins with a square hole in the centre; tumbaks, ceremonial lances with gilt tips; rombongs which are rice bowls containing 225 bolongs and covered by a cloth half-a-metre square, which has a small knife placed across it called a pangat; the fourth consists of coconut milk and red sugar. The rombongs are given to the mother of the bride and are symbolic of the milk she fed her as a baby; the pangat is for the father of the bride. The bolongs must be kept within the family and handed down from generation to generation. The coconut milk and sugar represent the bride and groom and they are eaten and drunk together by the two families in celebration of the union.

Payment of 1000 bolongs, three tumbaks, one rombong and two coconuts is the going price when the boy and girl both come from the highest caste; 5000 bolongs, four tumbaks, one rombong and two coconuts is the price demanded when a boy from the second caste marries a girl from the highest; and 10,000 bolongs, seven tumbaks, one rombong and two coconuts is necessary when boys from the third and fourth castes marry 'above' themselves.

Once this has been settled the wedding begins. Generally the bride and groom, dressed in ceremonial clothes, are carried through the streets on a sedan chair on long bamboo poles. Boys carrying tumbaks lead the procession and the sounds of the gamelan (known as the *barong tengkok*) mingle with the shouts and laughter of the guests as the couple are swooped up and down and around on their way to the wedding place. Throughout the whole ceremony the bride, in an enormous gold and flowered headdress and dark sunglasses, must look downcast and unhappy at the prospect of leaving her family.

When they arrive they are seated with their backs to a wall, the man's headdress is removed and gold tincture is rubbed into his body and the faces of each. Finally the couple are given a ritual bathing, and then perform a series of symbolic acts which includes feeding each other to demonstrate their new status and duties to each other.

Death

The Balinese inhabitants of Lombok hold cremation ceremonies identical to those on Bali when one of their community dies, but members of the Wektu Telu religion and Muslims have their own rituals. The body of the dead person is washed and prepared for burial by relations in the presence of a holy man, and then wrapped in white sheets and sackcloth. The corpse is placed on a raised bamboo platform while certain sections of the Koran are read out and relations pray to Allah and call upon the spirits of their ancestors. The body is then taken to the cemetery and interred with the head facing towards Mecca. During the burial passages of the Koran are read aloud in Sanskrit and afterwards more quotations from the Koran are recited in Arabic.

Relatives and friends of the dead place offerings on the grave – pieces of hand-carved wood called *tumbak* if it's a man or decorative combs if it's a woman. Various offerings which include combs and cloth are also made in the village. Several ceremonies are held on certain set days after the burial involving readings from the Koran. These are performed on the third, seventh, 40th and 100th days after the death and after 1000 days have elapsed a special ceremony known as *nyiu* is carried out. During nyiu the grave is sprinkled with holy water and the tumbak or combs removed and stones put in their place.

Contests

The Sasaks are fascinated by physical prowess and heroic trials of strength, fought on a one-to-one level. As a result they have developed a unique contest of their own and adopted and adapted others from nearby Sumbawa.

Peresehan This peculiar man-to-man combat is a great favourite all over Lombok. Usually held in the late afternoon in the open air, a huge crowd – all men apart from the occasional curious female traveller – gather together to watch two men battle it out with long rattan staves, protected only by small rectangular shields made from cow or buffalo hide. The staves are ceremoniously handed around the crowd lined up in a large roped-off area and then returned to the referee. With great drama the gamelan starts to play and two men, dressed in exquisite finery featuring turbans or head scarves and wide sashes at the waist, feign the movements of the contest about to be fought.

Having shown everyone how it is supposed to be done, the men look around the crowd for contestants, who are carefully chosen to match each other as closely as possible in height and strength. Skill is another matter altogether. Anyone can be chosen; some perform several times during the afternoon, others refuse to take part at all. While it is quite permissible to refuse, it is clearly of great status to win. Those who agree to participate must quickly find scarves to wrap around their heads and waists if they haven't already got them – the head gear and waist-sash are supposed to have magical powers of protection – take off their shirts and shoes, roll up their trousers and then pick up their staves and shields and begin to flay into each other.

The performance is umpired or refereed by the *pekembar*, usually one of the two men who select the contestants. If either of the fighters loses his headscarf or waistband the contest is stopped immediately until he puts it back on. It goes for three rounds – often five with more experienced fighters – or until one of the two is bleeding or surrenders. The pekembar can also declare the contest over if he thinks things are getting too rough. They often do, for though the movements are very stylised, there is absolutely nothing carefully choreographed or rigged about this – unlike western wrestling matches. Both contestants generally finish with great welts all over them, the crowd gets wildly excited and each fighter has his own groupies cheering him on. At the end of each contest the

winner is given a T-shirt or sarong, and the loser also gets some small token.

Before the event, as part of the spectacle and atmosphere, they often hold a greasy pole contest. Two tall poles are erected, topped by a gaily decorated, large wooden wheel with a number of goodies dangling from it like cloth, bags and shorts. Amid much mirth and merriment two small boys attempt to clamber up the slippery pole and untie the loot. Strictly speaking they are supposed to untie one article at a time, slide down to the bottom and then climb up again for the next one. But a lot of 'cheating' goes on, particularly when the crowd's attention is trained on the more violent spectacle of the peresehan, which generally starts before this is over.

Lanca This particular trial of strength originated in Sumbawa, but the Sasaks have also adopted it and perform it on numerous occasions, particularly when the first rice seedlings are planted. Like peresehan it is a contest between two well-matched men, who use their knees to strike each other. It involves a fair amount of skill and a lot of strength.

ARTS & CRAFTS

Lombok is renowned for its traditional weaving. The techniques are handed down from mother to daughter. Each piece of cloth is woven on a handloom in established patterns and colours. Some fabrics are woven in as many as four directions and interwoven with gold thread. Many take at least a month to complete. Flower and animal motifs of buffaloes, dragons, lizards, crocodiles and snakes are widely used to decorate these exquisite sarongs.

Several villages specialise in this craft and it is worth visiting one as often a wider selection of cloth is available. Sukarara, south of Cakranegara on the main road through Kediri and Puyung, and Pringgasela, in the mountains of east Lombok, are two villages that continue to produce fabrics using the Purbasari technique.

Lombok also has a fine reputation for plaited basketware, bags and mats. Loyok and Kotaraja are two villages in east Lombok where this ancient Sasak craft may still be practised.

MUSIC & DANCE

Lombok has some brilliant dances found nowhere else in Indonesia. But unlike Bali which encourages - in fact hustles - westerners to go along to its dances, getting to see any on Lombok depends on word of mouth or pure luck. Once again in western Lombok all the dances of Bali are performed, particular favourites being the Legong, Arja and Joget Bumbung. But there are also a wide variety of Sasak dances performed all over the island.

Cupak Gerantang

This is a dance based on one of the *Panji* stories, an extensive cycle of written and oral stories originating in Java in the 15th century. Like Arjuna, Panji is a romantic hero and this dance is popular all over Lombok. It is usually performed at *adat* celebrations and other festivities.

Kayak Sando

This is another version of a Panji story but here the dancers wear masks. It is only found in central and east Lombok.

Gandrung

This dance is about love and courtship - *gandrung* means being in love or longing. It is a social dance, usually performed outside by the young men and women of the village. Everyone stands around in a circle and then, accompanied by a full gamelan orchestra, a young girl dances dreamily by herself for a time, before choosing a male partner from the audience to join her. It is typical to Narmada in west Lombok, Suangi and Lenek in east Lombok and Praya in central Lombok.

Oncer

This is a war dance performed by men and young boys. It is a highly skilled and dramatic performance which involves the participants playing a variety of weird musical instruments in time to their movements. The severe black of the costumes is slashed with crimson and gold waist bands, shoulder sashes, socks and caps. It's performed with great vigour at *adat* festivals, both in central and east Lombok.

Rudat

Another traditional Sasak dance performed by pairs of men dressed in black caps and jackets and black-and-white check plaid sarongs. They are backed by singers, tambourines and cylindrical drums called *jidur*. This dance – music, lyrics, costume – is a combination of Islamic and Sasak cultures.

Tandak Gerok

Traditionally an east Lombok performance, it combines dance, theatre and singing to music played on bamboo flutes and the bowed lute called a *rebab*. Its unique and most attractive feature is that the vocalists imitate the sound of the gamelan instruments. It is usually performed after harvesting or other hard physical labour, but is also put on at adat ceremonies.

Genggong

Seven musicians are involved in this particular performance. Using a simple set of instruments which includes a bamboo flute, a rebab and knockers, they accompany their music with dance movements and stylised hand gestures.

Barong Tengkok

This is the name given to the procession of musicians who play at weddings or circumcision ceremonies.

RELIGION
Wektu Telu

Lombok has a unique religion, Wektu

Telu, which originated in north Lombok in a village called Bayan. Approximately 30% of the population of Lombok belongs to this faith, although the numbers are slowly diminishing as more and more young people turn to Islam.

The word *wektu* means 'result' in the Sasak language, while *telu* means 'three' and signifies the complex mixture of the three religions which comprise Wektu Telu: Balinese Hinduism, Islam and animism. Members of the Wektu Telu religion regard themselves as being Muslims, although they are not officially accepted by the Muslims as such.

The fundamental tenet of this faith is that all important aspects of life are underpinned by a trinity. One example of this principle is the trinity of Allah, Mohammed and Adam. Allah symbolises the one true God, Mohammed is the link between God and human beings and Adam represents a being in search of a soul. The sun, the moon and the stars are believed to represent heaven, earth and water; and the head, body, arms and legs, creativity, sensitivity and control. Another example involves the three methods of reproduction or multiplying through eggs, mammals and seeds.

On a communal basis the Wektu Telus hold that there are three main duties which they must fulfil: belief in Allah, avoiding the temptations of the devil and co-operating with, helping and loving other people. The faithful must also pray to Allah every Friday, meditate and undertake to carry out good deeds.

The Wektu Telus do not observe Ramadan, the month-long period of abstinence so important in the Islamic faith. Their concession to it is a mere three days of fasting and prayer. They also do not follow the pattern of praying five times a day in a holy place – mosque – laid down as one of the basic laws of the Islamic religion. While prayer and meditation are of supreme importance in their daily rituals, the Wektu Telus believe in praying from the heart as they feel it and wherever they are, not at appointed times in man-made edifices specifically built for worship. According to them all public buildings serve this purpose and all are designed with a prayer corner or contain a small room which faces Mecca. Their dead are buried with their heads facing Mecca, but it is unheard of for a Wektu Telu follower to go there.

As for not eating pork, the Wektu Telus consider everything which comes from Allah to be good.

Castes Like the Balinese Hindus the Wektu Telus have a caste system, which is one of the factors which distinguishes them from other Lombok inhabitants. There are four castes: the highest being *datoe*; the second *raden*; the third *buling* and the fourth *jajar karang*.

Islam

Over half the population of Lombok are Muslims, the majority living in the central and eastern parts of the island. There are a few closed Muslim settlements on Lombok, Labuhan Lombok being one.

Islam reached Indonesia in the 13th century through peaceful Gujarati merchants, not fanatical Arabs. It arrived on the eastern coast of Lombok via Sulawesi (the Celebes) and via Java on the west. Today it is the professed religion of 90% of the Indonesian people and its traditions and rituals affect all aspects of their daily life. Friday afternoon is the officially decreed time for believers to worship and all government offices and many businesses are closed as a result. Arabic is taught in all Indonesian schools so the Koran can continue to be read and studied by successive generations. Scrupulous attention is given to cleanliness including ritualistic washing of hands and face. The pig is considered to be unclean and is not kept or eaten in strict Muslim regions. Many Indonesian Muslims have more than one wife. There are also many who scrimp and save throughout their lives to make the pilgrimage to Mecca to circle the black stone Ka'aba seven times. Those who have done this, *haji* if they are men, *haja* if women, are deeply respected.

Islam not only influences routine daily living and personal politics but also has an affect on the politics of government. Orthodox Muslims demand that the whole population observe religious holidays and that the government protects and encourages Islam. Since independence was declared Indonesia has had two serious uprisings, both instigated by reactionary Muslim extremists. F...
th. 197...

including: a belief in a hell, a heaven, one true God, a creation theory almost identical to the Garden of Eden and myths like Noah's Ark and Aaron's Rod.

The expression 'there is no god but Allah and Mohammed is his prophet' is the fundamental tenet of Islam, which itself means submission. Islam is a faith that demands unconditional surrender to the wisdom of Allah and means far more than a mere set of beliefs or rules. It involves total commitment to a way of life, philosophy and law. Theoretically it is a democratic ...

... on is
... lual,
... cial
... ith
... nce
... s it
... ful
... ue
... a
... re
... ve
... of
... a
... n,
... e
... ...e

... ...age to Mecca. It is also a fatalistic faith in which everything is rationalised as the will of Allah.

... did not ... supernatural powers, but he did claim he was God's only teacher and prophet, charged with the divine mission of interpreting the word of God. Mohammed's teachings are collated and collected in the scripture of Islam, the Koran, which was compiled from his oral and written records shortly after his death. It is divided into 14 chapters and every word in it is said to have emanated from Mohammed and been inspired by God himself, in the will of Allah.

Much of the Koran is devoted to codes of behaviour, and much emphasis is placed on God's mercy to mankind. Mohammed's teachings are heavily influenced by two other religions, Judaism and Christianity, to the point where there are some extraordinary similarities

In Indonesia the dogma of Islam has become intermixed with aspects of animist and Hindu-Buddhist precepts, so it has a peculiar twist of its own. So intrinsic are they that they affect the Muslim way of life from peripheral details like architecture to fundamental attitudes like the treatment of women. Many Indonesian mosques do not have minarets and instead feature onion-shaped cupolas. The muezzin of Indonesia today are a dying breed, often pre-recorded tapes are sent out over a loudspeaker. Indonesian Muslims also pray in a distinctive manner with their hands pressed together, fingers extended, touching the chest, lips or forehead.

Muslim women in Indonesia are

Left: Thatched roof phone box, Mataram, Lombok (TW)
Right: Pura Meru temple from the Mayur water palace, Cakranegara, Lombok (TW)
Bottom: Kuta Beach, Lombok (TW)

Top: Kids in the rain, Lingsar, Lombok (TW)
Left: Rice barn, Sade, Lombok (TW)
Right: Heading towards Gili Trawangan, Lombok (TW)

allowed more freedom and shown more respect than their counterparts in other Third World countries. They do not have to wear facial veils, nor are they segregated or considered to be second-class citizens. There are a number of matrilineal and matriarchal societies and sometimes special mosques are built for women. What is more, Muslim men in Indonesia are only allowed to marry two women whereas Muslims in other parts of the world can have as many as four wives. Even then they must have the consent of their first wife. Throughout Indonesia it is the women who initiate divorce proceedings where necessary under the terms of their marriage agreement.

HOLIDAYS & FESTIVALS
Most of the religious festivals of Lombok take place at the beginning of the rainy season around October to December or at harvest time around April to May. During these periods there are celebrations in villages all over the island, people dress in their most resplendent clothes and flaunt status symbols like sunglasses and watches. Wooden effigies of horses and lions are carried in processions through the streets and the sound of the gamelan reaches fever pitch.

While most of these ceremonies and rituals are annual events, many of them do not fall on specific days. This means you have to keep your eyes open and listen carefully in order to find out when they are being held. The Muslim year is shorter than the western one so their festivals and events fall at a different time each year.

Wektu Telu
Puasa/Ramadan Three days of fasting and prayer in deference to the Muslim period of abstinence.

Perang Ketupat Annual rain festival held at Lingsar between October and December when the Wektu Telus and the Balinese Hindus give offerings and pray there, then come out and pelt each other with

ketupat, sticky rice wrapped in banana leaves (see Lingsar).

Hari Raya Ketupat Celebration held seven days after the end of Ramadan at Batulayar near Senggigi.

Islam
Puasa/Ramadan The ninth month of the Muslim calendar is often preceded by a cleansing ceremony *Padusan* to prepare for the coming fast. Traditionally people get up at 4 am for breakfast and then fast from sunrise to sunset. Many visit family graves and royal cemeteries, recite extracts from the Koran, sprinkle the graves with holy water and strew them with flowers. Special prayers are said at mosques and at home. During this time most restaurants are closed and foreigners eating or smoking in public are regarded with contempt that can border on aggression. By the time the end of the month is up many Muslims' tempers are frayed to snapping point. Try to avoid spending Ramadan on Lombok as there is little to do and less that is open.

Hari Raya The first day of the 10th month of the Muslim calendar and the end of Ramadan. This climax to a month of austerity and tension is characterised by wild beating of drums all night, fireworks and no sleep. At 7 am everyone turns out for an open-air service. Women dress in white and mass prayers are held followed by two days of feasting. Extracts from the Koran are read and religious processions take place. Gifts are exchanged in this time of joy and mutual forgiveness. Pardon is asked for past wrong-doings. Everyone dresses in their finest and newest clothes and neighbours and relatives are visited with gifts of specially prepared food. At each house visited tea and sweet cakes are served. It continues until all relatives have been seen.

For travellers it is a difficult time to get around. All public transport is booked out and bemos double in price, accommodation can also be difficult to find. If you're in Indonesia at this time, don't plan on travelling anywhere; stay put until the week is over.

Idul Adha This day of sacrifice is held on the 10th day of the 11th month of the Muslim calendar. People visit the mosque and recite passages from the Koran.

Maulid Nabi Mohammed/Hari Natal Mohammed's birthday is held on the 12th day of the 12th month of the Arabic calendar.

Mi'raj Nabi Mohammed A festival celebrating the ascension of Mohammed.

Bali Hinduism
Pujawali Celebration held every year at the Kalasa Temple at Narmada in honour of the god Batara, who dwells on Lombok's most sacred mountain, Gunung Rinjani. At the same time the faithful who have made the trek up the mountain and down to Lake Segara Anak hold a ceremony called *Pekelan*, where they throw gold trinkets and objects into the lake.

Perang Ketupat Festival held in conjunction with the Wektu Telus some time during October, November or December. (See Wektu Telus.)

Harvest Ceremony Held as a thanksgiving for a good harvest at Gunung Pengsong, nine km from Cakra some time around March or April. In this ceremony a buffalo is dragged up the steep hill and sacrificed.

Miru Temple A special ceremony is held every June at full moon in this splendid Balinese temple in Cakranegara.

Bersih Desa This festival occurs at harvest time. Houses and gardens are cleaned, fences white-washed, roads and paths repaired. Once part of a ritual to rid the village of evil spirits it is now held in honour of Dewi Sri, the rice goddess.

Other
Independence Day This marks the anniversary of Indonesian independence from Holland in 1945. It's celebrated all over Indonesia on 17 August and is the biggest Indonesian national holiday. Dances, public entertainment, performances, processions, sporting events, you name it, it all happens. School children and young girls and boys spend months preparing for it.

LANGUAGE
The people of Lombok are all bi-lingual, fluent in Bahasa Indonesia and their own ethnic dialect, Sasak. They are taught Bahasa Indonesia, the official language of the country, in their school curriculum and use it as their formal mode of communication. Sasak is the colloquial tongue and is not derived from Malay, nor does it have any relationship to Malay's modern successor, Bahasa Indonesia. So don't expect to be able to understand Sasak if you can speak Indonesian.

Very few people on Lombok speak English and this includes police and other officials. Travellers without a grasp of Bahasa Indonesia can get by, but some knowledge of it not only enhances an understanding of the island, but could also be invaluable in any emergency such as losing your passport or having an accident. Outside the main centres, finding anyone who can say more than a few phrases like 'hello', 'where do you come from' or 'good evening Mister', is extremely rare. If you can't speak Indonesian, arm yourself with a phrasebook and dictionary.

Getting Around Lombok

Lombok has an extensive network of roads, although there are many outlying villages that are difficult to get to by public transport. In the flatter areas between Gunung Rinjani and the southern highlands the roads are good and numerous and it's easy to get around. It's far more difficult to travel through the highlands of Rinjani and down the south coast to Kuta and environs where there are either no roads at all or else the roads are fine but public transport is very irregular.

Up in the north-east highlands the choice is either walking or going by motorcycle. If you are exploring these regions on foot or motorbike bear in mind two things: often food and drinking water are scarce so it's a good idea to carry supplies; secondly so few westerners have been in these parts you'll be regarded as a sensation by any villagers you come across. During the wet many roads are flooded or washed away, others are impassable because of fallen rocks and rubble, making it impossible to get to many of the out-of-the-way places.

Another impediment to getting around Lombok is that public transport is generally restricted to main routes, which means that if you want to explore places that are off the beaten track you have to walk or hire a *dokar* (horse cart) or motorcycle. The situation may be improving as the government has instituted an ambitious road improvement scheme as part of a long-term plan of putting Lombok on the tourist map. A new coastal road had been mooted and other roads are being built.

Like Bali, Lombok has the usual Indonesian methods of transport: bemos, buses, minibuses, colts, dokars and outrigger canoes (sampans and prahus) for short sea voyages – see the Getting Around Bali chapter for more details.

Taxis are also available on Lombok and either charge by the hour or a fixed sum for particular distances like getting to and from the airport.

Warning

Like many Indonesians, Lombokians don't travel well. In particular many of the women and children have extremely weak stomachs.

Most public transport stops at 10.30 or 11 pm, often earlier in more isolated areas. If you find yourself out in the sticks without your own wheels you can try to charter a bemo or just make yourself as comfortable as you can until sunrise.

BEMOS

The cheapest and most common way of getting around is by bemo or minibus for shorter distances or bus for longer stretches. There are several bemo terminals on Lombok including one at Cakranegara and another at Ampenan, but the main station is at Sweta, a couple of km out of Cakra. Here buses, minibuses, bemos and colts fan out to all points of the island: it's the sweaty, blaring hub of public transport on the island.

Public transport fares are fixed by the provincial government and at Sweta there is a list of fares to most places on the island prominently displayed. This does not stop the bus and bemo boys from trying to take you for a ride, so check the notice board before setting off. Otherwise watch what the locals are paying or ask someone on the bemo what the going rate is. Children on a parent's knee are free, up to about 11 they cost around half price.

As with all public transport in Indonesia drivers wait until their vehicles are crammed to capacity before they contemplate moving. Often there are people, produce, fighting cocks, caged birds, stacks of sarongs, laden baskets, even bicycles hanging out the windows and doors and at times it seems you're in danger of being crushed to death or at least asphyxiated. More often than not you won't be able to organise yourself to get a good vantage spot to see much of the countryside. However most people are very friendly, many offer to share their food with you, most ask where you come from – be prepared for lots of *dari manas* – and generally want to find out all they can.

Chartering Bemos

While you can get to most of the accessible places on Lombok by bemo, bus, dokar or a combination of all three, many trips involve several changes and a lot of waiting around. If you're pressed for time and can get a few people together hiring a bemo by the day or even from one village or place of interest to the next can be cheap and convenient.

These days hiring bemos is becoming almost as common on Lombok as on Bali so it's quite feasible and easy to arrange. Work out where you want to go and be prepared for some hard bargaining. Try to stick to your original plan but if you don't and stop off somewhere else on the way, be prepared to pay extra. As with Bali prices for chartering bemos are worked out roughly by the number of passengers a regular bemo carries – 12 – multiplied by the normal fare, or about 25 rp per person per km for a full load. Once again, like Bali, a reasonable price to pay for chartering a bemo for the day would be 20,000 to 25,000 rp.

You can probably arrange to charter a bemo through your losmen or hotel or alternatively you can simply go round to the bemo station and ask directly. Check the vehicle is roadworthy. Does it have good tyres? Do the lights and wipers work? A straightforward trip can quickly turn into a nightmare when you find yourself out after dark, in the rain, with a wiperless and lightless bemo!

DOKARS

Dokars are the jingling, horse-drawn carts found all over Indonesia. The two-wheel carts are usually brightly-coloured with decorative motifs and fitted out with bells that chime when they're in motion. The small ponies that pull them often have long colourful tassels attached to their gear. A typical dokar has bench seating on either side which can comfortably fit three people, four if they're all slim. I counted 15 passengers in one plus several bags of rice and other paraphernalia.

It's a picturesque way of getting around if you don't get upset by ill-treatment of animals – although generally the horses are looked after reasonably well, they're the owner's means of survival. Dokars are a very popular form of transport in many parts of Lombok and often go to places that bemos don't, won't or can't.

The minimum price is 50 rp but it's unlikely that you'll be taken anywhere for less than 100 rp. Count on paying around 100 rp per person per km.

PRAHUS & SAMPANS

These elegant, brilliantly painted, outrigger fishing boats, looking rather like exotic dragonflies, are used for short inter-island hops and from Bangsal Harbour to the Gili Islands.

MOTORCYCLES & BICYCLES

There are motorcycle and bicycle hire places in the main centres of Lombok but not as many as there are in Bali. They are also not as easy to find, you won't see the 'motorbike for hire' signs stuck up all over the place that you do in Bali. You have to ask around. However, there are individuals owners who rent out their bikes and a couple of specialist places in Ampenan and Mataram. The motorcycles and the rental charges are very similar to Bali. As in Bali the longer you hire one for, the cheaper it becomes.

A great advantage of having a motorcycle is that you can get to the more inaccessible places with relative ease and you can make side trips and stops when you feel like it. Once you get out of the main centres there's not much traffic on the roads, apart from people, dogs and water buffaloes, but you do have to contend with numerous potholes and men at work upgrading the roads. This can be particularly hazardous at night when you round a corner and come slap up against a grader, rocks piled into the middle of the road or 44-gallon drums of tar. They rarely, if ever, put up warning signs that there are roadworks in progress, and up in the mountains there are perilous and unprotected drops down sheer cliff faces to the valley below. Once off the main roads you will find yourself on dirt tracks and in for a rough ride.

Petrol can also be a problem. There are petrol stations around the larger towns but out in the villages petrol can be difficult to find. If you intend going to out-of-the-way places it may be advisable to

take some with you, so long as you can carry it safely. If not, it's available from small wayside shops – look out for signs that read *press ban*.

Try to get a motorcycle which is in good condition. This is a real problem in Lombok, first of all there aren't so many motorcycles available so they don't tend to be as well kept as the better ones in Bali.

Secondly you get 'off the beaten' track in Lombok, much more quickly than in Bali. It's a bad combination, potentially unreliable motorcycles and limited help when they go wrong. So if you've got a choice between a better more expensive bike and a worse but cheaper one, in Lombok the better one is the best bet.

The story on bicycle hire is much the same. Bicycles are for rent in and around the main centres of Lombok, but so far they are not a very popular form of transport around the island either among the locals or with travellers. This is probably because many of the local inhabitants could not afford them and those that have any money for such luxuries would save up for a motorcycle. If you want to explore Lombok by bicycle you probably have to bring your own or be prepared to do some maintenance work on one of the old rust buckets you will find here.

Distances from Sweta in km

Narmada	6 km
Kopang	25 km
Selong (East Lombok)	47 km
Pringgabaya	60 km
Labuhan Lombok	69 km
Sambelia	89 km
Airport	7 km
Pemenang	31 km
Bayan	79 km
Lembar	22 km
Ampenan	7 km
Suranadi	13 km
Sesaot	15 km
Praya	27 km
Tetebatu	46 km
Lingsar	10 km
Gunung Pengsong	8 km
Kuta	52 km
Batu Bolong	10 km

West Lombok

AMPENAN, MATARAM, CAKRANEGRA & SWETA

Although they are officially four separate towns Ampenan, Mataram, Cakranegara and Sweta actually run together and it's virtually impossible to tell where one stops and the next starts. Collectively they're the main 'city' on Lombok and you'll have to come here to handle any type of bureaucracy from changing money to buying airline tickets. They also have a few things to see but once that's out of the way most visitors head off to other places on the island. These days it's not even necessary to stay in the town, Senggigi Beach is easy commuting distance.

Ampenan

Once the main port of Lombok, Ampenan is now not much more than a small fishing harbour, though cattle are still exported from here to Jakarta, Surabaya, Hong Kong and Singapore. It's dirty and dusty and the stench of the open drains pervades the whole township at times. It's inundated with mosques which makes it impossible to get away from the raucous sound of the loudspeakers, calling the faithful to prayer. But it's also full of hustle and bustle and colour and life. The long main road through Ampenan-Mataram-Cakranegara does not actually reach the coast at Ampenan. Somehow it simply fades out, just before it gets to the port's grubby beach.

Ampenan has a curious mixture of people. Apart from the Sasaks and Balinese, there is also a small Arab quarter known as *Kampung Arab*. The Arabs (probably descendants of Arab merchants and Sasak women) living here are devout Muslims; they're inclined to hold themselves aloof from the other people on Lombok. They marry amongst themselves, are well educated and relatively affluent – many follow professions such as teaching and medicine, others are insurance agents or office workers. They're also extremely friendly towards foreigners.

Most of the Chinese living in Lombok today are based in Ampenan or up the road in Cakranegara – almost every shop and every second restaurant in Cakra is run or owned by the Chinese. The Chinese first came to Lombok with the Dutch as a cheap labour force, to work as coolies in the rice paddies. Later, as in other parts of the archipelago, the Dutch fostered them as economic middle men between themselves and the Indonesian population. The Chinese soon became a privileged minority and were allowed to set up and develop their own businesses. When the Dutch were ousted from Indonesia in 1949 the Chinese stayed and continued to expand their business interests. Many of those in eastern Lombok however, were killed in the aftermath of the attempted '65 coup. The massacres were perhaps as much anti-Chinese as anti-Communist.

Mataram

Mataram is the administrative capital of the province of Nusa Tenggara Barat which comprises Lombok and Sumbawa Islands. It is surprising how much money has been poured into unexpectedly impressive buildings like the Bank of Indonesia, the new post office and the governor's office and residence. There are also some surprisingly palatial houses around the outskirts of town, the homes of Lombok's elite.

Cakranegara

Now the main commercial centre of Lombok, Cakranegra is usually referred to as Cakra. Formerly the old capital of Lombok under the Balinese rajahs, Cakra today is a cacophony of bemos and motorbikes and people trying to keep

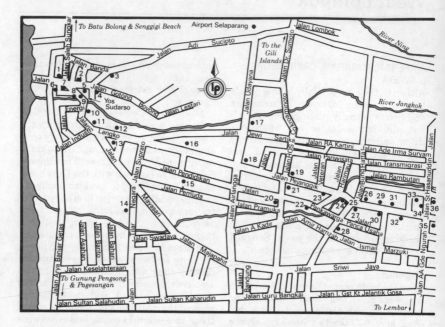

their heads above the exhaust fumes. It has a thriving community of Chinese as well as many Balinese residents. It's also a centre for craftwork and is particularly well known for its basketware and weaving. Check out the bazaar and watch the silver and goldsmiths at work. You may also be able to find some of the idiosyncratic clay animal figures and ceramics produced on Lombok.

Sweta

Seven km from Ampenan and only about 2½ km beyond Cakra is Sweta – the central transport terminal of Lombok. This is where you catch bemos, buses and minibuses to other parts of the island. There are several warungs here and numerous food, tobacco and drink vendors. Stretching along one side of the terminal is a vast covered market, the largest on Lombok. Wander through its dim alleys where stalls spill over with coffee beans, eggs, rice, fish, fabrics, fruit and hardware. There's also a bird market.

Information & Orientation

The division is effectively Ampenan the port; Mataram the administrative centre; Cakranegara the trading centre; and Sweta the transport centre. There's one main road running east from the port all the way to Sweta and it's one way until you get through Cakranegara. The road starts as Jalan Pabean in Ampenan but quickly becomes Jalan Yos Sudarso then changes to Jalan Langko, Jalan Pejanggik and Jalan Selaparang. Just as it's difficult to tell where one town merges into the next it's also difficult to tell where the road changes names. Indeed it seems that they actually overlap since some places appear to have more than one address.

A second one-way street, Jalan Sriwi Jaya which turns into Jalan Mahapahit, brings traffic back in the other direction and bemos run a shuttle service between

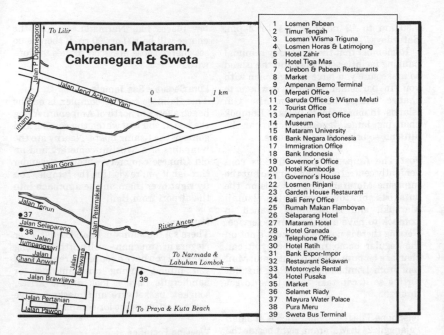

Ampenan, Mataram, Cakranegara & Sweta

To Lilir
To Lilit
Jalan P Diponegoro
Jalan Jend Achmad Yani
Bonjol
0   1 km
Jalan Gora
Jalan Peternakan
Jalan Tenun
Jalan Selaparang
● 37
● 38
Jalan Tumpangsari
Jalan Chanil Anwar
Jalan Bahwana
River Ancar
To Narmada &
Labuhan Lombok
Jalan Brawijaya
● 39
Jalan Pertanian
Jalan Pawon
To Praya & Kuta Beach

1   Losmen Pabean
2   Timur Tengah
3   Losman Wisma Triguna
4   Losmen Horas & Latimojong
5   Hotel Zahir
6   Hotel Tiga Mas
7   Cirebon & Pabean Restaurants
8   Market
9   Ampenan Bemo Terminal
10 Merpati Office
11 Garuda Office & Wisma Melati
12 Tourist Office
13 Ampenan Post Office
14 Museum
15 Mataram University
16 Bank Negara Indonesia
17 Immigration Office
18 Bank Indonesia
19 Governor's Office
20 Hotel Kambodja
21 Governor's House
22 Losmen Rinjani
23 Garden House Restaurant
24 Bali Ferry Office
25 Rumah Makan Flamboyan
26 Selaparang Hotel
27 Mataram Hotel
28 Hotel Granada
29 Telephone Office
30 Hotel Ratih
31 Bank Expor-Impor
32 Restaurant Sekawan
33 Motorcycle Rental
34 Hotel Pusaka
35 Market
36 Selamet Riady
37 Mayura Water Palace
38 Pura Meru
39 Sweta Bus Terminal

Getting back and forth is, therefore, dead easy. You can stay in Ampenan, Mataram or Cakra since there are hotels and restaurants in all three locales. Most budget travellers tend to head towards Ampenan, however, because it has a handy little enclave of cheap hotels and a choice of good places to eat.

The Mataram government buildings are chiefly found along Jalan Pejanggik. The main square, Lampangan Mataram, is bounded by Jalan Pejanggik and Jalan Cempaka. Art exhibitions, theatre, dance and wayang kulit performances are held in the square but it's by word of mouth that you'll find out about these shows. Alternatively swarms of police and military personnel are the most obvious sign of such an occasion.

Mataram has a small 'centre' near the river and a larger shopping area across the crossroads of Jalan Selaparang-Jalan Hasanuddin, where Cakra begins and where you will also find the market.

the bemo station in Ampenan and the big terminus in Sweta about seven km away.

Tourist Office The main tourist office on Lombok, the Kantor Dinas Pariwisata Daerah (tel 21866, 21730), is in Ampenan on Jalan Langko 70 on the left side heading towards Mataram, almost diagonally opposite the post office. The people at the office are helpful and reasonably well informed. They have a good map of Ampenan-Mataram-Cakranegara and of Lombok and a few other pamphlets and brochures in English with information on sights, customs, addresses and so on.

Banks There are a number of banks along the main drag through Mataram and into Cakra, all of them in impressively large buildings. Most appear to change travellers' cheques without any difficulty. The Bank Expor-Import seems to be open longer hours than some of the others – weekdays

7.30 am to 12 noon and 1 to 2 pm, Saturdays 7.30 to 11.30 am.

Remember that there are only minimal banking facilities elsewhere on the island so make sure you have enough cash with you. In particular there is nowhere to change foreign currency on the Gili Islands. In more remote parts of Lombok changing large denominations can be difficult so break down big notes.

Post The Ampenan post office is conveniently central on Jalan Langko but the imposing Mataram post office is on the outskirts of town on Jalan Ismail Marzuki, and is the only branch in Lombok to have a post restante service. Getting there is not easy since it's not on the regular bemo routes, but you can charter a bemo or dokar in Mataram. Mail sent from Lombok goes to Bali first for sorting so it can take some time to get through.

Telephone The telephone office is at Jalan Pejanggik 24 in Mataram, right beside the Bank Umum. It's in a very anonymous building so look for the bank as a landmark. The office is surprisingly efficient and you can get through to overseas in a matter of minutes.

Immigration Lombok's Kantor Immigrasi is on Jalan Udayana, the road out to the airport. They're a friendly and cooperative bunch.

Bookshops There are several bookshops on Jalan Pabean in Ampenan including Toko Buku Titian opposite the Ampenan bemo station. It has maps of Lombok for 750 and 900 rp. The *Jakarta Post* is also sold here, only a day out of date. Apart from that it's virtually impossible to pick up anything in English apart from English/Indonesian dictionaries. There is no Sasak/English dictionary.

Entry Charges Unlike in Bali, entry charges are not so common apart from a

few places like Narmada. Usually the charge will be 100 or 200 rp. If there is no set charge those are good figures to work with!

Pura Segara - Sea Temple
This Balinese temple complex is on the beach a few km north of Ampenan. Along the beach you can watch the coming and going of the fishing boats. Nearby are the remnants of a Muslim cemetery and an old Chinese cemetery - worth a wander through if you're visiting the temple. You fly right over them on the approach into the airport from Bali.

Museum
There's a museum on Jalan Banjar Tiler Negara in Ampenan - well worth browsing around if you have a couple of free hours. If you intend buying any antiques or handicrafts have a look at the krises, songket, basketware and masks to give you a starting point for comparison.

Weaving Factories
There used to be several weaving factories in Cakra open to anyone who wanted to wander in, but now most of them have closed. An exception is Selamet Riady on Jalan Ukirkawi, where women weave delicate gold and silver thread sarongs and exquisite ikats on looms that look like they haven't altered since the Majapahit dynasty. A bemo will drop you within a few metres of the factory and you're welcome to wander around - they seem to be quite used to visitors. It's worth checking out the prices in the shop but you're not obliged to buy anything - you can try to bargain but they won't lower prices by much. The factory is open from 7.30 am.

Mayura Water Palace
Just beyond the market, on the main road through Cakra, stands the Mayura Water Palace. It was built in 1744 and was once part of the Royal Court of the Balinese kingdom in Lombok. The centrepiece is

the large artificial lake covered in water lilies. In the centre of the lake is an open-sided hall connected to the shoreline by a raised footpath. The hall or floating pavilion (*bale kampung*), was used both as a court of justice and a meeting place for the Hindu lords. There are other shrines and fountains dotted around the surrounding park. Entrances to the walled enclosure of the palace are on the north and west sides.

Today the Balinese use it to graze their livestock, and as a place to unleash their fighting cocks and make offerings to the gods. It's a pleasant retreat from Cakra but less than a century ago this was the site of a bloody clash with the Dutch. In 1894 the Dutch sent an army to back the Sasaks in a rebellion against their Balinese rajah. The rajah quickly capitulated but the crown prince decided to fight on while the Dutch-backed forces were split between various camps.

The Dutch camp at the Mayura Water Palace was attacked late at night by a combined force of Balinese and west Sasaks. The camp was surrounded by high walls, and the Balinese and Sasaks took cover behind it as they fired on the exposed army, forcing the Dutch to take shelter in a nearby temple compound (the Pura Meru?). The Balinese also attacked the Dutch camp at Mataram, and soon after the entire Dutch army on Lombok was routed and withdrew to Ampenan where the soldiers, wrote one eye-witness, 'were so nervous that they fired madly if so much as a leaf fell off a tree'. The first battles had resulted in enormous losses of both men and arms for the Dutch.

While the Balinese had won the battle they had just begun to lose the war. Now they would not only have to continue to fight the east Sasaks but also the Dutch, who were quickly supplied with reinforcements from Java. The Dutch attacked Mataram a month after their initial defeat, fighting street to street not only against Balinese and west Sasak soldiers but also the local population. The Balinese crown prince was killed in the battle for the palace and the Balinese retreated to Cakranegara, where they were well-armed and where the complex of walls provided good defence against infantry. Cakra was attacked by a combined force of Dutch and east Sasaks, and as in Mataram Balinese men, women and children staged repeated suicidal lance attacks, only to be cut down by rifle and artillery fire. The Rajah and a small group of *punggawas* fled to the village of Sasari in the vicinity of the pleasure gardens at Lingsar. A day or two later he surrendered to the Dutch – but even the capture of the rajah did not lead the Balinese to surrender.

In late November the Dutch attacked Sasari and a large number of Balinese committed the traditional suicidal *puputan*. With the downfall of the dynasty the local population abandoned the struggle against the Dutch. The conquest of Lombok, thought about for decades, had taken the Dutch barely three months. The old rajah died in exile in Batavia in 1895.

Pura Meru

Directly opposite the water palace and just off the main road, is the Pura Meru – the largest temple on Lombok. It was built in 1720 under the patronage of the Balinese prince, Anak Agung Made Karang of the Singosari kingdom, as an attempt to unite all the small kingdoms on Lombok. Though now rather neglected looking, it was built as a symbol of the universe and is dedicated to the Hindu trinity of Brahma, Vishnu and Shiva.

The temple has three separate courtyards. The outer courtyard has a hall housing the wooden drums that are beaten to call believers to festivals and special ceremonies. In the middle court are two buildings with large raised platforms for offerings. The inner court has one large and 33 small shrines, as well

as three meru (the Balinese multi-roofed shrines). Each shrine is looked after by members of the Balinese community. The three meru are in a line, the central one of 11 tiers is Shiva's house, the one in the north with nine tiers is Vishnu's and the seven-tiered one to the south is Brahma's. In June each year a festival is held here.

Gunung Pengsong

This Balinese temple is built – as the name suggests – on top of a hill, nine km from Cakra and has great views overlooking the town below. Try to get there early in the morning before the clouds envelop Mt Rinjani. Once a year, generally in March or April, a buffalo is taken up the steep 100-metre slope and sacrificed to celebrate a good harvest. The *Bersih Desa* festival also occurs at harvest time – houses and gardens are cleaned, fences white-washed, roads and paths repaired. Once part of a ritual to rid the village of evil spirits, it is now held in honour of the rice goddess Dewi Sri.

Places to Stay – bottom end

The most popular cheap places to stay are in Ampenan. There is no shortage of choice elsewhere but few travellers bother to go further afield unless they intend to head straight out to beautiful Senggigi Beach, just 10 km to the north. From there it's easy to commute into town if there's any business to be done.

Losmen Pabean (tel 21758) at Jalan Pabean 146 is close to the centre of Ampenan and has reasonably clean and pleasant rooms – some with attached mandi – for 2500/3500 rp. It's almost directly opposite several of the popular rumah makans. Beware of the street name confusion in this area, Jalan Pabean is also known as Jalan Yos Sudarso at certain points.

Nearby and just south of Jalan Pabean (or Jalan Yos Sudarso if you prefer) is *Hotel Tiga Mas* (tel 23211) in the Kampung Melayu Tengah. It's basic and a bit grubby with singles/doubles at 1500/

2500 rp. It's also next door to a mosque so be prepared for noise.

At the first junction from Jalan Pabean/Jalan Yos Sudarso, Jalan Koperasi branches off to the north-east and if you continue far enough it takes you all the way to the airport. The other Ampenan cheapies are found along this road. A hop, skip and a jump from the town centre at Jalan Koperasi 12 is the very popular *Hotel Zahir* (tel 22403) with singles/doubles including breakfast for 2500/3500 rp or at 3000/4000 rp with attached mandi. The rooms each have a small verandah and are built around a central courtyard. The Zahir is run by friendly and helpful people.

Continue along the road to Jalan Koperasi 65 where *Losmen Horas* (tel 21695) is very clean and well kept and has rooms at 2500/3500 rp with spotlessly clean bathrooms. Virtually next door is the *Latimojong* at No 64. It's dirt cheap at 1000/1500 rp but this is a strictly bottom end place and very basic.

Continue along Jalan Koperasi and you reach the *Losmen Wisma Triguna* (tel 21705), about a km out from the centre of Ampenan. The Wisma Triguna is owned by the same helpful people as the Horas and it's quiet and pleasantly relaxed. The spacious rooms have attached mandis and open out on to the bright verandah. You can organise Rinjani climbs at the Horas or the Wisma Triguna.

There are other cheap places in Mataram and Cakra but there's really no pressing reason to search further afield than Ampenan. At Jalan Supratman 10 in Mataram the pleasant and cheap *Hotel Kambodja* (tel 22211) has rooms at 5000 rp. Nearby at Jalan Panca Usaha 18 the *Losmen Rinjani* (tel 21633) is slightly cheaper with rooms at 4500 rp. *Hotel Tenang* is also nearby but it's hidden away on Jalan Rumah Sakit Islam. Rooms are 7000/12,500 rp for singles/doubles and a western visitor is a rare occurrence.

On the Mataram/Cakra border there's the *Hotel Pusaka* (tel 23119) at Jalan Sultan Hasanuddin 23. They have a wide variety of rooms at 4000/5000 rp, 5000/6500 rp, 6500/8000 rp and 8000/10,000 rp. Close by at No 17 is the more basic *Losmen Merpati* with rooms at 1500/2500 rp, 3000/4000 rp and 4000/6000 rp.

Places to Stay – top end

There is a plentiful choice of more expensive hotels as well. *Hotel Granada* (tel 22275) is on Jalan Bung Karno, a little south of the centre in Mataram. Rooms here all have air-con, include breakfast and with discount cost 21,000, 25,000 or 35,000 rp. There's a swimming pool and the cheapest rooms are right beside it and excellent value. With its quiet location and pleasant gardens this is probably the best hotel in Ampenan-Mataram-Cakra. The only catch is the caged animals and birds dotted around the gardens. The Granada is undoubtedly the most heavily advertised hotel in Lombok, there are Hotel Granada signs everywhere you go from Kuta Beach to the Gili Islands.

At Jalan Yos Sudarso 4, right next to the Garuda airline office, the *Wisma Melati* (tel 23780) is a pleasant, well kept hotel with rooms ranging from 22,000 to 45,000 rp, all with air-conditioning. There's a restaurant and bar and all the rooms have a telephone and television.

Continue along the main road into Mataram and at Jalan Pejanggik 40-42 the *Selaparang Hotel* (tel 22670) has rooms ranging from 12,000/15,000 rp up to 22,000/25,000 rp with air-con. Across the road at No 105 there's the *Mataram Hotel* (tel 23411) with rooms starting at 12,500/15,000 rp and going up to 26,000/28,000 with air-con, hot water and other mod cons. Both these hotels have pleasant little restaurants but note that this is another area where the road mysteriously changes names, the street may also be called Jalan Selaparang.

Hotel Kertayoga (tel 21775) at Jalan Selaparang 82 is very pleasant with singles/doubles at 9000/12,000 rp. These middle price hotels are all comfortable and well kept with quiet courtyard gardens, they're typical of losmen style at its very best. The street names continue to jump back and forth so the next place is back at Jalan Pejanggik 127 where the *Hotel Ratih* (tel 21096) has rooms from 4000/6500 rp climbing slowly up to 12,500/17,500 rp with air-con. There's a pleasant garden area and breakfast is included, the scale and scope of the breakfast grows with each room price increment!

Places to Eat

Ampenan has several Indonesian and Chinese restaurants including the very popular *Cirebon* at Jalan Pabean 113. It has a standard Indonesian/Chinese menu with most dishes at 1000 to 2000 rp. Next door at No 111 the *Pabean* has very similar food and is run by the same family. You can get a cold beer at these places and the Cirebon menu even has steak & chips for 2000 rp. Meatball soup for 500 rp is very filling and the crab and asparagus soup has been recommended. The whole fish in sweet & sour sauce makes a good splurge.

Closer to the Ampenan bemo station is the *Rumah Makan Arafat* at No 64 with good, cheap Indonesian food. Other alternatives are the *Setia* at Jalan Pabean 129, the *Depot Mina* at Jalan Yos Sudarso 102 and the *Timur Tengah* at Jalan Koperasi 22, right across from the Hotel Zahir. There are lots of snack possibilities to be found in Ampenan market and there are also a couple of bakeries around town.

The Mataram shopping centre beside the river off Jalan Pejanggik, several hundred metres down the road from the Governor's residence has a couple of interesting restaurants. The *Garden House Restaurant* is a pleasant open-air place with nasi campur, nasi goreng and similar standard Indonesian dishes at 1000 to 1500 rp or others at 1500 to 3000 rp. They also have a variety of ice cream dishes from 300 to 400 rp, or casatta and

tutti-frutti for 750 rp. Nearby the *Taliwan* offers local dishes.

Continue further along the main road towards Cakra and you come to the *Rumah Makan Flamboyan*, a pleasant place with seafood and regular Indonesian dishes.

In Cakra the *Sekawan Depot Es* has cold drinks downstairs and a seafood and Chinese restaurant upstairs. Round the corner at Jalan Hasanuddin 20 is the shiny clean *Rumah Makan Madya 2* with Indonesian food. The older looking *Rumah Makan Madya* is right across the road. There are a number of other restaurants in this area, a handful of bakeries and, of course, plenty of other food opportunities at the market.

Things to Buy

There are a surprising number of antique and handicrafts shops in Lombok. Toko Sudirman in Ampenan is at Jalan Pabean 16A, across from the bemo station. They sell some excellent woodcarvings, baskets and traditional Lombok weavings, songket and so on.

Musdah at Dayan Penen, Jalan Sape 16 also has an interesting collection of masks, baskets, krises and carving. Describing how to get to this shop-in-a-home is virtually impossible but a series of signs leads you there from the Hotel Zahir or other places on Jalan Koperasi.

It's more difficult to bargain in Lombok than it is in Bali; you need to take your time – don't rush or be rushed. It's also harder to make an accurate evaluation of things, particularly antiques. You'll hear a lot of talk about special Lombok prices – these are supposed to be much cheaper than Bali prices – but unless you know what you're doing you can pay as much, if not more. Be very sure you want to buy before making an offer. Try to get the dealer to put a price on the object before starting to bargain. Always bargain for what you buy – particularly for items like cloth, basketware or antiques. If you manage to get the price down to half of the asking price then you're doing very well; it's more likely that you will end up paying about two-thirds of the starting price or only get a nominal amount knocked off.

If you want to mail things from Lombok you have to get customs clearance before they can be sent. You may need forms CP2 and five copies of form C2 and CP3 from the post office. Don't indicate on the form that anything you're sending is an antique. From the post office the maximum parcel size is three kg but you can send 10 kg from the GPO.

Getting There & Away
Air See the introductory Getting There chapter for details of the flights to and from Lombok. The Garuda office (tel 23762) is at Jalan Yos Sudarso 6 in Ampenan. There's a Merpati office (tel 21037) a little closer to the centre of Ampenan at Jalan Yos Sudarso 22 and a second Merpati office (tel 22670 & 23235) at the Hotel Selaparang at Jalan Pejanggik 40-42 in Mataram.

Bus The Sweta bus terminal is at the inland end of the Ampenan-Mataram-Cakra-Sweta development and is the main bus terminus for the entire island. It's also the eastern bemo terminus, bemos shuttle back and forth between Ampenan at one end and Sweta at the other. Check fares on the notice board at the office in the middle of the bus paddock before you're hustled on board one of the vehicles. Some distances and approximate bemo fares from Sweta to other parts of Lombok include:

East Direction (Jurusan Timor) Sweta to Narmada (6 km) 150 rp; Mantang 350 rp; Kopang (25 km) 400 rp; Terara 550 rp; Sikur 600 rp; Masbagek 700 rp; Selong (47 km) 700 rp; Aikmel 800 rp; Apitaik 900 rp; Pringgabaya (60 km) 900 rp; Labuhan Lombok (69 km) 1000 rp; Sambelia (89 km) 1200 rp; Tetebatu (46 km) 700 rp; Sesaot (15 km) 300 rp.

South & Central Direction (Jurusan Selatan dan Tenggara) Sweta to Kediri 150 rp; Gerung 300 rp; Lembar (22 km) 400 rp; Praya (27 km) 400 rp; Mujur 550 rp; Keruak 1000 rp; Tjoluar 800 rp; Rambang 900 rp; Labuhan Haji 1000 rp; Kuta (52 km) 900 rp; Tetebatu (46 km) 700 rp.

North Direction (Jurusan Utara) Sweta to Pemeneng (31 km) 500 rp; Tanjung 600 rp; Gondang 700 rp; Amor-Amor 900 rp; Desa Anyar 1200 rp; Bayan (79 km) 1200 rp.

Boat The introductory transport section also has full details on the KMP *Nusa Penida* ferry service between Bali and Lombok. The ferry actually docks at Lembar, some distance south of Ampenan. The SP Ferry office is at Jalan Pejanggik 49 in Mataram.

Getting Around
Airport Transport Lombok's Selaparang Airport is only a couple of km from Ampenan or Mataram, it costs about 3000 rp for a taxi. Alternatively walk out of the car park to the main road and No 7 bemos come by frequently and run straight to the Ampenan bemo terminal for 125 rp. It's not even necessary to go into town from the airport if you want to head out to Senggigi Beach or to the Gili Islands. See those sections for more details.

Local Transport Ampenan-Mataram-Cakra-Sweta is surprisingly sprawling, don't plan to walk from place to place. Bemos shuttle back and forth along the main route between the Ampenan terminal at one end and the Sweta terminal at the other. The fare is a standard 125 rp regardless of the distance. There are plenty of dokars to rent for shorter trips around town.

Bicycle, Motorcycle & Bemo Rental You can rent bicycles for 1500 rp a day from the Losmen Horas or Wisma Triguna in Ampenan.

Motorcycles can be rented in Mataram from Jalan Gelantik, off Jalan Selaparang near the junction with Jalan Sultan

Hasanuddin (at the Cakranegara end of Mataram). There are a bunch of motorcycle owners hanging around there with bikes to rent at 6000 to 10,000 rp a day. As usual the more you pay the better you get and it's wise to check a bike over carefully before saying yes. See the introductory Getting Around Lombok chapter for more details.

Chartering a bemo in Lombok is easy, count on about 25,000 rp a day but check the bemo over carefully as some of them are in decidedly poor condition. The introductory Getting Around Lombok chapter has more details. The bemo station in Ampenan is a good place to charter a bemo.

SENGGIGI BEACH

On a superb sweeping bay about 10 km north of Ampenan, Senggigi Beach has become *the* place to stay on Lombok and these days many travellers don't bother staying in town at all. Promotional work for the big Senggigi Beach Hotel has focused much more interest on Senggigi and Lombok as a whole.

Senggigi has a fine beach although it slopes off very steeply. There's some snorkelling off the point and in the sheltered bay across the headland. There are amazing views from Senggigi across Lombok Strait to Bali, dominated by mighty Gunung Agung. The sunsets are particularly wonderful.

Information

There's no place to change money or travellers' cheques at Senggigi although the Senggigi Beach Hotel will change for their guests. Eating there will probably qualify you as a guest, particularly if you don't have enough Indonesian currency to pay the bill!

Batu Bolong - Hollow Rock

This temple is about a km before Senggigi Beach, about eight km from Ampenan. While not terribly interesting in itself, the site of this large rock with a hole in it offers a fantastic view across Lombok Strait to Bali and Gunung Agung – and particularly good sunsets. Periodically the local people make offerings here and legend has it that beautiful virgins were once chucked into the sea from the top of the rock (virgins always get a rough deal). Locals like to claim that this is why the temple was built and why there are so many sharks in the water near Batu Bolong.

Places to Stay & Eat

The most popular travellers' centre at Senggigi is the *Pondok Senggigi* with rooms at 3000/4500 rp including attached mandi and toilet. The rooms run off a long verandah with a pleasant garden area in front. Along the other side of the garden there are comfortable individual bungalows at 7500 rp. Pondok Senggigi has an open air restaurant which is deservedly popular from breakfast time until late at night.

On the beach side, between the Pondok Senggigi and the Senggigi Beach Hotel, is the *Senggigi Holiday Inn* with rooms with a small mezzanine at 12,500/17,500 rp, two beds on each floor. Right next door *Mascot Bungalows* are pleasant individual cottages at 7500/10,000 rp. The Holiday Inn has a restaurant but it's not very busy.

Senggigi's one big 'international standard' hotel is right on the headland. Operated by Garuda Airlines the *Senggigi Beach Hotel* (tel 23430) has rooms at US$45/75, a beautiful setting, a swimming pool and other mod cons.

In the opposite direction the small *Pondok Melati Dua* is next door to the Pondok Senggigi and has rooms at 12,500 rp. Further along on the beach side of the road *Batu Bolong Cottages* is a brand new development. There will undoubtedly be more new places springing up as Senggigi becomes increasingly popular.

Continuing towards Ampenan you eventually come to the *Sasaka Beach Cottages*, about midway between Ampenan and Senggigi, close to the turn-off to Lendang Bajur. This up-market development never caught on and is now run down and neglected, the pool is empty and nobody stays there. If you really wanted to you can get a room for 10,000 rp.

Pondok Senggigi is far and away the number one dining attraction but you can also eat for a much higher cost, at the *Senggigi Beach Hotel* where main courses cost around 8000 rp plus 21% service and tax. Or there's the small *Warung Nasi Sederhana*, it was right next to Pondok Senggigi but may have moved further down the road. It makes a real effort to cater for visitors with an English menu. A new restaurant is also planned for across the road from the Pondok Senggigi.

Getting There & Away
Take a bemo from the Ampenan bemo terminal to Lendang Bajur, just north of the airport on the road to Pemenang and the Gili Islands. From there you can catch a bus to Senggigi, total fare about 400 rp. The direct road along the coast between Ampenan and Senggigi is actually quicker but there's no regular transport that way. Nevertheless there will often be bemos taking that route, again for about 400 rp, or you can charter one.

NARMADA
Laid out as a miniature replica of the summit of Mt Rinjani and its crater Lake Segara Anak, Narmada is a hill about 10 km east of Cakra, on the main east-west road crossing Lombok. It takes its name from a sacred river in India and the temple here, Pura Kalasa, is still used. The Balinese *Pujawali* celebration is held here every year in honour of the god, Batara, who dwells on Gunung Rinjani. At the same time the faithful who have made the trek up the mountain and down to Lake Segara Anak, hold a ritual called *Pekelan* in which they dispose of their gold trinkets and artefacts by ceremonially throwing them into the lake.

Narmada was constructed by the king of Mataram in 1805, when he was no longer able to climb Rinjani to make his offerings to the gods. Having set his conscience at rest by placing offerings in the temple he spent at least some of his time in a concealed spot on the hill lusting over the young girls bathing in the artificial lake.

It's a beautiful place to spend a few hours, though the gardens are neglected. *Don't* go there on weekends since it's overrun with the hordes. Apart from the lake there are two other pools in these grounds. One is an Olympic-size pool with changing rooms – admission is 200 rp for adults, 100 rp for children. Entry fee to Narmada itself is 100 rp (children 50 rp).

Along one side of the pool is the remains of a vast aqueduct built by the Dutch and still in use. Land tax was tied to the productivity of the land so the Dutch were keenly interested in increasing agricultural output. They did this by extending irrigation systems to increase the area under cultivation. The Balinese had already built extensive irrigation networks, particularly in the west.

The construction of roads and bridges was also given high priority, since from both a political and economic point of view it was in the Dutch interests to establish a good communication system. A large number of roads and tracks were constructed – like the aqueducts they were built and maintained with the unpaid labour of Lombok peasants.

Places to Eat
Right at the Narmada bemo terminal is the local market which sells mainly food and clothing and is well worth a look. There are a number of warungs scattered around offering soto ayam and other dishes.

Getting There & Away
There are frequent bemos from Sweta to Narmada, costing around 125 to 200 rp. When you get off at the bemo terminal at Narmada, the gardens are directly across the road. Walk 100 metres or so along a side road to the entrance gate. There are parking fees for bicycles, motorcycles and cars.

LINGSAR

This large temple complex, just a few km north of Narmada, is said to have been built in 1714. The temple combines the Bali Hindu and Islam Wektu Telu religions in one complex. Designed in two separate sections and built on two different levels, the Hindu pura on the north is higher than the Wektu Telu temple on the south.

The Hindu Temple has four shrines. The one on the left, Hyang Tunggal, looks towards Gunung Agung which is the seat of the gods in Bali – the shrine faces north-west rather than north-east as it would in Bali. On the right is a shrine devoted to Mt Rinjani, the seat of the gods in Lombok. Between these two shrines is a double shrine symbolising the union between the two islands. The left hand side of this shrine is named in honour of the might of Lombok. The right hand side of the shrine is dedicated to a king's daughter, Ayu Nyoman Winton, whom legend decrees gave birth to a god.

The Wektu Telu Temple is noted for its enclosed pond devoted to Lord Vishnu. It has a number of holy eels that can be enticed from their hiding places along the water ducts by persistent tapping of the walls and the use of hard-boiled eggs as bait. Apart from their outstanding size, they're rather unprepossessing – like huge swimming slugs. The stalls outside the temple complex sell boiled eggs – expect to pay around 200 rp or so. Next to the eel pond is another enclosure with a kind of large altar or offering place, bedecked in white and yellow cloth and mirrors. The mirrors were offered by Chinese business people asking for good luck and success. Many local farmers come here also with offerings or to feed eggs to the holy eels.

On the right as you enter the temple, running almost its entire length and hidden behind a wall, is a women's washing place. It's mainly a series of individual fountains squirting holy water and once again there are holy eels here. There's a men's mandi at the back. You can bathe here but Narmada is probably a better place to swim.

Once a year at the beginning of the rainy season – somewhere between October and December – the Hindus and the Wektu Telus make offerings and pray in their own temples. Then they come out into the communal compound and pelt each other with ketupat – rice wrapped in banana leaves. No-one quite knows what this ceremony is for – some say it's to bring the rain, others to give thanks for the rain. Be prepared to get attacked with ketupat from both sides if you visit Lingsar at this time.

Getting There & Away

There are frequent bemos from Sweta to Narmada for 125 to 200 rp. At Narmada catch another bemo to Lingsar for the same price and walk the short distance from here to the temple complex. Watch for the school on the main road, it's easy to miss the temple which is set back off the road.

There is a large square in front of the temple complex, with a couple of warungs to the right before you enter the main area and a small stall closer to the temple where you can buy snacks and hard-boiled eggs for the holy eels. If the temple is locked ask at one of the warungs for a key.

SURANADI

A few km east of Lingsar, Suranadi has one of the holiest temples on Lombok. This small temple, set in pleasant gardens, is noted for its bubbling, icy cold springwater and restored baths with ornate Balinese carvings. The eels have also been sanctified. Drop a hard-boiled egg into the water and watch the eels swim out of the conduits for a feed.

You can also swim here so bring your swimsuit. It is polite to ask permission before jumping in.

Places to Stay & Eat

The *Suranadi Hotel* (tel 23686) has rooms

at a wide variety of prices starting from 9000/11,000 rp and going up to 24,000/30,000 rp, plus 21% tax and service. There's a swimming pool, as well as a tennis court, restaurant and bar. People not staying at the hotel can use the swimming pool and tennis court for 500 rp (children 250 rp).

Apart from the restaurant in the hotel, there are also a few warungs in the main street.

SESAOT

About five km from Suranadi and worth a visit is Sesaot, a small quiet market town on the edge of a forest where wood-felling is the main industry. There's regular transport from Suranadi to Sesaot and you can eat at the warung on the main street which has simple but tasty food. By the bridge are separate bathing places for men and women.

South & East Lombok

LEMBAR

One of the two main ports of Lombok, this is where the ferries from Bali dock. Situated in a protected bay with palm-covered hills sweeping down to the edge of the harbour, Lembar is about 30 km south of Ampenan. Several small islands dot the narrow channel leading into the harbour.

Places to Eat

There's a canteen at the ferry wharf where you can buy snacks and drinks while waiting to catch the ferry. Lembar has no overnight accommodation, nor does it have any rumah makan.

Getting There & Away

See the introductory Getting There chapter for Lombok for information on the Bali-Lombok ferry service.

Regular buses and bemos from Sweta cost 400 rp during the day. If you arrive in Lembar on the afternoon ferry from Bali, buy a bemo ticket on the journey over. While you'll be paying more than the normal price, this will guarantee you transport to Ampenan, Mataram or Cakranegra. A minibus from the Zahir Hotel in Ampenan often meets the ferry.

Bemo drivers meeting travellers off this ferry often jack their prices up to over 1000 rp after dark. The ferry office is directly in front of where the bemo or bus puts you down.

SUKARARA

Twenty-five km south of Mataram on the Kediri-Puyung road is the small village of Sukarara. On the way to this traditional weaving centre you pass picturesque thatched-roof villages surrounded by rice fields. More unusual are the houses built from local stone found in Sukarara. Look out for Sasak women in their traditional black costumes around this area.

Lombok is renowned for its traditional weaving, the techniques for which have been handed down from mother to daughter for generations. Each piece of cloth is woven on a handloom in established patterns and colours. Some fabrics are woven in as many as four directions, interwoven with gold thread and can be so complicated that they take one person three months to complete. Many incorporate flower and animal motifs including buffaloes, dragons, lizards, crocodiles and snakes. Several villages specialise in this craft including Sukarara and Pringgasela.

Nearly every house in Sukarara has an old wooden handloom and along the main street you'll see displays of sarongs hanging in bright bands outside the houses. You can stop at one, watch the women weaving and buy direct. Another place worth trying is the Taufik Weaving Company on Jalan Tenun. The manager's name is Widasih and he has sarongs, songkets, Sasak belts, tablecloths and numerous other pieces.

Before you go to Sukarara it may be a good idea to check prices in the Selamat Riady weaving factory in Cakranegara and get some idea of how much to pay and where to start bargaining. If you're accompanied to Sukarara it will inevitably cost you more through commissions. Although the village is a regular stop for tour groups the people are very friendly and if you eat or drink at the warung you'll be surrounded by locals.

Places to Stay

Stay with the kepala desa or make a day trip. You could also check with the woman who runs the warung – she sometimes puts people up for the night and has a fine selection of cloth for sale.

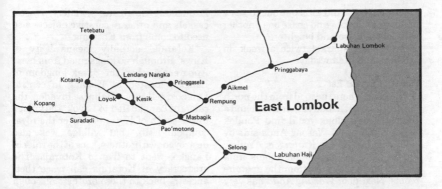

Getting There & Away

Bemos from Sweta to Puyung cost 350 rp. From Puyung take a dokar to Sukarara, the two-km ride will cost 200 rp.

REMBITAN & OTHER VILLAGES

From Sengkol down to Kuta Beach is a centre of traditional Sasak culture, and there are many relatively unchanged Sasak villages where the people still live in customary houses and engage in indigenous crafts.

Only a couple of km south of Sengkol is Rembitan, the best known village with a population of about 750. The Masjid Kuno, an old thatched roof mosque, tops the hill around which the village houses cluster. A short distance further south is Sade, a smaller and more traditional village with each house fronted by a rice barn. Dotted on the hills all around are other Sasak villages.

KUTA BEACH

Lombok's Kuta Beach is a magnificent stretch of sand with impressive hills rising around it but it's much less touristed than the better known version in Bali. At the annual nyale fishing celebration, people flock to Kuta but otherwise the small village is very quiet. Stinging seaweed makes swimming unpleasant at times but Kuta is also good for surfing and wind surfing.

The bay is flanked by a mountain chain to the west and an enormous rock about four km from the village to the east. If you climb this early in the morning you get superb views across the countryside.

Kuta isn't just one beach but a series of bays punctuated by headlands. Travelling east from Kuta the main centres are Segara Beach and Tanjung Aan. It's five km to Tanjung Aan where there's a market on Wednesday and Thursday. Gerupak is a fishing village about eight km from Kuta where there's a market on Tuesday. From there you can cross by boat to Bumgang. An alternative excursion from Kuta turns north just before Tanjung Aan but beyond Serneng the road deteriorates and you can get as far as Awang only with a motorcycle or on foot.

Information

Once a year a special Sasak celebration is held in Kuta for the opening of the nyale fishing season. On the 19th day of the 10th month in the Sasak calendar – generally February or March – hundreds of Sasaks gather on the beach and when night falls fires are built and the young people sit around competing with each other in rhyming couplets called *pantun*. At dawn the next morning, the first nyale are caught, after which it is time for the Sasak teenagers to have fun. In a colourful procession boys and girls put out to sea – in different boats – and chase one another with lots of noise and laughter.

Kuta has a market twice a week on Sundays and Wednesdays.

Places to Stay & Eat

At the point where the road from the north meets the coast, a road turns off east and a short distance along you'll find Pondok Sekar Kuning and Warung Anda side by side. *Pondok Sekar Kuning* or 'Yellow Flower Cottage' has double rooms from 5000 rp and a nice view from the upstairs rooms. Next door *Warung Anda* has very plain rooms for 4000 rp and a menu featuring nasi campur, nasi goreng and other straightforward Indonesian dishes.

A bit further along are the *Mandalika Seaview Cottages* or Mascot Cottages with rooms at 4000 rp, bungalows at 5000 rp and a pleasant grassy area beside the road. There's another place to stay at Tanjung Aan, they might decide to call it the *Tanjung Aan Hotel*. Accommodation is decidedly low key at Kuta, and at present there isn't much of it.

Getting There & Away

Although Kuta is just 45 km from Cakra, getting there by public transport is not easy. It's no trouble getting to Praya but beyond there it's a matter of waiting for transport to Sengkol and then again down to Kuta. Market day in Sengkol is Thursday when there may be more transport. The final five km to Kuta is a steep and winding descent which suddenly leaves the hills to arrive at the coast.

KOTARAJA

Basketware from Lombok has such a fine reputation in the archipelago that many Balinese make special buying trips to Lombok, selling it in Bali at inflated prices to foreigners. Kotaraja and Loyok villages in eastern Lombok used to be noted for their craftwork, particularly their basketware and plaited mats but it all seems to have disappeared today.

Exquisitely intricate jewellery, vases, caskets and other decorative objects also used to come from Kotaraja.

'Kotaraja' actually means 'City of Kings' although no kings ruled from here. Apparently when the Sasak kingdom of Langko, located at Kopang in central Lombok, fell to the Balinese invaders the rulers of Langko fled to Loyok, the village to the south of Kotaraja. After the royal compound in that village was also destroyed two brothers, sons of the ruler of Langko, went to live in Kotaraja. The aristocracy of Kotaraja can trace their ancestry back to these brothers although the highest caste title of raden has now petered out through intermarriage.

Places to Stay

If you want to spend the night in the area, stay with the kepala desa in Kotaraja. Otherwise it's a day trip from Ampenan, Mataram, Cakranegara or Sweta.

Getting There & Away

Kotaraja is 32 km from Sweta. If you go by bemo you have to change a couple of times. From Sweta you take a bemo to Narmada for 150 rp, and from there another bemo to Pomotong (also spelt Pao' Motong) for 400 rp. From Pomotong you can either get a dokar to Kotaraja or wait for another bemo (cheaper than dokars, but not as plentiful). There is a direct bus from Sweta to Pomotong but you may have to wait around for a while and it may actually be quicker and easier to take the bemos.

LOYOK

Loyok is a tiny village just a few km from Kotaraja and is noted for its fine handicrafts although it is very much off the trampled track. Most of the craftspeople work out of their homes and if you ask the dokar driver he will take you to where the basket weavers work although it's hard to find anything to buy.

Getting There & Away

To get to Loyok, you can get a bemo from Pomotong to take you as far as the turn-off to the village and then either walk the rest of the way or get a dokar for 150 rp per person. If you're setting out from Kotaraja for Loyok you've got the same options – either take a dokar or walk. Its a pretty drive with traditional thatched Sasak huts and lush rice terraces along the way.

TETEBATU

A mountain retreat at the foot of Gunung Rinjani, Tetebatu is 50 km from Mataram and about seven km north of Kotaraja. Like Loyok it was originally an offshoot settlement of Kotaraja. You can climb part way up Rinjani from here but the formerly magnificent stands of mahogany trees have virtually all disappeared. There are still lots of jet black monkeys to shriek at you.

Places to Stay & Eat

Wisma Sudjono is the only place to stay here – a couple of two-storey bungalows with separate living and sleeping areas, western-style toilets, and showers with hot and cold water. They charge around 10,000 rp for a bungalow, though there may be some cheaper rooms. Food here is excellent, but costs extra – they'll even pack lunch for you if you want to spend the day out walking. In fact everything here costs extra, they charge you to park a motorcycle while you have lunch! There are several warungs in Tetebatu.

Getting There & Away

Getting to Tetebatu involves a number of changes if you haven't got your own wheels. From Sweta take a bemo to Narmada for 200 rp, and then another to Pomotong for 400 rp. There are direct buses from Sweta to Pomotong but you may have to wait around for a while and in the long run it's probably quicker and easier to go by bemo. From Pomotong take a bemo or a dokar to Kotaraja, though a bemo is cheaper at 200 rp.

From Kotaraja there is a dirt road most of the way to Tetebatu – smoother than the old rocky road. Take a bemo from Kotaraja to Tetebatu for 150 rp – or alternatively a dokar for around 2500 rp for four people.

If you're not in a hurry and aren't carrying much of a load, it's a nice walk from Pomotong to Tetebatu through attractive country patched with rice fields. It will take you an easy 2½ to three hours.

LENDANG NANGKA

Lendang Nangka is a small village seven km from Tetebatu. Radiah, a local primary school teacher, will put you up at his house. He speaks excellent English and is a mine of information on the surrounding countryside and customs. He enjoys acting as guide and will drive you around to nearby villages and sights on his motorcycle.

Since the first edition of the *Bali & Lombok* guide Pak Radiah has written to us encouraging people to stay in Lendang Nangka, which he says is a traditional Sasak village and has similar surroundings to Tetebatu. He has a map for local walks. In the village and surrounding area you can see blacksmiths who still make knives, hoes and other tools using indigenous techniques. Jojang, the biggest spring in Lombok, is a few km away or you

Lendang Nangka

Radiah's House · Mosque · To Masbagik · To Kotaraja · Monument · Market · To Bagek Bontong

can walk to a waterfall with beautiful views or see the black monkeys in a nearby forest.

In August, at Lendang Nangka, you should be able to see the traditional Sasak form of boxing – a violent affair with leather-covered shields and bamboo poles. Local dances are a possibility at Batu Empas, one km away. At the village of Pringgasela the girls weave Sasak cloths, blankets and sarongs – it's only two km from Lendang Nangka – take a dokar or walk.

Places to Stay

Staying with Pak Radiah will cost you about 5000 rp per person, including three excellent meals per day of local Sasak food, and tea or coffee. You will get customary Sasak cake and fruit for breakfast, it's not cheap but highly recommended. His house is fairly easy to find in Tetebatu (see map) and has seven bedrooms for guests, each with attached bathroom and toilet. He and his family are very friendly and helpful.

Getting There & Away

Take a bemo from Sweta to Masbagik (42 km, 700 rp) and then take a dokar to Lendang Nangka (about four km, 250 rp). Lendang Nangka is about 4½ km from Pomotong and connected by a surfaced road – take a dokar for 250 rp (300 rp if you have a heavy load).

LABUHAN LOMBOK

There are fantastic views of mighty Rinjani from the east coast port of Labuhan Lombok. Ferries run from here to Sumbawa Island. It's a friendly, sleepy little place, a mixed bag of concrete houses, thatch shacks and stilt bungalows. You can climb the hill on the right-hand side of the harbour and watch the boats plying between here and Sumbawa.

If you walk about four km north from Labuhan Lombok towards Sembalia there is a reservoir and fishing village – the children either run away in fear or

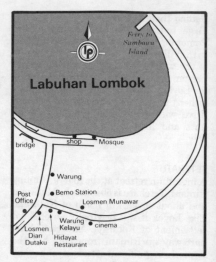

surround you and touch your white skin to see if it feels the same as brown skin.

South of Labuhan Lombok on the coast is Labuhan Haji which is supposed to have a good beach and is accessible by bemo and dokar.

Places to Stay

If you're just passing through Labuhan Lombok on your way to Sumbawa there's no need to stay overnight at all. You can catch an early bus from Sweta (5.30 am at the latest) and get to the port in time for the Sumbawa ferry. The Ampenan losmen are quite used to getting their guests on the road by that time.

If, however, you do want to stay for a day or two Labuhan Lombok has gone through an accommodation upheaval with the old Sudimampir finally closing down. New overnight options include the basic *Losmen Dian Dutaku* with rooms at 2000/3000 rp. Or on Jalan Khayangan there's *Losmen Munawar*, also pretty simple and basic, with rooms at 2500/5000 rp. Neither are anything to write home about but they're both quite habitable for a short stay.

Places to Eat

There are a couple of warungs around the bemo station, but they all feature a restricted menu and the food is not that good. You can always buy a fish at the market and get it cooked at a warung. The *Hidayat Restaurant*, across the road from the bemo station, is a friendly place. Alternatively there's the fairly clean *Warung Kelayu* next door.

Getting There & Away

Bus There are regular bemos and colts from Sweta, the 69 km trip costs 1000 rp and should take a bit less than two hours. It's possible to leave Ampenan early enough in the morning to get to Labuhan Lombok in time for the ferry departure to Sumbawa. The popular Ampenan travellers' losmen will organise this dawn departure for you. If you're zipping straight across Lombok bound for Bali you can take a bus via Sweta to Lembar for 1500 rp, a 97 km trip. Pancor, 37 km away, costs 600 rp.

Boat The ferry to Labuhan Alas on Sumbawa departs from a pier about a km from the bemo station. It's not far to walk if you've got little to carry – alternatively a dokar will cost you about 100 rp per person. The ferry departs around 7 to 8 am and the fare is 2100 rp. You can also transport motorcycles for about 2500 rp. The ticket office is by the pier and the trip takes about 3½ to four hours. See the Lombok introductory Getting Around chapter for more details.

There are a couple of stalls at the pier where you can buy biscuits or bananas and there are one or two warungs serving nasi campur. Guys come on board the boat selling fried rice wrapped in banana leaves and hard boiled eggs. Take a water bottle with you – it's a bloody hot ride! The ferry is a floating pile of closely compacted humanity – could be a good idea to get down to the dock early to get a seat – or bring a hat for sun protection and stretch out on the roof.

North Lombok

BAYAN

Midway between Desa Anyar and Senaro, Bayan is the birthplace of the Wektu Telu religion. Bayan is still an isolated village but the main road now extends to it. Traditional Hindu dances are still performed in Bayan, but getting to see them is a case of stumbling in at the right time, or asking around to find out when they're on. Bayan is also one of the main starting points for the climb up Mt Rinjani.

Places to Stay & Eat

Stay with the kepala desa here for around 2500 rp per person per night, including two meals. There are a couple of warungs in Bayan, one on the road to Senaro just off to the right. You can get fried chicken and rice here for 1500 rp.

Getting There & Away

Lombok's main north-south road ends at Bayan. There are several buses daily from Sweta to Bayan, the first leaving around 9 am. The fare is around 1200 to 1400 rp and it takes about three hours. The last bus back to Sweta departs Bayan around 6 pm.

SENARO

Perched high up in the foothills of Rinjani about nine km from Bayan, this small traditional village seems utterly unchanged from the time it evolved. It exudes a feeling of untainted prehistory that is quite unnerving. In fact it was less than 20 years ago that the villagers of Senaro saw their first westerners, and not many years before that that they began to have regular contact with people from the surrounding area. Until then they lived completely isolated from the rest of the world and are still very timid, making no attempt to communicate with strangers

and showing none of the overt curiosity that occurs in most parts of Lombok.

The village itself is surrounded by a high wooden paling fence and comprises about 20 thatched wooden huts in straight lines, some on stilts, others low to the ground. On the left, just before you come to the village, is a small coffee plantation. Unless accompanied by a local person it's polite to ask permission before entering Senaro. Nobody here speaks a word of English.

Many of the men from this village work in the nearby forests as woodcutters. Part of the ritual of climbing Rinjani is that guides usually stop at Senaro to stock up on betel nut. Young boys in the village thresh rice with long wooden mallets which reverberate like the sound of drums, adding to the primitive atmosphere. A large percentage of the population, which is less than 500, have goitre due to the lack of iodine in their diet and water.

There is a truck that picks up timber from Senaro regularly – usually on Sundays – so you may be able to get a ride down to Bayan on it. In Senaro you should be able to stay with the schoolmaster or at the warung for 1000 rp per person – but don't expect any privacy either way. There's a waterfall 2½ km from Senaro.

MT RINJANI

Both the Balinese and the local Sasak people revere Rinjani. To the Balinese it is equal to their own Gunung Agung, a seat of the gods, and many Balinese make a pilgrimage here each year. In a ceremony they call *pekelan* they throw gold jewellery into the lake and make offerings to the spirit of the mountain. As for the Sasaks some make several pilgrimages a year – full moon is the favourite time for them to pay their respects to the mountain and cure their ailments by bathing in its hot springs.

Rinjani is the highest mountain in Lombok, the second highest in Indonesia outside of Irian Jaya. At 3726 metres it soars above the island and dominates the landscape. Early in the morning it can be seen from anywhere on the island, but by mid-morning on most days the summit is shrouded in cloud. The mountain is actually an active volcano - though the last eruption was in 1901 - with a huge half-moon crater, a large slime-green lake and an extensive network of steaming hot springs said to have remarkable healing powers, particularly for skin diseases. The large caldera drops 200 metres below the rim and there's a new cone in the centre, beside the lake.

You should not tackle this climb during the wet season as it's far too dangerous. You need three clear days to do it and probably at least another day to recover. Don't go up during the full-moon because it will be very crowded. There are at least two ways of getting up Mt Rinjani. The first and apparently easier route is via Bayan, Batu Koq and Senaro in the north. The other route starts at Sapit in the east.

Guides & Equipment

You can do the trek without a guide, but in some places there's a confusion of trails branching off and you could get lost. The other advantage of guides is that they're informative, good company, and also act as porters, cooks and water collectors. When you're doing this walk with a guide make sure you set your own pace - some of them climb Rinjani as many as 20 or 30 times a year and positively gallop up the slopes!

It's worthwhile talking to Mr Batu Bara, at the Losmen Wisma Triguna, in Ampenan. For US$75(!) he will organise the complete trip for you - food, tent, sleeping bag and a guide. But if you don't want to come at that he will tell you how to go about it on your own. He'll explain

what food to take, and will rent you a two or three person tent for 10,000 rp and a sleeping bag for 7500 rp - steep prices but a sleeping bag and tent are absolutely essential.

He will also write a letter to the school teacher in Batu Koq, Raden Kertabakti (known locally as Guru Bakti). He is a very nice man who will not only arrange a guide but feed you, put you up on the first night and more than likely on the evening you get down from the mountain. To stay here overnight costs around 2500 rp per person. The food is good and there's plenty of it. There are two rooms, in one of the school buildings, that have double beds with ground sheets and pillows. There are no toilets here, but the children will show you where to go.

Food & Supplies

You need to take enough food to last three days - including food for your guide. It's better to buy most of it in Ampenan, Mataram or Cakra as there's more choice available. Take rice, instant noodles, sugar, coffee, eggs (lots - if you stay at Mr Batu Bara's losmen he will lend you a container to carry the eggs in), tea, biscuits or bread, some tins of fish or meat, onions, fruit and anything else that keeps your engine running.

It's also a good idea to take plenty of matches, a torch (flashlight), a water container and some cigarettes. The teacher and guide will provide water and containers for you, but it's good to be able to have some handy. Even if you don't smoke the guides really appreciate being given cigarettes. If you have any food left over, leave it at the school.

Getting There & Away

Ampenan to Bayan If you're setting off from Ampenan get to the bus terminal at Sweta before 9 am - there's a bus that leaves for Bayan around then. The 70-km journey to Bayan costs 1200 rp, takes approximately three hours and goes through some spectacular country - it's the same road to

Pemenang for the Gili Islands – so get a window seat up front if possible. The new coast road may be even more picturesque.

Bayan to Batu Koq When you get to Bayan you either have to walk the four or five km up the road to Batu Koq where the school teacher lives or take a truck. The latter is a far better alternative as you will probably arrive here in the middle of the day and it's a hot, dusty walk – there's not much shade along this road and you'll could be carrying a fair amount of junk as well as food for three days. Trucks go up and down here with regular irregularity. There are a couple of warungs near where the bus stops and the odd shop where you can buy last minute bits and pieces if necessary. Once you get to Batu Koq numerous children will rush out shouting their 'Hello Misters' and take you to the school teacher. Westerners are still seven-day-wonders here.

Make sure you go to the magnificent waterfall near Batu Koq – it can be heard from far away. It's a pleasant hour's walk partially through forest, and along the side of an irrigated water course for much of the way. Watch for the sleek, black monkeys swinging through the trees. Splash around near the waterfall – the water cascades down the mountain slope so hard and so fast that it's strong enough to knock the wind out of you.

Ascending the Mountain
Day 1 Depart Batu Koq about 8 am for base camp. The climb takes about six hours and is relatively easy going through dappled forest, the quiet only broken (*shattered*) by the occasional bird, animal, bell or woodchopper. At base camp pitch the tent, collect wood and water and if you have enough energy left climb up to the clearing and watch the sunset. The ground is rock hard at base camp and it's very cold so bring thick woollen socks, a sweater and a ground sheet with you. If a flock of 30-odd Lombokians arrives unexpectedly out of

the gloom the chances of seeing the lake and the hot springs at their solo-in-the-wilderness best are gloomy indeed. Go somewhere else and try again another day.

Day 2 Set off at about 8 am again and after approximately 1½ hours you will arrive at the rim of the volcano, an altitude of 3025 metres.

Rinjani is covered in dense forest up to 2000 metres, but at around this height the vegetation changes from thick stands of mahogany and teak trees to the odd stand of pine. As you get closer to the rim the pines become sparser and and the soil rubbly and barren. The locals cut down the mahogany and teak trees with handaxes (no chainsaws yet) and then carry the huge logs down the steep slopes, by hand! Monkeys, wild pigs, deer and the occasional snake inhabits the forest. Once you get above the forest and up to the clearing the going is hot as there's not much shade – the land here is harsh and inhospitable – but you have superb views across to Bali and Sumbawa.

From the rim of the crater it takes between five and six hours to get down to Lake Segara Anak and around to the hot springs. The descent from the rim into the crater is quite dangerous – for most of the way the path down to the lake clings to the side of the cliffs and is narrow and meandering. Watch out for rubble – in certain spots it's very hard to keep your footing. Close to the lake a thick forest sweeps down to the shore. There are several places to camp along this lake, but if you head for the hot springs there are many more alternatives. The track along the lake is also narrow and very slippery – be careful and take it slowly. There are a number of different kinds of small waterbirds on the lake – but no fish in it.

After setting up camp at the lake it's time to soak your weary body in the springs and recuperate. It's not as cold here as it is at base camp, but it is damp and misty from the steaming springs. Despite the hundreds of local people around it can still be an eerie place. Watch your step on the paths – although this is a holy place the locals have few inhibitions or qualms about relieving themselves when and wherever they need to – they don't even bother to move off the main paths.

Day 3 Departure time is approximately 8 am once again, and you walk more or less all day, arriving at Batu Koq in the late afternoon. It's a hard eight to 10 hour walk.

Day 4 If you get back to Batu Koq late in the afternoon, it's preferable to stay overnight with the school teacher. Even if you can get a lift down to Bayan by truck, the last bus from there to Cakra departs around 6 pm and there's a good chance you'll miss it. This means that you'll be stuck in Bayan until the following morning without anywhere to stay after a tiring trip, unless you can find the kepala desa. If you do stay overnight at Batu Koq it's a good idea to leave early in the morning before the sun gets too hot. You may have to walk down to Bayan but there's a bus to Cakra from here at about 8.30 am. If you miss this one there are frequent other buses during the day.

A Solo Climb

It's easy enough to do the climb without a guide although we thought the climb to the rim from the north and not bothering with the actual peak was just as good value and easy to do. But a traverse across the mountain is also perfectly feasible. Sign the book in Senaro and collect water since it's scarce along the track. Hundreds of paths lead uphill from Senaro so if you get lost ask *several* locals and take the most logical advice. One guy pointed back to Bayan when I asked him which was the path to Gunung Rinjani!

The track is erratically numbered from 0 to 200 (200 is the crater rim). You can camp at about 65-75, 110, 170 and 185. The last is an excellent spot above the bushline with fabulous views and only half an hour from the rim for

sunrise the next morning. Water is only available at 114 and 185.

From the crater rim to Lake Segara is steeply downhill. From here across the top and down to Sapit takes two to three days. A tent and sleeping bag are essential.

Mark Austin, New Zealand

To the Very Top

The first two days were pretty much as described but on the third day we warmed up in the springs before making a three-hour climb to a shelter by the path just before the junction with the summit route. This shelter is just a hollow scooped out of the ground and lined with dry grass. A few old sheets of iron serve as a roof. It fits three people, or maybe an intimate four.

There is wood that can be used for a fire – useful, as the shelter must be at 3000 metres or more and as soon as the sun goes down it gets very cold.

The next morning we watched the sun rise over Sumbawa from the junction of the paths, before starting the final ascent. The view from the rim is great, but it's nothing compared to the view from the very top! From the top, you look down into the crater which fills up with 'cotton wool' cloud streaming through the gap in the crater wall at the hot springs. In the distance, you look over Bali in one direction and Sumbawa in the other.

It's a difficult three-hour climb from the shelter; the air gets thinner and the terrain is horrible to walk on. It's powdery to start with, then you find loose stones on a steep slope (offering little support for your weight). It's a case of climbing one step up, then sliding two-thirds of a step back down, and the peak always looks closer than it is! Climbing without strong-toed shoes or boots would be masochistic.

Richard Tucker, England

SEMBULAN BUMBUNG & SEMBULAN LAWANG

High up on the eastern slopes of Mt Rinjani is the cold but beautiful Sembulan Valley. The inhabitants of the valley claim descent from the Hindu-Javanese and a relative of one of the Majapahit rulers is said to be buried here. Whilst it seems unlikely that Java ever controlled Lombok directly, similarities in music, dance and language have suggested that Lombok may have come under some long-lasting Javanese influence several hundred years ago.

In the valley, five km apart, are the traditional Sasak villages of Sembulan Bumbung and Sembulan Lawang. It's only a 45 minute walk from one village to the other and there are many pleasant walks in the surrounding area. From Sembulan Bumbung there is a steep 1½ hour climb to a saddle with a beautiful view all round. Five hours' walk from Sembulan Bumbung, first through rainforest, later coffee, paw paw, rice and vegetable fields, you arrive at a small village close to the village of Sapit. From there you can take a bemo to Pringgabaya and on to Labuhan Lombok.

You can reach the summit of Rinjani direct from either Sembulan Bumbung or Sembulan Lawang, but you must come prepared with sleeping bag, tent, food and other supplies – or walk the five hours from Sembulan Lawang to Sapit and trek to the summit from there. You can walk from Senaro to Sembulan Lawang but you have to start early; it's a long way and would take around 12 hours. Sometimes there are trucks between Bayan and Sembulan Lawang – walking takes a day.

Places to Stay

Stay with the kepala desa in Sembulan Lawang – expect to pay about 2500 rp per person, possibly more. Accommodation with the kepala desa in Sembulan Bumbung is more basic but will probably cost less than in Sembulan Lawang.

The Gili Islands

Off the north-west coast of Lombok are three small coral-fringed islands – Gili Air, Gili Meno and Gili Trawangan – with superb, white sandy beaches, clear water, coral reefs, brilliantly coloured fish – and the best snorkelling on Lombok. It's a toss up which you prefer and they're so close together it's quite easy to try each in turn. Although they're still relatively untouched these delightful dots on the map are rapidly becoming a major attraction.

Apart from Gili Trawangan's hill all three islands are pancake flat. Fishing, raising cattle and goats and growing corn, tapioca and peanuts are the main economic activities. Along with the growing number of tourists.

There are few facilities on these islands although some of the places to stay have their own electricity generators and there are small shops with a bare minimum of supplies. You may want to bring a few basic supplies with you like toilet paper, matches, a packet of biscuits or whatever. You can usually get a cool to cold beer at most places. There is no place to change money on the islands, in fact the nearest place to change money is back at Ampenan-Mataram. If possible bring your own snorkelling equipment although these days most of the losmen have some to lend.

Places to Stay & Eat

Most places on all three islands come out of the standard mould – you get a plain little bungalow, raised off the ground on stilts, with a small verandah out front. Inside there will be one or two beds with mosquito nets, the verandah will probably have a table and a couple of chairs. Mandi and toilet facilities are shared. The nightly costs are typically 7000/10,000 rp for singles/doubles and that includes breakfast, lunch and dinner plus tea or coffee on call. The food is simple but healthy and fresh, you live well here and it's certainly cheap! You might prefer the places with a communal dining area since there's more conversation and opportunity to meet people there. Some of the smaller places bring meals to your bungalow.

Getting There & Away

Within a couple of hours of leaving Ampenan or the airport, you can be sunbaking on one of the Gili Island beaches. However the trip involves several stages – unless you opt to simply charter a bemo from Ampenan, not a bad move between a group of people.

Usually the first step is a bemo from the airport or the city to Rembiga for 125 rp. Out of the airport turn left, it's not much over a km. From there it's 500 rp for a bus to Pemenang. The 25 km trip takes one to 1½ hours, a scenic journey past numerous small villages and through lush, green forest with monkeys by the side of the road. From Pemenang it's a km or so off the main road to the harbour at Bangsal, 150 rp by dokar.

There's a small information office at the harbour where they charge the official fares out to the islands – 400 rp to Gili Air, 600 rp to Gili Meno, 700 rp to Gili Trawangan. It's a matter of sitting and waiting until there's a full boat load or until the official departure times, which may depend on the tides. It's a good idea to try to get to Bangsal by 10 am. If you have to hang around that's no problem as it's a pleasant place to while away some time and the shaded warungs like the *Parahiangan Coffee House* have good food and coffee.

Boats go less frequently to Gili Trawangan, the furthest island. There's usually one in the late morning and it takes about 45 minutes to an hour. Services to Gili Air with its larger

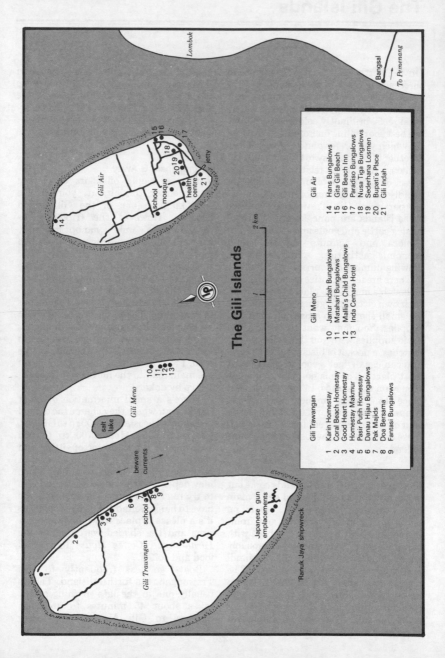

The Gili Islands

Lombok

Bangsal

To Pemenang

Gili Air

jetty

14

15
16
17
18
19 20
21

school
mosque
health
centre

2 km

0
1

Gili Meno

salt lake

10
11
12
13

beware currents

Gili Trawangan

1

2

3
4 5

6

7
8
9

school

Japanese gun emplacements

Ranuk Jaya shipwreck

Gili Trawangan
1 Karin Homestay
2 Coral Beach Homestay
3 Good Heart Homestay
4 Homestay Makmur
5 Pasir Putih Homestay
6 Danau Hijau Bungalows
7 Pak Majids
8 Doa Bersama
9 Fantasi Bungalows

Gili Meno
10 Janur Indah Bungalows
11 Matahari Bungalows
12 Malia's Child Bungalows
13 Inda Cemara Hotel

Gili Air
14 Hans Bungalows
15 Gita Gili Beach
16 Gili Beach Inn
17 Paradiso Bungalows
18 Nusa Tiga Bungalows
19 Sederhana Losmen
20 Bupati's Place
21 Gili Indah

population are more frequent and only take 20 minutes to half an hour.

Boats can be chartered for official prices of 12,000 rp to Gili Air, 14,000 rp to Gili Meno and 16,000 rp to Gili Trawangan. In practise you can usually beat those prices down a bit.

Getting Around

It's easy enough to charter boats to get around the islands if you want to try the other beaches. People often get a group together and spend a day exploring the islands.

On the islands themselves walking is the way to get around although there is a single dokar on Gili Air and a few bicycles; no doubt the first motorcycle will arrive soon.

GILI AIR

Gili Air is closest to the coast, the smallest and most densely populated island with around 600 people in an area of about one square km. The beach runs right around the island and there's a small village at the southern end. Homes and small farms are dotted amongst the palm trees which cover the island.

Places to Stay & Eat

Most of the accommodation is down at the southern end of the island at the harbour. *Gili Indah* is one of the bigger places on the Gili Islands with singles/doubles at 6500/10,000 rp, 7000/12,000 rp or some larger rooms with attached mandi for 8500/15,000 rp. There's a big open-air dining area where they offer to prepare potatoes fried, rösti, mashed, croquette and duchesse!

Bupati's Place is very popular and charges 5000 rp per person. Nearby is the *Sederhana Losmen* and *Nusa Tiga Bungalows* but the *Paradiso Bungalows* seem to be out of operation at present. *Gili Beach Inn* and *Gita Gili Beach* are two tiny little places with a pretty beach location.

Right up at the north is *Hans Bungalows*, with a beautiful outlook on the beach, attractive little bungalows and an open air dining area. It's quiet, relaxed and well away from everything but also a very convivial place to stay; some nights dinner may include as much banana wine as you can drink, and still stand up! Costs are 7000/10,000 rp for singles/doubles including all meals. You can arrange to be dropped off right at Hans, to save the walk from the harbour.

GILI MENO

Gili Meno is the middle island in size and location but has the smallest population, around 300. There's a salt lake in the middle of the island where salt is produced when it dries up in the dry season. It's said to cause mosquito problems at some times of year. Otherwise the island is much like the others with lots of palm trees and some fine snorkelling just off the beach.

Places to Stay & Eat

The accommodation here is all on the east beach and it's more varied than on the other islands. At the southern end there's the brand new *Inda Cemara*; planned to be the largest and most expensive hotel on the Gili Islands it's run by the Gazebo Hotel at Sanur, Bali. This is an indication that big time tourism has noticed what's happening here.

Next up is *Mallia's Child Bungalows* with straightforward rooms at 5000/10,000 rp or larger rooms at 7500/12,000/18,000 rp for a single/double/triple. One bungalow has rooms upstairs on a common verandah, ideal for a family. Then there's *Matahari Bungalows* and the *Janur Indah Bungalows* at similar prices to Mallia's Child. Again the bungalows here are a bit bigger than usual and Janur Indah also has triples.

GILI TRAWANGAN

Gili Trawangan is the largest island, with a population of about 400 and an area of about 3½ square km. It can be very dusty and dry at some times of the year but the snorkelling off the east coast here is simply superb. You just step out of your room, stroll across the beach and into the water, swim a few strokes out from the shore and there are fish everywhere. There's a nice little drop-off not far from the shore with lots of coral.

Beware of the rip which runs between Gili Trawangan and Gili Meno at the change of tide. The locals have got so used to foolish *orang turis* getting caught in it that they seem to have an outrigger ready and waiting to go and save their guests when necessary! On the other hand strong swimmers sometimes swim across to Gili Meno.

Like the other islands most of Gili Trawangan is very flat and much of the island has far fewer trees than Gili Air or Gili Meno. However, Gili Trawangan also has a hill rising abruptly at the south of the island. On the western flanks of the hill you can find traces of a couple of Japanese WW II gun emplacements. Down below on the reef is the wreck of the *Ranuk Jaya*, a Bugis schooner which went aground in 1985. In a few more years it will probably be totally demolished. It's quite easy to walk right around the island in a few hours.

Places to Stay & Eat

The accommodation on Gili Trawangan is also along the east coast of the island, fronted by that wonderful beach. Starting at the south again there's *Fantasi Bungalows* and *Doa Bersama*, both in the standard format at the standard price of 7000/10,000 rp. *Pak Majid* is the original Gili Trawangan losmen and still deservedly popular. Pak's Javanese wife Suparmi cooks up a storm and it's a friendly place to stay with lots of fellow travellers to chat to. As well as the bungalows there are some cheaper and plainer rooms.

Continuing north other places are *Danau Hijau Bungalows, Pasir Putih Homestay, Homestay Makmur, Good Heart Homestay, Coral Beach Homestay* and away at the northern tip of the island *Karin Homestay*. Homestay Makmur is another of the early places and over the years a number of people have written to recommend it as being a friendly place with good food.

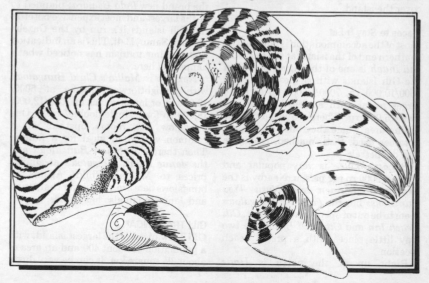

Glossary

Adat – traditional laws and regulations

adegan – effigy used in cremation ceremony as a symbolic container for the soul

Agung, Gunung – the great volcano in the east of Bali which is both Bali's highest and holiest mountain

Airlangga – an 11th century king of considerable historical and legendary importance in Bali

Air panas – hot springs

aling aling – guard wall behind the entrance gate to a Balinese family compound; demons can only travel in straight lines so the aling aling prevents them from coming straight in through the front entrance

Alun Alun – main public square of a town or village

Alus – 'refined', high standards of behaviour and art, characters in Wayang Kulit performances are traditionally alus or kasar

Anak Agung – 'child of Agung', honourable title of a member of the former Balinese royalty

Anjing – dog

Angklung – the portable form of the gamelan, used in processions as well as in other festivals and celebrations

Antaboga – cosmic naga

antakaranasarira – the soul which is released during a cremation

Arak – colourless distilled palm-wine firewater

Arja – a particularly refined form of Balinese theatre

Arjuna – a hero of the Mahabharata epic and a popular temple gate guardian image

Ayodya – Rama's kingdom in the Ramayana

Babad – early chronicle of Balinese history

Babi guling – spit-roast suckling pig, a great Balinese delicacy

Bahasa – language

Bale – pavilion, house or shelter, a meeting place

Bale banjar – the communal meeting place of the village banjar, a sort of social club where all the local communal activities are organised

Bale gede – the reception room or guest house of a wealthy Balinese' house

bale kambang – floating pavilion or hall

Bali Aga – the 'original' Balinese, the people who managed to resist the new ways brought in with the Majapahit migration

Balian – see dukun

Banjar – the local area of the village in which community activities are organised

Banyan – holy tree. See waringin

Bapak – father, also a polite form of address to any older man

Baris – warrior dance

Barong – mythical lion-dog creature, star of the Barong dance and a firm champion of the good in the eternal struggle between good and evil

Barong Landung – the enormous puppets known as the 'tall barong'. You can see them at an annual festival on Serangan Island

Barong Tengkok – Lombok name for portable form of gamelan used for wedding processions and circumcision ceremonies

Baruna – god of the sea

Batara – title used to address a deceased spirit, particularly that of an important person

Batik – cloth made by coating part of the cloth with wax, then dyeing it and melting the wax out. The waxed part is not coloured and repeated waxings and dyeings builds up a pattern. This is a craft of Java not Bali but the Balinese also produce batik

Bayu – god of the air

Bedaulu, Dalem – legendary last ruler of the Pejeng dynasty

Bedawang – the cosmic turtle on which the world rides

Bemo – popular local transport in Bali and Lombok, a bemo is traditionally a small pickup-truck with a bench seat down each side in the back. The traditional bemos are now disappearing in favour of small minibuses

Betutu bebek – a Balinese delicacy, roast duck

Bima – another hero of the Mahabharata, biggest and strongest of the Pandava brothers

Blimbing – starfruit

Boma – son of the earth, temple guardian figure

Brahma – the creator, one of the trinity of Hindu gods

Brahmana – the highest caste, the caste of priests; although all priests are Brahmanas not all Brahmanas are priests

Brem – rice wine

Bu – shortened form of ibu

Bukit – hill, also the name of the southern peninsula of Bali

Bupati – government official in charge of a regency (kabupaten)

Buta – demon or evil spirit

Camat – government official in charge of a district (kecamatan)

Candi – shrine of originally Javanese design, also known as prasada

Candi Bentar – split gateway entrance to a temple

Caste – the Balinese have castes, as in India, but it's nowhere near as firmly entrenched and important. There are basically four castes – three branches of the 'nobility' and the common people

Catur Yoga – ancient manuscript on religion and cosmology

Cili – decorative motif, a stylised girl

Cokorda – male title of a Satria

Colt – minibus, popular form of public transport in Bali and Lombok

Condong – attendant to a noblewoman in a dance-drama, including the legong

Dalang – the story teller who operates the puppets, tells the story and beats the time in a wayang kulit shadow puppet performance, a man of varied skills and considerable endurance

Danau – Lake, as Danau Batur

Desa – the village

Dewa – a deity or supernatural spirit

Dewa Agung – title of the royal family of Klungkung, at one time they were thought of as the kings of Bali

Dewi – goddess

Dewi Danau – goddess of the lakes

Dewi Sri – goddess of rice

Dokar – horse cart, still a popular form of local transport in many towns and larger villages throughout Bali

Dukun – 'witch doctor' actually a faith healer and herbal doctor

Durga – goddess of death and destruction and consort of Shiva

Durian – 'the fruit that smells like hell and tastes like heaven'

Erlangga – see Airlangga

Fingernails – many Balinese men have very long nails on the fingers of one hand, it's done to indicate that they don't have to exert themselves in any sort of hard manual labour! This is no new trend, Covarrubias mentions it in his pre-WW II book on Bali.

Gado Gado – a popular Javanese dish of vegetables with a peanut sauce

Gajah Mada – famous Majapahit prime minister who defeated the last great king of Bali and extended Majapahit power over the island

Galungan – great Balinese holy day which comes every 210 days

Gambuh – classical form of Balinese theatre

Gamelan – traditional Balinese orchestra, usually almost solely percussion with large xylophones and gongs

Ganesh – Shiva's elephant-headed son

Gang – alley or footpath, Poppies Gang at Kuta Beach is a well known one

Garuda – mythical man-bird, the vehicle of Vishnu and the modern symbol of Indonesia

Gringsing – rare double ikat woven cloth of Tenganan

Gunung – mountain, as Gunung Agung or Gunung Batur

Gusti – the polite title for members of the Wesia caste, third ranked of the Balinese castes

Hanuman – the monkey god who plays a major part in the Ramayana

Holy Water – a lot of holy water gets sprinkled around during Balinese dances and other occasions. It's often a high priest who does the sprinkling. Holy water is produced with incantations and blessings or by more direct methods – like dipping a Barong's beard in the water at the end of a Barong and Rangda dance

Homestay – a small family run losmen

Ibu – mother, also polite form of address to any older woman

Ida Bagus – honourable title for a male brahman

Ider-Ider – long strips painted in the wayang style, used as temple decorations

Ikat – cloth where the pattern is produced by dyeing the individual threads before weaving; ikat can be of the warp or the weft or even of the warp and the weft but this rare 'double ikat' is only found in one place in all of Indonesia, the village of Tenganan in east Bali

Indra – king of the gods

Jaffle – a popular snack in travellers' restaurants in Bali, an Australian invention a jaffle is a toasted sandwich made with a jaffle iron which 'welds' the edges of the two pieces of bread together

Jalan – street

Jalan Jalan – to walk

Jidur – large cylindrical drums played widely throughout Lombok

Jukung – prahu

Kabupaten – regency

Kain – wrap around sarong-style article of clothing

Kaja – Balinese 'north' which is always towards the mountains. In a temple the most important shrines are always on the kaja side

Kala – demonic face often seen over temple gateways with outstretched hands to stop evil spirits from entering although kalas are themselves evil spirits

Karma – belief that one's destiny is controlled by the total of all one's previous actions, the law of cause and effect

Kasar – the opposite of alus

Kawi – classical Javanese, the language of poetry

Kawin – married

Kebaya – Chinese long-sleeved blouse with plunging front and embroidered edges

Kelod – opposite of kaja, the side of a temple oriented away from the mountains and toward the sea

Kemban – woman's breastcloth

kepala desa – village headman

Kepeng – old Chinese coins with a hole in the centre, they were the everyday money during the Dutch era and can still be obtained quite readily from shops and antique dealers for just a few cents

Ketupat – a kind of sticky rice cooked in a banana leaf. The Balinese Hindus and Islamic Wektu-Telus of Lombok pelt each other with ketupat in a mock war held annually at Lingsar. This ceremony is to honour the rainy season

Kosala – see Ayodya

Kretek – Indonesian clove cigarettes, a very familiar odour in Bali

Kris – wavy bladed traditional dagger, often held to have spiritual or magical powers

Kulkul – the hollow tree trunk drum used to sound a warning or call meetings

Kulkul tower – the tower in which a kulkul is housed

Kuningan – holy day celebrated throughout Bali 10 days after Galungan

Ladang – a non-irrigated field for dry-land crops

Lamak – decorated palm-strips hung up in temples during festivals

Langse – traditional paintings used as decorations in palaces or temples

Leyak – a witch who can assume fantastic forms by the use of black magic

Lontar – type of palm tree, traditional books were written on the dried leaves of the lontar palm

Losmen – small Balinese hotel, often family run and similar in design to a traditional Balinese house

Mahabharata – one of the great Hindu holy books, tells of the battle between the Pandavas and the Korawas

Majapahit – the last great Hindu dynasty in Java, pushed out of Java into Bali by the rise of Islamic power they are responsible for much of Bali's amazing creative and artistic energy

Mandi – usual Indonesian form of bath, consists of a large water tank from which you ladle water to pour over yourself like a shower

Mantra – chanted magical formula

Manusa Yadnya – ceremonies which mark the various stages of Balinese life from prior to one's birth right through to after one's cremation

Mapadik – marriage by request, as opposed to *ngrorod*

Merapik – popular form of marriage by elopement in Lombok

Meru – multi-roofed shrines in Balinese temples, takes its name from the Hindu holy mountain Mahameru

Mukur – see nyekah

Naga – a mythical snake-like creature

Names – apart from the nobility most Balinese only have four first names, the first born is Wayan, second Made, third Nyoman, fourth Ketut, from five on they repeat

Ngrorod – marriage by elopement, a traditional 'heroic' way of getting married in Bali

Nusa – island, as Nusa Penida

Nyale – worm-like fish caught off Kuta Beach, Lombok. A special ceremony is held each year around February/March in honour of the first catch of the season

Nyekah – second funeral ceremony held either 12 or 42 days after the cremation in order to release the soul

Nyepi – a day of complete stillness and rest in preparation for chasing out evil spirits in an annual festival

Odalan – the temple festival held every 210 days, the Balinese 'year'

Offerings – these are put out every day to appease evil spirits. Little woven baskets with a few flower petals and grains of rice are scattered on the ground. They're often placed at the entrance to buildings and homes, at road or path junctions or at other 'dangerous' places. The evil spirits are thus persuaded not to enter the buildings or to cause accidents

Padmasana – temple shrine, throne for the sun god Surya

Paduraksa – covered gateway to a temple

Paibon – shrine in a state temple for the royal ancestors

Pak – shortened form of bapak

Palan Palan – slowly

Palinggihs – shrine in a temple which consists of a simple little throne, they are intended as resting places for the gods when they come down to the temple for festivals

Pandanus – palm plant used to make mats

Pande – blacksmiths who are treated somewhat like a caste in their own right

Pantun – ancient Malay poetical verse in rhyming couplets

Pasar – market

Patih – prime minister

Pedanda – high priest

Pekembar – umpire or referee in the traditional Sasak trial of strength known as peresehan

Pemangku – temple guardian and priest for temple rituals, not necessarily of high caste

Pendet – formal offering dance made when offerings are presented at a temple festival

Penjors – during festivals or ceremonies these long bamboo poles arch over the road or the pathway with decorations hung from the end

Perbekel – government official in charge of a village (desa)

Peresehan – popular form of one-to-one physical combat peculiar to Lombok in which two men fight armed with a small hide shield for protection and a long rattan stave as a weapon

Pigs – unlike the Muslims, who predominate in most of Indonesia, the Balinese have no scruples about pork and pigs are a common sight in every village. But what pigs! – Balinese pigs are weirdly ungainly sway-backed creatures whose spines seem to sag so much that their bellies literally drag along the ground, they taste fine

Prahu – traditional Indonesian outrigger boat

Prasada – see candi

Pratima – figure of a god used to 'stand in' for the actual god's presence during a ceremony

Pulaki – the sparsely populated, dry and hilly west end of Bali

Puputan – a warrior's fight to the death, ceremonial if necessary and akin to the suicidal *jauhar* of the rajput warriors of India

Pura – temple

Pura dalem – temple of the dead

Pura desa – temple of the village for everyday functions

Pura puseh – temple of the village founders or fathers, honouring the village's origins

pura subak – temple of irrigation society

puri – palace

puseh – the place of origin

Rajah – lord or prince

Ramayana – one of the great Hindu holy books, stories from the Ramayana form the keystone of many Balinese dances and tales

Rangda – the widow-witch, the evil black magic spirit of Balinese tales and dances

Rattan – hardy, pliable vine used for handicrafts, furniture and weapons such as the staves in the spectacular trial of strength ceremony peresehan in Lombok

Rebab – bowed lute

Regency – 'provinces' into which Bali is divided

Rinjani, Gunung – active volcano on Lombok, the island's holiest and highest mountain and one of the highest in Indonesia

Rudat – traditional Sasak dance overlaid with Islamic influence

Rumah makan – restaurant, literally 'house to eat'

Sakti – magic power

Sampan – small sailing vessel used primarily for island hops or short journeys

Sanghyang – trance dance in which the dancers impersonate a local village god

Sanghyang Widi – the Balinese supreme being is never actually worshipped as such; one of the 'three in one' or lesser gods stand in

Sarira – the three bodies burnt during cremation

Sasak – native of Lombok

Satria – the second Balinese caste, below the Brahmanas and above the Wesias

Sawah – an individual rice field

Sebe – polluted, spiritually unclean

Shiva – one of the three great Hindu gods, Shiva is the creator and destroyer

Sirih – betelnut, chewed as a mild narcotic

Songket – silver or gold threaded cloth, hand woven using floating weft technique

Stulasarira – the material body which is burnt during a cremation

Subak – the village association that organises the rice terraces and shares out the irrigation water, each owner of a sawah must be a member

Sudra – the lowest or common caste to which the majority of Balinese belong

Suksmasarira – the body of feelings and thoughts, burnt during a cremation

Sunguhu – a low-caste priest whose function is chiefly limited to looking after evil spirits

Taman – 'garden with a pond', ornamental garden

Tjili – see cili

Trisakti – the 'three in one' – Brahma, Shiva and Vishnu

Uang – money

Vishnu – one of the three great Hindu gods, Vishnu is the preserver

Wallace Line – the imaginary line between Bali and Lombok which marks the end of Asian and beginning of Australasian flora and fauna. In reality the line is a fuzzy one.

Wantilan – open pavilion used to stage cockfights

Waringin – banyan tree, the holy tree found at many temples, a large shady tree which sends out drooping branches which root and can produce new trees. It was under a banyan tree (the bo tree) that the Buddha achieved enlightenment

Warung – food stall, a sort of Indonesian equivalent to a combination of corner shop and snack bar

Wayang kulit – puppet shadow play

Wayang wong – masked drama playing scenes from the Ramayana

Wektu Telu – religion peculiar to Lombok which originated in Bayan and combines many tenets of Islam and aspects of other faiths

Wesia – the third caste, the military caste and most numerous of the noble castes

Widadaris – celestial nymphs

Index

232

MAPS

Temperature

To convert °C to °F multiply by 1.8 and add 32

To convert °F to °C subtract 32 and multiply by ·55

Length, Distance & Area

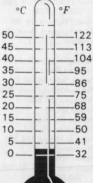

	multiply by
inches to centimetres	2.54
centimetres to inches	0.39
feet to metres	0.30
metres to feet	3.28
yards to metres	0.91
metres to yards	1.09
miles to kilometres	1.61
kilometres to miles	0.62
acres to hectares	0.40
hectares to acres	2.47

Weight

	multiply by
ounces to grams	28.35
grams to ounces	0.035
pounds to kilograms	0.45
kilograms to pounds	2.21
British tons to kilograms	1016
US tons to kilograms	907

A British ton is 2240 lbs, a US ton is 2000 lbs

Volume

	multiply by
Imperial gallons to litres	4.55
litres to imperial gallons	0.22
US gallons to litres	3.79
litres to US gallons	0.26

5 imperial gallons equals 6 US gallons
a litre is slightly more than a US quart, slightly less
than a British one

Lonely Planet

Lonely Planet published its first book in 1973. Tony and Maureen Wheeler had made a lengthy overland trip from England to Australia and, in response to numerous 'how do you do it?' questions, Tony wrote and they published *Across Asia on the Cheap*. It became an instant local best-seller and inspired thoughts of a second travel guide. A year and a half in South-East Asia resulted in their second book, *South-East Asia on a Shoestring*, which they put together in a backstreet Chinese hotel in Singapore in 1975. The 'yellow book', as it quickly became known, soon became *the* guide to the region and has gone through five editions, always with its familiar yellow cover.

Soon other writers started to come to them with ideas for similar books – books that went off the beaten track and took an adventurous approach to travel, books that 'assumed you knew how to get your luggage off the carousel,' as one reviewer described them. Lonely Planet grew from a kitchen table operation to a spare room and then to its own office. It also started to develop an international reputation as the Lonely Planet logo began to appear in more and more countries. In 1982 *India – a travel survival kit* won the Thomas Cook award for the best guidebook of the year.

These days there are over 60 Lonely Planet titles. Nearly 30 people work at our office in Melbourne, Australia and another half dozen at our US office in Oakland, California.

At first Lonely Planet specialised exclusively in the Asia region but these days we are also developing major ranges of guidebooks to the Pacific region, to South America and to Africa. The list of walking guides is growing and Lonely Planet is producing a unique series of phrasebooks to 'unusual' languages. The emphasis continues to be on travel for travellers and Tony and Maureen still manage to fit in a number of trips each year and play a very active part in the writing and updating of Lonely Planet's guides.

Keeping guidebooks up to date is a constant battle which requires an ear to the ground and lots of walking, but technology also plays its part. All Lonely Planet guidebooks are now stored and updated on computer, and some authors even take lap-top computers into the field. Lonely Planet is also using computers to draw maps and eventually many of the maps will be stored on disk.

The people at Lonely Planet strongly feel that travellers can make a positive contribution to the countries they visit both by better appreciation of cultures and by the money they spend. In addition the company tries to make a direct contribution to the countries and regions it covers. Since 1986 a percentage of the income from each book has gone to aid groups and associations. This has included donations to famine relief in Africa, to aid projects in India, to agricultural projects in Nicaragua and other Central American countries and to Greenpeace's efforts to halt French nuclear testing in the Pacific. In 1988 over $40,000 was donated by Lonely Planet to these projects.

Lonely Planet Distributors

Australia & Papua New Guinea Lonely Planet Publications, PO Box 617, Hawthorn, Victoria 3122.
Canada Raincoast Books, 112 East 3rd Avenue, Vancouver, British Columbia V5T 1C8.
Denmark, Finland & Norway Scanvik Books aps, Store Kongensgade 59 A, DK-1264 Copenhagen K.
Hong Kong The Book Society, GPO Box 7804.
India & Nepal UBS Distributors, 5 Ansari Rd, New Delhi – 110002
Israel Geographical Tours Ltd, 8 Tverya St, Tel Aviv 63144.
Japan Intercontinental Marketing Corp, IPO Box 5056, Tokyo 100-31.
Netherlands Nilsson & Lamm bv, Postbus 195, Pampuslaan 212, 1380 AD Weesp.
New Zealand Transworld Publishers, PO Box 83-094, Edmonton PO, Auckland.
Singapore & Malaysia MPH Distributors, 601 Sims Drive, #03-21, Singapore 1438.
Spain Altair, Balmes 69, 08007 Barcelona.
Sweden Esselte Kartcentrum AB, Vasagatan 16, S-111 20 Stockholm.
Thailand Chalermnit, 108 Sukhumvit 53, Bangkok 10110.
UK Roger Lascelles, 47 York Rd, Brentford, Middlesex, TW8 0QP
USA Lonely Planet Publications, PO Box 2001A, Berkeley, CA 94702.
West Germany Buchvertrieb Gerda Schettler, Postfach 64, D3415 Hattorf a H.
All Other Countries refer to Australia address.

Guides to South-East Asia

Burma - a travel survival kit
Burma is one of Asia's friendliest and most interesting
countries, but for travellers there's one catch – you can
only stay for seven days. This book shows you how to make
the most of your visit.

Indonesia - a travel survival kit
This comprehensive guidebook covers the entire
Indonesian archipelago. Some of the most remarkable
sights and sounds in South-East Asia can be found
amongst these countless islands and this book has all the
facts.

Malaysia, Singapore and Brunei
- a travel survival kit
These three nations offer amazing geographic and
cultural variety – from hill stations to beaches, from Dyak
longhouses to futuristic cities – this is Asia at its most
accessible.

The Philippines - a travel survival kit
The 7000 islands of the Philippines are a paradise for the
adventurous traveller. The friendly Filipinos, colourful
festivals, superb natural scenery, and frequent travel
connections make island hopping addictive.

Thailand - a travel survival kit
Beyond the Buddhist temples and Bangkok bars there is
much to see in fascinating Thailand. This extensively
researched guide presents an inside look at Thailand's
culture, people and language.

South-East Asia on a shoestring
For over 10 years this has been known as the 'yellow bible'
to travellers in South-East Asia. The fifth edition has
updated information on Brunei, Burma, Hong Kong,
Indonesia, Macau, Malaysia, Papua New Guinea, the
Philippines, Singapore, and Thailand.

Also Available:
Indonesia phrasebook, *Burmese phrasebook*, *Pilipino
phrasebook* and *Thai phrasebook*

Guides to The Pacific

Australia – a travel survival kit
Australia is Lonely Planet's home territory so this guide gives you the complete low-down on Down Under, from the red centre to the coast, from cosmopolitan cities to country towns.

New Zealand – a travel survival kit
Visitors to New Zealand find a land of fairytale beauty and scenic contrasts – a natural wonderland. This book has information about the places you won't want to miss, including ski-resorts and famous walks.

Fiji – a travel survival kit
This is a comprehensive guide to the Fijian archipelago. On a number of these beautiful islands accommodation ranges from camping grounds to international hotels – whichever you prefer this book will help you to enjoy the South Seas.

Tahiti & French Polynesia – a travel survival kit
The image of palm-fringed beaches and friendly people continues to lure travellers to Polynesia. This book gives you all the facts on paradise, and will be useful whether you plan a package holiday, or to travel the islands independently.

Micronesia – a travel survival kit
Amongst these 2100 islands are beaches, lagoons and reefs that will dazzle the most jaded traveller. This guide is packed with all you need to know about island hopping across the north Pacific.

Papua New Guinea – a travel survival kit
Papua New Guinea is truly 'the last unknown' – the last inhabited place on earth to be explored by Europeans. This guide has the latest information for travellers who want to find just how rewarding a trip to this remote and amazing country can be.

Also Available:
Papua New Guinea phrasebook

Lonely Planet Guidebooks

Lonely Planet guidebooks cover virtually every accessible part of Asia as well as Australia, the Pacific, Central and South America, Africa, the Middle East and parts of North America. There are four main series: 'travel survival kits', covering a single country for a range of budgets; 'shoestring' guides with compact information for low-budget travel in a major region; trekking guides; and 'phrasebooks'.

Australia & the Pacific
Australia
Bushwalking in Australia
Papua New Guinea
Papua New Guinea phrasebook
New Zealand
Tramping in New Zealand
Rarotonga & the Cook Islands
Solomon Islands
Tahiti & French Polynesia
Fiji
Micronesia

South-East Asia
South-East Asia on a shoestring
Malaysia, Singapore & Brunei
Indonesia
Bali & Lombok
Indonesia phrasebook
Burma
Burmese phrasebook
Thailand
Thai phrasebook
Philippines
Pilipino phrasebook

North-East Asia
North-East Asia on a shoestring
China
China phrasebook
Tibet
Tibet phrasebook
Japan
Korea
Korean phrasebook
Hong Kong, Macau & Canton
Taiwan

West Asia
West Asia on a shoestring
Trekking in Turkey
Turkey

Mail Order

Lonely Planet guidebooks are distributed worldwide and are sold by good bookshops everywhere. They are also available by mail order from Lonely Planet, so if you have difficulty finding a title please write to us. US and Canadian residents should write to Embarcadero West, 112 Linden St, Oakland CA 94607, USA and residents of other countries to PO Box 617, Hawthorn, Victoria 3122, Australia.

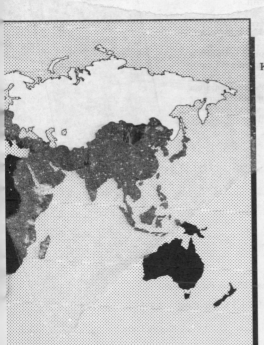

Lonely Planet Update

We collect an enormous amount of information here at Lonely Planet. Apart from our research there's a steady stream of travellers' letters full of the latest news. For over 5 years much of this information went into a quarterly newsletter (and helped to update the guidebooks). The paperback *Update* includes this up-to-date news and aims to supplement the information available in our guidebooks. There are four editions a year (Feb, May, Aug and Nov) available either by subscription or through bookshops. Subscribe now and you'll save nearly 25% off the retail price.

Each edition has extracts from the most interesting letters we have received, covering such diverse topics as:

- how to take a boat trip on the Yalu River
- living in a typical Thai village
- getting a Nepalese trekking permit

Subscription Details

All subscriptions cover four editions and include postage. Prices quoted are subject to change.

USA & Canada – One year's subscription is US$12; a single copy is US$3.95. Please send your order to Lonely Planet's California office.

Other Countries – One year's subscription is Australian $15; a single copy is A$4.95. Please pay in Australian $, or the US$ or £ Sterling equivalent. Please send your order form to Lonely Planet's Australian office.

Order Form

Please send me

☐ One year's sub. – starting current edition.   ☐ One copy of the current edition.

Name (please print) ....

Address (please print) ....

....

....

Tick One

☐ Payment enclosed (payable to Lonely Planet Publications)

Charge my   ☐ Visa   ☐ Bankcard   ☐ MasterCard   for the amount of $ ....

Card No .... Expiry Date ....

Cardholder's Name (print) ....

Signature .... Date..

US & Canadian residents
   Lonely Planet, Embarcadero West, 112 Linden St,
   Oakland, CA 94607, USA
Other countries
   Lonely Planet, PO Box 617, Hawthorn, Victoria 3122, Australia